THE OTHER SIDE OF WESTERN CIVILIZATION

Readings in Everyday Life

Second Edition

VOLUME II

The Sixteenth Century to the Present

Edited by

Peter N. Stearns

Carnegie-Mellon University

 HARCOURT BRACE JOVANOVICH, INC.

New York / San Diego / Chicago / San Francisco / Atlanta

ISBN: 0-15-567649-0

Library of Congress Catalog Card Number: 78-60215

Printed in the United States of America

Picture Credits

cover   Chimney sweep, Bethnal Green, England, 1931.
Radio Times Hulton Picture Library

p.   16   Kunsthistorisches Museum, Vienna
p. 102   The Times, London/Pictorial Parade, Inc.
p. 176   Gernsheim Collection
p. 254   Guy Le Querrec/Magnum
p. 334   Henri Cartier-Bresson/Magnum

For Wendy and Julie

PREFACE

The second edition of *The Other Side of Western Civilization*, Volume II, focuses on the involvement of the common people of Europe in some of the massive social changes that have occurred over the past three hundred years as Western society became more urban and industrial. In addition, the book provides an opportunity to measure the considerable progress made by historians in getting to the roots of the modern social process. Unlike most surveys, this volume's major concern is not with the leaders of society, the prominent people whose names and deeds are well known and whose importance is obvious. Instead, it treats the masses of ordinary people, the "inarticulate," whose impact on history is not well documented. The intent is to provide some insight into the impact of change on the daily lives of these people, and through this insight to promote a better understanding of the nature and evolution of modern society.

In order to make valid judgments about how liberating or oppressive modernization has been, the nature of premodern society must first be analyzed and evaluated. In addition, the origins of social change must be ascertained: Was change imposed on the masses by forces beyond their control, or did the people actively participate in the construction of modern society? The opening selections represent a number of different interpretations of these issues so that students may assess for themselves the impact of change, the adjustments it promoted, and the resistance it provoked.

Although this collection focuses on only some of the many facets of the modern history of Europe's people, the selections can be enhanced by additional essays, and the bibliographies provide numerous suggestions for further reading.

Some of the topics dealt with in this volume are relatively familiar: the meaning of political involvement in the modern world, the nature of industrial work, and the plight of the industrial worker. Other subjects covered are less common: the evolution of the family, the impact of modernization on women, innovation and continuity in health practices, new attitudes toward madness and deviant social behavior, and the changing nature of sexual relationships. The essays included here were chosen with an eye to recent research presented in a stimulating manner and with an awareness of the major conceptual problems involved. Collectively, they suggest important debates over the nature of modern life. Topics that would hardly have been mentioned five years ago, such as the history of sex, now have a diverse literature. Today the history of women receives more sophisticated treatment as historians reach directly into the lives of women in the past. The history of leisure roles is receiving new attention, perhaps a sign that we are trying to come to terms with the meaning of leisure in our own lives.

Undergirding the treatment of novel topics, developments in the study of the common people in Western society show a concern for the popular mentality and for the ideas, values, and impulses that motivated measurable behavior. Though the actions and values of most people were undoubtedly affected by the policies set forth by society's leaders (and a number of essays in the book discuss this connection), the masses of people shaped society through their own actions. Ultimately, the effort to reach back to the minds of our forebears, to their attitudes toward health, children, or death, and to the possible unities in an approach to life, represents an exciting chance to place ourselves in context; to understand how, to what extent, and in what directions we are really changing beneath the obviously new trappings of an advanced industrial society.

A number of people provided vital assistance in the preparation of this book. I am grateful to those who read and commented on the original plan for this work: J. Kim Munholland, University of Minnesota; James T. Sheehan, Northwestern University; Mack Walker, Johns Hopkins University; Edward Shorter, University of Toronto; Donald Sutton, Carnegie-Mellon University; John Gillis, Rutgers University; Louise Tilly, University of Michigan; and William Weber, California State University, Long Beach. The editorial and production staffs at Harcourt Brace Jovanovich were of great aid. For suggesting readings and for other assistance, I also thank Howard Zehr, Peter Meyers, and my wife, Carol. I am, finally, grateful to the many students, both graduate and undergraduate, at Rutgers University and Carnegie-Mellon University, who have helped me apply some of the key problems of modernization to the study and teaching of European social history.

Peter N. Stearns

CONTENTS

3 Mature Industrial Society 1850-1918

4 The Twentieth Century 1918-Present

5 The Nature of Modern People

Topical Table of Contents

Introduction

Most of the people who lived in the past rarely appear in historical studies. Instead, histories of European civilization concentrate on rather small groups of people—the thinkers, the artists, the political leaders. Of course, the importance of these elites is undeniable. They have left unusually clear records, so that historians can study them without too much difficulty. But their acts and ideas form only a part of human history. This book focuses on the other, and possibly the more important, part. It deals with groups of people who are rarely heard from in surveys of Western civilization—women and workers, criminals and the insane, soldiers and peasants. They are a diverse lot, but they have in common the fact that contemporary social elites and later historians usually regarded them as inarticulate. Periodically, popular revolutions brought them into the scheme of history, but in normal times they were largely ignored.

The result of such disregard is incomplete history. More to the point, it is the kind of history that lacks relevance. We do not judge our present on the basis of the doings of the elite and their formal institutions alone, though of course these are vital. When we take our social temperature we think of the stability of families, the condition of women, the fate of the work ethic, the problems of commercialized leisure—in other words, activities whose evaluation depends on knowledge of what various kinds of people, and large numbers of people, are doing. These activities, and the folk who engage in them, have histories. These histories in turn can be as important as, and possibly more interesting than, the narrow accounts of the politics of the past. They can help us to understand ourselves.

Most elites in the past, and most historians more recently, have tended to place ordinary people and their activities in rather simple categories. This does not necessarily mean that they were insensitive to them, but it does suggest that they knew rather little about them. Until the nineteenth century most ordinary people in Europe were peasants, a word that immediately suggests a formless, stolid mass, in terms of the little that most conventional historical surveys say about peasants. According to the simplest definition, peasants normally valued tradition and stability and rebelled, as they did occasionally, against change and in the name of the past. But did peasants have a real history, or were they a mindless constant beneath the surface of great events? In fact, from time to time peasant families changed; their economic habits and values changed; their definitions of crime and morality changed. Peasant families rose and fell in social standing, often with great rapidity. Many of them were geographically mobile; many welcomed new ideas and methods, and some even produced them, although peasants tended to resist novelty. We should not be content with merely occasional references to the millions of people who were peasants in Europe as Western civilization developed. Although we cannot know the details of their individual lives and ideas, we must seek to fill in broader generalizations. We must keep in mind that simply knowing that a peasantry existed means little unless we also know what trends were operating in each major period and area. In some periods peasants regularly practiced infanticide because they could not support the children born to them; in others they were eager to have many children, and not just because of special economic opportunities. It is from the variety and evolution of peasant culture in western Europe that much of modern civilization sprang.

The masses of people in the last two centuries have received more attention, if only because they have impinged more often on the political process. But still, many aspects of their lives are ignored, while others are subjected to judgments by people who are remote from their ordinary existence. Working-class families have decayed, say conservatives who deplore modern times. Many socialists, seeking to condemn the disruptive effects of capitalism, agree. Few scholars have even tried to look at the actual evolution of family patterns. With rare exceptions, until recently, the history of the masses received attention only when the masses rocked the boat, annoying conservatives and giving heart to radicals. But protest, although important, can prove too difficult for people whose lives are so demanding even in the best of times. Consequently, most of the history of people long went unrecorded.

A great deal of historical research is now being devoted to the history of "inarticulate" people. It is now clear that historians have regarded these people as mute in part because they themselves have not tried to listen. To be sure, it is much more difficult to know what "the workers" thought than it is to outline the philosophy of Descartes. Some speculation, some historical intuition is essential if we are to get at popular ideas, which means that there is considerable room for disagreement. The history of the inarticulate is a rather new field of study. It is rife with debate (and it is exciting for this very reason), but already some points are reasonably well established. Aspects of popular behavior can be measured with some precision, even if the outlook that prompted the behavior is more difficult to determine. The common people had ideas, and they left their own kinds of records. In protest, in crime, in family behavior, and in religious practices we can discern the mentality of the broad masses of people, even those who lived centuries ago. We can know how many people were born and died, how they structured their families, how often they rioted. Now that historians are looking for them, the sources of information about the inarticulate are proving abundant, even overwhelming. They are different kinds of sources from those historians have been accustomed to. Many of them reveal information only about large groups of people rather than about individuals. But there are individual records as well, to rescue this new kind of history from impersonality. Criminals, workers, and many others have left statements of what their lives were like and what they thought about.

So we can learn about the common people. But why should we want to? E. P. Thompson has argued eloquently that the common people must be rescued from "the enormous condescension of posterity." He means, among other things, that history, even when written by radical historians, has usually had an upper-class bias, regarding the mass of humanity as a silent lump to be shaped or abused by the elites. This is a valid point, which does not mean that one has to appreciate the history of the inarticulate only to demonstrate democratic or socialist purity.

Because it adds a vast new dimension to what we can learn about people, the history of the inarticulate fascinates many students of the past —but not all. Many historians and students of history continue to be most interested in great men and great ideas. Some people, however, who were never able to get terribly excited about the "greats" can now find a new meaning in history through studying the masses; others who began with a conventional interest in history may decide that the real meaning of history lies in this new approach and the issues it raises.

Reactions of this sort are personal, of course. But whether or not one is really enthusiastic about studying the history of the inarticulate, there are three reasons why students should know something about it. First, the history of the common people provides one measure of the nature and quality of civilization. Did peasants and artisans gain a new outlook during the Italian Renaissance? Did their lives change, and, if so, did the changes follow the same direction as those of the political and intellectual elites? Many thinkers of the Enlightenment believed in humanitarianism and in progress. When and to what extent did such beliefs enter the popular mentality? We cannot fully determine the historical importance of great men and great ideas unless we know what impact they had on the bulk of society. Often the process of disseminating the effects of "greatness" is more important than the initial cause.

Furthermore, we must dispel the notion that the masses of people have not themselves been active agents in history, although perhaps they have reacted to outside forces more than they have acted spontaneously. In many of the readings in this volume, this point is implicitly debated. Did the common people adopt more modern attitudes toward work and sex because they were prodded and compelled to do so by forces from above, or did they have, to some extent at least, their own reasons for changing their outlook? There is no question that the common people had an important voice in determining exactly how they adapted to change. They often resisted change as well, and their resistance was an important historical force in its own right. When masses of people changed their views about their sexual goals or about how many children to have, they played a direct role in altering the course of history.

These arguments apply to the history of the common people at any place and time. There is a final, more specific reason for studying the common people in modern times. The simple fact is that most of us, as ordinary citizens, judge modern society by different criteria from those most historians have used in judging the past. Many of us think of our own time more in terms of divorce rates and crime rates than in terms of, say, artistic achievements. We think in terms of the quality and nature of life of *most people,* and this means that we need histories of precisely these areas. Has the suicide rate been rising or falling in modern societies? Has child abuse increased or decreased as families have grown smaller and attitudes toward child-rearing changed? Perhaps some day students of modern history will have as much information on patterns of this sort, and as satisfactory explanations for major changes in these patterns, as they now have about formal political theory and the development of new forms of government.

We return here to the point that historians have ignored many significant kinds of activities in the past. What has been studied in most Western civilization survey courses is vitally important, but it is incomplete. We are left without genuine historical knowledge of many of the features of our own society that are closest to us. Hence, in a real sense, we cannot assess the direction our society is taking. For example, until recently historians have virtually ignored the history of crime, while piling study upon study of the details of diplomatic interchanges. Historians are empiricists. They learn from observation and therefore need sources; sources from diplomats are more abundant than sources from criminals. So historians tend to study diplomats, although it might be argued that criminals are at least as important in shaping society. (Some might even argue that the different labels exaggerate the differences between the two groups.) But the fact that historians honor diplomats more than criminals leads us to assume that diplomats' historical importance is greater, until we consider our own times and realize that most of us devote a great deal of attention to crime and its significance for us personally and for our society.

This is not to say that every current opinion reflects an important historical reality. Some historians who demand that history be "relevant" really mean only that it should reinforce their own views of what should happen from here on. But history is relevant. We can't understand crime today if we don't know about crime in the past, for we have no sense of direction or means of comparison. We have no way of knowing if crime is rising, falling, changing in nature, or staying the same. Yet contemporary comments on crime often assume a historical knowledge. Newspaper accounts, for example, talk about a rising crime rate as an inescapable aspect of modern urban society. This is a historical judgment. But in view of how little is generally known about the history of crime, it is an invalid historical judgment. Modern urbanization has not necessarily produced more crime; the situation is more complex.

The readings in this book stress topics that are not generally considered in historical surveys, such as popular health attitudes, and large groups, such as youth, factory workers, and thieves. However it is important to realize that these are not separate strands of history, but rather part of a larger social process. Increasingly, social historians, who claim a special interest in the inarticulate and in mundane social activities, are realizing their kinship with students of culture and politics. Topics like crime or groups such as housewives should be juxtaposed to more familiar historical phenomena. The modern criminal mentality, for example, may have developed in relationship to ideas of the Enlightenment about material well-being and individualism. New behavior of women in the nineteenth century altered the character of religion; for as men left religious activities increasingly to their wives, religion became gentler, less riveted for example, on condemnation of evil, and certainly more inclined to equate womanhood with purity.

This collection is not, then, merely a sample of interesting insights into the history of much that concerns us today, much less a hymn to unfairly neglected groups in European history. The readings have been selected and organized to relate to a large, unifying theme in the history of the last four centuries, the transition from a traditional to a modern society, the process broadly termed *modernization*. The hypothesis here is that there is something of a pattern to the development of Western society in recent centuries. This pattern links various groups in society, although not necessarily in simple ways, so that some common developments can be seen among paupers and among the rich. It also links the various facets of human activity, so that changes in sexuality bear some relationship to changes in attitudes toward health, and in turn to developments in the world of formal ideas and politics. It gives coherence to our recent past and relates our present to it integrally; it might even cast some light on our probable future.

Modernization, however, the model used to assess the less familiar side of Western civilization since 1550, is a sticky term and concept. The word itself invites confusion; we are by definition modern in the sense of existing right now, so what is special about seeing modernization as a process? The term has been variously described in social science and historical literature as "too big and slippery for deft manipulation," "historically crude," "better than no model at all," "elusive," and "inadequate . . . for comprehending the diversity of the human experience during several centuries of social transformation." The present collection of essays is in one sense an effort to have cake and eat it, too, by invoking modernization while raising questions not only about what its definition is, but whether it existed as a process at all. It will be perfectly possible to emerge from the following readings with a firm belief that social changes over the last four centuries have no coherent direction, much less a "modern" one, and certainly possible for any two readers to disagree vigorously over what modernization has been and where it is heading. And the best method to launch discussion is by way of introduction.

As a concept, modernization was devised by social scientists, mostly Americans, eager to predict where nonwestern societies were heading and where they should head. See what we in the West have done? Surely Japan or Turkey or Nigeria must/should/will do the same. Many of the criticisms of modernization result from ethnocentrism. But we are concerned here with Western society. We must first find out if a coherent process of modernization has occurred in the West and what the conditions for it were. We may then wish to see if it suggests patterns for understanding what is happening elsewhere in the world now. For there may in fact be interconnections such that societies which industrialize, for example, also develop Western practices about women. Here, certainly, would be an important reason to grasp the Western model. But modernization may be useful simply to put our own present in context, suggesting ongoing trends in the West itself. It is this effort at self-understanding that is the focus of the varied views that follow.

Modernization raises a number of objections or questions when applied to Western civilization directly. When did it begin? Many people equate the process with clear structural change. We know that, in the late eighteenth and early nineteenth centuries, western European countries began to industrialize (a relatively definable phenomenon), to urbanize, and so on. Some would date modernization using these phenomena. But, increasingly, some historians are claiming that before this, indeed as a precondition for structural change, values were altered; people, or at least some people in key positions, began to think in new ways. These historians push modernization back to the early eighteenth century or even the seventeenth century. But can one talk of a coherent process that has spanned such a long and diverse period, and which began with changes too difficult to pin down and measure? Here is one source of the claim that modernization is too fuzzy and all-inclusive, that it gives a false sense of pattern to the very diverse realities of human life in the past.

Modernization encounters geographical objections as well, even within Western society. How different was English modernization from French or German modernization? How does one fit specific national phenomena—German Nazism, or the English public school experience—into a single basic package? (And if the United States were added, as is the case in a few of the essays that follow, what additional complexity: How do specifically American patterns of crime, divorce, or race relations fit any broader model?) The essays in this collection deal variously with single countries or regions, or with a number of areas. In combination, they do suggest that some basic changes overrode and still override national boundaries. But it is certainly legitimate to argue, as many conven-

tional historians would, that a region or
analysis, putting its own vital stamp on gen[
cities or factory industry, and that the trees
the woods.

Periodization is a problem as well. Is
phenomenon, starting in the seventeenth o
ing ever upward (or downward, or in sor
definite stages of modernization? The ide
has some support: a period of early tech
limited introduction of factories followe
relevant technology, with appropriate levels of urbaniza.... .
ganization, and so on to match. But modernization, so much more amor-
phous in including basic behavior patterns and values, may not lend
itself to this kind of approach. How, for example, does the twentieth century fit after the nineteenth? Are we witnessing further gains of modernization or a souring of the process or a reversion to older, premodern
patterns? The essays in this book offer support for all of these views.
Twentieth-century woman may be seen as entering the modern world in
new ways, and gaining a more clearly modern mentality in the process.
Phenomena such as Nazism and, one selection argues, basic trends within
the contemporary family suggest a sharp deterioration from nineteenth-
century patterns. Modernization, if applicable at all, would here be seen
not as a straight-line development, but a series of curves, differentiating
the nature and quality of life in one period from those in another. Or,
as another judgment holds, the contemporary family, after considerable
innovation and disruption in the nineteenth century, is returning to something like a premodern structure, notably as both husband and wife
participate in economic production as they did in the seventeenth century but did not in the nineteenth. Modernization would seem scarcely
applicable in this view at all, for family behavior proves more cyclical
than directional in quality.

But the overriding issue surrounding modernization relates to its
capacity to integrate developments in diverse areas of human activity. Are
all trends in a modernizing society linked, moving in some definable direction (whether for better or for worse)? Or are some phenomena simply
immune to modernization? Leisure is a case in point. Some observers see
leisure as a distinctly modern activity, different from traditional recreation, notably in being open to freer choice. Others point to vast continuities, with contemporary leisure expressing a traditional social need to
give outlets to youth, to male violence, to courtship. But if modernization
is not a whole package, if older values persist along with the development of new ones, where do we draw the lines that define modernization?

One approach to this problem suggests a distinction between structural and behavioral modernization, that is, between changes in the human environment (urbanization, industrialization) and changes in the way
people act, particularly in private areas over which they have most control, and the values they apply to their acts and to their environment.

...estion that the framework of life has greatly changed since
...th century, and that many of the changes are interlinked.
...ociety has industrialized, moved to the cities, developed greater
...more bureaucratic apparatus, and higher literacy. Broadly speak-
...ach aspect of this structural modernization seems to involve the
...ers, although the precise mix may vary from one society to the next.
...he essays in this book do not deal primarily with structural modernization, but with the more complex issue of how, or whether, behavior and
attitudes have changed. Here, modernization theory normally holds that,
as part of structural modernization, people become more rationalistic,
individualized, acquisitive. But how do values of this sort apply to groups
such as workers or youth, to activities such as leisure? Does the structure
of modern society compel a particular kind of behavior on the part of
women? The basic question is this: Does modernization describe a process by which now normal personalities have been produced over the
last few centuries? Is there some coherence to the interaction of various
groups in modern society, in their various activities, relating one to another and to modern structures? We cannot expect simplicity. Modernization of outlook and behavior may reach some groups before others (the
periodization problem again), and may take different, precise forms from
one segment of society to another. Will modernized men and women
turn out to share the same viewpoint and, with due qualifications for a
bit of biology, behavior forms? Or should we expect distinct gender patterns in modernization? And again, some activities, possibly some definable groups, may not modernize at all, but can best be seen in a different kind of interaction with modern structures or moving in a cyclical
fashion or not changing at all.

With all this undeniable complexity, why not just give up on modernization? Some scholars clearly have done so. They talk of specific changes,
not a grand pattern. They warn of the danger in seeing direction in history instead of the hodgepodge that the past really is. (How, for example,
can we speak in the same breath of modernization as the expansion of
bureaucracy and modernization as greater individualization?) Western
civilization, even before modern times, has undeniably tended to see a
direction in history, moving toward a final coming of Christ, a better
society, new knowledge, improved medicine—the goals vary greatly, but
the desire for a goal is deep within us. Perhaps, if we were honest, we
could admit that the past gives us no direction, no real interconnected-
ness among our various activities. But the desire to see some sense, some
pattern, runs deep. And just possibly, in a sophisticated concept of modernization, a pattern really has been there. A careful reading of the kinds
of essays in the present collection will, it is hoped, give some basis for
judgment.

But if modernization existed, if there has been some coherent movement in the thoughts and behavior of people in the modern centuries,
the problems are not over. What caused modernization, and its specific
manifestations both in structures and mentalities? Indeed, which came

first: Did structures change, forcing or encouraging people to think differently, or did some tentative changes in ideas prompt developments such as industrialization? Modernization is not a clear statement of causation; rather, it describes and summarizes major changes. Yet several of the selections in this book go beyond summary to an assessment of cause, which includes careful attention to those elements of premodern society that could permit change.

Even more pervasive is the question of the quality of modernization. Critics of the concept properly note its teleological implications: History has a purpose. But while most formal advocates of modernization as a construct have been optimists (modern society is not just different from, but better than, traditional society), many other analysts, implicitly agreeing that modernization has differentiated our society from the past in coherent and definable ways, are profoundly pessimistic. We have changed, but we have lost in basic human values.

Hence a study of the impact of modernization on the common people, whether in Europe or elsewhere, invites some value judgments, and a word must be said about these in advance. The term modernization may be a loaded one, suggesting a kind of blanket approval of change, for many people have been conditioned to believe that what is modern is what is good. This is profoundly different from the traditional outlook, which tended to look to the past for standards. We know that formal Christianity saw a golden age in the past (although, significantly, it looked forward to a brighter future as well). Before the onset of modernization, peasants tended to believe that rural society had been better in past ages; artisans looked back to the ideals of the early guilds. Indeed the common people had little historical sense and tended to merge past with present. Since modernization, however, we have become acutely, perhaps exaggeratedly, conscious of how different we are, and often how much better we are than our predecessors. So when we talk of something becoming more modern, we may be too quick to praise or at least to find the development entirely natural and easily understandable. For example, one important aspect of modernization is the development of a belief in the possibility and desirability of material progress, for oneself as well as for society as a whole. Most Americans probably find this a good change, at least when contrasted with the resignation and stagnancy of a more traditional view. A minority—those concerned about the ecological damage that material progress can cause, for instance—would find this aspect of modernization dangerous. But almost everyone would find it natural. It's hard for us to believe that people might think anything else. Economic thought from the early nineteenth century onward has assumed that the goal of "economic man" is to maximize his wealth. Yet, even applied to most people in the nineteenth century, this is not a proper historical view. Interest in material improvement constituted a profound change in the popular mentality. It came slowly and, in fact, has not yet been completed. "Modernization" is probably not a sufficiently neutral word to describe what it must describe, but we have not yet found a better one.

Our focus on the common people may appeal to a different set of values, leading to a condemnation of trends within modern society itself. Debates over the effects of industrialization and urban growth on the lower classes, for example, began a century and a half ago, and they continue today. Historians still argue over whether material conditions improved during the first stage of British industrialization, and the topic is significant in the history of any area undergoing the initial stages of an industrial revolution. This is an important question, for conditions in such a formative stage of working-class life may have influenced outlook to such an extent that attitudes and behavior persisted even after the material setting changed. But our concern is broader, for we are trying to assess general outlook and style of life, and not just of workers but of other groups as well. Still, some of the problems of interpretation are similar, for if one dislikes contemporary society, it is easy to emphasize how much people have suffered since its inception; or, if one finds current conditions improving, it is tempting to assume a constant process once traditional society began to break down. In the British standard of living debate, historians favorable to capitalism and convinced of the essential soundness of the modern world generally try to show that conditions were improving even during early industrialization. Leftist historians, who dislike capitalism and commiserate with the workers, invariably look for signs of deterioration. Note that the connection between political judgment and historical judgment is not entirely logical. One could well argue that capitalism has proved a good thing in the long run and that modern life is lovely, even for the workers, while admitting that in the first stage of industrialization conditions deteriorated. Or one could urge the need for fundamental reforms in modern life while admitting that conditions have improved somewhat compared with preindustrial times. Obviously, ideological commitments can predetermine an approach—and most of us have an ideology, even if it is not neatly labeled. Changes in mood can also change our historical perspective. What American, in the 1970s, after a decade of riot and assassination, followed by one of political corruption and economic malaise, can blithely assume our superiority to Europe? Yet twenty-five years ago it was normal for intelligent historians to focus on Europe's instability, bellicosity, and economic inferiority. Perspectives change quickly, as do historical trends, which means that it may be impossible to offer a simple characterization of any of the developments affecting the common people during the modernization process. But the most common impulse, among historians who have dealt with the inarticulate, is to find an example to support one's own reaction to modern life, whether that example is valid or invalid.

The readings that follow present a variety of approaches, some commending the liberating aspects of modernization, others stressing the deterioration. Few historians who deal with these vital topics content themselves with simply saying that things have changed, which might be the most objective view. They generally try to assess the quality of that change. Try to study the modern history of women, for example, without asking whether things have been getting better or worse. Many now argue that with modernization and the decline in the family as a productive unit, woman's inferior status became more pronounced, for her economic utility was less obvious and her dependence on her husband greater. Others point to better education and the declining birth rate as indications of improvements in woman's lot.

Each student of history must make up his own mind about trends. Two preliminary points should be kept in mind. First, most historians who have been drawn to the study of the common people have sympathized with their lot. They tend to dwell on their hardships and to see their subjects as victimized by some outside force—workers by capitalists, women by men, and so on. It is important also to study the ways in which the common people adjusted to their situations and the values they used and changed in doing so. It is important to see the common people as an active force, not just in protest—though this is a significant aspect of their lives—but also in shaping family structure, recreational patterns, and so on. This view is quite consistent with an emphasis on the hardships of life, but it goes beyond a dreary catalogue of exploitation. More generally, any judgment of trends must use some basis of comparison. Too often this basis is not clearly spelled out. If a historian argues that the horizons of middle-class women in Victorian England were becoming more limited, he must describe an antecedent situation in which they were less so. Overall, most large evaluations of modernization involve an implicit or explicit comparison with premodern life. We have to know where we came from to know where we are going.

In fact, whether one is a historian or not, it is impossible to study modernity without asking "where from?"—which is of course a historical question. Any journalist or politician who claims that values or behavior patterns are changing or that violence is rising or falling or that a situation is unprecedented is making a historical judgment, and it would be well if he made it intelligently. Some of the judgments are short term, of course. It is possible and useful to compare crime rates and patterns of the 1960s with those of the 1920s. But the larger evaluations, those, for example, which are concerned with the nature of industrial life or of urban man, involve or should involve a knowledge of the premodern world. We have no other way to assess the direction of change, and we are far from agreeing on the direction, for our knowledge of facts is limited. So is our ability to cut through biases and slogans. We hear of the loosening of family ties. We therefore assume that premodern families were closeknit and jolly—but has the subject really been studied? Only a historical view can tell us the extent to which present problems are recent and human-caused, as opposed to being durable reflections of human nature or at least the nature of Western man. Divorce, for example, is a rather new institution, but does it signify a really new problem in family life or does it represent a new answer to a persistent tension? We must look at the past to find out. We might avoid a lot of nonsense from advocates of the brand new as well as from critics of the present if we required every statement of "never before" or "a sign of these troubled times"—unquestionably judgments of present in terms of past—to be backed by solid historical evidence. This book stems from the need to approach key trends in modern life in the only way they can really be understood.

The book does not cover all the major topics in the history of the common people during the centuries of modernization. It largely avoids the study of modern states and institutional structures, vital topics in their own right, in favor of activities normally closer to the common people. Even many of the topics dealt with in this book have only been outlined. There is insufficient information on some of them; there is a great disagreement on others. We are not in total ignorance, though, and the whole issue of modernization is so essential that we cannot constantly beg off on grounds of insufficient data. If we are to understand ourselves and our society, we must venture a genuine historical view of such topics as the evolution of family life or the situation of women. Confusing signals and outright disagreement add spice to our effort to know.

The readings are arranged more or less chronologically, but they can also be grouped into topics that cover essential aspects of the formation of a modern outlook in the general population. Readings on rural society discuss the nature of preindustrial life, which was overwhelmingly agrarian, and allow an assessment of the changes in the countryside in recent times. A section on modern attitudes presents varying interpretations of where we are now. Two large groupings of the inarticulate, women and workers, receive extensive treatment. The readings on workers also discuss the nature of industrial work in general. Children and youth are considered as groupings as well. The family is elaborately studied, for, although its nature has changed in a number of aspects, it was and remains a basic institution in the lives of most people. The family must be understood if we are to comprehend what values children bring into adulthood: If modernization has produced a new personality type, or as some would argue a succession of new types, then new child-raising practices must be involved. More generally, the strengths or weaknesses of the family help us measure the extent to which key groups were able to adapt to modernization at various points. Readings on education and popular culture deal both with the formal values taught to the lower classes and with new and old types of recreation that played a growing role in life outside of work. Health practices, a new and exciting area of social history, receive explicit attention. Discussions of crime and insanity consider changes in forms of individual protest and maladjustment and how modern society defines deviance. Readings on protest concern the evolution of the forms and goals of collective action.

The focus is for the most part on western Europe, where the process of modernization began, and where it has gone farthest. The history of modernization in other regions is equally interesting and important, but many of the major issues and trends can be suggested within the more familiar context of Britain, France, and Germany. Even this zone is by no means homogeneous; and this involves the problem of the geographic coherence of modernization. If the process of modernization has important general features in common, national and regional differences are surely important in any detailed study. Although not explicitly comparative, the readings allow some assessment of the differences in rates and patterns of change from one country to the next. But the main focus is on developments of wide applicability, even where regional variations would modify the basic generalizations to some extent.

Because historians are just beginning to sketch the history of the common people, we cannot easily pinpoint when decisive time breaks occurred. Conventional periodization (1715–63, 1870–1914, and so on) has little relevance, for the lives of most people were not always decisively shaped by the doings of diplomats and politicians. Indeed, we should probably seek a decade or more in which some measurable change occurred—when rapid population growth began or waned, for example —rather than a single year. The chronological organization of this book is meant to be loose and suggestive, but it does provide a necessary framework. The first section, 1550–1750, allows an understanding of the society and the traditions that were to change. But the period itself saw important developments that set the basis for modernization. Between 1750 and 1850 the confrontation between tradition and change was extremely intense. Industrialization began but was not yet dominant, while the attitudes of ordinary people began to take more modern form. Between 1850 and 1914 the nature of industrial society became clearer. Problems of adaptation remained, but they were more subtle. To many Europeans, at least in retrospect, this period seemed a golden age. However, those who lived through it, outside of the upper classes, may have judged it differently. The period from 1918 to the present opened with the intense dislocation caused by the First World War. The confused nature of European society between the two world wars is important in its contribution to more enduring social trends. But the overriding theme of the twentieth century is the extent to which a new society is taking shape and what kind of society it is. Many observers talk of a postmodern or postindustrial age; we must try to find out what this means in human terms. And of course the whole issue of the coherence of modernization, from one major period to the next, should be considered. There is even a possibility that a sense of the direction of modernization might allow a glimpse toward the future. What, for example, is the probable fate of the family as modernization progresses? But some analysts, accepting modernization as a pattern for the recent past, would disclaim the ability to forecast.

The history of the common people is a new kind of history in many ways, but it is not a total departure. It involves a testing of many conventional historical themes to see what impact major ideas and political forms had on the masses. Hence, while the readings do consider some unusual subjects, they can and should be linked to the more obvious developments in modern European history. Rural society was clearly affected by religious doctrine and organization. The spread of popular education involved a deliberate attempt to inculcate in the peasant attitudes such as nationalism, liberalism, and a belief in science and progress. New forms of protest related to changes in political ideology, most obviously the rise of socialism. The world that workers lived in was conditioned by the actions of the state and of employers. These can in turn be assessed in terms of liberalism and other political doctrines. Connections of this sort are not always simple. One cannot assume that liberal ideas about the treatment of workers fully represent the actual ideas of employers, even employers who claimed to be liberal. But the connections are there, and they clearly relate the history of the common people to history in general. Other links can be found as well. We will see how the rise of rationalism changed the definition of madnes and, therefore, the attitudes toward the treatment of insanity. Changes in the family or in sexual behavior cannot be understood solely in terms of formal ideas or political activities, but they are not entirely independent either. By the late eighteenth century, people in Europe seemed to have gained a new interest in romantic, or at least sexual, love. Surely this must have helped cause the rise of romanticism, or at least that aspect which stressed human emotions. The historian deepens his understanding of the common themes in political and intellectual history by understanding their relationship with the world of the common people.

Modernization, if it works at all as a concept, may allow us to interpret the familiar and the unfamiliar in our past, and, as a result provide some basis for assessing what we are now, and how the various facets of our society relate to each other. Or a sophisticated assessment of modernization may suggest that contemporary society is painfully unintegrated, with groups and activities pulling in different, perhaps contradictory, directions. Students of the basic process of modern society are trying to fathom what we have become, and why. The quest is one of the most exciting developments in historical study.

BIBLIOGRAPHY

A bibliography follows the introduction to each section, to provide further reading on each of the topics covered. There is no general survey of the period from 1600 to the present that satisfactorily covers the subjects included in this volume. For the first part of the period, Fernand Braudel, *Civilisation matérielle et capitalisme (XVe-XVIIIe siècle)* (Paris, 1967), constitutes a major study. Henry Kamen, *The Iron Century: Social Change in Europe 1550–1660* (New York, 1971), stresses developments among the lower classes. Important works on industrialization include David Landes, *The Unbound Prometheus: Technological Change and Industrial Development in Western Europe from 1750 to the Present* (New

York, 1969), and Alexander Gerschenkron, *Economic Backwardness in Historical Perspective* (Cambridge, Mass., 1962). W. W. Rostow, *The Stages of Economic Growth* (New York, 1960), is a controversial work that suggests an economic periodization possibly related to major stages in the broader modernization process. Cyril Black, *The Dynamics of Modernization: A Study in Comparative History* (New York, 1966), offers a historical sketch of the general process. A major interpretation of basic types of modernization is Barrington Moore, *Social Origins of Dictatorship and Democracy* (Boston, 1966). A more general survey is Peter N. Stearns, *European Society in Upheaval,* 2nd ed. (New York, 1975).

On modernization, see Richard D. Brown, *Modernization: The Transformation of American Life* (New York, 1976); Samuel N. Eisenstadt, *Tradition, Change, and Modernity* (New York, 1973); Daniel Lerner, *The Passing of Traditional Society* (Glencoe, Ill., 1958); Edward B. Harvey, ed., *Perspectives on Modernization* (Toronto, 1972); and Myron Weiner, *Modernization: The Dynamics of Growth* (New York, 1966). A trenchant criticism is Dean C. Tipps, "Modernization Theory and the Comparative Study of Societies: A Critical Perspective," *Comparative Studies in Society and History* (1973), pp. 199–227.

Part 1

PREMODERN PEOPLE

1550-1750

Pieter Bruegel the Elder, *The Peasant Dance* (detail), c. 1567, Kunsthistorisches Museum, Vienna

The modern world, young as it is in the span of human history, has broken decisively with the past. Yet we must begin with the past to understand modernity.

One of the key assumptions of most modernization theory posits the existence of a definable traditional society to be changed. In many pictures, traditional society appears as a virtual antithesis of modernity: static, wedded to the past, superstitious, and of course, in terms of structure, poor, agricultural, and aristocratic and/or monarchical in political form. Can premodern society be captured so neatly? Many historians argue that it cannot, pointing to great regional variations, even within western Europe, and great fluctuations in the situation of individuals and groups over time. They would find the label traditionalist a great oversimplifier.

If there was a definable entity, a traditional society, then other questions follow. Was preindustrial society a pleasant or unpleasant place? (Most people who claim to like the trends of modern society tend to emphasize the constraints of traditionalism, while many critics look with nostalgia on this more remote past; but it would be possible to argue that preindustrial society was neither better nor worse, overall, just different.) Did preindustrial society have characteristics so valuable, perhaps even so natural to the human species, that we should look for efforts, and possibly successful efforts, to preserve them amid the later structural changes of modernization? We might, in other words, look to our preindustrial past not simply as a contrast to our own day, but as the source of much that remains viable, in areas like family life.

The impulse to see preindustrial society as static, capable of change but not fundamental change, obviously raises the issue of how and when modernization began. Some historians are now pushing back the quest for modernization into the seventeenth century (thus touching base with older traditions in intellectual history, which stressed the importance of the new science). But if the historians' view is valid, does modernization gain or lose as a model of change? Some would contend that it becomes so extended and gradual, if originating so early, as to be meaningless, for clearly many of the features of modern society were long absent. Others find the idea of a new mentality as the first assignable source of change attractive, deepening the concept of modernization beyond questions of economic and political structure.

Causation itself, like chronology, is a complex problem. If modernization is vastly different from preindustrial society, then we need to ask what jolted the latter toward the former; did some huge external force compel a break, and to whom did it apply? Yet, at the same time, what was there in traditional Western society, particularly in that of Great Britain, that allowed the only spontaneous, nonimitative modernization that the world will ever know? Might change in fact have occurred within? Both questions turn us squarely to what was going on in the century or so before clear structural changes, such as the early factories, were on the scene. It is certainly possible to see causes of fundamental change in the seventeenth and early eighteenth centuries. Premodern society was never static; many new trends developed in Europe between 1550 and 1750. Since the end of the Middle Ages, Europe had witnessed important shifts in population levels, social structure, and popular culture. By the sixteenth and seventeenth centuries, some of the changes began to point toward the formation of modern society. Under absolutism, governments became more centralized and efficient. Most of these governments encouraged economic change, if only in the interest of augmenting the tax base for the royal coffers. By the early eighteenth century, several governments were promoting the cultivation of new crops, such as the potato, and establishing new factories, which encouraged the utilization of new machinery.

During the seventeenth and eighteenth centuries, the tone of intellectual life was dramatically altered. Leading intellectuals vaunted man's power to reason and the possibility of progress. They urged further scientific and technological advances. The new world of the intellectuals was aggressively secular. God and religion receded in importance, and in some cases were directly attacked. The scientific revolution merged into the new general Enlightenment.

Somewhat apart from both government and intellectuals, a variety of businessmen and landowners, primarily in Great Britain and Holland, were experimenting with new farming and manufacturing techniques and new forms of economic organization. New crops, drainage methods, and farming equipment began to increase agricultural production. Many landowners—and not just those who directed great estates—began to produce primarily for sales to distant markets. In business, the most spectacular innovators were the merchants who organized great trading companies for worldwide commerce. New systems of investing and accounting developed. Manufacturing changed more slowly, but by the eighteenth century, manufacturers were rapidly extending the systems of rural production, drawing hundreds of thousands of peasants into a new market system. The manufacturers provided raw materials and sold the finished products. Rural workers set up looms or spindles in their homes and produced what they were told to produce. Never before had so many people been involved in a capitalistic production system.

Governments, intellectuals, and entrepreneurs are three obvious and significant sources of change, though historians still debate their relative importance and their interconnections, and are still far from understanding the dynamics of initial modernization. Many new entrepreneurs, for example, knew little about scientific discoveries or the growing belief in progress. They increased industrial production by applying new techniques, but most of the techniques were devised by artisans. It is more likely that the success of the new technology led industrialists to their belief in science and progress rather than the other way around. The essays that follow, however, deal with groups that were remote from the most obvious sources of change. The majority of Europe's preindustrial people were rural—the peasant is rightly seen as the archetypical preindustrial group—and were wedded to a belief in a stable society. The rural population was diverse, including landowning peasants, near-landless cottagers, and artisans. But the common people of the countryside, as well as most of their counterparts in the cities, shared a set of values that was fundamentally opposed to change.

Even a brief glimpse at Europe's preindustrial people returns us to two vital and related issues. First of all, a judgment about the nature of preindustrial life is essential in order to assess the impact of modernization. If rural life was in fact comfortable and secure, surely the advent of industrialization and urban life must have been profoundly disruptive. If, on the other hand, rural life was marked by persistent tension and frustration, perhaps change was welcome. (We need not, of course, regard the preindustrial lower classes as homogeneous. Certain areas, personality types, or even age groups may have been particularly restless.)

The second issue that must be dealt with is the extent to which the common people of Europe, or at least of western Europe, actively contributed to modernization. We might assume that most change came from above—from the state, the new philosophers, the pioneering businessmen—and that the common people were forced into new political and economic roles. This approach would presumably be the most compatible with a belief that modernization imposed profound dislocation on most people. But perhaps some change was spontaneous, stemming from the values of the common people themselves. There is evidence that these values were changing. During the eighteenth century, for example, the spread of domestic manufacturing, although sponsored in part by urban capitalists, found a quick response in the countryside. Rural workers learned new consumption habits. They adopted more urban styles of dress and bought processed food products such as tea and sugar. This was the first step, perhaps, in a new esteem for material acquisitions that would ultimately prove vital to the industrialization process. Family patterns also changed, since many rural workers began to marry at an earlier age.

In other words, the lower classes in preindustrial western Europe may have been ripe for change. Although no one can deny that disruption was involved—bringing not only material hardship, but intense psychic stress—the common people may have been more than passive victims in the modernization process. Indeed, it was from their ranks that some of the key innovators stemmed. The ancestors of most of the dynamic factory owners of the early nineteenth century could be found, a hundred years earlier, among the peasants and artisans. Their rise was unusual, but it may have drawn on an openness to change that was more widely shared and that served to cushion the shock of modernization for those who remained in the lower classes.

So we are trying to determine both the distance ordinary Europeans had to travel to become "modern" and the extent to which they launched the process themselves in the seventeenth and eighteenth centuries. Obviously, any discussion of the values of the "common" people is a chancy business, even for the present day. For the premodern period, historians must use very fragmentary records. In a few cases there is good statistical evidence on behavior patterns—size of families, for example—but the question of the motives and values that gave rise to the patterns is open to speculation.

This means that the historian's own preconceptions can take on added importance. There has been a constant tendency to idealize the past. As far back as the beginning of the nineteenth century, many people turned to the preindustrial past as a solace from the evils of the present. Even late into the nineteenth century, workers retained a nostalgia for the countryside, although they seldom acted on it. In the United States, as in Europe, "back to the land" impulses continue to appear, based at least in part on a belief in the purity and simplicity of preindustrial existence. Not surprisingly, many of the historians who try to assess this existence have similar yearnings. Since the peasants and artisans left few direct records of their thoughts, making it impossible ever to be absolutely certain how they viewed their own life, it is all too easy for nostalgic historians to fill in the gaps with their own projections of what preindustrial life must have been like.

The study of preindustrial society, in America and in Europe, is being actively pursued on a number of fronts. Our knowledge is increasing. We can already come to some tentative conclusions about why modernization began on the shores of the Atlantic, in western Europe and North America, and what impact it had on the people involved.

BIBLIOGRAPHY

Studies of preindustrial rural society are somewhat sparse. In addition to the works by Le Roy Ladurie and Laslett, see Marc Bloch, *French Rural History* (Berkeley, 1970), and Pierre Goubert, *Louis XIV and Twenty Million Frenchmen* (New York, 1969). B. H. Slicher Van Bath, *The Agrarian History of Western Europe, A.D. 500–1850* (New York, 1963), and Robert Trow-Smith, *Life from the Land: The Growth of Farming in Western*

Europe (New York, 1967), deal with the traditional rural economy. Traian Stoianovich, *A Study in Balkan Civilization* (New York, 1967), outlines a society unique in some respects, but one perhaps more genuinely "premodern" than the society of western Europe. Early changes in English rural life are discussed in Joan Thirsk, ed., *The Agrarian History of England 1500–1640* (Cambridge, Eng., 1967); Charles Wilson, *England's Apprenticeship* (New York, 1965); and G. R. Mingay, *English Landed Society in the Eighteenth Century* (Toronto, 1963). John Lough, *An Introduction to Seventeenth Century France,* 2nd ed. (New York, 1969), is a valuable survey of French society and politics. For one aspect of material culture, Olwen Hufton, *The Poor of Eighteenth Century France* (New York, 1975). Although it deals with the end of the eighteenth century, Charles Tilly, *The Vendée* (New York, 1967), shows the impact of economic change on peasants and the readiness of some to come to grips with it in contrast to the bitter resistance of others—a division that depended on an earlier exposure to a market economy. Finally, for an effort at a general statement on the nature of the peasantry, Eric Wolf, *Peasants* (Englewood Cliffs, N.J., 1966).

Toward an understanding of premodern attitudes, including popular religion and superstition: Christopher Hill, *The World Turned Upside Down: Radical Ideas During the English Revolution* (New York, 1972); Alan Macfarlane, *The Family Life of Ralph Josselin* (New York, 1970), and *Witchcraft in Tudor and Stuart England* (London, 1970); Philip Greven, *The Protestant Temperament* (New York, 1978); E. William Monter, *Witchcraft in France and Switzerland* (Ithaca, 1976); and Natalie Davis, *Society and Culture in Early Modern France* (Stanford, 1975). An interesting effort to connect new ideas with early industrial technology is A. E. Musson and Eric Robinson, *Science and Technology in the Industrial Revolution* (Toronto, 1969).

There are few historical studies of madness. Michel Foucault, *Madness and Civilization,* trans. Richard Howard (New York, 1965), offers a sweeping interpretation. George Rosen has published other works on the history of the insane and their treatment in his collection *Madness in Society: Chapters in the Historical Sociology of Mental Illness* (New York, 1968). Changes in attitude toward the insane in America are suggested in David Rothman, *The Discovery of the Asylum: Social Order and Disorder in the New Republic* (Boston, 1971), and Gerald N. Grob, *The State and the Mentally Ill: A History of the Worcester State Hospital in Massachusetts* (Chapel Hill, 1966).

The preindustrial family is beginning to receive considerable attention. A pioneering work, with an important general thesis about the development of the modern family, is Philippe Ariès, *Centuries of Childhood: A Social History of Family Life* (New York, 1962). On family structure, Peter Laslett and R. Wall, *Household and Family in Past Time* (New York, 1972). Two histories of French villages provide important information on family structure: Thomas Sheppard, *Lourmarin in the Eighteenth Century: A Study of a French Village* (Baltimore, 1971), and

Patrice Higonnet, *Pont-de-Montvert: Social Structure and Politics in a French Village, 1700–1914* (Cambridge, Mass., 1971). Another major work on the period, though with an American focus, is Philip J. Greven, Jr., *Four Generations: Population, Land, and Family in Colonial Andover, Massachusetts* (Ithaca, 1970).

On the nature of work, leisure, and of changes in both with early modernization, E. P. Thompson, *The Making of the English Working Class* (New York, 1964); W. G. Hoskins, *The Midland Peasant: The Economic and Social History of a Leicestershire Village* (New York, 1957); and three classic studies by J. L. and Barbara Hammond: *The Village Labourer, 1760–1832* (New York, 1970 [reprint of 1911 edition]), *The Town Labourer, 1760–1832* (New York, 1968 [reprint of 1917 edition]), and *The Skilled Labourer, 1760–1832* (New York, 1970 [reprint of 1919 edition]).

The Peasants of Languedoc

EMANNUEL LE ROY LADURIE

The peasantry was the key ingredient of preindustrial society in terms of its numbers and the prominence of its value systems among the common people. Yet it proves an elusive entity when examined with any precision. The peasant world was varied, differing greatly from one region to the next, and it changed significantly over time. Even its basic wealth could alter. Too easily we imagine uniform material conditions for the peasantry, when in fact there were significant gradations within a single region. In western Europe, the peasant economy usually maintained some contact with the market, even though many peasants produced enough for their own needs, with only a bit of surplus to cover tax obligations and landlord exactions. There were peasant owners, peasant employers, as well as peasants who hired themselves out as laborers or sharecroppers. The peasant economy as a whole is often termed a subsistence operation, producing only basic human needs. Yet periodically there was a surplus beyond that necessary to support a small upper class. On this basis, among other things, population could grow.

Yet, although it was capable of change, the peasant economy was not a dynamic one; certainly it could not readily support massive population growth. The very fact of occasional surplus meant there was ample possibility for cycles of shortage. The following selection deals with one such cycle, during the eventful sixteenth century, in a large area of southeastern France. It is not a typical area—there is no totally typical peasant region—but it convincingly demonstrates what could be a grim reality for peasants in many places. Languedoc was no placid, changeless peasant world. Changes in material standards, whereby growing misery brought on rising death rates, and currents of religious upheaval such as Protestantism (in a region that had often deviated from mainstream Catholicism), played on the peasant mind. Nevertheless, from the vantage point of modernization, peasant turbulence can seem rather directionless. Crisis did not produce the kind of mentality that would open itself to a new economy, to new methods of work, and to new levels of productivity. Relying as it did on elements of traditional peasant ritual, bitter protest did not suggest a turn to modernity. Sixteenth-century Languedoc was not a pleasant place, and should be compared with more favorable images of the premodern rural world presented in subsequent selections. We can see, in the material life of the peasantry, in the omnipresence of misery and death, ample reason why some peasants might welcome a different economic system. But there was no motive to impel the development of a new system. Change of a fundamental sort could not come from within, and Languedoc long remained a backward (although still turbulent) region in the French economy and society. If we can describe a traditional order, in terms of economic behavior and outlook, to contrast with later modernization, it would not be in terms of passiveness, tranquility, or even a steady level of poverty, but rather in terms of this locked-in quality, in which distress would only confirm the existing economic system. This raises, of course, the question of the causes of ultimate modernization; what kind of peasants could accept, much less produce, fundamental change? And, lest we turn too easily to modernization as a steady source of progress, we must ultimately ask if modernization does not produce its own varieties of distress, which the system itself, for all its dynamic tone, cannot resolve.

At the bottom of the social ladder, among the great mass of the populace, twin processes of pauperization were raging. The first process attacked the smallholders whose numbers had multiplied as a result of land subdivision without a sufficient increase in real income per unit to compensate for shrinking individual land parcels; the second affected the salaried workers and resulted from the decline in real wages. It is certain that the same individuals and the same families were very often victims of both processes. The cases of mixed income in which the peasant lived off his wages plus a small plot of land are numerous. It is enough to leaf through the notaries almost at random. In a certain large village of the Cévennes in about 1555, for example, many wageworking *travailleurs* also owned diminutive mountain plots and "half a pair of oxen" (sic). It is true that there were also landless wageworkers, but these were the regular hired hands on the estate farms, not the village day laborers.

In the last analysis, this twofold impoverishment represents history's radical solution to the Malthusian dilemma. Because population had taken wing while production was marking time, a double system of rationing went into effect: a rationing of land that confined the peasant to tinier and tinier plots and a rationing of money, because employers cheerfully exploited the economic conjuncture to distribute lower and lower wages to their workers. The living standards of the poor succumbed to this double system of restraints and sank to the vital minimum, and the subsistence crises deepened.

From E. Le Roy Ladurie, *The Peasants of Languedoc* (Paris: Flammarion et Cie, 1969). Trans. copyright © 1974 by the Board of Trustees of the University of Illinois. Reprinted by permission of the University of Illinois.

In fact, the poor harvest years (one out of every three or four in this dry region) had relatively benign effects on the sparse population of 1480–1500, whose tenures were ample and whose wages were substantial, but their ravages spread as population grew, landholdings contracted, and wages shrank. A harvest failure about 1550–90 affected living standards that were already depressed and impoverished. For this reason it created acute shortages and sometimes famine.

If our analyses of landownership and wages in the preceding pages are exact, one would expect to encounter, during the course of the century, scarcities and famines of increasing frequency and intensity and at the same time appropriate modifications in the provisioning policies of the authorities. This hypothesis corresponds to reality, at least as far as the century between 1460 and 1560 is concerned. (After 1560 the civil wars, by creating artificial famine conditions, may serve to vitiate the results). In general, it is possible to distinguish three periods: one of relative plenty (1460–1504), one of initial difficulties (1504–26), and one of grave crises (after 1526). The three stages suggest a process of deterioration; the mounting demographic tide was submerging the weak defenses of agricultural production.

First we have the period of plenty from 1460 to 1504, of which the Estates of Languedoc were fully conscious. The delegates had not yet succumbed to the timorous, prohibitionist attitude they would adopt after 1504 and especially after 1526. They did nothing to restrict the exportation of grain from the province. On the contrary, they encouraged it, and they complained of the king's agents who first set restrictions on exports and then granted export licenses "under the table" to their special friends. It was for this reason that the provincial governor, the sieur de Chabannes, was censured by the Estates in 1492. In this first period the regional assembly imposed an embargo on grain exports on only three occasions: in 1496, in 1498, and in 1501. In normal years the province enjoyed a surplus. The grain market was strangely becalmed. What a far cry from the human overcharge and recurrent famines of the first half of the fourteenth century, prior to 1348.

There were omens of what was to come, however. To begin with, there was the harvest failure of 1474 in the region of Toulouse. It seems to have spared Mediterranean Languedoc, unlike the one born of cold and rain that devastated the whole of France south of the Loire in 1482/83. At Montpellier the beggars were penned up and given three hundred loaves of bread to share with the plague victims of that same year. Then the curtain falls; for the next fifteen years there was not a single famine alert. In this period of plenty without precedent, the demographic resurgence of Languedoc, which had long been brewing, could materialize under the most favorable of circumstances.

With the mediocre harvests of 1495–96, and especially of 1497, the first discordant notes of *esterillité de vivre* (food shortage) were sounded. The towns were full of panderers and roving packs of hungry roughnecks. The

Genoese wanted to buy grain, but the Estates imposed an embargo on the ports. Mule drivers with their pack animals came flocking from the poverty-stricken Rouergue and from the whole mountainous amphitheater of the south-central plateau in the hope of making off with some of the meager stocks of the Mediterranean littoral. These starving wretches were indeed a pitiful sight to behold. There were a few other alarms (the mediocre crop of 1501 caused a brief price flurry), but afterwards everything returned to normal. On the whole, periods of scarcity were rare during these forty-four years.

The second period (1504–26) began with a poor harvest year, which initiated a new phase of austerity. The following winter the Estates placed an embargo on exports. Clients near at hand who were also short of provisions—Genoese, Florentines, and natives of the Dauphiné—were refused grain. The twenty-two bishops sitting in the assembly even confiscated two hundred *charges* of wheat destined for "Our Holy Father the Pope." Throughout the winter of 1504/1505 the cathedral chapters and commanderies distributed alms to a swarm of paupers. The situation remained tense following the harvest of 1505. By fall, food hoarding and shortages were rife. The harvest of 1506 was not much better. In January, 1507, with the new harvest still months off, the Estates panicked and forbade the export of grain. Similar measures followed the harvest of 1507, when exports of grain to Aragon or other destinations were outlawed. The run of bad luck continued; the harvest of 1508 must have been another disappointment if in the spring of 1509 commissioners were appointed to prevent the circulation of grain from seneschalsy to seneschalsy. This phase of uncommon scarcity, lasting from 1504 to 1508, was signaled by a plateau of high prices on the *mercuriale* of Montpellier.

A new hunger cycle set in after a very short lapse of time (something unheard of before 1504), with three lean years in succession (1513, 1514, and 1515). This time it was clear that Languedoc's position as a grain-exporting region was seriously compromised—that the grain market was somehow out of order. The fortunate late fifteenth century—when five or ten or sometimes even fifteen years passed without the slightest hint of scarcity, when export restrictions were measures of exception and were never renewed from year to year—was a distant memory. In fact, if the structure of the market changed, if barriers were raised between the regional economies in a spirit of exclusiveness, it was because there were many more mouths to feed. The "full contingents" of the period around 1500 weighed heavily on the demand side of the supply and demand equation, creating conditions of scarcity.

The situation was irreversible and was getting worse. Export embargoes were imposed in 1517, 1519, 1520, 1522, and 1525. Henceforward, hidden lean periods recurred every second year, like fallowing. Beginning in 1526 the "tragedy of wheat"—a veritable famine cycle—got under way. A period of recurring difficulties gave way to one of permanent crisis. The Estates' laissez-faire attitude was a forgotten memory, and the free grain market of the fifteenth century was dead and buried. For ten years running (1526–36) the provincial assembly prohibited the export of cereals.

A Crisis in Depth

In 1526 the harvest was mediocre; in 1527 disaster struck. A cyclonic period lasting several years (with rainy summers and mild winters that caused the grain to rot in the ground) descended on Europe and the Mediterranean. The harvest of 1527 was a total loss. In August the Estates—ignoring the entreaties of grain buyers from Provence, Florence, and Genoa—prohibited cereal exports. But important personnages like the abbot d'Aniane, who was too close to the court to be refused a favor, managed nevertheless to market their grains abroad at high prices and handsome profits. By April of 1528 famine was raging in Languedoc, and wheat had to be imported from overseas via the port of Marseilles. It sold for two *livres* and ten *sous* in the towns and three *livres* in the villages, always the last to be served. Dearth was attended by plague.

The usurers were having a field day. In the foothills they lent scarce grain to the poor at high interest. This was the way the *sieur de Carlencas* responded to the appeals of a number of hungry weavers in that sinister April of 1528.

June, 1528: the new harvest was not good. Hunger persisted and stocks remained low. August, November, 1528: "*rarité des bleds, cherté plus que ne fut oncques*" ("shortage of grain, prices higher than ever"). The price curve had been climbing steadily since 1525. The borders of the province remained sealed. The spring of 1529 was therefore a difficult time; the Parlement of Toulouse finally beseeched the notables, "for charity's sake unlock your granaries, cart your grains to market, lower your prices." But it was a case of "famine," and the implacable order also went out to "expel the vagabonds and foreigners."

The harvest of 1529 did not succeed in exorcising the shortage of bread. In November the Estates, assembled in the lower hall of a large hospital, rejected the appeals for grain emanating from the cities of Lyons, Avignon, and Arles. The harvest of 1530 was still inadequate, given the growing need and the empty granaries. In September, 1530, restrictions were imposed on nonresident grain buyers. In November exports were again prohibited. The spring of 1531 was one of scarcity and even famine; a reward was posted for denouncing secret stocks. In May requisitioning began, and the price of grain was frozen in the face of the intolerable scarcity and the growing multitude of destitute poor. At Montpellier, for that matter, the seasonal highs of 1529 and 1531 broke all previous records on the price curve. They would not be equaled again until 1545. New prohibitions against exports were promulgated by the Estates in 1531, 1532, 1533—when a bad dry spell paralyzed the sowing—and finally in 1535.

The passage from a free-trade mentality to self-serving protectionism on the part of the notables of Languedoc is evident. Their about-face connotes a simple awareness of economic realities and also a psychological adjustment. Thirty years earlier abundance had been the rule; now it was chronic scarcity. Henceforth, there were too many mouths to feed and not enough bread to go around.

It is necessary to dwell at some length on these ten lean years (1526–35), in the first place because they mark a major turning point in the grain policy of the Estates of Languedoc. In other sectors, that of wine for example, the provincial assembly remained faithful to its fifteenth-century free-trade principles. The export of wine was permitted because there was never a shortage of it, but in the case of grain, freedom to export was only an exception reserved for the bumper harvest years (1536, 1542, 1547, 1549, 1554, and 1556). Interdiction had become almost an automatic reflex. In the period 1537–60, the Estates suppressed (at least in theory) all cereal exports from the province three years out of four. Languedocian wheat after 1526 was in reality a prisoner, if sometimes free on parole.

The crisis of 1526–35, moreover, also marked a social turning point. Vagrancy became a veritable scourge and was, for the first time, systematically suppressed. In 1532, following five years of dearth, the province was full of vagabonds—"murderers guilty of innumerable homicides." According to the Estates, the inhabitants of the region no longer dared go to their fields. In 1533 the countryside of Nîmes was "infested with beggars as a result of the extreme misery that has reigned here in recent times."

Ritual complaints, perhaps? But there was nothing ritual about the following. In 1533 for the first time in their history, the Estates of Languedoc, all out of patience with the profusion of poor wretches, determined to wipe out pauperism by force. They wrote the king that too many poor sought refuge in the lands of Languedoc, that too many of them refused to work, and that they encumbered the churches, troubled the divine service, and disturbed the meditations of the faithful during the elevation of the Host by their clamor—not to mention the sicknesses that followed in their wake.

Francis I granted the petition. From Compiègne, he signed an edict dated April 15, 1534, providing for the arrest of all healthy individuals who "for a certain time" have gone to beg and panhandle (*belistrer*) in the territories of Languedoc. And thenceforth, almost every year up to 1560, the question of the errant poor, "thieves, robbers and evildoers" (*"volleurs, larrons et malvenans"*), "vermin who proliferate day after day in the towns, fields, roads and lanes," led to anxious deliberations in the Estates or in the Parlement of Toulouse.

What was true of Languedoc, where the long subsistence crisis of 1526–35 aggravated by demographic factors led to mass vagrancy and to its repression by the authorities, was also true of the rest of Europe. Everywhere in the west the problem of the poor became acute about 1525–30 because of demographic ground swell, the succession of poor harvests, and the cycle of high grain prices. In 1525 Zwingli set up his relief plan for the indigent population of Zurich. In 1526 Juan Luis Vives published *De subventione pauperum*, a work conceived at Louvain and Oxford. In 1530 Henry VIII promulgated the first antivagrancy statute. By royal order, sturdy beggars were yoked to carts, were whipped until the blood ran, were mutilated by having an ear cut off, or were sometimes hung. In 1537 Charles V took similar measures in the Low Countries. It was precisely in these years that monopolized the people's purchasing power. Meat was omitted from the popular diet, and the livestock industry suffered the backlash.

Finally, it is necessary to invoke a third factor to explain the crisis in stock raising, one that was likewise inseparable from the general movement of the society. Land reclamation reduced sheepwalks. Olive and chestnut plantings, terraces, and stone enclosures restricted common pasture. For all these reasons, stock raising leveled off and then declined. In traditional peasant agriculture, where forage plants were unknown—or confined to gardens—it was impossible for livestock and field crop production to develop simultaneously, since both were competing for the remaining free land which was daily becoming more circumscribed. In the absence of an organization like the Spanish *Mesta* to defend the interests of the graziers, the livestock industry in an expanding preindustrial society was sacrificed without ado.

Once again, the turning point occurred about 1520–30. Grazing rights on the commons and fallow had been liberally accorded stockherders prior to that time, and the Parlement of Toulouse, between 1445 and 1519, had shown itself to be the leading champion of the ancient customs. In 1520 came the first discordant note. Parlement's attitude changed in connection, specifically, with the recent spread of vine and olive cultivation. In that year the inhabitants of Gignac were forbidden to pasture their animals in the vineyards and olive orchards. This was the first time Parlement took such measures. In 1528 the inhabitants of Lunel suffered the same restrictions. The question was henceforth one of public concern, and faced with a choice between livestock and cash crops like wine and olives, one did not hesitate to sacrifice animals to plants—the peasant's common rights to the farmer's private interests. In 1530, for the first time in their history—and then again in 1531 and 1532—the local notables sitting in the Estates demanded the off-limits posting of vineyards, olive orchards, meadows, woods, copses, and fruit trees and the interdiction of common pasture in these posted areas, or devès, without the owner's permission. At Pézenas, too, measures against collective grazing in the plantings—decreed in 1306 but fallen into disuse during the Wüstungen period of 1350–1500 when stock was king—were resurrected in 1533; overpopulation and land hunger infused new life into the ancient pre-Wüstungen legislation dating from an earlier cycle of demographic congestion, vine and tree plantings, and agrarian particularism. And under the pressure of circumstances, the attitude of the public authorities changed radically about 1520–30; by a single impulse, both free trade in grain and common grazing rights were repudiated or restricted. The precious bread cereals and certain cash crops were the objects of every solicitude, while cattle and sheep were regarded with hostility. The reign of the graziers drew to a close.

The livestock industry of Languedoc never recovered from the crisis of 1530. Between the start of the sixteenth century and the civil war, the nominal returns from the carnencs passed from an index of 60 to an index of 100—a nominal increase, but a regression in real terms because in the same interval the price of dressed meat rose 130 percent. This deterioration of real income from the carnencs is a sure sign of shrinking herds. While the human population was doubling and food crop production was rising slightly, or at least holding its own, stock raising collapsed, and the popular consumption of meat, as reflected in wages and tithes, caved in.

The period 1526–35, in short, was one of deep crisis arising from the contradictions inherent in the development of the society itself. It was a crisis that affected every aspect of life from its biological foundation to its psychological superstructure.

With regard to biology, the plague of 1530, which proliferated in the wake of hunger and malnutrition, was one of the most violent of the sixteenth century (this at a time when the plague tended to become less virulent in the French Midi). In 1530 Montpellier mobilized practically all its revenues to fight the contagion. The case was almost unique in the financial history of the city, a measure of the seriousness of the epidemic.

With regard to psychology, beginning in 1526 Protestant propaganda evoked a powerful response in a population tormented by material adversity and envious of the wealthy clergy. It was during the Christmas of 1527 and the terrible Lent of 1528, a winter and spring of stark hunger, that the Reformation took root in the Vivarais and in Languedoc with the first heretical preaching of the Cordeliers before excited crowds and the earliest persecutions of religious propagandists in a region heretofore untouched by heresy. In November, 1528, Lutheran sectarians appeared as far away as Toulouse, "invoking the devil," it was said, and "uttering execrable blasphemies." The rural Cévennes, a future bastion of heresy, was already "infected." In 1529 the Rebeine insurgents of Lyons, contemporaries of the Anabaptists of the North, staged food riots, attacked the convents, and mutinied against the tithes. The influence of the Rebeine was perceptible throughout the southeast, a region linked to Lyons by a multiple network of commercial relations. Beginning in 1530, the satiric theme of the monk's head with ass's ears was popularized as a decorative motif by the stonemasons of Languedoc. The peasant masses were contaminated. In 1532 in the Bas-Rhône, entire villages—led by their syndics, regents, and priests—embraced the Reformation. The heresy was thus implanted at the height of a social crisis. It took firm root, giving promise of a brilliant future; five years later its practitioners were beyond counting.

The years 1526–35 were therefore a pivotal crisis, a nodal point of social history as the Fronde was later and elsewhere and in an entirely different context. As a result of these years, the abstract economic indices—the disparities noted in rates of growth and the analyses of landownership and wages—assume a concrete significance, finding embodiment in the great popular disturbances. The crisis first dramatized the lessons of immoderate demographic advance attended by insufficient economic growth. During and after this paroxysm, the popular and rural masses "could no longer live as before"—could no longer work, eat, pray, think, and die as in the past. On the threshold of the second generation of expansion, the crisis of 1530 marked the end of good times and the twilight of a happy age.

Languedoc was not alone. In Spain, Germany, the Low Countries, and England the decade of the 1520's or 1530's commenced the long travail of the old-style proletariat, the repression of the peasants and the poor. In Italy the decade of the 1520's, especially 1528–29, was a time of terrible famine, of the *gran fame*, the "great hunger," at Venice. "What were obliterated in these difficult years were the brightest flowers of the early Renaissance."

A Certain Capitalism Miscarries

It remains for us to consider—over and against the question of poverty—the triumphant history of profits and wealth. To understand the latter, the studies of land and income, the horizontal and vertical analyses, have to be compared and integrated "in their multiple complexity and the reciprocity of their interrelations" (Sartre). In the world of the poor, a comparison of the two angles of vision leads to converging and cumulative results. The two kinds of pauperization, in wages and in land, reinforced one another. The "little man" was impoverished twice over, as a wageworker and as a smallholder. At the other end of the scale, at the level of profits and wealth, the story was different. There, the land or "horizontal" perspective and the social or "vertical" perspective were no longer complementary but apparently contradictory. From the vertical perspective of types and levels of income, land rent held its own while profits rose. Did this signify that rural capitalism was making progress?

In a certain measure, yes. But it remained confined within narrow limits because the surplus value on which it depended was not derived, except in a small way, from a rapidly growing aggregate product, as was to be the case after 1750 and especially after 1850. For once our picture-book clichés happen to be true. That surplus value was extracted drop by drop from the sweat of the impoverished workers, and the good fortune of profits was conditioned by the misfortune of wages. A "growth of wealth" of this type is necessarily limited, for pauperization quickly reaches the level of bare subsistence and can proceed no further. In order to release important sources of surplus value, production would have had to increase on a massive scale, as was the case in neighboring Catalonia in the eighteenth century. But in sixteenth-century Languedoc the process of economic growth was not yet really under way.

The other profit impasse derived from the land structure itself and from its characteristic evolution. True, entrepreneurial profits grew in the sixteenth century, but only within the immutable confines of a given domain. The capitalist class, in order to allow the process ample scope, should have consolidated its lands—enlarged its territorial base. There should have been more and more great estates, big landowners, and large-scale tenant farmers. Land concentration, in other words, should have been the dominant phenomenon.

Practically nothing of the kind occurred. There were, of course, a few attempts at land consolidation, but these constituted exceptions to the rule. Take the case of Eutrope Fabre, of Gaillac, a miserly priest who died in 1532. In a lifetime of saving he barely managed to piece together five or six plots of land, a miserable seven hectares in all. This "magnificent" property, moreover, was destined to be parceled out again to his prolific grandnephews. The basic movement of the sixteenth century is to be sought elsewhere, in the process of land subdivision which dismembered those land units capable of generating capitalistic profits. The great estates of the sixteenth century constituted an isolated archipelago lost (and sometimes swallowed up) in a rising sea of destitute, diminutive smallholds.

Rural capitalism appropriated a greater share for itself on the vertical plane at the expense of the farm worker, but it was largely unsuccessful on the horizontal plane, where success was a question of land aggrandizement. It failed to appropriate the peasant smallholds. To the extent that this process was taking place at all in the sixteenth century, it was limited to the countryside of Paris or London and was hardly characteristic of the regions around Nîmes or Narbonne. The south of France, between 1490 and 1600, was refractory to land engrossers.

There are three possible sources of surplus value in agriculture: increased production, land concentration, and reduced wages. Rural capitalism in Languedoc in the sixteenth century really only explored the most primitive and the least humane of these three possibilities, the third. In these circumstances it was able to accomplish modest and limited progress at best. The regional economy, notwithstanding the enormous sacrifices of the rural laborers, remained incapable of secreting a capitalistic social system—capitalism is not built on poverty.

Languedoc and Catalonia

A comparison between Languedoc in the sixteenth century and Catalonia in the eighteenth century is perhaps relevant in this connection. The common features stand out in relief. In both cases population doubled in less than a century—two examples of the incredible demographic resiliency of the Mediterranean peoples, cast into the depths by misery and disease only to reemerge with renewed vitality. Another trait in common was the accelerated subdivision of landholdings that went hand in hand with the rising tide of population.

At this point, however, the comparison breaks down. In Catalonia production kept pace with and sometimes outdistanced the increase in population. An ingenious irrigation policy unchained income per land unit, eliminated fallowing, and transformed the rural landscape into an enchanted world of meadows, *huertas*, and cash crops like flax, maize, rice, alfalfa and clover, and garden plants. Vineyards were planted, stock multiplied, and the heavy plow ousted the scratch plow. The demographic increase served as a multiplier of real wealth. The overall tithe, income, living standards, land rent, profits—all "rode up together, on the tide" and at a much faster rate than prices. Wages were no longer the pariah of economic expansion. They clung to the price curve, picking up momentum and managing even to leave prices behind during the prosperous years of the French Revolution. This was true economic growth in the modern sense, and it contributed to the growth of urban and industrial capitalism. Peasant savings, sustained by Mexican piastres, financed the expansion of the port of Barcelona, a city of one hundred thousand inhabitants, upsetting the old economic balance and paving the way for an industrial "takeoff."

Nothing of the sort occurred in our mid-sixteenth-century Languedoc. The one dominant factor, alas, was demography. Economic attitudes remained immutable, and Malthusian "scissors" were opening up on every side: between population and production, between agriculture and stock raising, between wages and prices. Wage rationing and land rationing were instituted. The meager savings realized from the squeeze on rural wages were insufficient to initiate large-scale agricultural investment and failed at the same time to stimulate urban development. The biggest "cities" of Mediterranean Languedoc in about 1550, Nîmes and Montpellier, each counted two thousand houses or about ten thousand inhabitants, a quarter of whom were peasants and farm laborers. They were still, in reality, just small country towns.

The Catalonian expansion of the age of the Enlightenment was a modern type of development, the source of individual economic enrichment. The Languedocian expansion of the Renaissance was of the ancient kind, a multiplier of poverty. . . .

Carnival at Romans

Around 1580, on both banks of the Rhône—in Languedoc and Dauphiné (the provincial frontiers are of no importance in this connection)—a colorful and impassioned peasant insurrection flared up. It was ignited by hardship and misery and the price of bread: "In that same year, 1580, and since the year 1579, a great multitude of starving poor, more than four thousand men, women and little children came here from the Vivarais country weeping and wailing" and so hungry they were devouring the beans in the fields. Hunger and revolt were brewing everywhere in the Rhône region, from the Languedocian Vivarais—the movement's point of departure—to the countryside of Romans in the Dauphiné, an old Huguenot stronghold where the uprising would reach its climax. In this region of the middle Rhône— where for twenty years the authorities had been denouncing the contagious influence of the Swiss leagues and even certain infiltrations of revolutionary Anabaptism—the parochial youth societies in charge of the popular festivals, or *reynages*, were the active cells of the insurrection. The revolt was first "sworn" in a few Protestant villages, and its initial objectives were modest: to force the soldiers and brigands to respect the peace and to reduce the taille that left the taxpayers with nothing to their names but "rocks and clay." But soon both the base and the program of the movement were broadened. A working alliance was concluded between the peasants ("the village faction") and the artisans of Romans, "an infinity of carders and other mechanical people," led by a local athlete, king of the arquebus, the "wicked draper" Jean Serve, better known as Paulmier ("Handballer"), who was "a coarse and clownish fellow." Serve was so "insolent" that he refused in 1579 to kneel before Catherine de Médicis, who was visiting Romans. The insurgent peasants of the "communes," encouraged by these urban reinforcements, raised their demands, declaring "that they did not wish to pay anything at all," that in 1579 "they had won the tailles and part of the tithes and that the said year following they would win the rest of the said tithes and the quitrents and rights that they owed the lords." Tithe, quitrents, and taille, the three pillars of the traditional order, were being called into question. The peasants grew bolder. They occupied Châteaudouble, a bandit hideout, where we see them "inflated with vainglory" and "threatening the gentlefolk" with dirty and wicked words to "turn their houses upside down." Châteaux and manorial registers went up in flames, "and there was not a yokel who did not behave as if he were as great a lord as his lord." Simultaneously, the project of social inversion which would give the Rhône rebellion its ultimate meaning began to take form.

The episode began as a popular revolution; it ended as an Elizabethan tragedy arrayed in the bright colors of the Renaissance. In the winter of 1580, in fact, excitement began to mount at Romans, which had become the nerve center of the whole movement. The artisans and peasants, incited by the approach of Carnival, acted out their revolt in the streets of the city. "They organized several great feasts, street dances and masquerades, and throughout the week in their dances and masquerades they proclaimed that the rich of their town had grown rich at the expense of the poor people." This popular ballet expresses better than words the latent motivations of the rebels. Certain dancers with Swiss drums and bells on their feet brandished naked swords; others flourished rakes, brooms, threshing flails, and death shrouds (the massacre of the rich by flogging them to death—a simple fantasy or sometimes actually perpetrated—would remain a significant theme of agrarian revolt up to the Spanish Civil War).

And so these flail bearers cried at the top of their voices that "before three days are out Christian flesh will be selling at six *deniers* the pound." These words alone struck terror into people's hearts, and the judge Guérin, our probable narrator, scarcely dared repeat them. Paulmier, for his part—dressed in a bearskin like Spartacus, a detail which seems to have terrified the bourgeois—seized possession of the seat of the consulate, whence he expelled the representatives of the ruling classes. It was an upside-down world in which a pound of rancid tuna and wormy wine cost twenty to twenty-five *sous*, while "partridge à *l'orange* and roast woodcock" and the most exquisite dishes (not to mention Christian flesh) cost only four or five *deniers*, at least according to a long, ludicrous, and *carnavalesque* "price list" composed by the "gentlefolk" and intended to hold Paulmier up to ridicule. It was precisely these "gentlefolk" who, for their part, seized the occasion of Carnival to trick themselves out in tinsel, which symbolized their appetite for power, ostentation, and intimidation and at the same time their desire to forge an alliance with the brutal forces of a virile repression, Turkish style, against the "Scythian" barbarism of the rebels. The members of the "law and order" party, therefore, disguised themselves as king, chancellor, archbishop, high judge, arquebusiers, Swiss, and turbaned Turks. Returning from the Mass, their procession intersected one of the popular party, already dressed in mourning for the people they regarded as their oppressors. The herald of Paulmier's men was disguised as death's messenger in red and blue (the mourning colors) and mounted on an ass, and his followers were crying over and over, "Christian flesh for six (or four) *deniers*." The rich interpreted this scandalous slogan as the expression of cannibalistic intentions in their regard. Nobles, magistrates, bourgeois, and merchants credited the crowd of artisans and peasants with a horrible design to kill them all, if not to eat them, on the day of Mardi Gras in order to marry their wives and divide up their property—a shadowy motive in various revolts. The whole thing was seen as a heinous conspiracy, a Feast of Fools, a bloody buffoonery of a Mardi Gras (or *Gradimars*) which would literally turn the world upside down and confound the meanings of words and the sense of things.

Justified or not, what had become a deep-rooted fear incited the gentle-folk of Romans to take punitive action. They chose as their leader a certain Laroche, the bosom friend of Jean Serve and his comrade in arms during the civil wars, who would become, as sometimes happens, his mortal enemy. The city divided into hostile factions corresponding to the different quarters, rich or poor, and to the animal totems which constituted the prizes in their respective folk festivals—the sheep, hare, and capon parties (the peasants and craftsmen led by Jean Serve), and the cock, eagle, and partridge parties (of the gentlefolk). Laroche was invited, metaphorically, to "embrace" the partridge.

It will be observed that the animals chosen by the poor—contrary to those in the bestiary of the rich, which were delicate or rare (the partridge) or more often virile (the cock, the eagle)—were weak and emasculated, or "bad omens," as the notary Eustache Piémond, who was nevertheless sympathetic to the rebels, remarked. The insurgents did not seem exactly determined to win at all costs. The mourning rites they employed (the psychological sig-nificance of which is quite obscure, as far as that is concerned) indicate that they experienced a certain regret (mixed with hatred, of course) at the eventual demise of their masters. In fact, it was they, the downtrodden, who, on the day of the massacre following the death of Paulmier, let themselves be overpowered and slaughtered by the nobles without offering resistance "like a bunch of pigs."

Carnival, in any case, preserved its rights (the final butchery would not take place until a little later by the light of Mardi Gras candles brandished in the hands of children), and it constituted for the two parties an inspired pretext for theatrical exaggeration. Both sides organized jousts, tilting at the ring, balls, and marvelously ordered banquets, whence there issued reciprocal letters of defiance and challenges. All these festivities were a prelude to the bloody combat in which the factions finally fell upon one another to the strains of music. The occasion for the massacre was furnished the night preceding Mardi Gras by the last parade of the partisans of the partridge, with gamboling, masquerades, and a procession of four kings and a queen so richly dressed "that she was all aglitter." Did those of the capon faction try to attack this queen and pillage the procession? Whatever the case, the gentlewomen at the masked ball of the partridge faction were seized by panic. A band of Mardi Gras sword wielders, armed by the in-furiated rich, left the ball, and at dawn the same day (February 15, 1588) they felled Paulmier, who was taken by surprise, with the blow of a pickax to the face. The other leaders of the popular faction were forced to scale the walls with ropes or swim for their lives in the icy waters of the Isère. Fifteen hundred peasants of the surrounding countryside, alerted by the sound of the tocsin, hurried to the aid of the artisans, but they were too late. Inside the sealed ramparts of Romans, the massacre lasted three days, and it was thus that the gentlefolk were "liberated from the tyranny of the peasants and the Leaguers." The butcher La Fleur and eight other ringleaders were hung. The cadaver of Paulmier, "too putrefied and stinking" to be strung up, was cast into the city dump. The gentlemen finally took their revenge on the rebels, "whom they butchered like hogs." In this way the Carnival of Romans, an abortive episode of social inversion, came to an end. Everything was set right side up again; the dominant classes, for a moment topsy-turvy, landed back on their feet. The better to affirm the return of order, the judges had an effigy of Jean Serve, the rebel chief, hung upside down by the heels.

The bloody Carnival of Romans, a long series of symbolic demonstrations, was a sort of psychological drama or tragic ballet whose actors danced and acted out their revolt instead of discoursing about it in manifestos. The whole was composed like a work of art, giving immediate access to the creations of the unconscious. Since it lacked an interposed ideological screen of the sort that filters and obscures, it was capable of revealing, in the insurrection and in its repression—in the swordplay of reciprocal fears—a certain unformulated content which, in the case of ordinary and less expressive revolts, remained masked from view.

At the same time, thanks to the very richness of its themes and their precise articulation, the Rhône revolt justifies a comparative, thematic study of other medieval and postmedieval revolts that also occurred in the Languedocian, Provençal, and Franco-Provençal region. For example, the public sale of human and Christian flesh, the undeniable cannibalistic fantasies, and the related theme of wife exchange that one meets with at Romans in the anxieties of the rich for a certainty, and probably also in the threats of the poor, are already encountered at the time of the Tuchins, during the Montpellier revolts of 1380, in much the same order and in almost the same sacrilegious terms. "The fomenters of sedition," according to one account, "quartered the bodies of the king's officers with knives and ate the *baptized flesh* like savage animals or threw it to the beasts." Not content with devouring the flesh of the husbands, these rebels, too, were accused of wanting to possess the bodies of the wives. The poor of Béziers in 1381, according to a chronicler, planned to murder their own spouses in order to replace them with the beautiful consorts of the rich. Even if they are exaggerated, such accusations represent a significant element in the accounts of these revolts and, consequently, in the obsessions of the narrators who served as the spokesmen of their age. In fact, the abduction of rich ladies and noble maids by the poor is a constant and recurring theme in the popular revolts of the past as late as the uprisings of lower Brittany in 1675. Young Karl Marx saw in this the peculiar mark of a then outdated primitive communism.

In regard to the related theme of sacrilegious cannibalism by men and beasts—a theme sometimes connected to hysterical episodes of castration—it is attested to not only at Romans and Montpellier, as we have seen, but also during the Huguenot sack of Lodève in 1573 and in the revolt of the boatmen of Agen in 1635—not to mention the popular saturnalia that accompanied the quartering of Ravaillac in 1610.

A new psychohistory will someday have to elucidate the various symptoms of "identification" that crop up in the threats, in the anxieties, and sometimes in the actual deeds attending these plebeian and peasant uprisings. For us, the important thing is to underscore, thanks to the fascinating example of Romans, the enormous emotional charge released in the southern revolts of the second half of the sixteenth century. These rebellions were extremely audacious. They called into question, as we shall see later, institutions that earlier insurrections respected. But if they were more daring from a social point of view, both revolts and repressions also seem to have been more ferocious. Their political objectives were more far-reaching, but at the same time they awakened the most deep-seated impulses of the human psyche.

Religion and the Decline of Magic

KEITH THOMAS

The first clear signs of society's changing mentality are found in the seventeenth century, and they antedate clear structural change such as new technology involved in modernization. The scientific revolution, along with the political and economic attitudes that accompanied it, has long been seen as a key development in intellectual history. Keith Thomas here argues that it decisively changed the framework for popular outlook as well. The following excerpt briefly outlines the nature and function of traditional superstition, indicates the means by which it began to be superseded, and raises the important question of why the massive change in culture occurred.

The selection also suggests two other issues. The new mentality developed at the top of society, among intellectuals and their immediate audience. How far did it penetrate? It is not possible to go too simply from the new science to new business forms or agricultural techniques, for the people responsible for the latter were not directly exposed to the cutting edge of science. Modernization has long been seen as splitting society, leaving many people with a traditional set of beliefs and others, the more powerful, with a new, activist outlook. How many people remained traditionalists, and why? And what happened to them as structural modernization (economic and political change, most obviously) took hold? This leads to the second issue: How thoroughly has modernization altered traditional belief even today? Is society still divided between modern and unmodern people? Do we all harbor a magical approach to nature and society that is now usually clad in the guise of science?

England was the first society to industrialize. Thomas suggests a basic cause was a prior modernization of belief systems. Countries able to copy England's industrialization might not have the same popular mentality with which to work. In other words, questions on the extent of modernization of attitudes, difficult to answer for England, are even more difficult to answer for other European countries. Even for England, Thomas suggests the key problem is one of assessing the extent of change, particularly since there was such a long period in which a new mentality was not accompanied by a new control of the environment. What could impel human beings to put themselves through this transition? In the final analysis, perhaps traditional kinds of faith were applied to new objects; and perhaps we have, or need, some of this faith still.

What the scientific revolution did was to supersede this type of reasoning and to buttress up the old rationalist attitude with a more stable intellectual foundation, based on the mechanical philosophy. It did not matter that the majority of the population of eighteenth-century England had possibly never heard of Boyle or Newton and certainly could not have explained the nature of their discoveries. At all times most men accept their basic assumptions on the authority of others. New techniques and attitudes are always more readily diffused than their underlying scientific rationale. "The average man of today," wrote the psychoanalyst, Ernest Jones, "does not hesitate to reject the same evidence of witchcraft that was so convincing to the man of three centuries ago, though he usually knows no more about the true explanation than the latter did." Most of those millions of persons who today would laugh at the idea of magic or miracles would have difficulty in explaining why. They are victims of society's constant pressure towards intellectual conformity. Under this pressure the magician has ceased to command respect, and intellectual prestige has shifted elsewhere.

It is thus possible to argue that these primitive beliefs declined because they had come to be seen as intellectually unsatisfactory. But it must be confessed that the full details of this process of disillusion are by no means clear. One cannot simply attribute the change to the scientific revolution. There were too many "rationalists" before, too many believers afterwards, for so simple an explanation to be plausible. Let us therefore examine the question from a different point of view. Instead of concentrating on the intellectual status of these beliefs let us consider them in their social context. . . .

The most important cause of man's recourse to magic is his lack of the necessary empirical or technical knowledge to deal with the problems which confront him. "Magic is dominant when control of the environment is weak." When the appropriate techniques become available, magic grows superfluous and withers away. Only in the case of those problems to which men still have no adequate solution does it retain its appeal. It is science and technology which make magic redundant; the stronger man's control of his environment, the less his recourse to magical remedies.

This explanation does not of course make clear why magical rituals should take one form rather than another, for it leaves aside the origin of the mental ingredients which go to make up individual magical fantasies and beliefs. But it does offer an explanation of why magic is invoked at one time rather than another. When applied to the facts of sixteenth- and seventeenth-century society, it makes a good deal of initial sense. The purposes for which most men had recourse to charms or cunning men were precisely those for which an adequate alternative technique was lacking. Thus in agriculture the farmer normally relied upon his own skills; there are no magical charms extant for such automatic tasks as reaping corn or milking cows. But when he was dependent on circumstances outside his control—the fertility of the soil, the weather, the health of his animals—he was more likely to accompany his labours with some magical precaution. There were all the traditional fertility rites and seasonal observances: Plough Monday to ensure the growth of corn; wassailing to bless the apple trees; Rogation processions and Midsummer fires for the crops; corn dollies at harvest time. In Colchester in 1532 a smith's wife was said to practise magic "to make folks believe they should have a sely [lucky] plough." In the absence of weed-killers, there were charms to keep weeds out of the corn, and, in place of insecticide and rat-killers, magical formulae to keep away pests. There were also charms to increase the land's fertility.

Similar precautions surrounded other potentially uncertain operations. Care was taken to time such tasks as sowing corn or cutting trees to harmonise with the phases of the moon or some other propitious factor. There were divinatory systems for ascertaining the weather or the future price of corn. There were charms to make horses work harder, to protect cows from witchcraft, to procure healthy stock, and even to influence the sex of future calves. Bee-keeping and chicken-raising had their semi-magical precautions. So did the making of bread, beer, yeast and butter—spheres in which witchcraft was particularly feared. Ritual precautions surrounded other household operations: no menstruating woman, for example, could ever pickle beef or salt bacon. Similar prescriptions related to hunting and fishing, both speculative activities; in the fishing trade the fear of witchcraft lingered until the nineteenth century. There was also magic designed to counter human deficiencies, moral and physical: charms to prevent the crops being robbed, herbs to allay weariness at the plough, devices like spitting on one's hands to give renewed energy for work.

In many other occupations magical aids were also invoked when problems were too great to be solved by human skill. The dangers of seafaring made sailors notoriously superstitious and generated a large number of ritual precautions designed to secure favourable weather and the safety of the ship. The risks of military adventure encouraged the use of amulets and protective talismans of many kinds. The deficiencies of contemporary medicine drove the sick into the hands of the cunning men and wise women. The slowness of communications and the lack of a police force fostered dependence upon village wizards for the recovery of stolen goods and missing persons. Ignorance of the future encouraged men to grasp at omens or to practise divination as a basis for making decisions. All such devices can be seen as attempts to counter human helplessness in the face of the physical and social environment.

Correspondingly, the decline of magic coincided with a marked improvement in the extent to which this environment became amenable to control. In several important respects the material conditions of life took a turn for the better during the later seventeenth century. The pressure of population, which had caused much hardship during the previous hundred years, now slackened off. Agricultural improvement brought an increase in food production; in the later seventeenth century the country became virtually self-sufficient in corn, while increased imports were used to keep down prices at times of dearth. The growth of overseas trade and the rise of new industries created a more diversified economic environment. There was no major plague epidemic after 1665 and in the 1670s the disease disappeared from England altogether. By 1700 Englishmen enjoyed a higher level of material welfare than the inhabitants of any other country in the world, save Holland. General circumstances of this kind must have done something to increase human self-confidence. Moreover several further developments may have borne a particular responsibility for the declining appeal of the magical solution.

The first of these was a general improvement in communications. Printed news-sheets began in the early seventeenth century, proliferated during the Interregnum and, though checked until 1695 by the licensing laws, had become an indispensable feature of London life by the end of the century. Thereafter they spread to the provinces. Between 1701 and 1760 a hundred and thirty provincial newspapers had made at least a temporary appearance, and they emanated from no fewer than fifty-five different towns. A penny post was introduced in London in 1680 and the letter-carrying service greatly improved thereafter. These developments were accompanied by an increase in popular literacy which may have reached a peak in the third quarter of the seventeenth century, when nearly forty per cent of the adult male population may have been able to read. Changes in the mobility of the population are harder to measure, but it is clear that even in Tudor England the village population was never constant. In the later seventeenth century mobility may have increased with the growth of new industries and the constant movement in and out of London. The general effect of all these trends was to keep the provinces more closely in touch with the metropolis, to break down local isolation and to disseminate sophisticated opinion.

Also important were the advertisements which the newspapers had begun to carry. Notices about lost property and missing persons were a feature of the Commonwealth news-sheets and continued thereafter. Lost dogs, stolen horses, runaway apprentices, suspected thieves—all could now be notified to a wider public than the village wizard or town crier had ever been able to command. In 1657 a projector announced the foundation of an Office of Public Advice with eight branches in the London area to deal with inquiries about lost goods and a weekly bulletin of runaway servants and apprentices. From May to September of that year the sixteen-page *Publick*

Adviser was devoted to weekly advertisements of this kind; and it had a rival in *The Weekly Information from the Office of Intelligence*, which appeared in July and was also made up of advertisements. There were many later attempts at developing such advertising agencies. For the urban middle classes the coffee-house or newspaper office had become the obvious place to which to refer problems about lost goods. The need for the cunning man was accordingly reduced.

Meanwhile certain devices were introduced to lessen the incidence of human misfortune. Greater security for men of property was provided by the rise of deposit banking, but nothing yields greater testimony to the new spirit of self-help than the growth of insurance at the end of the seventeenth century. Of course, schemes designed to cushion sufferers from theft, fire, sickness or other disasters were not without precedent. Many of the gilds of medieval England had operated as friendly societies, taking common responsibility for the cost of burying their members or recompensing their losses by fire. Manorial customs of inheritance often provided for the maintenance of the elderly. But the gilds had disappeared and manorial customs were being eroded. For most inhabitants of late Tudor and Stuart England fire, flood, or the sudden death of a close relative could mean total disaster.

Steps to provide artificial security against such hazards were first taken by merchants and shipowners. Marine insurance developed in fourteenth-century Italy and had taken root in England by the mid-sixteenth century. In 1574 indeed the notaries were claiming to have registered policies "time out of mind." But for a long time the system remained rudimentary. Underwriting was done by individuals rather than companies and most traders only thought about insuring their goods when the ship was already overdue. The insurance of ships as well as the goods they carried did not become common until the reign of William III. The law relating to the arbitration of insurance disputes also remained unsatisfactory. In such circumstances many merchants preferred to lighten their risks by dividing ownership of the ship and its goods between a number of different individuals. All these uncertainties were reflected in the numerous insurance problems which were brought to astrologers like William Lilly. But in the early eighteenth century the situation changed, with the development of Lloyds coffee-house as a regular meeting-place for underwriters and the foundation in 1720 of two substantial joint-stock companies devoted to marine insurance, the London Assurance and the Royal Exchange. . . .

Contemporaries thus gradually grew less vulnerable to certain kinds of disaster. They also developed new kinds of knowledge to supersede mystical explanations of misfortune in terms of witches, ghosts or divine providence. Here the social sciences were as important as the natural ones. Embryonic economics and sociology had developed considerably during the period. By the end of the seventeenth century, it was commonplace for intellectuals to reveal their awareness of the extent to which economic and social hardships could be attributed to impersonal causes, and of the way in which education and social institutions could explain the differences between different peoples and different social classes. This was to be of the main themes of the Enlightenment. The explanatory aspirations of astrological inquiry were taken over by these new disciplines. They rejected the notion that social phenomena were purely random; every event, they held, had a cause, even if it was still hidden. This was why Bacon listed Fortune as a non-existent entity. It was to be replaced by new historical laws. "No government is of so accidental or arbitrary an institution as people are wont to imagine," thought James Harrington, "there being in societies natural causes producing their necessary effects as well as in the earth or the air." The immediacy of the doctrine of divine providence was inevitably much reduced by this assumption that God had bound himself to work through sociological causes as well as physical ones. Witch-beliefs, by contrast, were less affected at first, for they were concerned to explain individual misfortunes, whereas the aim of the social sciences was to account for social developments as a whole. But in the long run psychology and sociology were to supersede the idea of witchcraft by providing a new way in which the victim could blame others for his fate. Instead of accusing witches, he could attribute his misfortunes to the way in which his parents had brought him up, or to the social system into which he had been born.

A further development undermining more primitive explanations of misfortune was the growing awareness, particularly among mathematicians, of the way in which even chance and misfortune were subject to statistical laws and thus capable, up to a point, of being rationally predicted. The formulation of theories of probability was the work of a long series of European mathematicians—Cardan, Fermat, Huygens, Pascal, the Bernouillis and de Moivre. But Englishmen made a distinctive contribution through the empirical study of mortality tables by Graunt, Petty and Halley; and the Royal Society showed considerable interest in the subject. In the last decade of the seventeenth century probability theory was widely discussed in English scientific circles. It was also in the later seventeenth century that the word "coincidence," in the sense of the juxtaposition of causally unrelated events, first appeared. In 1692 John Arbuthnot made the new theories available to a wider public in a translation of Huygens's treatise on gaming odds. A chance event, he declared in the preface, was merely one whose causes were not known; but it was possible to calculate the probability of its taking one form rather than another, even when human beings were involved. For what was politics, but "a kind of analysis of the quantity of probability in casual events"? There were, thought Arbuthnot, very few topics incapable of being reduced to mathematical reckoning.

It was this nascent statistical sense, or awareness of patterns in apparently random behaviour, which was to supersede much previous speculation about the causes of good or bad fortune. Today it is even possible to predict the likely number of fatal accidents or crimes of violence in the coming year. We take steps to hedge ourselves against misfortunes, but if they happen to us we do not feel the need to seek mystical causes for their occurrence. No doubt few of us today are capable of stoical acceptance of the random caprices of misfortune, but it is the awareness that they are indeed random which distinguishes us from our ancestors.

The decline of magic was thus accompanied by the growth of the natural and social sciences, which helped men to understand their environment, and of a variety of technical aids—from insurance to fire-fighting—by which they were able to increase their control of it. Yet the more closely Malinowski's picture of magic giving way before technology is examined, the less convincing does it appear. For the correspondence between magic and social needs had never been more than approximate. It is true that magic was seldom invoked when a technical solution was available. But the corollary was not true: the absence of a technical remedy was not of itself sufficient to generate a magical one. For magic was conservative in subject-matter, as well as in its techniques. The village wizards of our period had little in their repertoire to distinguish them from their medieval or, possibly even their Anglo-Saxon predecessors. Their remedies were traditional and so were the problems for which they catered. The astrologers similarly offered answers to questions which had originally been drawn up by Arabs, living in a different social environment. English magic, in other words, did not automatically expand to fill all new technological gaps, in the way Malinowski suggested. Society's magical resources were the result of its cultural inheritance, as much as of its current problems. Magic has always had to come from somewhere. In Tudor and Stuart England it came from the medieval and classical past, and it was slow to adapt itself to new situations.

This brings us to the essential problem. Why was it that magic did not keep pace with changing social circumstances? Why did its sphere become more limited, even as the English economy was expanding into new domains? For the paradox is that in England magic lost its appeal before the appropriate technical solutions had been devised to take its place. It was the abandonment of magic which made possible the upsurge of technology, not the other way round. Indeed, as Max Weber stressed, magic was potentially "one of the most serious obstructions to the rationalisation of economic life." The technological primacy of Western civilisation, it can be argued, owes a sizable debt to the fact that in Europe recourse to magic was to prove less ineradicable than in other parts of the world. For this, intellectual and religious factors have been held primarily responsible. The rationalist tradition of classical antiquity blended with the Christian doctrine of a single all-directing Providence to produce what Weber called "the disenchantment of the world"—the conception of an orderly and rational universe, in which effect follows cause in predictable manner. A religious belief in order was a necessary prior assumption upon which the subsequent work of the natural scientists was to be founded. It was a favourable mental environment which made possible the triumph of technology.

There is inevitably a chicken-and-the-egg character to any debate as to whether economic growth produces its appropriate mental character or is produced by it. Most sociologically-minded historians are naturally biased in favour of the view that changes in beliefs are preceded by changes in social and economic structure. But so far as magic and technology are concerned, it seems indisputable that in England the former was on the wane before the latter was ready to take its place. The fourteenth-century Lollards who renounced the Church's supernatural protection against disease and infertility had no effective alternative to put in its place. Their doctrines gave them spiritual security, but no new means of material aid. Neither did the Reformation coincide with any technological revolution: the men of the sixteenth century were more or less as vulnerable in face of epidemics, bad harvests, illness, fire, and all the other environmental hazards as their medieval predecessors. Yet many were able to discard the apparatus of the Church without devising a new magic in its place.

In the later seventeenth century the more general rejection of magic was still unaccompanied by the discovery of new remedies to fill the gap. It is often said that witch-beliefs are a consequence of inadequate medical technique. But in England such beliefs declined before medical therapy had made much of an advance. It is true that the seventeenth century witnessed notable contributions to the study of physiology, anatomy and botany. No history of medicine can omit mention of the work of Harvey on the circulation of the blood, of Glisson on rickets, Willis on the nervous system, and Sydenham on epidemics. The invention of the microscope enabled Robert Hooke to pioneer the study of the cell and paved the way for the eventual discovery of bacteria and the formulation of the germ theory of disease. Robert Boyle's chemical inquiries destroyed the whole basis of the old humoral physiology.

But so far as actual therapy was concerned, progress was negligible. Harvey's great discovery had no immediate practical consequences. "It seemed to illustrate the theory of medicine," declared a contemporary, "yet it made no improvement in the practice thereof." The sad truth, wrote another, was that although physicians had laboured mightily in chemistry and anatomy, they had added almost nothing to the diagnosis of disease (and, we might add, even less to its cure). "It was necessary to obtain clear concepts of the action of the body in health," explains a modern historian of medicine, "before venturing into discussion of its action in disease." Indeed it has recently been argued that, with the exception of smallpox inoculation, introduced in the eighteenth century, medical innovations did little to increase the expectation of life until at least the nineteenth century, and made no substantial contribution, sanitary reform apart, until the second quarter of the twentieth. This may be unduly pessimistic. But it seems clear that the expectation of life at birth was *lower* in the late seventeenth century than it had been in the reign of Elizabeth I; it did not regain its mid-Tudor level until the late eighteenth century.

The difference between the eighteenth and sixteenth centuries lies not in achievement but in aspiration. For the intervening period had seen the beginning of positive efforts to improve the level of medical therapy. The Paracelsians introduced new mineral remedies. Bacon wanted a systematic drive to raise the expectation of life and improve therapeutic medicine. Sydenham pioneered epidemiology, looking forward to the time "when the world, valuing learning for that only therein which is necessary for the good of human life, shall think as well of him that taught to cure disease as those that taught to discourse learnedly about them." Growing overseas trade with the East made possible a new pharmacology; the volume of drugs imported by the end of the seventeenth century was at least twenty-five times what it had been at the beginning. Only a few of these, such as quinine for malaria and guiacum for syphilis, were to gain a permanent place in the medical pharmacopoeia, but their introduction reflected a significant urge to experiment. The eighteenth century saw the founding of nearly fifty new hospitals. Whether these institutions did more to spread disease than to cure it is debatable. But, whatever their merits, they helped to displace the amateur, the empiric and the wise woman. They also reflected a new practical, optimistic attitude. . . .

We are, therefore, forced to the conclusion that men emancipated themselves from these magical beliefs without necessarily having devised any effective technology with which to replace them. In the seventeenth century they were able to take this step because magic was ceasing to be intellectually acceptable, and because their religion taught them to try self-help before invoking supernatural aid. But the ultimate origins of this faith in unaided human capacity remain mysterious. We do not know how the Lollards were able to find the self-reliance necessary to make the break with the Church magic of the past. The most plausible explanation seems to be that their spirit of sturdy self-help reflected that of their occupations. Few of these early heretics were simple agriculturalists dependent on the uncontrollable forces of nature. In the fifteenth century most of them were artisans—carpenters, blacksmiths, cobblers, and, above all, textile-workers. They spoke of religion in practical terms, rejecting the miracle of the Mass, because "God made man and not man God, as the carpenter doth make the house, and not the house the carpenter"; or asserting that "Ball the carpenter or Pike the mason could make as good images as those which were worshipped." Their trades made them aware that success or failure depended upon their unaided efforts, and they despised the substitute consolations of magic. . . .

It is therefore possible to connect the decline of the old magical beliefs with the growth of urban living, the rise of science, and the spread of an ideology of self-help. But the connection is only approximate and a more precise sociological genealogy cannot at present be constructed. Too many of the participants in the story remain hidden from view and the representative status of those who are visible is too uncertain. The only identifiable social group which was consistently in the van of the campaign against certain types of magic is the clergy, but their attitude to supernatural claims in general was highly ambivalent. It does not seem possible to say whether the growing "rationalism" of natural theology was a spontaneous theological development or a mere response to the pressures of natural science. It would make sense, no doubt, if one could prove that it was the urban middle classes, the shopkeepers and artisans, who took the lead in abandoning the old beliefs, but at present there seems no way of doing so. An equally convincing claim could be made for the Arminian clergy of the early seventeenth century or the aristocratic sceptics of the Restoration period.

What can, however, be clearly seen is that by the mid-seventeenth century the new intellectual developments had greatly deepened the gulf between the educated class and the lower strata of the rural population. Of course, evidence of the disdain felt by intellectuals for popular "superstition" can be found from classical times. But in the seventeenth century the gulf was emphasised by the appearance of well-born collectors of popular folklore, like Sir Thomas Browne in his *Vulgar Errors* or John Aubrey in his *Remaines of Gentilisme and Judaisme;* for despite their tolerance towards the old ways such men were acutely conscious of belonging to a different mental world. Aubrey himself was convinced that it was during the Civil War period that old beliefs had lost their vitality. But there is plenty of evidence to suggest that in rural areas there was still much life left in these ways of thought. "Notwithstanding the great advances in learning and knowledge which have been made within the last two centuries," declared a preacher in 1795, "lamentable experience but too clearly proves how extremely deep these notions are still engraven upon the minds of thousands." Nineteenth-century students of popular folklore discovered everywhere that the inhabitants of rural England had not abandoned their faith in healing wells, divination, cunning folk, witchcraft, omens or ghosts. "Those who are not in daily intercourse with the peasantry," it was reported from Lincolnshire in 1856, "can hardly be made to believe or comprehend the hold that charms, witchcraft, wise men and other like relics of heathendom have upon the people."

Nor had popular religion necessarily changed either. The religion of the nineteenth century, said Jacob Burckhardt, was "rationalism for the few and magic for the many." The belief in "judgments" was frequently upheld by influential clergymen, while many persons who incurred misfortune continued to ask what they had done to "deserve" it. The conviction that religion "worked" and that prayer got results sustained innumerable people in adversity. Every kind of religious enthusiasm—mystical healing, millenarian prophecy, messianic preaching—made its periodic return, and not only at a working-class level. Many of the nineteenth-century middle classes were interested in spiritualism and automatic writing, astrology, haunted houses and all the paraphernalia of the occult. Even the fear of witchcraft, that is of occult damage as a result of another's malignity, was revived in Mary Baker Eddy's concept of "malicious animal magnetism." Today astrologers and fortune-tellers continue to be patronised by those for whom psychiatrists and psycho-analysts have not provided a satisfactory substitute. The presence of horoscopes in the newspapers and of lucky mascots in cars is consistent with a recent investigator's conclusion that "about a quarter of the population . . . holds a view of the universe which can most properly be designated as magical." This is a much smaller figure than any which could ever be produced for the seventeenth century, were such analysis possible, but it is not a trivial one.

Indeed the role of magic in modern society may be more extensive than we yet appreciate. There is a tautological character about Malinowski's argument that magic occupies the vacuum left by science, for what is not recognised by any particular observer as a true "science" is deemed "magic" and vice versa. If magical acts are ineffective rituals employed as an alternative to sheer helplessness in the face of events, then how are we to classify the status of "scientific" remedies, in which we place faith, but which are subsequently exposed as useless? This was the fate of Galenic medicine, which in the sixteenth century was the main rival to folk-healing. But it will also be that of much of the medicine of today. Sociologists have observed that contemporary doctors and surgeons engage in many ritual practices of a nonoperative kind. Modern medicine shares an optimistic bias with the charmers and wise women and it has similar means of explaining away any failure. In many other spheres of modern life we also put our trust in activities designed to "work" (for example, in diplomatic conferences as a means of avoiding war), when all the evidence, if we wished to consider it, suggests that they do not.

Anthropologists today are unsympathetic to the view that magic is simply bad science. They stress its symbolic and expressive role rather than its practical one.

They would therefore maintain that the wizard's conjurations or the wise woman's charms were not really comparable with pseudo-science. In so far as the two activities had a different pedigree and a different intellectual status this is obviously true. But all the evidence of the sixteenth and seventeenth centuries suggests that the common people never formulated a distinction between magic and science, certainly not between magic and medicine. "We go to the physician for counsel," argued contemporaries, "we take his recipe, but we know not what it meaneth; yet we use it, and find benefit. If this be lawful, why may we not as well take benefit by the wise man, whose courses we be ignorant of?" The modern working-class woman who remarks that she doesn't "believe" in doctors is acknowledging the fact that the patient still brings with him an essentially uninformed allegiance. Usually he knows no more of the underlying rationale for his treatment than did the client of the cunning man. In such circumstances it is hard to say where "science" stops and "magic" begins.

What is certain about the various beliefs discussed in this book is that today they have either disappeared or at least greatly decayed in prestige. This is why they are easier to isolate and to analyse. But it does not mean that they are intrinsically less worthy of respect than some of those which we ourselves continue to hold. If magic is to be defined as the employment of ineffective techniques to allay anxiety when effective ones are not available, then we must recognise that no society will ever be free from it.

Madness in Society

GEORGE ROSEN

A number of scholars, including several historians, have maintained that a decisive change in the definition of madness is one key feature of modernization. George Rosen finds the beginnings of a new outlook in the seventeenth and eighteenth centuries, when more rigorous concepts of rationality led to new and more restrictive notions of what "normal" behavior was. He discusses some of the reasons for the shift and views the results in terms of the treatment of the insane. (He suggests that further changes were to come in the nineteenth century, with the rise of humanitarianism, but these would only modify the "modern" definition of madness, not change its direction.) In contrast to the medieval tolerance of insanity and its integration of the insane into family and community life, modern man insists on defining madness as something apart. The fact that this new definition developed so early points up once more the complexity of the origins of modernization.

The history of madness is a somewhat offbeat subject, with many questions still to be answered. How quickly did the new attitudes toward the insane spread to ordinary people? Rosen, after all, is talking mainly about definitions by formal theorists and institutional leaders. But there is little doubt that the new definition ultimately became widespread and that it constitutes a major feature of the modern mentality.

To some observers, the decline in the tolerance of madness is a major weakness of modern society. This is open to debate. What does seem clear is that the insane themselves have been losers in the modernization process. To what extent do we moderns mark off a fragile sanity by labeling difference as madness, thereby proving ourselves by the new intolerance to the insane?

In 1785 Jean Colombier, inspector-general of French hospitals and prisons, summed up the situation of the mentally ill in a succinct, devastating statement.

From George Rosen, *Madness in Society* (New York: Harper & Row, 1968), pp. 151–57, 158–61, 162–65. Copyright © George Rosen 1968. Reprinted by permission of Harper & Row, Publishers, Inc., and Routledge and Kegan Paul Ltd., London.

Thousands of lunatics are locked up in prisons without anyone even thinking of administering the slightest remedy. The half-mad are mingled with those who are totally deranged, those who rage with those who are quiet; some are in chains, while others are free in their prison. Finally, unless nature comes to their aid by curing them, the duration of their misery is life-long, for unfortunately the illness does not improve but only grows worse.

The validity of this picture is generally supported by other contemporary evidence. Indeed, one historian of psychiatry was led to conclude from such evidence that up to the end of the eighteenth century there were no real hospitals for the care and treatment of the mentally ill, only "places where they were *kept* . . ." Moreover, he attributed the sad lot of the mentally ill to a psychological factor, to the view that they were "step-children of life," a social attitude which survived in the community as an atavistic inheritance from the primitive past.

Yet the situation was not so simple, nor can it be explained solely in terms of an atavistic but potent psychological factor which has operated through the ages. Various sources clearly indicate that not all those who were mentally or emotionally disturbed were treated in the manner described by Colombier. At the very same time there were to be found in Paris, on the street or in cafés, individuals whose peculiarities of dress or behaviour did not attract undue notice. Without much astonishment, Sebastien Mercier encountered a crack-brained maker of projects in a coffee-house, simply remarking that there were others like him who had the public weal at heart "but who unfortunately were addlepated." Diderot's brilliant portrayal of Rameau's nephew presents another social deviant who is a strange mixture of good sense and folly. Delineated with great acuteness and intelligence, he was, according to Diderot, "one of the most bizarre fellows in a country where God has seen to it that there is no lack of them."

Mentally disturbed individuals occur as social personages, as distinctive characters on the social landscape not only in the later eighteenth century but in earlier periods as well. Consciousness of public responsibility for the mentally deranged was limited to the medieval period. Custody of the mentally ill generally rested with their relatives and friends; only those who were considered dangerous or socially disturbing were dealt with by the community. In some places it was customary to receive persons who were acutely disturbed and agitated into general hospitals. Harmless lunatics were permitted to roam the streets and roads; others were whipped out of town.

William Langland described the "lunatick lollers" wandering over the countryside and referred compassionately to their sad state. Another instance in point was depicted by Thomas More in 1533. Writing of a poor lunatic, he stated that he was one which after that he had fallen into these frantick heresies, fell soon after into plaine open franzye beside. And all beit that he had therefore bene put up in Bedelem, and afterward by beating and correccion gathered his remembraance to him and beganne to come again to himselfe, being thereupon set at liberty, and walkinge aboute abrode, his old fransies beganne to fall againe in his heade. I was fro dyvers good holy places advertised, that he used in his wandering about to come into the churche, and there make many mad toies and trifles, to the trouble of good people in the divine service, and especially woulde he be most busye in the time of most silence, while the priest was at the secrets of the masse aboute the levacion . . . whereupon I beinge advertised of these pageauntes, and beinge sent unto and required by very devout relygious folke, to take some other order with him, caused him, as he came wanderinge by my doore, to be taken by the counstables and bounden to a tree in the streets before the whole towne, and ther they stripped [striped] him with roddes therefore till he waxed weary and somewhat lenger. And it appeared well that hys remembraunce was goode ineoughe save that it went about in grazing [wool-gathering!] til it was beaten home. For he coulde then verye wel reherse his fautes himselfe, and speake and treate very well, and promise to doe afterward as well. And verylye God be thanked I heare none harme of him now.

A characteristic group among the vagrants and wandering beggars of Tudor England were the Abram-men or Toms o' Bedlam. They were patients discharged from Bethlem Hospital, sometimes not entirely recovered, who were licensed to beg. As a means of quickly identifying those allowed to solicit alms, they wore a metal plate as a badge on the left arm. The Bedlam beggars were a familiar sight throughout England until well into the later seventeenth century. According to John Aubrey,

Till the breaking out of the Civil Warres, Tom o' Bedlams did travell about the countrey. They had been poore distracted men that had been putt into Bedlam, where, recovering to some sobernesse, they were licentiated to goe a-begging . . . they wore about their necks a great horn of an oxe in a string or bawdric, which, when they came to an house for almes, they did wind, and they did put the drink given to them into their horn, where they did put a stopple.

Some of these beggars were undoubtedly impostors, and by 1675 the license to beg had been revoked. The ubiquitous presence of these vagrant mental patients is fully reflected in the literature of the Elizabethan and early Stuart periods. Illustrative are the close of the third scene in the second act of *King Lear* when Edgar announces his intention of becoming a Bedlam beggar, and the mad songs, "Loving Mad Tom," and "Old Tom of Bedlam."

Social attitudes towards the mentally and emotionally disturbed have clearly not been uniform at all times but have exhibited modulations and nuances. During the medieval period and the Renaissance, forms of unreason were considered fundamental elements in the fabric of the universe and of man. Medieval men believed that there were compelling forces making for righteousness and perfection, not only within the individual but as well in nature. Moreover, there were norms in nature which should not be violated, for their transgression led to vice. The later Middle Ages, particularly from the thirteenth century onwards, placed madness in the hierarchy of the vices. Another view of mental derangement is implied by the passage in the Prologue of *Piers Plowman* where a lunatic speaks up to praise the ideal king, while an angel speaks from heaven. The implication that only madmen and angels can speak the truth is related to the idea of holy madness, the idea that the ultimate of Christian truth is revealed to Christ's fools, to those who throw themselves utterly on God. Actually this view is very old and is based on the *New Testament* (I Corinthians 1:18ff.).

Numerous students of the waning Middle Ages have commented on the feeling of melancholy and pessimism which marked the period. A sense of impending doom hung over men and women, intensified by a belief that the end of time was approaching and that the last days were at hand. Nor was this apocalyptic sense of anxiety and urgency unjustified. A world was indeed disintegrating, and in its midst a new order, the shape of which could be seen only dimly, was agonizing towards birth. The feudal order was yielding to absolute monarchy and the early nation state. The all-embracing Christian commonwealth, fashioned and guided by the Church of Rome, was wracked by dissension, hatred, and violence. Abuses in the Church brought forth a desire to return it to its pristine state, to a new birth of life. The need for renewal was felt by many, and to perceptive men the troubles of the time were evidence that the age was at hand which would usher in the Last Judgement. The prevalence and spread of heresy, popular mysticism and personal piety in the later fourteenth and fifteenth centuries were hardly an accident. History was moving towards renewal and divine fulfilment, and men looked for signs and interpretations that warned sinners and encouraged the just.

Within this context madness through its linkage with the revelation of religious truth became a means of achieving knowledge. Madness was a primitive force of revelation, revealing the depths of menace, destruction, and evil that lurked beneath the illusory surface of reality. Unreason revealed the unbearable, the things in the world upon which one could not otherwise bear to look. Madness was on the increase, clearly a sign that the end of the world was at hand. But it was also a cause, for human folly had unleashed forces of disorganization and destruction that could end only in ultimate catastrophe. These forces were loose in a world that had succumbed to self-delusion, a world grown callous, hard-hearted, and rotten with selfishness, where people maddened with fear were pressed to the very brink of existence, a world which must therefore inevitably end in frenzied self-destruction. This theme of cosmic madness is a major element in the art and literature of the fifteenth and sixteenth centuries. Grünewald's Temptation of St. Anthony, the Lisbon painting by Bosch on the same subject, as well as his Millennium, provide evidence on this point. Writers as diverse as Pierre Ronsard and Sebastian Brant dealt with madness as a cosmic phenomenon, as a cause of the troubles which seemed to herald the end of the world. Ronsard combined these ideas in his *Discours des misères de ce temps*, denouncing the senseless errors of belief that turned the world upside down so that reason and justice were replaced by violence, hate, and death, and even God was no longer secure in his own dwelling. Similarly, the episode in Brant's *Narrenschiff*, where a furious storm drives the ship off its course and wrecks it, symbolized a world driven mad and its coming catastrophic end.

Irrationality personified in the figure of Folly loomed large in the Renaissance, but there was little discrimination between species of folly. Erasmus speaks of foolish persons and of the insane without clearly differentiating between them. He has Stultitia remark that the latter are the happiest of all; perhaps he was referring to harmless deranged folk, perhaps to mental defectives. In large measure this identification of stupidity with irrationality reflects an attitudinal shift from the idea of madness as a cosmic phenomenon to the view that madness is born in the hearts of men. Sebastian Brant published his highly popular satire, *Das Narrenschiff*, in 1494. In it he pilloried the follies connected with a whole gamut of human activities. Irrational desires and behaviour become objects of ridicule in this context and are exposed to the laughter and scorn of the world. Folly is no longer a vice and a punishment, but only a defect of human nature appropriate for castigation by the moralist. For Erasmus, irrationality is no longer a menace but a necessity to make the wheels of the world go round. In the *Moriae encomium*, which appeared in 1511, Folly wearing a fool's cap and bells points out how prosaic is her rule in the affairs of mankind.

Even religion seems to have some affinity with a certain kind of folly. Did not Paul say, "The foolishness of God is wiser than men"? This touches on the old Christian theme that the world is folly in the eyes of God, a theme that was revived in the sixteenth century and explored by thinkers as different as Calvin and Sebastian Franck. According to Calvin,

> as long as our views are bounded by the earth, perfectly content with our own righteousness, wisdom and strength, we fondly flatter ourselves, and fancy we are little less than demigods. But, if we once elevate our thoughts to God, and consider his nature, and the consummate perfection of his righteousness, wisdom, and strength, to which we ought to be conformed— what before charmed us in ourselves under the false pretext of righteousness, will soon be loathed as the greatest inequity; what strangely deceived us under the title of wisdom, will be despised as extreme folly; and what more the appearance of strength, will be proved to be most wretched impotence.

When compared to the limitless reason of God, human reason is fallacious and irrational. Man can endeavour to reach God by breaking the chains which bind his spirit and thus escaping into the liberty of other-worldliness. However, in so doing he fathoms the depths of unreason and enjoys the highest wisdom. Heavenly bliss is the greatest madness, and is achieved when man transcends the gap between the things of this world and their divine essence, when he reconciles the cruel contradictions which God created.

Thus, in the sixteenth century, from the humanistic as well as from the Christian viewpoint, irrationality is not regarded as having any absolute existence in the world. Folly exists only in relation to some form of reason, whether it be that of God or of man. Indeed, folly itself becomes a form of reason, even though distorted. ". . . Reason has taught me," wrote Montaigne, "that to firmly condemn something as false and impossible is to assume that one knows the bounds and limits of God's will and of the power of our Mother Nature; and that there is no more notable folly than to reduce these things to the measure of our capacity, and self-conceit."

> Men fail to recognize the malady of their mind. It does nothing but pry and seek, and keeps spinning about incessantly, constructing and becoming enmeshed in its own work, like our silkworms, and is suffocated in it. A mouse in pitch. It thinks that it sees from afar some apparent gleam of imaginary light and truth; but while it is running to it, so many difficulties, obstacles, and new quests cross its path that they mislead and intoxicate it.

Folly and madness had become integral elements of the world of people and things. It is certainly no coincidence that the literature of the late sixteenth and early seventeenth centuries is so rich in the portrayal of distraught and insane characters. . . . The shift in social attitudes towards mental illness which took place in Europe at this time can be analysed and explained in terms of socioeconomic, philosophical, and moral factors. Furthermore, this attitudinal change is closely linked with the character of the institutions developed and used during the seventeenth and eighteenth centuries for the mentally and emotionally deranged. These institutions must be seen first in relation to the evolution of the hospital. At various periods in history the need to care for the needy and the dependent, the sick and the disabled, has crystallized sufficiently in terms of attitude, theory, and practice so that one may speak of characteristic institutional models. In this sense, the history of the hospital may be seen in terms of certain types that have predominated in given historical periods. While knowledge concerning the healing shrines and the secular healing institutions of antiquity is not complete enough to be generalized, this is not the case for the medieval period. The medieval hospital in all its varied forms was essentially an ecclesiastical institution, not primarily concerned with medical care. This type was eventually replaced in the sixteenth century by another kind of hospital whose goals were not religious but primarily social. That is, the hospital from the sixteenth into the nineteenth century was intended chiefly to help maintain social order while providing for the sick and the needy. To achieve this aim the medieval hospital was to a large extent secularized, placed under governmental control, and its activities were accepted as a community responsibility.

From the thirteenth century onwards the hospital had begun to come increasingly under secular jurisdiction. As cities in Europe prospered, and the bourgeoisie grew wealthy and powerful, municipal authorities tended to take over or to supplement the activities of the Church. In part this was politically motivated, a desire of the civil authorities to be independent of clerical domination or to render the ecclesiastical power subordinate to themselves. This does not mean that the clergy were eliminated. Monks and nuns continued to provide nursing care as they had done before. Administratively, the municipal authorities were responsible for the hospital facilities, but the Church might participate in some way.

Secondly, hospitals and related establishments were considered increasingly inadequate to deal with situations in which problems of health and welfare were considered from a new viewpoint. From the medieval standpoint the poor, the sick and the infirm might almost be considered necessary for the salvation of the donor of charity. They did the almsgiver a service. Such an attitude, however, accepted the beggar as a necessary part of society and tended to encourage begging. Small consideration was given to bettering the condition of the poor and the infirm. During the late Middle Ages, and especially following the Reformation, the whole approach to this problem changed.

Though the causes of poverty changed but little from the thirteenth to the sixteenth century, economic and social circumstances altered their significance and intensified their impact. As a result the condition of the poor, which was bad in the earlier period, had become worse by the early sixteenth century. Increased unemployment, higher prices, enclosures of peasant lands and related factors brought into being the problems of unemployment, vagrancy, and beggary which confronted governments from the fourteenth to the eighteenth centuries. Vagrancy appeared in the Netherlands and Germany even earlier than in England and France and then assumed increasingly large dimensions in all countries. In their endeavours to eke out a livelihood many vagrants pretended to be crippled or diseased so as to be able to beg with impunity and to obtain admission to a hospital. Some were professional beggars, frequently organized in gangs, such as those that frequented the Cours des miracles in Paris. There is little doubt that the large number of poor and sick wanderers overtaxed the facilities available in various communities. Furthermore, whether or not these vagrants were sick, there was a great deal of economic and social distress by the sixteenth century, and the problem was what to do about it. As Simon Fish put the case in 1529 in his famous *Supplicacyon for the Beggars:* "But whate remedy to releve us your poor sike lame and sore bedemen? To make many hospitals for the relief of the poore people? Nay truely; The moo the worse, for ever the fatte of the hole foundacion hangeth on the prestes berdes." Fish also proposed a solution— that the clergy be expropriated and the hospitals and related facilities taken in hand by the king.

In fact, this was the course followed, a course influenced essentially by the Reformation, mercantilist thought, and the rise of absolute monarchy. While the intervention of the civil authorities in matters of welfare and health before the sixteenth century has been noted, the notion that poor relief including medical care was a community, not a Church, responsibility was definitely established during the Reformation period. Those who wished to bring some order into the area of welfare and health, whether Vives in Bruges or Zwingli in Zürich, were guided by the same principles and oriented to the same goals: elimination of beggary, organization of effective agencies of public assistance, and unification of all facilities and resources (hospitals, domiciliary relief, and the like) in the hands of local or national authorities. With variations, the process and its consequences can be seen in England and on the continent.

This desire to bring some kind of order into the field of assistance went hand in hand with an equally great enthusiasm for the repression of idleness. Condemnation of idleness was, of course, not new; indolence and lassitude had been condemned in ancient and medieval thought. The main difference was that the concerns of the seventeenth century were chiefly political and economic, rather than moral. Most seventeenth-century thinkers accepted the idea that governments should use their power to compel all persons capable of engaging in production to do some work. As a result of this view, the economic literature of this period, in England and on the continent, teems with proposals for dealing with idleness. In general, the proposed remedies fall into two groups: the repression of idleness by corrective or punitive legislation, and the creation of institutions which would provide work for the poor and punishment for those who refused to work. From this viewpoint, charity in the medieval sense was to be discouraged, for it led to idleness and beggary. On the other hand, the idle poor, properly employed, would help to make the nation rich and strong. . . .

To deal with the problems of the poor, the dependent, and the vagrant, a policy of internment and indoor relief was generally adopted, and institutions developed to put it into practice. Thus there were workhouses and houses of correction in England, *Zuchthäuser* in Germany, and *hôpitaux généraux* in France. Many of these institutions were not new creations; they evolved out of preexisting facilities and in response to problems that occurred at various times. However, it was in the later seventeenth century and in the eighteenth century that they achieved their fullest development.

The course of events in France is illuminating in this respect. From the sixteenth century on, royal action to deal with welfare and health problems occurred along two lines, one concerned with finances, the other, with administrative discipline and efficiency. A series of reform regulations from 1544 on turned over the administration of each hospital to a commission composed of merchants, burghers, and artisans who had to give an annual accounting to the local representatives of the king. In addition to endowments and other sources of income, the king authorized or imposed a communal tax. The first of these measures was issued by Henri II in 1551. Moreover, to insure financial stability, institutions were merged or were put under a general administrative board. As early as the reign of Henri IV plans had been made to establish such institutions for the relief of the poor and needy, but little was achieved. Finally, in 1656 a royal decree was issued founding the *Hôpital Général* of Paris. (It had been preceded by the welfare bureau of Lyon and its affiliated hospital, which dated from 1613–1614.) The purposes of the institution were threefold. In part they were economic: to increase manufactures, provide productive work for the able-bodied, and to end unemployment; in part, social: to punish wilful idleness, restore public order, and rid Paris of beggars; and in part, religious and moral: to relieve the needy, the ill and suffering, to deal with immorality and antisocial behaviour, and to provide Christian instruction.

The creation of such institutions was not limited to Paris. It was a solution to the problem of poor relief which was tried all through France. Indeed, developments at Paris had been anticipated in the provinces. The *Hôpital Général* at Toulouse dated from 1647, that at Béziers from 1654, and that at Caen from 1655. Most of the provincial general hospitals were established under royal authorization. At Le Mans in 1658 all the hospitals, hostels, and *maisons-Dieu* were united into a general hospital by royal letters patent. This trend was carried further by Colbert, and slowly but steadily general hospitals came into existence throughout France.

The very nature of the functions which these institutions were intended to perform required some kind of involvement with health problems. Though the *Hôtel-Dieu* was supposed to take care of the sick, the *Hôpital Général* took care of old people, people with venereal diseases, epileptics, and the mentally ill. Thus, in the course of time the general hospital combined the characteristics of a penal institution, an asylum, a workshop, and a hospital.

An important purpose was to deal with immorality and antisocial behaviour. All individuals who were defined as asocial or socially deviant were segregated by internment. This procedure is analogous to the manner in which the leper was treated in the medieval period. By separating such individuals from society, by exiling them to the *Hôpital Général*, they were consigned to a social and psychological situation of which the dominant character is alienation. A separate socio-psychological lifespace was created for those who removed themselves from or transgressed the moral order considered appropriate to their social position, occupation, or family relationship. Thus, on 20 April 1690 regulations were instituted, providing

> that children of artisans and other poor inhabitants of Paris up to the age of twenty-five, who used their parents badly, or who refused to work through laziness, or, in the case of girls who were debauched or in evident danger of being debauched, should be shut up, the boys in the Bicêtre, the girls in the Salpêtrière. This action was to be taken on the complaint of the parents, or, if these were dead, of near relatives, or the parish priest. The wayward children were to be kept as long as the directors deemed wise and were to be released only on a written order signed by four directors.

At the same time arrangements were made to incarcerate prostitutes and women who ran bawdy houses; they were to be kept in a special section of the Salpêtrière.

The consequence of this policy was described by Tenon in his account of the Salpêtrière in 1788.

> The Salpêtrière [he wrote] is the largest hospital in Paris and possibly in Europe: this hospital is both a house for women and a prison. It receives pregnant women and girls, wet nurses and their nurselings; male children from the age of seven or eight months to four and five years of age; young girls of all ages; aged married men and women; raving lunatics, imbeciles, epileptics, paralytics, blind persons, cripples, people suffering from ringworm, incurables of all sorts, children afflicted with scrofula, and so on and so forth.
>
> At the centre of this hospital is a house of detention for women, comprising four different prisons; *le commun*, for the most dissolute girls; *la correction*, for those who are not considered hopelessly depraved; *la prison*, reserved for persons held by order of the king; and *la grande force*, for women branded by order of the courts.

In short, what had happened by the later seventeenth century was not only or simply an evolution of institutions; it was more than that. It was a change in the social perception of irrationality and madness based on criteria derived from a new view of human nature. Today, the idea of a personal self appears as an indispensable assumption of existence. Actually, like other views of human nature, it is in large measure a cultural idea, a fact within history, the product of a given era. At any given period certain criteria are employed to establish normal human nature, as well as any deviation from it.

For the seventeenth and eighteenth centuries, the touchstone was reason and its right use. Reason provided the norm; any divergence from the norm was irrational. Pascal said that he could conceive of a man without hands, feet, or head, but he added, "I cannot conceive of a man without thought; that would be a stone or a brute." Moreover, from the context in which this statement is made, it is clear that Pascal has rational thought in mind. Montaigne had still been able to accept and to discuss reason and unreason as related, interwoven facets of human behaviour. By the fourth decade of the seventeenth century, however, a sharp line of separation was being drawn between reason and unreason. Descartes, for example, recognized that reason and irrationality are encountered together, that dreams and errors of various kinds are associated with madness, but he decided to rely upon reason and to avoid the irrational. Thus, unreason and madness were exiled in thought on the basis of a conscious decision.

From this viewpoint, irrationality took on a new aspect; it could be regarded as a matter of choice, as a matter of volition. Unreason, and with it insanity, were related primarily to the quality of volition and not to the integrity of the rational mind. Endowed with reason, man was expected to behave rationally, that is, according to accepted social standards. Rational choice was his to make by virtue of his nature. Eccentric or irrational behaviour, actions which diverged from accepted norms, were considered as rooted in error or as derangements of the will and therefore subject to correction.

The World We Have Lost

PETER LASLETT

In the following selection the author seeks to define the essential characteristics of preindustrial society, which he regards as sharply differentiated from its modern counterpart. He shows us a carefully controlled social environment, dominated by small units of organization in which affectionate ties prevail. The family is obviously crucial, and although the author notes the tensions that family life can create, he is preoccupied with the family's success as an emotional as well as economic unit. The essence of modernization, correspondingly, is a change in the family, and presumably a weakening of ties. Factories have replaced families as units of production. The author does not spell out the relationship, if any, between the rise of factories and changes in family structure, but he has no doubt that industrialization has severely altered what the family has to offer modern people.

This is an intelligently nostalgic picture. The author admits the importance of material limitations, even outright misery, and acknowledges such vital aspects of preindustrial life as high mortality rates. But in terms of human relationships it is clear that the author thinks the modern world has lost a great deal. The picture of preindustrial life he paints is one of stability and close personal ties. There can be little doubt, if this picture is accurate, that most people suffered profound disruption as they entered modern society—or rather, as they were forced into it, since there is no clear motive in this preindustrial society spontaneously to seek change. Note that the author judges preindustrial society to be rather homogeneous in its basic values. Important class differences existed, but they did not interfere with a common devotion to religion and a patriarchal family structure.

Laslett's views regarding the quality of preindustrial life and the causes and impact of change should be compared with those of Le Roy Ladurie. Laslett is writing about a later period than Le Roy Ladurie. England was undergoing more rapid changes than France in terms of the rise of market agriculture and the disruption of established religious and political patterns (see the selection by Keith Thomas). Laslett himself, elsewhere in his study, points to substantial mobility in rural society. Yet he insists on the integrity and adequacy of traditional values. What then would cause change? And how could people tolerate the advent of modernity? It would be easy to go from Laslett to a view that modern life is hopelessly disruptive, if the strengths of premodern society were as great as this selection suggests.

In the year 1619 the bakers of London applied to the authorities for an increase in the price of bread. They sent in support of their claims a complete description of a bakery and an account of its weekly costs. There were thirteen or fourteen people in such an establishment: the baker and his wife, four paid employees who were called journeymen, two apprentices, two maid-servants and the three or four children of the master baker himself. Six pounds ten shillings a week was reckoned to be the outgoings of this establishment of which only eleven shillings and eightpence went for wages: half a crown a week for each of the journeymen and tenpence for each of the maids. Far and away the greatest cost was for food: two pounds nine shillings out of the six pounds ten shillings, at five shillings a head for the baker and his wife, four shillings a head for their helpers and two shillings for their children. It cost much more in food to keep a journeyman than it cost in money; four times as much to keep a maid. Clothing was charged up too, not only for the man, wife and children, but for the apprentices as well. Even school fees were claimed as a justifiable charge on the price of bread for sale, and it cost sixpence a week for the teaching and clothing of a baker's child.

A London bakery was undoubtedly what we should call a commercial or even an industrial undertaking, turning out loaves by the thousand. Yet the business was carried on in the house of the baker himself. There was probably a *shop* as part of the house, *shop* as in *workshop* and not as meaning a retail establishment. Loaves were not ordinarily sold over the counter: they had to be carried to the open-air market and displayed on stalls. There was a garner behind the house, for which the baker paid two shillings a week in rent, and where he kept his wheat, his *sea-coal* for the fire and his store of salt. The house itself was one of those high, half-timbered overhanging structures on the narrow London street which we always think of when we remember the scene in which Shakespeare, Pepys or even Christopher Wren lived. Most of it was taken up with the living-quarters of the dozen people who worked there.

It is obvious that all these people ate in the house since the cost of their food helped to determine the production cost of the bread. Except for the journeymen they were all obliged to sleep in the house at night and live together as a family.

The only word used at that time to describe such a group of people was "family." The man at the head of the group, the entrepreneur, the employer, or the manager, was then known as the master or head of the family. He was father to some of its members and in place of father to the rest. There was no sharp distinction between his domestic and his economic functions. His wife was both his partner and his subordinate, a partner because she ran the family, took charge of the food and managed the women-servants, a subordinate because she was woman and wife, mother and in place of mother to the rest.

The paid servants of both sexes had their specified and familiar position in the family, as much part of it as the children but not quite in the same position. At that time the family was not one society only but three societies fused together: the society of man and wife, of parents and children and of master and servant. But when they were young, and servants were, for the most part, young, unmarried people, they were very close to children in their status and their function. Here is the agreement made between the parents of a boy about to become an apprentice and his future master. The boy covenants to dwell as an apprentice with his master for seven years, to keep his secrets and to obey his commandments.

> Taverns and alehouses he shall not haunt, dice, cards or any other unlawful games he shall not use, fornication with any woman he shall not commit, matrimony with any woman he shall not contract. He shall not absent himself by night or by day without his master's leave but be a true and faithful servant.

On his side, the master undertakes to teach his apprentice his "art, science or occupation with moderate correction."

> Finding and allowing unto his said servant meat, drink, apparel, washing, lodging and all other things during the said term of seven years, and to give unto his said apprentice at the end of the said term double apparel, to wit, one suit for holydays and one suit for worken days.

Apprentices, therefore, were workers who were also children, extra sons of extra daughters (for girls could be apprenticed too), clothed and educated as well as fed, obliged to obedience and forbidden to marry, unpaid and absolutely dependent until the age of twenty-one. If apprentices were workers in the position of sons and daughters, the sons and daughters of the house were workers too. John Locke laid it down in 1697 that the children of the poor must work for some part of the day when they reached the age of three. The sons and daughters of a London baker were not free to go to school for many years of their young lives, or even to play as they wished when they came back home. Soon they would find themselves doing what they could in *bolting*, that is sieving flour, or in helping the maidservant with her panniers of loaves on the way to the market stall, or in playing their small parts in preparing the never-ending succession of meals for the whole household.

We may see at once, therefore, that the world we have lost, as I have chosen to call it, was no paradise or golden age of equality, tolerance or loving kindness. It is so important that I should not be misunderstood on this point that I will say at once that the coming of industry cannot be shown to have brought economic oppression and exploitation along with it. It was there already. The patriarchal arrangements which we have begun to explore were not new in the England of Shakespeare and Elizabeth. They were as old as the Greeks, as old as European history, and not confined to Europe. And it may well be that they abused and enslaved people quite as remorselessly as the economic arrangements which had replaced them in the England of Blake and Victoria. When people could expect to live for only thirty years in all, how must a man have felt when he realized that so much of his adult life, perhaps all, must go in working for his keep and very little more in someone else's family?

But people do not recognize facts of this sort, and no one is content to expect to live as long as the majority in fact will live. Every servant in the old social world was probably quite confident that he or she would some day get married and be at the head of a new family, keeping others in subordination. If it is legitimate to use the words exploitation and oppression in thinking of the economic arrangements of the pre-industrial world, there were nevertheless differences in the manner of oppressing and exploiting. The ancient order of society was felt to be eternal and unchangeable by those who supported, enjoyed and endured it. There was no expectation of reform. How could there be when economic organization was domestic organization, and relationships were rigidly regulated by the social system, by the content of Christianity itself?

Here is a vivid contrast with social expectation in Victorian England, or in industrial countries everywhere today. Every relationship in our world which can be seen to affect our economic life is open to change, is expected indeed to change of itself, or if it does not, to be changed, made better, by an omnicompetent authority. This makes for a less stable social world, though it is only one of the features of our society which impels us all in that direction. All industrial societies, we may suppose, are far less stable than their predecessors. They lack the extraordinarily cohesive influence which familial relationships carry with them, that power of reconciling the frustrated and the discontented by emotional means. Social revolution, meaning an irreversible changing of the pattern of social relationships, never happened in traditional, patriarchal, pre-industrial human society. It was almost impossible to contemplate.

Almost, but not quite. Sir Thomas More, in the reign of Henry VIII, could follow Plato in imagining a life without privacy and money, even if he stopped short of imagining a life where children would not know their parents and where promiscuity could be a political institution. Sir William Petty, 150 years later, one of the very first of the political sociologists, could speculate about polygamy; and the England of the Tudors and the Stuarts already knew of social structures and sexual arrangements, existing in the newly discovered world, which were alarmingly different from their own. But it must have been an impossible effort of the imagination to suppose that they were anything like as satisfactory.

It will be noticed that the roles we have allotted to all the members of the capacious family of the master-baker of London in the year 1619 are, emotionally, all highly symbolic and highly satisfactory. We may feel that in a whole society organized like this, in spite of all the subordination, the exploitation and the obliteration of those who were young, or feminine, or in service, everyone belonged in a group, a family group. Everyone had his circle of affection: every relationship could be seen as a love-relationship.

Not so with us. Who could love the name of a limited company or of a government department as an apprentice could love his superbly satisfactory father-figure master, even if he were a bully and a beater, a usurer and a hypocrite? But if a family is a circle of affection, it can also be the scene of hatred. The worst tyrants among human beings, the murderers and the villains, are jealous husbands and resentful wives, possessive parents and deprived children. In the traditional, patriarchal society of Europe, where practically everyone lived out his whole life within the family, often within one family only, tension like this must have been incessant and unrelieved, incapable of release except in crisis. Men, women and children have to be very close together for a very long time to generate the emotional power which can give rise to a tragedy of Sophocles, or Shakespeare, or Racine. Conflict in such a society was between individual people, on the personal scale. Except when the Christians fought with the infidels, or Protestants fought with Catholics, clashes between masses of persons did not often arise. There could never be a situation such as that which makes our own time, as some men say, the scene of perpetual revolution.

All this is true to history only if the little knot of people making bread in Stuart London was indeed the typical social unit of the old world in its size, composition and scale. There are reasons why a baker's household might have been a little out of the ordinary, for baking was a highly traditional occupation in a society increasingly subject to economic change. We shall see, in due course, that a family of thirteen people, which was also a unit of production of thirteen, less the children quite incapable of work, was quite large for English society at that time. Only the families of the really important, the nobility and the gentry, the aldermen and the successful merchants, were ordinarily as large as this. In fact, we can take the bakery to represent the upper limit in size and scale of the group in which ordinary people lived and worked. Among the great mass of society which cultivated the land, and which will be the major preoccupation of this essay, the family group was smaller than a London craftsman's entourage. . . .

. . . One reason for feeling puzzled by our own industrial society is
that the historian has never set out to tell us what society was like before industry came and seems to assume that everyone knows.

We shall have much more to say about the movement of servants from
farmhouse to farmhouse in the old world, and shall return to the problem
of understanding ourselves in time, in contrast with our ancestors. Let us
emphasize again the scale of life in the working family of the London baker.
Few persons in the old world ever found themselves in groups larger than
family groups, and there were few families of more than a dozen members.
The largest household so far known to us, apart from the royal court and the
establishments of the nobility, lay and spiritual, is that of Sir Richard Newdigate, Baronet, in his house of Arbury within his parish of Chilvers Coton in
Warwickshire, in the year 1684. There were thirty-seven people in Sir
Richard's family: himself; Lady Mary Newdigate his wife; seven daughters, all
under the age of sixteen; and twenty-eight servants, seventeen men and boys
and eleven women and girls. This was still a family, not an institution, a staff,
an office or a firm.

Everything physical was on the human scale, for the commercial worker
in London, and the miner who lived and toiled in Newdigate's village of
Chilvers Coton. No object in England was larger than London Bridge or St.
Paul's Cathedral, no structure in the Western World to stand comparison
with the Colosseum in Rome. Everything temporal was tied to the human
life-span too. The death of the master baker, head of the family, ordinarily
meant the end of the bakery. Of course there might be a son to succeed, but
the master's surviving children would be young if he himself had lived only
as long as most men. Or an apprentice might fulfil the final function of
apprenticehood, substitute sonship, that is to say, and marry his master's
daughter, or even his widow. Surprisingly often, the widow, if she could,
would herself carry on the trade. . . .

We may pause here to point out that our argument is not complete.
There was an organization in the social structure of Europe before the coming of industry which enormously exceeded the family in size and endurance.
This was the Christian Church. It is true to say that the ordinary person,
especially the female, never went to a gathering larger than could assemble in
an ordinary house except when going to church. When we look at the aristocracy and the church from the point of view of the scale of life and the im-
permanence of all man-made institutions, we can see that their functions
were such as make very little sense in an industrial society like our own. Complicated arrangements then existed, and still exist in England now, which
were intended to make it easier for the noble family to give the impression
that it had indeed always persisted. Such, for example, were those intricate
rules of succession which permitted a cousin, however distant, to succeed to
the title and to the headship, provided only he was in the male line. Such

was the final remedy in the power of the Crown, the fountain of honour, to declare that an anomalous succession should take place. Nobility was for ever.

But the symbolic provision of permanence is only the beginning of the social functions of the church. At a time when the ability to read with understanding and to write much more than a personal letter was confined for the most part to the ruling minority, in a society which was otherwise oral in its communications, the preaching parson was the great link between the illiterate mass and the political, technical and educated world. Sitting in the 10,000 parish churches of England every Sunday morning, in groups of 20, 50, 100 or 200, the illiterate mass of the people were not only taking part in the single group activity which they ordinarily shared with others outside their own families. They were informing themselves in the only way open to them of what went on in England, Europe, and the world as a whole. The priesthood was indispensable to the religious activity of the old world, at a time when religion was still of primary interest and importance. But the priesthood was also indispensable because of its functions in social communication. . . .

Not only did the scale of their work and the size of the group which was engaged make them exceptional, the constitution of the group did too. In the baking household we have chosen as our standard, sex and age were mingled together. Fortunate children might go out to school, but adults did not usually go out to work. There was nothing to correspond to the thousands of young men on the assembly line, the hundreds of young women in the offices, the lonely lives of housekeeping wives which we now know only too well. We shall see that those who survived to old age in the much less favourable conditions for survival which then were prevalent, were surprisingly often left to live and die alone, in their tiny cottages or sometimes in the almshouses which were being built so widely in the England of the Tudors and the Stuarts. Poor-law establishments, parochial in purpose and in size, had begun their melancholy chapter in the history of the English people. But institutional life was otherwise almost unknown. There were no hotels, hostels, or blocks of flats for single persons, very few hospitals and none of the kind we are familiar with, almost no young men and women living on their own. The family group where so great a majority lived was what we should undoubtedly call a "balanced" and "healthy" group.

When we turn from the hand-made city of London to the hand-moulded immensity of rural England, we may carry the same sentimental prejudice along with us. To every farm there was a family, which spread itself over its portion of the village lands as the family of the master-craftsman filled out his manufactory. When a holding was small, and most were small as are the tiny holdings of European peasants today, a man tilled it with the help of his wife and his children. No single man, we must remember, would usually take charge of the land, any more than a single man would often be found at the head of a workshop in the city. The master of a family was expected to be a householder, whether he was a butcher, a baker, a candlestick maker or simply a husbandman, which was the universal name for one whose skill was in working the land. Marriage we must insist, and it is one of the rules which gave its character to the society of our ancestors, was the entry to full membership, in the enfolding countryside, as well as in the scattered urban centres.

But there was a difference in scale and organization of work on the land and in the town. The necessities of rural life did require recurrent groupings of households for common economic purposes, occasionally something like a crowd of men, women and children working together for days on end. Where the ground was still being tilled as open fields, and each household had a number of strips scattered all over the whole open area and not a compact collection of enclosures, ploughing was co-operative, as were many other operations, above all harvesting, and this continued ever after enclosure. We do not yet know how important this element of enforced common activity was in the life of the English rural community on the eve of industrialization, or how much difference enclosure made in this respect. But whatever the situation was, the economic transformation of the eighteenth and nineteenth centuries destroyed communality altogether in English rural life. The group of men from several farmsteads working the heavy plough in springtime, the bevy of harvesters from every house in the village wading into the high standing grass to begin the cutting of the hay, had no successors in large-scale economic activity. For the arrangement of these groups was entirely different in principle from the arrangement of a factory, or a firm, or even of a collective farm.

Both before and after enclosure, some peasants did well: their crops were heavier and they had more land to till. To provide the extra labour needed then, the farming householder, like the successful craftsman, would extend his working family by taking on young men and women as servants to live with him and work the fields. This he would have to do, even if the land which he was farming was not his own but rented from the great family in the manor house. Sometimes, we have found, he would prefer to send out his own children as servants and bring in other children and young men to do the work. This is one of the few glimpses we can get into the quality of the emotional life of the family at this time, for it shows that parents may have been unwilling to submit children of their own to the discipline of work at home. It meant, too, that servants were not simply the perquisites of wealth and position. A quarter, or a third, of all the families in the country contained servants in Stuart times, and this meant that very humble people had them as well as the titled and the wealthy. Most of the servants, moreover, male or female, in the great house and in the small, were engaged in working the land.

The boys and the men would do the ploughing, hedging, carting and the heavy, skilled work of the harvest. The women and the girls would keep the house, prepare the meals, make the butter and the cheese, the bread and the beer, and would also look after the cattle and take the fruit to market. At harvest-time, from June to October, every hand was occupied and every back was bent. These were the decisive months for the whole population in our damp northern climate, with its one harvest in a season and reliance on one or two standard crops. So critical was the winning of the grain for bread that the first rule of gentility (a gentleman never worked with his hands for his living) might be abrogated. . . .

The factory won its victory by outproducing the working family, taking away the market for the products of hand-labour and cutting prices to the point where the craftsman had either to starve or take a job under factory discipline himself. It was no sudden, complete and final triumph, for the seamstresses were working in the garrets right up to the twentieth century, and the horrors of sweated labour which so alarmed our grandfathers took place amongst the out-workers, not on the factory floor. It was not a transformation which affected only commerce, industry and the towns, for the hand-work of the cottages disappeared entirely, till, by the year 1920, rural England was an agrarian remnant, an almost lifeless shell. The process was not English alone, at any point in its development, and its effects on the Continent of Europe were in some ways more obviously devastating than ever they were amongst our people. But ours was the society which first ventured into the industrial era, and English men and women were the first who had to try to find a home for themselves in a world where family and household seemed to have no place.

But Marx and the historians who have followed him were surely wrong to call this process by the simple name of the triumph of capitalism, the rise and victory of the bourgeoisie. The presence of capital, we have seen, was the very circumstance which made it possible in earlier times for the working family to preserve its independence both on the land and in the cities, linking together the scattered households of the workers in such a way that no one had to make the daily double journey from home to workshop, from suburb to office and factory. Capitalism, however defined, did not begin at the time when the working household was endangered by the beginnings of the factory system, and economic inequality was not the product of the social transformation which so quickly followed after. Though the enormous, insolent wealth of the new commercial and industrial fortunes emphasized the iniquity of the division between rich and poor, it is doubtful whether Victorian England was any worse in this respect than the England of the Tudors and the Stuarts. It was not the fact of capitalism alone, not simply the concentration of the means of production in the hands of the few and the reduction of the rest to a position of dependence, which opened wide the social gulf, though the writers of the eighteenth and nineteenth centuries give us ample evidence that this was observed and was resented—by the dispossessed peasantry in England especially. More important, it is suggested, far more likely a source for the feeling that there is a world which once we all possessed, a world now passed away, is the fact of the transformation of the family life of everyone which industrialism brought with it.

In the vague and difficult verbiage of our own generation, we can say that the removal of the economic functions from the patriarchal family at the point of industrialization created a mass society. It turned the people who worked into a mass of undifferentiated equals, working in a factory or scattered between the factories and mines, bereft forever of the feeling that work, a family affair, carried with it. The Marxist historical sociology presents this as the growth of class consciousness amongst the proletariat, and this is an important historical truth. But because it belongs with the large-scale class model for all social change it can also be misleading, as we shall hope to show. Moreover it has tended to divert attention from the structural function of the family in the preindustrial world, and made impossible up till now a proper, informed contrast between our world and the lost world we have to analyse. . . .

European society is of the patriarchal type, and with some variations, of which the feudal went the furthest, it remained patriarchal in its institutions right up to the coming of the factories, the offices and the rest. European patriarchalism, we may notice, was of a rather surprising kind, for it was marked by the independence of the nuclear family, man, wife and children, not by the extended family of relatives living together in a group of several generations under the same patriarchal head. Yet society was patriarchal, nevertheless, right up to the time of industrial transformation: it can now no longer be said to be patriarchal at all, except vestigially and in its emotional predisposition. The time has now come to divide our European past in a simpler way with industrialization as the point of critical change.

The word alienation is part of the cant of the mid-twentieth century and it began as an attempt to describe the separation of the worker from his world of work. We need not accept all that this expression has come to convey in order to recognize that it does point to something vital to us all in relation to our past. Time was when the whole of life went forward in the family, in a circle of loved, familiar faces, known and fondled objects, all to human size. That time has gone for ever. It makes us very different from our ancestors.

. . . In every one of the village communities too, the families of craftsmen, labourers and paupers tended to be smaller than the families of yeomen, and those of the gentry to be largest. The traffic in children from the humbler to the more successful families shows up in the relative numbers in the various groups. Poverty, in our day, or, at least, in the very recent past, was associated with large numbers of children, but . . . in the seventeenth century exactly the reverse was true. The richer you were, the more children you had in your household. In [the village of Goodnestone] in 1676, the gentry with children had an average of 3.5 in their families, the yeomen 2.9, the tradesmen 2.3, the labourers 2.1 and the paupers 1.8.

These figures from Goodnestone are too good to be true and it is common enough to find humble families with many children at home, too many for the meagre resources of the wage-earner and a promise of destitution for his widow if he should die too soon. Nevertheless, the association of few children with modest position and resources is almost as marked a feature of social structure in the traditional world as the association of smaller families generally with the poor. It was not simply a matter of the poor offering up their children to the rich as servants; they probably also had fewer children born to them, and of those which were born, fewer survived. It is likely that works on the expectation of life and size of the biological family will confirm what early impressions seem to show, which is that poor men and their wives could not expect to live together long enough to have as many offspring as the rich. This loss of potential labour-power was a matter of consequence, for it always must be remembered that the actual work on most of the plots of land was done by the working family, the man, his wife and children.

At harvest-time, of course, there was a difference: the individual farming family could no longer cope with the work. From the making of the hay in June until the winning of the corn and pease in late September, every able-bodied person in the village community was at work on everyone's land. How much co-operation there was is difficult to say, but when the crisis of the agricultural year came round, right up to the time of mechanized farming, the village acted as a community. When all was in, there was harvest home.

> It is usual, in most places, after they get all the pease pulled or the last grain down, to invite all the workfolks and their wives (that helped them that harvest) to supper, and then they have puddings, bacon, or boiled beef, flesh or apple pies, and then cream brought in platters, and every one a spoon; then after all they have hot cakes and ale; for they bake cakes and send for ale against that time: some will cut their cake and put it into the cream, and this feast is called cream-pot, or cream-kit; for on the morning that they get all done the workfolks will ask their dames if they have good store of cream and say they must have the cream-kit anon.

This was the Yorkshire custom in the 1640's when it was necessary, at harvest-time, to go even beyond the carpenters, the wheelwrights and the millers, in order to bring in the sheaves off the fields. The richer men had to make a home in the barns during harvest for folk, pastoral in their ways, who came down from the wild moorland. Migration of labour at harvest was common enough in the eighteenth century, but eating and drinking together was a universal characteristic of rural life at all times. Whatever the churchwardens or the overseers of the poor did, when the church-bell was rung in celebration, or the churchyard mowed, there was an entry in the ill-written accounts for ale drunk on the occasion. . . . The meticulous, unpopular Rector of Clayworth in the last quarter of the seventeenth century, entertained the *husbandry* of the two settlements in his parish separately to dinner every year.

When the curate of Goodnestone returned the names of all his parishioners in April, 1676, "according to their families, according to their quality and according to their religion," he did as he was bid and told his lordship, the bishop, how many of them had been to holy communion that Eastertide. Apart from sixteen exceptions every person in the community known by their priest to be qualified for the sacrament had actually taken it at some time during the festival, which fell in that year between March 19th and 26th: 128 people communicated that is to say, out of a population of 281. Even the defaulters had promised to make amends at Whitsuntide, all but the one family in the village which was nonconformist. But William Wanstall, senior, one of the absentees, was given no such grace; he had been "excluded the Holy Sacrament for his notorious drunkenness, but since hath promised reformation." Francis Nicholson, the priest-in-charge, was evidently a devoted pastor, for he could give an account of every one of the absentees. Mrs. Elizabeth Richards, the widowed head of one of the households of gentry, was excused as "melancholy," and Barbara Pain since she was "under a dismal calamity, the unnatural death of her husband," who had left her at the head of a yeoman family, three children and two servants.

This . . . draws attention to a feature of the village community and of the whole of the world we have now half-forgotten which has scarcely been mentioned so far. All our ancestors were literal Christian believers, all of the time. Not only zealous priests, such as Francis Nicholson, not only serious-minded laymen, but also the intellectuals and the publicly responsible looked on the Christian religion as the explanation of life, and on religious service as its proper end. Not everyone was equally devout, of course, and it would be simple-minded to suppose that none of these villagers ever had their doubts. Much of their devotion must have been formal, and some of it mere conformity. But their world was a Christian world and their religious activity was spontaneous, not forced on them from above. When Francis Nicholson refused the cup to William Wanstall, in March, 1676, the scores of other people in the church that morning no doubt approved of what he did, as no doubt Wanstall deserved this very public rebuke. When William Sampson, the formidable Rector of Clayworth, did exactly the same thing in April, 1679, to Ralph Meers and Anne Fenton "upon a common fame that they lived and lodged together, not being married," he also had the community behind him. He knew what he was doing too, for Anne Fenton's first baby was christened two months later, only a week or two, presumably, after she had married Ralph Meers.

It has been shown only very recently how it came about that the mass of the English people lost their Christian belief, and how religion came to be a middle-class matter. When the arrival of industry created huge societies of persons in the towns with an entirely different outlook from these Stuart villagers, practically no one went to church, not if he was working class and was left untouched by religious emotion. Christianity was no longer in the social air which everyone breathed together, rich and poor, gentleman, husbandman, artificer, labourer and pauper. So much has been written about the abuses of the clergy in earlier times, so much about the controversies and doubts, about the revivals, especially the Wesleyan revival, that the religious attitude of common folk has been lost sight of. Perhaps the twelve labourers who lived at Goodnestone in 1676 did not know very clearly what Our Lord's Supper meant, and perhaps they felt that it would displease Squire Hales if they stayed away, but every single one of them took communion. Their descendants in the slums of London in the 1830's, '40's and '50's did not do so: they already looked on Christianity as belonging to the rural world which they had lost. It was something for their employers, something for the respectable, which, perhaps, they might go in for if ever they attained respectability and comfort. This was not true of the hard-working, needy, half-starved labourers of pre-industrial times.

Premodern Families

DAVID HUNT

Much of our image of premodern society depends on an evaluation of the family. A sense that family life is decaying goes back to the beginning of industrialization and continues to the present day, making it sometimes difficult to understand how anything remains to deteriorate further. The family as an economic unit has undoubtedly declined. The question is, what has happened to it as a unit of affection?

Peter Laslett stressed the bonds of love that united the family. More recent work, however, emphasizes the tensions that existed within the family. There is evidence of serious discord between young adults and their parents, as the young people generally could not marry or even enjoy adult status until their parents died or retired, leaving them with the land. Laslett himself suggests one possible result of this friction: the practice of putting children into the service of other families.

There is also serious question about the attitudes toward and the treatment of young children in the early modern family. The following selection relies for its evidence primarily on documents from the upper classes, particularly the account of the upbringing of Louis XIII when he was dauphin. But the author generalizes about French society as a whole, a dangerous practice but perhaps necessary in this murky area. He also applies some of the theories of modern psychology (notably those of Erik Erikson) to a decidedly unmodern family structure. This approach, too, can be criticized; it might be argued that premodern families produced a different set of psychological problems. (Hunt clearly suggests they produced a different personality, but he bases his views on modern notions of personality.) If we cannot apply psychological theories to the past, or develop them in relationship to the past, though, we clearly restrict our claims to a full knowledge of history and of personality alike; this is a serious issue in dealing with human behavior.

Hunt's picture, if correct, has a number of implications for the history of modernization. In contrast to Laslett's view, it suggests that in the seventeenth century the family as an affectionate unit was barely developed. In other words, the picture of preindustrial life as emotionally and psychologically satisfying must be seriously qualified—there may not have been as much for industrialization to disrupt as some authorities claim. And as a more affectionate family did develop, it may well have added important new dimensions to human experience, thus serving as some compensation for whatever new stresses modernization did produce.

At the same time, certain aspects of family life had to change before modernization was possible. In particular, there is evidence that the extremely authoritarian treatment of children, designed to break their will and to retard individual initiative and innovation, did begin to change in the eighteenth century. Swaddling (tightly wrapping an infant in strips of cloth), for example, was abandoned in France. It is also possible that the affection for young children increased. Only the outlines of these changes have as yet been established, but they have important implications. Why did they occur? Some historians have argued that in the late seventeenth century the upper classes began to develop new emotions about young children and that these new attitudes filtered down to the lower classes. David Hunt mentions that the thinkers of the Enlightenment urged greater affection and specifically criticized practices such as swaddling. Declining child mortality rates in the eighteenth century may have encouraged parents to make a greater emotional investment in their children. The reasons are not fully clear, and we cannot at this point be sure that the lower-class outlook toward children did actually change significantly during the eighteenth century. Again the question is whether the common people began to revise their own attitudes before they were caught up in externally imposed change. In any event, the long-term changes in behavior toward children suggest the need to reinterpret the role of the family in modernization.

For every new-born infant, whether he was from a rich family or a poor one, whether he was raised by a nurse, a governess, or by his parents, the major difficulty in the first months of life was getting enough to eat. Without bottles or good baby foods, adults were very hard pressed to nourish children fully and safely. Our effort to understand childhood in the seventeenth century ought to begin with a discussion of this fundamental issue.

The experience of Louis XIII, as recorded by Héroard, provides a good starting point. From the beginning, the dauphin had feeding problems. The difficulty was first attributed to the "fiber" (filet) under the infant's tongue. His surgeon, Jacques Guillemeau, cut this fiber in the hope of making it easier for the young prince to suck properly. In the days that followed, attention shifted to the nurse. She did not seem to have enough milk to satisfy the baby, who sucked in "such great gulps . . . that he drew more in on one try than others did in three." The woman attempted to correct this deficiency by eating more than usual, a tactic which succeeded only in giving her an upset stomach. A supplementary nurse was brought in and then almost immediately

Excerpted from *Parents and Children in History: The Psychology of Family Life in Early Modern France*, by David Hunt, pp. 113–17, 119–23, 124–30, 154–57. © 1970 by Basic Books, Inc., Publishers, New York.

dismissed because enemies at court managed to discredit her with the queen. When Louis was eleven weeks old, and obviously undernourished, a medical conference was summoned to consider further remedies. This situation gives occasion for some sober thought. With unlimited resources at their disposal, and with the child enjoying the best possible living conditions available at that time, the doctors nonetheless found themselves confronted with a case of virtual starvation: the muscles of the dauphin's chest were "completely wasted away," and his neck was so thin that the folds in the skin had disappeared. A third nurse arrived, but she lasted only a short time; people thought she was not "clean." The fourth and permanent nurse was not in place until the baby was sixteen weeks old.

This account is in no way extraordinary. For example, the operation on the dauphin's tongue was routinely performed. Almost all the medical authorities mentioned it, with Guillemeau giving the fullest explanation:

> In children that are newly borne there are commonly found two strings: the one comes from the bottome of the tongue, and reacheth to the very tip and end thereof. This string is very slender and soft and it hindreth the child from taking the nipple . . . so that he cannot sucke well. This string must be cut with a sizzer within a few daies after he is borne.

Paré agreed with this advice, adding that, if not cut, the "string" would later cause the child to stutter. These comments were not dictated by the surgeon's desire for an extra commission; Vallambert's remark that the cutting was well performed with one's thumbnail indicates that the doctors thought anyone could do the job. One folklorist has maintained that the custom of cutting the infant's *filet* persisted into the twentieth century in rural France.

The trouble with the nurses was also common, and in fact Louis' appetites were rather modest when compared to those of other children in the royal line. Michelet claimed that as an infant Henri IV went through eight nurses; Louis XIV may have had as many as nine. In the *livres de raison*, several families hired and discarded one nurse after another because no one among them was able to satisfy the demands of the infant she had been contracted to feed. These accounts give us another perspective on the use of the nurse. In a situation where breastfeeding was clearly the best and the safest way to nourish children, the financial ability to employ a nurse, or better yet a whole string of them, was a major advantage for a family anxious about the welfare of its offspring. If something happened to the mother nursing her own children, if she became ill or if another pregnancy interrupted the regime of breastfeeding (it was felt that carrying a child and feeding one at the same time was too taxing an undertaking for a woman to attempt), she could fall back on her family's economic reserves and bring in a nurse to help out. In a number of cases, the mother shared from the moment of birth feeding chores with a nurse, so that there were always two women available to her infant.

Since their families could not afford nurses, most children must have been forced to work even harder than the dauphin to get enough to eat. Mothers seem to have felt that, because of their many other duties, they were not in a position to devote a great deal of time even to very young children. The medical literature was almost unanimously in favor of feeding children on demand, but of all the pieces of advice offered by the experts this suggestion was among the most academic. The doctors indicate that the common practice was to limit feeding to particular times and places determined by the women rather than by their offspring. Even if the poor mother managed to stay with her child at all times, it was thought that she still would not have enough milk to satisfy him. As Vallambert observed: "Because of their continual labor and poor life, [these mothers] do not have a lot of milk, so that they would not be capable of feeding the child if he did not take other nourishment in addition to the milk from the breast."

This "other nourishment" was "gruel" (bouillie), a combination of cow's or goat's milk with wheat flour or the crumbs of white bread soaked in water. The mixture was to be baked until it thickened, then served to the infant on his mother's or nurse's finger. This staple appears to have been very widely used. Dionis commented: "There are no women who do not know how to make bouillie." Yet the doctors were very suspicious of it. Bouillie was too "viscous and thick," causing "indigestion and constipation." Women made the mixture carelessly, not sifting the flour or neglecting the baking stage.

However, in a characteristic way, these experts would break their discussion in two parts. Recognizing the strength of the custom, and apparently deciding to make the best of a bad situation, they would add all sorts of recommendations on the use of bouillie, for example, that egg yolk or honey added to the mixture would serve as a purgative, counteracting the "obstruction" normally caused by the food. Several of them were content with very modest prohibitions against its use, forbidding bouillie in the first two weeks of a child's life. Mauriceau's belief that it should not be added to the infant's diet until the second or third month seems utopian by comparison.

Badly prepared bouillie, fed to the infant on the end of his mother's finger, must have created serious problems for untested digestive systems. However, the use of this staple was unavoidable:

> Long before the first teeth appear, even before the age of three months, . . . the women of the countryside, and the other poor women of the towns [give bouillie to their children] because if the latter took no other nourishment besides milk, they would not be able to go so long without sucking as they do, during the time when mothers are absent and held down by their work.

Even the dauphin was given *bouillie* only eighteen days after birth. Here, as elsewhere, the experience of the most precious child in the kingdom enables us to imagine the even more somber circumstances of his less fortunate peers. A squad of nurses barely managed to feed the dauphin, and his diet had to be filled out with *bouillie* before he was three weeks old. In spite of all the efforts of the household, Louis almost succumbed. We might well wonder how other children survived the precarious first months of life.

In fact, when the infant did not get enough milk at the breast and was unable to digest the *bouillie*, he starved. The willingness to have children suckled by farm animals (a practice condoned in the medical literature) indicates the gravity of the food problem. In this respect, the story of the feeding of children represents very well the insecurity of their situation as a whole. For whatever reason, a shocking number of children died. This mortality rate has been fairly conclusively documented. In one rural area during the seventeenth century, more than one-quarter of the children born at a given time did not reach the age of one, and almost a half died before the age of four. There are no equally reliable statistics for urban areas within France during this period, but from what we know of European cities in general, it seems safe to conclude that rates there would have been at least as high. The fact that infants were so vulnerable, that it was tremendously difficult to feed them properly and to protect them from disease and death, is the fundamental precondition which we of a more comfortable milieu must grasp if we are to understand what childhood was like in the seventeenth century. . . .

With these thoughts in mind, it is interesting to turn to actual descriptions of very small children in the seventeenth century. In fact, grownups had a highly developed awareness of the infant's tireless capacity for appropriation, of his tenacious parasitism. The picture Héroard sketched of a greedy Louis gulping in huge swallows of milk is not without a tinge of the sinister. It was commonly believed that birth was prompted by the hunger of the infant who, because he could no longer satisfy himself in the womb, tried "with great impetuousness to get out." Avarice was the child's principal trait: "All children are naturally very greedy and gluttonous." At the same time that they called for feeding on demand, the doctors cautioned mothers against overfeeding. While being indulgent, they could not let the unquenchable appetite of the infant hold full sway.

These opinions take on their full significance when we note that the experts thought the mother's milk was actually whitened blood. They do not seem to have understood the fact that secretion of milk in the mother's body is a self-sustaining process designed specifically to meet the special demands of the new-born infant. The nursing situation was not seen as a cooperative effort, but as a struggle in which the interests of the two parties were at least to some extent at odds. In fact, the infant prospered at the expense of his mother, from whose body he sucked the precious substance he needed for his own survival. These views explain why breastfeeding was seen as a debilitating experience for a woman, why she was counseled to hire a nurse after a difficult delivery, or if she again became pregnant. Only the healthy mother could afford to sacrifice a part of herself for the welfare of her children.

In a world where people believed that resources of all kinds were fixed and in short supply, the prosperity of one person or group was always linked to the bad luck of others. From this perspective, adults were naturally disturbed by the incessant demands of small children. For example, I think that such sentiments underlie the story recorded by Louise Bourgeois about a Strasburg mother who fell asleep while nursing her child. A snake with poisonous fangs attached itself to her breast and began to suck. The woman and her husband could not remove the animal for fear that it would bite, and for ten months it continued to suck, growing to monstrous proportions on the strength of this nourishment. Bourgeois thought the incident showed "how much substance there is in woman's milk." The mother was forced to put her child out to nurse and to go everywhere with the unwelcome guest, carrying it in a basket. The child at the breast had been transformed into a serpent, symbol of evil. At the end of the story, only the magic charms of a sorceress succeeded in tempting away this covetous intruder.

The fear of being bitten expressed in the story was manifested more generally by adults in a great deal of anxiety about teething. Parents reacted very specifically to this step in infantile development and regarded teething as a serious disease which might lead to all sorts of complications: diarrhea, fevers, epilepsy, spasms, and even death. Paré wrote:

> Monseigneur de Nemours sent to fetch me to anatomize his dead son, aged eight months or thereabouts, whose teeth had not erupted. Having diligently searched for the cause of his death, I could not find any, if not that his gums were very hard, thick and swollen; having cut through them, I found all his teeth ready to come out, if only someone had cut his gums. So it was decided by the doctors present and by me that the sole cause of his death was that nature had not been strong enough to pierce the gums and push the teeth out.

Remedies abounded for this "disease," and parents were advised to rub the sore gums with all sorts of magical panaceas. If this did not help, Guillemeau suggested: "Rub the legs, thighs, shoulders, backe and nape of the child's necke, drawing still downwards, thereby to alter and turne the course of humours which fall downe upon the gummes and passages of the throat." As a last resort, the surgeon was supposed to cut the gums so that the teeth might more easily emerge.

In these comments, doctors stress the fact that teeth are the infant's first aggressive tools, although they limit themselves to discussing the ways in which children themselves can be harmed by such sharp instruments. However, I think that the tone of the discussion, the awe with which doctors analyze the eruption of teeth, indicate an underlying fear of the child's biting impulses, the potentially dangerous use he can make of his mouth. In this respect, the interpretation of teething is consistent with the tendency to see children as gluttonous little animals and with the belief that they were sucking away the mother's blood. Collecting together these images, we have a picture of the small child as a predatory and frightening creature capable of harming the woman whose duty it was to care for him. Returning to [Erik] Erikson's hypothesis, we can say that in the eyes of his elders the seventeenth-century infant was an "oral sadist."

I have no doubt that similar themes appear in the childrearing literature of all cultures. In fact, they are built into the breastfeeding relationship: the infant does suck with striking intensity, because his life depends on it; women are to some extent tied down by the demands of their very small offspring; and breastfeeding is always complicated by the child's teething. At the same time, I believe that images of the child as a greedy little animal had a special power in the seventeenth century and that they exerted a relatively pronounced negative influence on efforts to feed the very young.

I picture a mother, who herself probably did not get enough to eat, and who was forced to work long and difficult hours, turning to the task of breastfeeding with mixed feelings. The child was a parasite; he did nothing and yet his appetites seemed to be endless. He was sucking a vital fluid out of her already depleted body. This situation must have been tremendously difficult for mothers to tolerate. In turn, children sensed the anxiety of their providers, perhaps in the tense way they were held, in the tentativeness of the breast being offered to them. Aware of the unreliability of this source of life, they redoubled their efforts to "get" as much as possible. These efforts impressed mothers as especially gluttonous and devouring, and in reaction they developed an image of children as greedy little animals, who were harmful to their guardians. These fantasies worked to undermine the resolution of mothers, whose gathering ambivalence would be communicated to children, who in turn would become all the more peremptory in their demands for more milk.

Some hypothesis along these lines is necessary to account for the frequent breakdown in efforts to feed little children. The poverty of the society, while it provided the necessary, and very powerful, initial impetus for the process by which mother and child became wary of each other, is not in itself a sufficient explanation for the problem. Mothers in equally poor societies manage to keep their children close by and to feed them on demand. Medically speaking, there is no reason why a woman, even if she is relatively undernourished, cannot adequately breastfeed a child. Further, we know that lactation does not weaken mothers who undertake it. This analysis is not intended as a critique of seventeenth-century mothers. Given their situation, it is entirely natural that they should have been ambivalent about children. My point is that economic or physiological arguments do not in themselves explain the great difficulty experienced in getting enough food into the child's belly. These difficulties make sense only if we picture the specifically economic factors overlaid with a set of disturbing fantasies about children at the breast. The problem was first of all in the seventeenth-century economy, but at the same time it was also in the minds and the deportment of parents.

This point is clearly illustrated in the royal court, and in the houses of the rich, where nurses, who almost certainly got enough to eat, were often unable to produce enough milk for the children they were supposed to breast-feed. Poor living conditions cannot explain these failures which the literature documents with such regularity and which adults of the time seem to have accepted as a matter of course. The situation of the nurse must have created conflicts of its own. Given their low status, and the constant critical scrutiny of people like Héroard, who were alert to any sign of their inadequacy as providers, these women may well have had trouble relaxing and devoting themselves wholeheartedly to the task of feeding the children of their superiors. On the other hand, I suspect that some part of the problem was independent of the woman's identity as a nurse, but instead grew out of her image of children, her sense of them as demanding and dangerous little animals, a sense she shared with all other mothers, of the time. . . . In his analysis of the first phase of childhood growth, Erik Erikson maintains that the incorporative mode of behavior is expressed most obviously through the mouth, but that it is also manifested in the activity of the infantile organism as a whole. The child must be seen as a personality, facing a total existential situation, and not simply as an oral creature who must be fed. By contrast, in the seventeenth century infantile experience was grasped by adults primarily in terms of feeding. The discussion of the doctors concentrated heavily on the problem of how best to nourish the child. In the same spirit, parents contracted with nurses to serve simply as suppliers of milk, rather than as maternal figures in a broader sense, because they believed that the infant's alimentary needs were the only ones worthy of serious attention. The fact that small children needed conversation, companionship, and play, as well as nourishment of a more tangible sort, was not well understood by adults of the period.

Of course parents were amused and diverted by infants and did take notice of them in situations other than those connected with feeding. On the other hand, I think it is significant that in the seventeenth century the notion of "playing" with children had an ambiguous ring. Some critics thought that in this play adults betrayed a careless, self-indulgent attitude. In casting about for the words to describe their impressions, these observers hit upon a comparison which we have already encountered in the discussion of feeding: parents treated children like pets, or little animals. Montaigne argued: "We have loved [infants] for our own amusement, like monkeys, not like human beings." And Fleury commented: "It is as if the poor children had been made only to amuse the adults, like little dogs or little monkeys."

This comparison of the child to an animal is something more than a useful device, a way of characterizing the infant at the breast. The image appears throughout seventeenth-century literature on children. In a total sense, the small child was an intermediate being, not really an animal (although he might often be compared to one), but on the other hand not really human either. This quasi-evolutionary model of the ages of life was so ingrained that adults often hardly noticed its presence in their own speech. Thus in describing the battle of Paris, Jean Burel wrote that the Parisians "were besieged by the King of Navarre so closely that they were forced to eat animals: dogs, horses, everything right up to, and almost including, little children." In the chain of being, a separate link—infancy—connected the animal and the human worlds without belonging completely to either one.

I have already argued that, with respect to the specifically oral forms of this image of the child as little animal, in an area where infant survival was very much at stake, parents struggled with their negative feelings and managed to stay in touch with their offspring. Once the child had been safely fed, however, it is possible that adults gave vent to their aversion and disgust and treated the infant with the callousness which his subhuman station deserved. We must try to ascertain whether the feeding of infants was somehow special, or if, on the other hand, parental attitudes in that area carried over into the whole of relations with the child during the first year of life.

I think the best way to approach this problem is through an examination of the practice of swaddling. The eighteenth-century philosophes have already experimented with a similar tactic. In turning their attention to child-rearing, they found evidence of negligence on every side, but nowhere more obnoxiously manifested than in the practice of swaddling. In detailing the evils of the custom, these critics conjured up a whole gallery of cruel images: the infant was wrapped up tight and tossed "in a corner"; or the nurse hung a crying baby in swaddling clothes from a nail on the wall, so that the bands tightened, suffocating the child and choking off his cries; or the nurse placed the swaddled baby in his cradle and rocked him until he fell into a groggy sleep. In all these instances, swaddling represented a general point of view toward children, a deficiency in that sympathy or generosity which the philosophes thought a child had a right to expect from his elders. While reserving judgment on the exact meaning of the practice, I follow the eighteenth-century critics by discussing swaddling in this symbolic sense, as a key to understanding what adults thought of the first stage of life.

The swaddling of infants, which to us is one of the most exotic features of childrearing in the seventeenth century, was utterly taken for granted by the adults of that period. Doctors, who showed such a lively interest in the various controversial issues of childrearing, barely took notice of swaddling and offered only a few scraps of advice on the subject; as Mauriceau put it, "There are no women who do not know all about something which is so common." In describing Louis' birth, Héroard mentions that the infant was swaddled soon after being washed and fed, but he never refers to the clothes again. In an account otherwise rich in detail, there is nothing on the regime of swaddling: how the wrapping was done, when during the day the clothes were removed, not even a hint as to when in the life of the dauphin the practice was terminated. Although swaddling has almost completely disappeared in modern France, the custom was once so deeply rooted in everyday life that it was put into practice almost automatically. This combination of factors makes it a particularly useful, as well as difficult, subject for the historian interested in the distinctive qualities of childrearing in the old regime.

The swaddling band (called the *maillot*) was a roll of cloth about two inches across. The infant was wrapped up with this length of cloth, arms straight at his sides and legs extended, with a few extra turns around the head to hold it steady, so that only a small circle of his face would be left exposed. Doctors advised that the pressure of the band should be equal on all parts of the body, to avoid crippling the infant, and that especial care should be taken in wrapping the chest and stomach so that breathing would not be impeded. The swaddling was left in place at all times during the first weeks of an infant's life except when it was necessary to clean and change him. Vallambert suggested that if an infant cried excessively, one could "unswaddle him, and massage and move his limbs, for that often causes the crying and the screaming to stop." At some time early in his life (according to doctors, between the first and fourth month), the infant's arms would be freed and the wrappings applied only to his legs and torso. Finally, when he was eight or nine months old, or at the latest around his first birthday, the infant would be left unswaddled for good.

Intuitively—and wrongly—we imagine that such a regime would leave infants deformed or retarded. Actual details on the physical development of babies in the seventeenth century are very scarce, but Héroard's *Journal* does suggest something of the dauphin's progress in this respect and helps to show that swaddling did not stunt the growth of children. At first, the doctor describes Louis performing acts compatible with a regime of swaddling: listening, staring, speaking, laughing. At four months, Louis was "playing" with the king and queen, and in one session Henri studied the feet of his son, which, he had been told, resembled his own. At five and a half months, "he dances gaily to the sound of a violin." Obviously this was not real dancing, but perhaps some rhythmic movement of the arms. A week later, he stretched out his hand for an object (a book) for the first time. Louis was throwing things at the age of six months and was also being put to bed with his arms free (it will be remembered that while he was teething Héroard sat up holding his hand). At eight months, the dauphin was fitted for his first pair of shoes, and six weeks later the "leading strings" (lisières), which would be used by adults to help him learn to walk, were attached to his clothes.

This circumstantial evidence seems to fit well enough the schedule suggested by the doctors. No later than five and a half months after his birth, Louis' arms were left unswaddled so that he was free to "dance," to grasp a book, to be held by the hand. In fact, he may have been completely unswaddled by this time since Henri IV was able to study his feet; but it is also possible that the dauphin was specially unwrapped for his parents' visit. In any case, the maillot was definitively discarded by eight or nine months when Louis was fitted for shoes and lisières.

Swaddling had little effect on subsequent motor development. Apparently children did not spend much time crawling. There are almost no pictorial representations of a stage between swaddling and walking, and, on the other hand, every effort seems to have been made to help children learn how to walk. Around his first birthday, the dauphin was indeed walking with "firmness, held under the arms." When Louis was nineteen months old, Héroard describes him running, and in going from place to place he was now led (mené) as often as carried (porté). The descriptions offered of his play corroborate the impression of the dauphin's rapidly growing dexterity, "fencing" with Héroard (ten months), playing the violin and the drum (about a year and a half), and striking a blow of fifty-five paces with his "bat" (palemail) when he was just over two.

Swaddling obviously did not cripple children. In fact the practice performed a number of positive functions. From the recent literature on the subject, we know that (like a high-walled cradle or a play-pen) swaddling limits potentially dangerous motor activity; that (like a carriage) it makes children easier to carry; and that it provides a measure of security and reassurance by relieving the infant of responsibility for the control of his limbs in a period when he does not yet have sufficient physical mastery to handle the job completely on his own.

All of these reasons may have been considered in the seventeenth century, but they were not mentioned by experts in their terse discussions of the practice. Among the reasons which were given for swaddling, the first and most important seems to have been that it kept the baby warm:

> Nor then forget that wrappers be at hand,
> Soft flannels, linen, and the swaddling band,
> T'enwrap the babe, by many a circling fold,
> In equal lines, and thus defend from cold.

This function was very important; we are dealing with a world in which even the royal palaces were so poorly insulated that children had to be admonished to stay close to the fireplace on the coldest days. One doctor cautioned against freeing the child's arms during the winter. Even if he was past the age of three or four months, the baby was to remain fully swaddled "until he is older and it is not so cold."

Doctors also argued that swaddling was necessary to help the infant's limbs grow straight. Apparently this belief in the effectiveness of the wrapping is not unfounded, especially when one considers the prevalence of rickets among young children at that time. There was also some notion that swaddling prevented the child from hurting himself by striking a hard object or by falling. More generally, swaddling immobilized the child under reasonably beneficial circumstances and thus served as a substitute for the constant attention which the unhindered baby would have required from its elders. This substitution may often have been dictated by a lack of interest in children and could therefore be interpreted (in the tradition of the philosophes) as a sign of parental neglect. However, in this respect as in others, we must be careful to distinguish matters of choice from those of necessity. For many poor women, the *maillot*, no less than *bouillie*, was an essential device which enabled them to spend long periods of time at work and away from their infants. For any society which could not afford to be too child-centered, swaddling, or some other practice which relieved adults of the need for constant supervision of children, was inevitable and can hardly be construed as a sign of some special parental malice and neglect.

In fact, swaddling can be interpreted as an antidote to the more extreme forms of parental ambivalence. We have seen how much contempt adults were likely to feel for children and how they seemed to regard their offspring as little animals. Swaddling allowed parents to defend against the consequences of their own distaste. This distinctive custom helped to place infants. It defined with a more reassuring precision the limbo of childhood, leaving it distinct from the sphere of adult life, but also firmly marking it off from the animal kingdom. As Mauriceau observed, children were swaddled for fear they would otherwise never learn to stand erect, but would always crawl on all fours like little animals. Swaddling embodied the promise of a future humanity and saved infants from a descent to that animal world into which their own strangeness and frailty threatened to propel them.

In the same spirit, adults wanted children either in swaddling clothes or walking on two feet. Crawling was discouraged precisely because it made more ambiguous that distinction between infants and animals which adults knew in their hearts they had to maintain. We have already seen how a kind of collective repression protected parents from their fear of the predatory appetites of growing infants. With its numerous benefits, and as a means of defining the first stage of life, swaddling operated on an even more general plane as a way of caring for infants and at the same time of binding up the anxiety which adults experienced in dealing with the animality of small children. . . .

I would maintain that in the seventeenth century people felt strongly the contrast between the loyalties and duties incumbent upon them as a consequence of their station in society on the one hand, and their natural inclinations on the other. Institutional arrangements always implied a gradation of rank and were thus held to be incompatible with friendship, in which equality between the partners was so important. Far from accepting the fact that personal relations were almost always arranged according to hierarchical principles, individuals were made acutely uncomfortable by this situation. In personal letters, writers often distinguished sincere and spontaneous affection from the more perfunctory good will which went with the formal relationship to their correspondent. Thus Madame de Sévigné, in sending good wishes to her daughter, stipulated that, "In this case, maternal love plays less of a part than inclination."

As the quote indicates, the family was caught up in this system. To be a brother, son, or wife was a status, with its special obligations, its place in a grid of rule and submission. Members of the family were supposed to love one another; paternal, maternal, fraternal love were all often cited as models of human fellow feeling. At the same time, even within the family, it was terribly hard to imagine a relationship of mutual affection which was not simultaneously one of ruler and ruled. Like the bond between master and servant, between seigneur and peasant, between king and subject, family ties, while steeped in a folklore of pious harmony, implied as well the power to dominate others, to claim rewards, or, on the contrary, the awareness of a helpless dependence.

This line of argument will help to explain further the distinction which, as we have seen, observers made with such clarity between marriages of love and those of interest. Marriages of love implied spontaneous affection between the two lovers, who were concerned primarily with their own happiness. Marriage of interest involved social and financial considerations to be arranged for the benefit of families. These observers understood very well that in a social system which attempted to subordinate the wishes of marriageable children to the ambitions of their parents, and in which the wife was regarded simply as the means of cementing alliances between families, marriage could not at the same time be expected to provide for the happiness and the emotional satisfaction of the partners.

Fraternal relations were compromised by similar pressures. As the dauphin was being forced to acknowledge himself as his father's valet, it was also being pointed out to him that his brothers, who were younger and hence subordinate, would serve him just as he served the king. Books of etiquette often struggled with the problem of fraternal affection and the rights of primogeniture. How do you reconcile "natural" ties with the principle which arranges brothers one above the other in a hierarchy of prerogatives? Corneille built the play *Rodogune* around this dilemma. The twins Seleucus and

Antiochus are the model of fraternity. Since they do not know who is older (the oddity of the situation demonstrates how hard it was in the seventeenth century to conceive of real equality), they can be familiar and trusting in relations with one another. Their mother, however, decides to disclose the order of birth, and the two brothers are thrown into a panic. They know that if this information is revealed, one will become the arrogant master, the other, his resentful servant (full of "shame and envy"), and their accord will be ruined.

We can see that gradations of rank within the household were interpreted simply as a matter of power and of usage, and that people believed this situation discouraged close and mutually satisfying relationships among family members. Ideally, those of lower rank should have accepted the eminence of their superiors and been warmed by the benefits they received from an admittedly unequal partnership. In fact, inequality within the domestic unit filled people not with love and warmth, but with resentment and a feeling of "shame and envy."

Among the members of the family, the infant is the most prone to these feelings. His physical and intellectual inferiority is a basic fact of nature as is his subjection to the will of older, stronger adults. Precisely because it is so completely unearned by any merit, but instead is derived from an amoral biological fact, parental authority might legitimately be expected to embody whatever sense of justice adults profess to respect. The child has to obey; in what ways do grownups persuade him that he ought to obey?

It seems to me that no one could deny the paramount importance of force and intimidation in the upbringing of the dauphin. The beating Louis received at the hands of his father demonstrated the lengths to which adults were willing to carry the matter: an obstinate child was in physical danger. Grownups relied heavily on their ability to frighten the young prince. They rightly assumed that he remembered what had happened the last time he had been too defiant. Childish fears were exploited in a variety of petty ways. For example, when it was discovered that Louis was afraid of someone (a hunchbacked member of the guard, or a mason in the king's service), that person would be summoned whenever it was necessary to make Louis toe the line.

The whippings continued, gradually settling into a fixed ritual. Louis was beaten first thing in the morning the day after his infractions: "Scarcely were his eyes open when he was whipped." Often he would get up early and hide or block the door in order to avoid these sessions. When it became impossible for Madame de Montglat to handle the dauphin, his father instructed soldiers of the guard to hold him while the whippings were administered. Louis was beaten even after becoming king of France, and at the age of ten, he still had nightmares about being whipped. As late as January, 1614, adults continued to threaten Louis with the switch, but by this time his physical development was at last putting a stop to such means of punishment.

As I suggested earlier, formalized coercion was probably better for the infant than the erratic and unrestrained cruelty which no doubt characterized discipline in families where parents had to deal directly with their offspring. But even in the royal household, it is obvious that fear was one of the principal forces steering the child into that social role which adults required him to assume. Such fear was not incompatible with love. Louis always demonstrated an intense feeling for his father, and it would be foolish to pretend that their relationship was entirely negative. Yet this love (corresponding to the sentiment which many historians have thought tied together master and servant in the old regime) does not change the fact that terrorizing children was inhumane and wrong. At the core of its domestic life, I think we find a telling indictment of the old regime.

We now have a better idea of how life cycles "interlocked" in the seventeenth century. It is no accident that fathers whipped their sons for their own good, because they themselves were whipped as children. These fathers had been thwarted in their own infantile efforts to be autonomous. Punished for attempting to establish selfhood, and deprived of control over their bodies, they were left with a pervasive sense of shame and doubt. Such sentiments fit the adult life they could lead in a hierarchical society indifferent to the dignity of the individual and held together principally by coercive means. In turn, people formed along these lines were necessarily going to respond to their children's search for independence with rigid counterassertions and panicky violence. The inability of the king himself, the only man in the society who was without a master, to break out of this vicious circle attests to the power of the cycle of unfreedom.

Popular Recreations in English Society

ROBERT W. MALCOLMSON

What options have we lost in losing the traditional world of recreation? Historians are just beginning to return to this question, as they grapple with the proper meaning and function of leisure in modern life. Yet laments for the lost gaiety of village festivals began with the rise of industrial society, for the nineteenth century, with its stern work ethic and its middle-class fear of unruliness, unquestionably cut into a host of popular pastimes.

Traditional recreations are not without their modern critics. Historians dealing with the European continent, more than with England, have claimed that leisure in its truest sense is actually a modern phenomenon. They point out that before industrialization few people had much time for extensive nonwork activities. Free time, consisting principally of festival days, was rigorously controlled by community custom, allowing no individual choice of leisure forms. Also, it is valid to ask if the criticisms levied against modern leisure cannot also be directed against its preindustrial counterpart: undue violence; undue concentration on youth; manipulation by the upper classes to keep the masses in line; undue conformity (although to custom rather than the media of our own day).

Preindustrial recreation was clearly not pure joy. Instead, it had a variety of social functions. Are these functions—outlets for youth, community feeling, acceptable hostility against the ruling class, acceptance of death—as necessary in modern society, and if so, are they as well served by modern leisure? Again, the question is how much have we lost.

Perhaps, we have lost little after a period of adjustment to urban and industrial life in the nineteenth century. Leisure may be a phenomenon that does not modernize, serving basic human needs that have not greatly changed. For, without question, we have preserved or revived many of the games and pastimes of preindustrial England, including the sacred football game—and, quite possibly, for many of the same purposes.

. . . Many recreations arose directly out of the fabric of common interests and common sentiments among the working people themselves. The fundamental social basis for several of the calendar festivities was the relatively small, tightly-knit rural community, and it was in this kind of community that a large number of labouring men spent most of their time and developed their basic sense of social identity. It was a world of face-to-face contacts, deriving its unifying forces from the common experiences of daily (and yearly) routine and a shared oral culture. The people's social relationships stemmed mostly from the ties of family, the ties of neighbourhood (a village, a hamlet, one end of town), and the ties which were formed in the course of their work. The range of their social encounters was normally fairly limited; in most rural areas, aside from the market towns, they would have had relatively infrequent contact with complete strangers. Some of their recreations reflected the personal character of their day-to-day experiences. During the Christmas season friends from the parish, and perhaps relatives from nearby, were in the habit of gathering together at a public house or in each others' cottages. It was said that on Christmas Day "at Danby Wisk in ye North-Riding of Yorkshire, it is the custom for ye Parishioners after receiving ye Sacrament, to goe from Church directly to the Ale House and there drink together as a testimony of Charity and friendship." A morris dance in the market place or through the village streets would have attracted an audience from the bulk of the inhabitants, many of whom would have known one another personally. There was a communal basis for the ritual. The community's sense of solidarity might also have been expressed in some athletic competition—the village hero contending in a wrestling match, a football game against a neighbouring parish. Some festive occasions arose out of a consciousness of mutual interests among people of the same trade. St Crispin's feast, the 25th of October, was regularly celebrated by the shoemakers in Knaresborough; Plough Monday was an occupational holiday for the ploughmen, St Andrew's Day (November 30th) for the lacemakers; February 3rd was widely observed by the woolcombers with parades and merry-makings, in honour of their patron saint, Bishop Blaze.

The ties of kinship, friendship, and neighbourliness among the common people were especially important as supports for the annual wake, probably the principal occasion for individuals to come together in order to reaffirm their social relationships. Henry Bourne remarked that at the time of a wake the people "deck themselves in their gaudiest Clothes, and have open Doors and splendid Entertainments, for the Reception and Treating of their Relations and Friends, who visit them on that Occasion, from each neighbouring Town"; and in September 1738 a contributor to the *Gentleman's Magazine* declared that "I hear of one [parish feast] every Sunday kept in some Village or other of the Neighbourhood, and see great Numbers of both Sexes in their Holiday Cloaths, constantly flocking thither, to partake of the Entertainment of their Friends and Relations, or to divert themselves with the rural Games and athletick Exercises." John Clare also wrote of the social connections which underlay the wake:

The woodman and the thresher now are found
Mixing and making merry with their friends
Children and kin from neighbouring towns around
Each at the humble banquet pleas'd attends
For though no costliness the feast pretends
Yet something more than common they provide
And the good dame her small plum pudding sends
To sons and daughters fast in service tied
With many a cordial gift of good advice beside

The feast was pre-eminently a time of hospitality and generous provision. It was said in 1759 that in Fallow, a hamlet of the parish of Sparsholt in Berkshire, "the feast day at the old chapel at Fallow, now demolished, had been on the Sunday following the feast of St James, which day the neighbourhood of Fallow keep in the way of having better cheer and open hospitality." At the wakes in Stamford, "An abundance of good cheer, which every individual in the parish provides, whose circumstances will permit him to obtain it, supplies his table nearly the whole of the week, to which a host of ready cousins, friends, and neighbours, are welcome: and on the Saturday night, the round of festivity is commonly concluded with ass races and dancings." Similarly, Samuel Bamford recalled that on the Sunday of the wake "the very best dinner which could be provided was set out . . . and the guests were helped with a profusion of whatever the host could command. It was a duty at the wakes to be hospitable, and he who at that time was not liberal according to his means, was set down as a very mean person."

On many festive occasions the most active participants, as one might expect, were men and women in their teens and early twenties. John Aubrey reported that the Michaelmas fair at Kington St Michael, Wiltshire was "much resorted unto by the young people," a feature which was noticed of many other fairs. "Here met the village youths on pleasure bent," wrote James Withers of the annual petty fair in his Cambridgeshire village. Since almost all servants were single, young people were especially prominent at hiring fairs. Guy Fawkes Day seems to have been particularly associated with the revelries of younger men; Shrove Tuesday was traditionally the special holiday of apprentices, and May Day was primarily for the benefit of young men and women.

The most important reason for the prominent involvement of young people in recreational events was the fact that they served as occasions for courtship and sexual encounters. This was most noticeably the case at fairs and feasts. On 29 October 1781 Sylas Neville referred in his diary to the "country Beauties and their sweethearts enjoying themselves at the fruit stalls and mountebank's stage" at a fair in Burton-upon-Trent; and at Norwich on 8 April 1784 he wrote of a "fair on Tombland for toys etc., full of Beaux and Belles before dinner." An observer of the hiring fair at Studley, Warwickshire, noticed that "towards evening each lad seeks his lass, and they hurry off to spend the night at the public houses." It was said that at the fairs and statutes in Cumberland "it is customary for all the young people in the neighbourhood to assemble and dance at the inns and alehouses"; after a hiring, with "fiddlers tuning their fiddles in public houses, the girls begin to file off, and gently pace the streets, with a view of gaining admirers; while the young men . . . follow after, and having eyed the lasses, pick up each a sweetheart, whom they conduct to a dancing room, and treat with punch and cake." The feast at Pudsey was reported to be a major occasion for match-making. Dancing was always a standard attraction at wakes and pleasure fairs and it provided a focal point for courting and flirtation. John Clare, for instance, wrote of the dancing at a village feast:

> Where the fond swain delighteth in the chance
> To meet the sun tann'd lass he dearly loves
> And as he leads her down the giddy dance
> With many a token his fond passion proves
> Squeezing her hands or catching at her gloves
> And stealing kisses as chance prompts the while

It would have been strange if many holiday gatherings had not catered to the special interests of unmarried men and women. Festive assemblies offered them some of the best opportunities for establishing new contacts and for pursuing acquaintances already made; they widened the range of choice, and because of their free and easy and relatively uninhibited textures, they encouraged the kinds of gallantries and personal displays which were not usually possible in everyday life. Eustace Budgell must have had this sort of setting in mind when, in his portrayal of a football game at a country wake, he noted that one "Tom Short behaved himself so well, that most People seemed to agree it was impossible that he should remain a Batchelour till the next Wake." Sir Thomas Parkyns was assuming a similar set of circumstances when he was publicizing the satisfactions which were to be gained from his favourite sport:

For the most Part our Country Rings for Wrestlings, at Wakes and other Festivals, consist of a small Party of young Women, who come not thither to choose a Coward, but the Daring, Healthy, and Robust Persons, fit to raise an Offspring from: I dare say, they sufficiently recommend themselves to their Sweet-hearts, when they demonstrate that they are of hail Constitutions, and enjoy a perfect state of Health, and like the Fatigue of that Day . . .

In the same vein, John Gay's The Shepherd's Week had the maid Marian speak warmly of how

Young *Colin Clout*, a Lad of peerless Meed,
Full well could dance, and deftly tune the Reed;
In ev'ry Wood his Carrols sweet were known,
In ev'ry Wake his nimble Feats were shown.
When in the Ring the Rustic Routs he threw,
The Damsels Pleasures with his Conquests grew;
Or when aslant the Cudgel threats his Head,
His Danger smites the Breast of ev'ry Maid . . .

However, although the young may have been particularly active on many holidays and even dominant on a few, they seldom monopolized the pleasures of a festive gathering. On most occasions there would have been ample room for the participation, in some form or other, of the middle-aged and the elderly. On 9 July 1715 Nicholas Blundell reported that at Little Crosby "the Little Boyes and Girles of this Town diverted themselves with Rearing a May-pole in the West-Lane, they had Morrys dansing and a great many came to it both old and young." Similarly, John Denson of Waterbeach claimed that "both old and young participated" in the afternoon diversions of May Day—the rites of the morning were exclusively for the young people—"and those whom age and infirmity prevented, appeared to enjoy our sports as they sat at their cottage doors." On those occasions when youth enjoyed the limelight there was nothing to prevent the older people from looking on. At the annual harvest feast in Warton, Lancashire, during the early eighteenth century "the Old People after Supper smoak their Pipes, and with great Pleasure and Delight behold the younger spending the Evening in Singing, Dancing, etc." On Midsummer Eve, according to Henry Bourne,

> it is usual in the most of Country Places, and also here and there in Towns and Cities, for both Old and Young to meet together, and be Merry over a large Fire, which is made in the open Street. Over this they frequently leap and play at various Games, such as Running, Wrestling, Dancing, etc. But this is generally the Exercise of the younger Sort; for the old Ones, for the most Part, sit by as Spectators, and enjoy themselves and their Bottle.

Matrons would watch the games and dancing at a wake and older men would be keen observers at a match of football, wrestling, or cudgelling. "Aged men also, hardly able to walk, were to be seen moving towards this scene of riot," complained a clergyman of the bull-running at Stamford, "anxious to witness a repetition of such exploits as they, when young, had often performed."

Even when the young were the most vigorous participants, then, it is clear that a good many older people attended a festive event as spectators— often to gossip, to pronounce judgements, and to display the wisdom of experience. James Withers wrote of how at a village fair, "The old folks talked of times when they were young, / And the same songs, year after year, were sung." Indeed, the crowds at many fairs and most feasts were drawn from all age groups of the population. Moreover, there were a number of holidays and diversions which placed no special premium on youth. The celebrations of the Christmas season, for instance, were appropriate for people of all ages. Several of the principal pastimes favoured no particular age group: bull-baiting and cock-fighting retained an appeal for many older men, and bell-ringing could be enjoyed and practised by people of almost any age. Sex, in fact, was probably a social determinant of greater weight than age, for while many of the major holidays involved women almost as much as men, most of the sporting events assumed that women would attend only as spectators, or not at all. . . .

During much of the eighteenth century the dominant attitude of the gentry towards the recreations of the people seems to have been one of acquiescence and tolerance. To a certain extent gentlemen shared some of the same recreational interests as the common people, and there was only limited room for conflict when their tastes were often so similar. The common denominator was particularly noticeable in the practice of animal sports. Although there were murmurings of disapproval before the middle of the century, there is no indication that any substantial number of gentlemen had as yet become seriously opposed to them; in fact, they were more likely to be keen spectators, and sometimes even participants. "My Black-Bull was Baited at Mrs Ann Rothwells," wrote Nicholas Blundell on 8 September 1712, "there played but three right Doggs and two of them were ill hurt." On 20 October 1714 the physician Claver Morris gave 1s. 6d. for the bull-baiting at a public house; and on 5 September 1759 James Woodforde wrote that "I went to the Bear-baiting in Ansford" (his father was rector of the parish). During the festivities on the day of the mayor's election in Liverpool it was said that "every house and window in the vicinity of the spot where the bear was baited, was adorned by the appearance of the most elegant ladies and gentlemen in the town"; and an observer of the Stamford bull-running probably had men of substance in mind when he claimed in 1785 that "I have heard some of the natives, who have lived in the metropolis, aver that they never saw any diversion there comparable to it, and if they were to pay a visit to their friends, have construed to come down a little before this day in order to become actors in it." Cock-fighting drew its followers from genteel as much as from plebeian sportsmen; and the informal field sports, especially fishing and coursing, sometimes brought together a diversity of social ranks.

The point to bear in mind is that, during the first half of the eighteenth century in particular, many gentlemen were not entirely disengaged from the culture of the common people. They frequently occupied something of a half-way house between the robust, unpolished culture of provincial England and the cosmopolitan, sophisticated culture which was based in London. Most of the country houses were not yet principally seasonal extensions of a polite and increasingly self-conscious urban culture, and many of their occupants remained relatively uncitified. They still retained some of the characteristics of rusticity, traits which they shared with the common people. The fact that the drama of the late seventeenth and earlier eighteenth centuries was full of booby-squires (boobies from London's point of view) is an indication, not that the characterization was necessarily accurate, but that there actually were a large number of gentlemen whose modes of thought and behaviour were deeply imbedded in the experiences of rural life. There were points at which genteel and plebeian experiences overlapped, and many a gentleman must have been prepared to accept the traditional customs of that community on which he himself depended for some of his satisfactions—not only economic, but psychic and social as well. He too was often a traditionalist, a cultural as well as a political conservative. Moreover, as one student of the period has justly observed, "to an English landowner popularity was of real importance," and the less social insulation was possible, the more was popularity valued. Nicholas Blundell cannot be regarded as a typical squire of the early eighteenth century—he was a Catholic and he lived in a relatively remote part of the country—but his diary is certainly an instructive testimony of the extent to which one gentleman was involved in those traditional activities which were also shared by the common people of the community. An intimate involvement in rural culture imposed certain common experiences on lord and labourer alike.

The paternalism and tolerance which did exist was not, of course, entirely disinterested. Sometimes it was very much in a gentleman's own interest to accommodate himself to the customary expectations of the common people. Despite the reservations which he may have held, it would often have been inexpedient to fly in the face of popular tradition. It was just this kind of self-interest which one observer had in mind when he wrote in 1759 of the custom of providing harvest feasts:

> These rural entertainments and usages . . . are commonly insisted upon by the reapers as customary things, and a part of their due for the toils of harvest, and complied with by their masters perhaps more through regards of interest, than inclination. For should they refuse them the pleasures of this much expected time, this festal night, the youth especially, of both sexes, would decline serving them for the future, and employ their labours for others, who would promise them the rustic joys of the harvest supper, mirth, and music, dance, and song.

There was, in other words, the need to accept a certain amount of give and take. It is often difficult, however, to determine how much of the gentry's behaviour was motivated by an awareness of their own self-interest and how much resulted from their uncritical acceptance of traditional practice. At times certainly there must have been a tension between the conflicting pulls of two inclinations, the one traditional and the other "progressive." Sir Joseph Banks seems to have felt this sort of tension when he wrote from Revesby, Lincolnshire, on 20 October 1783 that "This is the day of our fair when according to immemorial custom I am to feed and make drunk everyone who chooses to come, which will cost me in beef and ale near 20 pounds." His conformity to the customary obligations was probably prompted largely by the desire to maintain his reputation. Certainly some popular traditions must have been ambivalently regarded by the gentry: although many customs served to keep the people contented and sympathetically attached to their social superiors, they also assumed the expenditure of time and money. The crucial distinction, it seems, was between those who accepted the traditional practices, more or less willingly and without much consideration (probably the more common disposition), and those who regarded them as impediments to their freedom of action, as unacceptable and anachronistic popular impositions. The latter view, as we shall see, was to become increasingly powerful as the century advanced. . . .

Festive gatherings could also serve as a medium for the direct expression of hostility against the prevailing structures of authority. In these instances an active defiance was displayed against norms and constraints which were imposed from above; recreations became opportunities for irreverence, occasions for challenging conventional proprieties. This was one of the objections which was advanced against popular festivities by a writer in the mid-seventeenth century. Recreational events sometimes included incidents of aggression specifically intended to embarrass and irritate men of higher rank. The Swiss visitor César de Saussure complained in the 1720s of the populace "throwing dead dogs and cats and mud at passers-by on certain festival days." This sort of aggressiveness was commonly observed at the time of Derby's Shrovetide football match, for it was customary for unpopular or just well-dressed persons among the spectators to be "dusted" with bags of soot or powder. The ritual celebrations of November the 5th were sometimes employed to castigate some prominent individual in the community, usually by substituting the person's effigy for that of Guy Fawkes. On 5 November 1831, for example, the effigies of several bishops were paraded and burnt in a number of towns, a popular protest against their opposition to the Reform Bill.

Popular assemblies were potential threats to the gentry's tranquility, and occasionally a disturbance materialized. "I went to drink Tea at Mr Knapp's at Shenley," reported William Cole on Sunday, 30 August 1767, "where was the Feast and great Rioting, fighting and quarreling: some of the People affronted Mr Knapp [the rector] as he returned from Church." On many holidays the common people were animated by a confidence which stemmed in part from numbers (plebeian crowds, they knew, had to be treated more respectfully than plebeian individuals), and as a result they were able to neglect for the moment the habit of deference; they could more easily insult established authorities and mollify, or even reverse, the perquisites of social rank. . . .

As well as functioning as outlets for hostile feelings, popular recreations also served to foster social cohesiveness and group unity. Competitive team sports, for instance, often reinforced the sense of solidarity of the communities from which the opposing players were drawn. One observer said of the traditional sports of the people, no doubt with some exaggeration, that "the victory obtained by their parish or hundred, served them for the next half-year, till another holiday brought another trial of strength." At times when a community's aggressiveness was externally directed, its feeling of unity was likely to be enhanced. Moreover, when internal conflicts were well modulated, there was often a binding force in the competition itself, if only because the attention of many individuals was concentrated on one widely-embracing social event. It was said of the Derby football match that

> No public amusement is calculated to call forth so high a degree of public excitement. Horse races and white apron fairs must not be named in comparison with it. The aged and the young are drawn from their homes to witness the strife in which the robust and vigorous population of the town and immediate neighbourhood engage with all the energy of eager but amicable competition.

The rituals which were observed on certain holidays—club day feasts, Plough Monday processions, weavers' parades, Bishop Blaze festivities—were affirmations of common interests and common sentiments, and always helped to consolidate group pride. Parish feasts, as we have noticed, encouraged social cohesiveness through their emphasis on fellowship, hospitality, and good cheer. Indeed, most festive occasions which were rooted in the small community served to articulate a vision of the social harmony for which its members wished; festivities celebrated those ideals which transcended self, they reinforced the individual's sense of his social identity. "Games and amusements," a French social historian has concluded, "extended far beyond the furtive moments we allow them: they formed one of the principal means employed by a society to draw its collective bonds closer, to feel united."

Another function of popular recreations was that they provided realistic opportunities for the common people to acquire prestige and self-respect. Through them the people were able to create, as one writer has aptly put it, "small-scale success systems of their own." Even a critical observer of Derby's Shrovetide football match could reveal some of this rationale for the game's popularity: "I have seen this coarse sport carried to the barbarous height of an election contest; nay, I have known a foot-ball hero chaired through the streets like a successful member, although his utmost elevation of character was no more than that of a butcher's apprentice." A clergyman complained in 1830 of the Stamford bull-running that "he who is the most daring, in facing the enraged animal, gains a sort of enviable notoriety among his fellows, which urges him on to fresh feats of adventure." It was said that during games of camping "the spirit of emulation prevails, not only between the adverse sides, but [also] among the individuals on the same side, who shall excel his fellows." John Clare had a similar competitive mood in mind when he wrote of the wrestling at a village wake:

> For ploughmen would not wish for higher fame
> Than be the champion all the rest to throw
> And thus to add such honours to his name
> He kicks and tugs and bleeds to win the glorious game

Football, cricket, boxing, running, wrestling, cudgelling: all these sports provided channels for gaining personal recognition. In fact, they were among the few kinds of opportunities which labouring men had to perform publicly for the esteem of their peers.

Part 2

EARLY INDUSTRIAL-IZATION

1750–1850

The Potteries, early factories, Staffordshire, England

The rate of social change in western Europe greatly increased after 1750. The industrial revolution began in England in the late eighteenth century and spread to France and other nearby countries after 1820. Its central feature was the application of power machinery to manufacturing, but it involved much more than this. The introduction of machines and factories necessarily imposed new systems of work. Rapidly rising production required new forms of consumption. Industrialization led to urbanization; many cities grew phenomenally. People were on the move. In the cities they found themselves surrounded by strangers, other new arrivals, and an unfamiliar environment. Urban life had always been different from rural. Now more people than ever before would experience these differences, ranging from greater sexual activity to greater literacy.

The industrial revolution was in part the product of other developments affecting the common people. Most important, the population began to increase rapidly in the eighteenth century. This forced people to seek new ways of making a living. Parents at all levels of society had to figure out what to do with and for children who in the past would not have survived. These same children, as they reached adulthood, often had to seek out new livelihoods, for there were not enough traditional jobs to go around. Here was a powerful disruptive force, challenging every social group and institution.

Partly because of population pressure, many economic activities became increasingly commercialized. Domestic manufacturing spread—here was one means of supporting excess rural labor. More and more peasants became involved with production for the market. By specializing in cash crops, they could hope to maintain growing families. In the cities, many artisan masters altered their business methods, treating their journeymen as paid employees rather than as fellow craftsmen. Journeymen found it harder to become masters because established masters reserved their places for their own children. This general commercialization of the economy affected far more people than did the early stages of the industrial revolution and very likely was profoundly disturbing to people accustomed to traditional economic relationships. Even the necessity of dealing with strangers, which commercialization required of peasants engaged in market agriculture or domestic manufacturing, may have been upsetting.

Obviously, then, the leading question for this period of European history concerns the impact of change. Was change simply imposed on the common people? Many peasants entered cities and factories only with the greatest reluctance, since population pressure and other economic factors left them no other means of earning a living. A large number of these people endured a massive deterioration in their conditions before making a move. But other peasants may have been more eager for a change. Tensions with their parents (most migrants to the city were in their late teens or early twenties, an age at which disputes in a peasant household were particularly likely) or an active desire for a better life may have drawn them away from the countryside. Without question, some of the forces of change were beyond the control of the common people, but there may have been positive attractions as well. There are signs, too, that rural values themselves were changing, leaving some people better able to cope with a new life style.

Furthermore, although the industrial revolution brought about a huge and rapid transformation, it did not occur overnight. We must not imagine there were modern factory conditions during this period. Early factories were small and sometimes rather informal. Many had no more than twenty workers and therefore were not necessarily impersonal or rigidly organized. Actually, most people were not working in factories at all, but rather in agriculture or in the crafts. Life for peasants and artisans was changing, but traditions yielded slowly. The common people themselves found ways to modify the shock of new conditions. Most people who moved to cities in this early period did so gradually: one generation moved to a village closer to a big city, the next to the city outskirts, and so on. Factory workers found ways to take time off so that they would not have to surrender their own notions of work and leisure completely.

So along with the shock and disturbance of change, we must consider successful resistance and positive adaptation. Which reaction predominated depended on the particular circumstances—specific economic conditions, for example—and personality types. Few people could adapt to the new life without regret; but probably most people were not completely confused by it either. Even in their outright protests the common people began to show signs of accepting the industrial system, for protest gradually moved away from traditional goals toward demands for greater rewards within the new social order.

The century after 1750 saw the most dramatic structural changes associated with modernization, although usually still in incomplete form. Industrial technology and organization were accompanied by significant political change, including more representative parliaments, wider suffrage, and government involvement in areas such as education. In addition there was the rapid population growth—something new to Europe and rather temporary, though producing great dislocation and the effervescence of new numbers of young people. The key questions of the period, in terms of the lives of people, relate to the interaction between values and the new structures. What caused change? Impersonal forces and a few social groups such as factory owners, who had developed new or newly vigorous values, may have imposed them on the bulk of the population. But there were probably some advantages in this first wave of modernization that gave even ordinary people a motivation to change. How extensive and how damaging was the dislocation? The thread of persistence must be assessed here. Many groups, although deeply affected by new structures, may not have changed their outlook or their basic hopes and expectations much at all. Their efforts would show in protest, perhaps, but also in an uneven pattern of change. This pattern was so uneven that many observers would prefer not to use a blanket term like modernization, as opposed to labels for separate processes such as urbanization, to cover the diversity of situations compatible with the new industrial and urban framework. Not only peasants and artisans—still a majority of the population in 1850—but also many big-city residents might differ little in their views on health, for example, from their preindustrial ancestors. Against this, others would argue that immense changes, associated particularly with demography and the family, can be seen, suggesting that in the popular mind, the preindustrial world was already lost.

BIBLIOGRAPHY

On population growth, E. A. Wrigley, *Population and History* (New York, 1969), is an excellent general introduction. See also Thomas Mc-Keown, *The Modern Rise of Population* (New York, 1976). Several explanations of population growth that differ from that of William Langer are presented in Michael Drake, ed., *Population in Industrialization* (New York, 1969). Another convenient survey is Carlo Cipolla, *Economic History of World Population* (Baltimore, 1962). These demographic studies, in discussing rising fertility rates in the eighteenth century, bear some relation also to the history of sex, which is only now acquiring a bibliography of its own.

On sexuality specifically, Peter Laslett, *Family Life and Illicit Love in Earlier Generations* (New York, 1977), and Lawrence Stone, *Family, Sex and Marriage in England, 1500–1800* (New York, 1977). See also Louise Tilly, Joan Scott, and Miriam Cohen, "Nineteenth Century European Fertility Patterns and Women's Work," *Journal of Interdisciplinary History* (1976), pp. 447–76. On children, see Ivy Pinchbeck and Margaret Hewitt, *Children in English Society* (London, 1973).

Despite the currency of generalizations about the middle class, there have been surprisingly few real studies of this group. Charles Morazé, *The Triumph of the Middle Classes* (New York, 1968), interprets modern history in the light of middle-class ascendancy. See also W. J. Reader, *Professional Men* (London, 1966). The key issue of contacts between middle-class values and the lower classes is taken up in Reinhard Bendix, *Work and Authority in Industry: Ideologies of Management in the Course of Industrial Labor* (New York, 1956); Sidney Pollard, *The Genesis of Modern Management* (Cambridge, Mass., 1965); and Peter N. Stearns, *Paths to Authority* (Urbana, 1978). The question of what the middle class was, and therefore how unified its approach to the working class was, needs further exploration; outlines of a debate can be followed in Lenore O'Boyle, "The Middle Class in Western Europe," *American Historical Review* (1966), pp. 826–45, and Alfred Cobban, "The 'Middle Class' in France, 1816–1848," *French Historical Studies* (1967), pp. 42–51.

The topic of popular health and medicine is just beginning to receive attention. See the *Journal of Social History* (June 1977) for a variety of approaches to the topic in Europe and the United States. Two useful books are John S. Haller and Robin M. Haller, *The Physician and Sexuality in Victorian America* (New York, 1977), and Charles Rosenberg, *The Cholera Years* (Chicago, 1962).

Very little work is yet available on the history of crime. Louis Chevalier, *Dangerous Classes and Laboring Classes* (New York, 1972), deals, like Tobias, with qualitative evidence rather than firm statistics. He believes that crime rose in Paris before 1850 and that middle-class fear of crime increased even more. Michel Foucault, *Discipline and Punish: The Birth of the Prison* trans. Alan Sheridan (New York, 1977), is an important interpretation; see also his *I, Pierre Rivière, Having Slaughtered My Mother, My Sister and My Brother: A Case of Parricide in the Nineteenth Century* (New York, 1975). Also interesting is Mary S. Hartman, *Victorian Murderesses* (New York, 1974). Two novels convey the flavor of traditional big-city crime: Victor Hugo, *Notre Dame de Paris,* and Charles Dickens, *Oliver Twist.* On both protest and crime, the essays in Hugh D. Graham and Ted R. Gurr, eds., *Violence in America* (New York, 1970) are suggestive; some deal with Europe directly. For some changes in criminal patterns in the twentieth century that so complicate a modernization model in this area, see F. H. McClintock and N. Howard Avison, *Crime in England and Wales* (New York, 1969).

A rich literature is developing on preindustrial and early industrial protest. A good general statement is George F. Rudé, *The Crowd in History, 1730–1848* (New York, 1964). See also Eric J. Hobsbawm, *Primitive Rebels* (New York, 1965). Specific studies include Malcolm I. Thomis, *The Luddites: Machine-Breaking in Regency England* (Hamden, Conn., 1971); Eric Hobsbawm and George Rudé, *Captain Swing* (New York, 1968); and Robert Bezucha, *The Lyon Uprising of 1834* (Cambridge, Mass., 1974), all of which allow discussion of the persistence of traditional values. Peter N. Stearns, *Revolutionary Syndicalism and French Labor* (New Brunswick, N.J., 1971), dealing with a later period, questions the suddenness of the transition to modern protest. Peter N. Stearns, *1848: The Tide of Revolution in Europe* (New York, 1974), is a standard survey of the early part of the period covered in Tilly's essay. An important general assessment is Edward Shorter and Charles Tilly, *Strikes in France, 1830–1968* (Cambridge, Eng. 1974).

The Population Revolution

WILLIAM LANGER

The massive increase in population that began in western and central Europe around the middle of the eighteenth century was the most obvious stimulus for change in other aspects of life among the European people. It provided new markets and an expanded labor force and caused growing competition for the number of "places" society had to offer. Prestigious government positions did not increase as rapidly as did the population that might aspire to them. The same was true, at a lower social level, of secure artisan jobs. The population surge was profoundly unsettling. By increasing competition for jobs and land, it caused great grievance and was one of the major factors leading to the wave of revolutions that in turn furthered political modernization. Population increase may explain the various innovations, such as new inventions, that more directly furthered the modernization process in Europe by prompting at least a significant minority of people to think in new ways and aspire to new goals. It may also help account for the spread of earlier ideas, such as those spawned by the scientific revolution, to larger groups and areas of Europe.

What caused this population rise? A variety of factors, surely. But were these factors largely independent of human choice, or were prior changes in values responsible?

One line of argument stresses that a new, perhaps more affectionate attitude toward the family, leading people to marry early and have more babies, was the most important cause of the population revolution. It has also been argued that economic changes and dislocations—the enclosure movement, the spread of new industry—broke down traditional barriers to large families.

William Langer takes a different view, although he acknowledges that the change in family patterns had a limited role to play. Langer paints a bleak picture of the common people in the later eighteenth century: trapped in growing misery, which the new food crops, particularly the potato, ironically allowed them to survive, the lower classes responded by increasing their traditional use of infanticide and abandonment—yet the population kept growing. Europeans were caught in a dilemma they could not understand. To be sure, they had made a decision, encouraged in some cases by their governments, to plant new crops, but having done this they lost control of their lot as an unprecedented percentage of children survived into adulthood. Population increase was virtually a worldwide phenomenon in the eighteenth century, although Europe's rate was higher than that in most other places. In this sense, even Langer's generalization may be judged inadequate, for the potato did not spread so widely (though some other new world crops did). More important, population increase outside Europe and North America did not stimulate modernization. Only in Europe did industrialization and new political forms directly follow. This means that some aspects of European culture—either traditional culture or more recent developments—were distinctively appropriate for modernization, when triggered by the demographic revolution.

The use of the dramatic term "explosion" in discussions of the present-day population problem may serve to attract attention and underline the gravity of the situation, but it is obviously a misnomer. The growth of population is never actually explosive, and as for the current spectacular increase, it is really only the latest phase of a development that goes back to the mid-eighteenth century.

Prior to that time the history of European population had been one of slow and fitful growth. It now took a sudden spurt and thenceforth continued to increase at a high rate. From an estimated 140,000,000 in 1750 it rose to 188,000,000 in 1800 to 266,000,000 in 1850, and eventually to 400,000,000 in 1900. The rate of increase was not uniform for all parts of the Continent, but it was everywhere strikingly high. Even in Spain, where there had been a remarkable loss of population in the seventeenth century, the population grew from 6,100,000 in 1725 to 10,400,000 in 1787 and 12,300,000 in 1833.

This tremendous change in terms of European society has received far less attention from historians than it deserves. In the early nineteenth century it troubled the Reverend Thomas Malthus and precipitated a formidable controversy over the problem of overpopulation and the possible remedies therefor. But the discussion remained inconclusive until reopened in more recent times by British scholars, making use of the rather voluminous English records and directing their attention almost exclusively to their own national history. It is not unlikely that this focusing on the British scene has had the effect of distorting the issue, which after all was a general European one.

The point of departure for recent attacks on the problem was the publication, in the same year, of two closely related books: G. T. Griffith's *Population Problems in the Age of Malthus* (Cambridge, Eng., 1926) and M. C. Buer's *Health, Wealth and Population in the Early Days of the Industrial Revolution* (London, 1926). To these should be added the keen corrective

From William Langer, "Europe's Initial Population Explosion," *American Historical Review*, Vol. 69, No. 1 (October 1963), pp. 1–5, 6, 7–9, 9–10, 11–12, 13–14, 16. Reprinted by permission of William Langer.

criticism of T. H. Marshall's essay, "The Population Problem during the Industrial Revolution."

Taken together, these writings provided a coherent, comprehensive analysis. Based on the proposition that the unusual increase of the population in the late eighteenth century was due primarily to a marked decline in the death rate, they attempted to show that this decline must, in turn, have been due to an alleviation of the horrors of war, to a reduction in the number and severity of famines, to an improvement in the food supply, and finally to a falling off of disease as a result of advancing medical knowledge and better sanitation.

These conclusions were not seriously challenged until after the Second World War, when a number of demographic and sociological analyses by British and American scholars called various items of the accepted theory seriously into question. Because of the inadequacy of the statistical data some aspects of the problem can probably never be disposed of definitively. However, the very foundation of the Griffith thesis has now been badly sapped. A number of specialists have come to the conclusion that the spectacular rise in the European population may have been due not so much to a reduction in the death rate as to a significant rise in the birth rate which, according to Griffith, did not vary greatly throughout the period.

From these excellent studies of fertility and mortality there has not, however, emerged any satisfactory explanation to replace the argumentation of Griffith and Buer about underlying causes. It may not be amiss, then, for a historian to join the debate, even though he must disclaim at the outset any professional competence in demography or statistics.

From the strictly historical standpoint none of the previous interpretations of the initial spurt of the European population has been satisfactory. At the time it was commonly thought that the so-called "Industrial Revolution," with its high requirement for child labor, may have induced larger families. This explication could at best apply primarily to Britain, where the demographic revolution was roughly contemporaneous with industrialization. Since the rate of population increase was just as striking in completely unindustrialized countries like Russia, a less parochial explanation was clearly required. At the present time it seems more likely that industrialization saved Europe from some of the more alarming consequences of overpopulation.

Griffith's theses, inspired by Malthusian doctrine, are unacceptable, for the historical evidence provides little support for the notion of a marked decline in the death rate. Take, for instance, the mortality occasioned by war. Granted that no conflict of the eighteenth or early nineteenth centuries was as deadly as the Thirty Years' War is reputed to have been, there is yet no evidence of a difference so marked as to have made a profound change in the pattern of population. It is well known that nations usually recover quickly from the manpower losses of war. If it were not so, the bloody conflicts of the French revolutionary and Napoleonic periods should have had a distinctly retarding effect on the growth of the European population.

Not much more can be said of the argument on food supply. What reason is there to suppose that Europe suffered less from famine? We know that there were severe famines in the first half of the eighteenth century and that the years 1769–1774 were positively calamitous in terms of crop failures. The early 1790's and the years immediately following the peace in 1815 were almost as bad, while at much later periods (1837–1839, 1846–1849) all Europe suffered from acute food shortages. Even in Western and Central Europe famine was a constant threat until the railroads provided rapid, large-scale transportation.

Griffith was convinced that the important advances in agronomy (rotation of crops, winter feeding of cattle, systematic manuring, improved breeding of livestock, and so forth) as well as the practice of enclosure all made for more productive farming and greatly enhanced the food supply. But even in Britain, where agriculture was more advanced than elsewhere, these improvements did not make themselves generally felt until the mid-nineteenth century. There were many progressive landlords, on the Continent as in Britain, and no doubt there was improvement in grain production, but it was too slow, and grain imports were too slight to have had a decisive bearing on the rate of population growth. Even in mid-nineteenth-century Britain the three-field system was still prevalent, ploughs and other implements were old-fashioned and inefficient, grain was still cut by sickle or scythe and threshed with the flail, and ground drainage was primitive. Of course, more land had been brought under cultivation, but the available data reflect only a modest increase in the yield of grain per acre in this period.

Crucial to the argumentation of Griffith and Buer was the proposition that improved health entailed a significant reduction in the death rate. The disappearance of bubonic plague, the falling off of other diseases, the advances in medical knowledge and practice (especially in midwifery), and progress in sanitation were in turn alleged to have produced the greater health of the people.

No one would deny that the disappearance of plague in the late seventeenth and early eighteenth centuries rid the Europeans of their most mortal enemy, and so reacted favorably on the development of the population. For the repeated plague epidemics had been fearfully destructive of life, especially in the towns. In the Black Death of 1348–1349 fully a quarter of the population had been carried away, while even as late as the epidemic of 1709–1710 from one-third to one-half of the inhabitants of cities such as Copenhagen and Danzig fell victims. In Marseilles in 1720 there were 40,000 dead in a total population of 90,000. In Messina in 1743 over 60 per cent of the population was carried off.

But whatever may have been the gains from the disappearance of plague they were largely wiped out by the high mortality of other diseases, notably smallpox, typhus, cholera, measles, scarlet fever, influenza, and tuberculosis. Of these great killers smallpox flourished particularly in the eighteenth century and tuberculosis in the eighteenth and nineteenth, while the deadly Asiatic cholera was a newcomer in 1830–1832.

Smallpox, though it reached up on occasions to strike adults, even of high estate, was primarily a disease of infancy and early childhood, responsible for one-third to one-half of all deaths of children under five. In 1721 the practice of inoculating children with the disease, in order to produce a mild case and create immunity, was introduced into England. It was rather widely used by the upper classes, but quite obviously had little effect on the epidemiology of the disease. There appears to have been a gradual falling off of the disease after 1780, but even the introduction of vaccination by Edward Jenner in 1798 did not entirely exorcise the smallpox threat, though vaccination was offered gratuitously to thousands of children and was made compulsory in England in 1853. Mortality remained high, especially in the epidemics of 1817–1819, 1825–1827, 1837–1840, and 1847–1849. In the last great epidemic (1871–1872), when most people had already been vaccinated, the toll was exceedingly heavy: 23,062 deaths in England and Wales, 56,826 in Prussia in 1871 and 61,109 in 1872. Small wonder that opponents of vaccination stamped it a dangerous and futile procedure. . . .

Considering the terrible and continuing ravages of disease in the days before the fundamental discoveries of Louis Pasteur and Robert Koch, it is hard to see how anyone could suppose that there was an amelioration of health conditions in the eighteenth century sufficient to account for a marked decline in the death rate.

Recent studies have pretty well disposed also of the favorite Griffith-Buer theme, that advances in medical knowledge and practice served to reduce mortality, especially among young children. Doctors and hospitals were quite incompetent to deal with infectious disease. The supposed reduction in child mortality was certainly not reflected in the fact that as late as 1840 half or almost half of the children born in cities like Manchester or even Paris were still dying under the age of five. . . .

In this context it may be said that in Europe conditions of life among both the rural and urban lower classes—that is, of the vast majority of the population—can rarely have been as bad as they were in the early nineteenth century. Overworked, atrociously housed, undernourished, disease-ridden, the masses lived in a misery that defies the modern imagination. This situation in itself should have drastically influenced the population pattern, but two items in particular must have had a really significant bearing. First, drunkenness: this period must surely have been the golden age of inebriation, especially in the northern countries. The per capita consumption of spirits, on the increase since the sixteenth century, reached unprecedented figures. In

Sweden, perhaps the worst-afflicted country, it was estimated at ten gallons of *branvin* and *akvavit* per annum. Everywhere ginshops abounded. London alone counted 447 taverns and 8,659 ginshops in 1836, some of which at least were visited by as many as 5,000–6,000 men, women, and children in a single day.

So grave was the problem of intemperance in 1830 that European rulers welcomed emissaries of the American temperance movement and gave full support to their efforts to organize the fight against the liquor menace. To what extent drunkenness may have affected the life expectancy of its addicts, we can only conjecture. At the very least the excessive use of strong liquor is known to enhance susceptibility to respiratory infections and is often the determining factor in cirrhosis of the liver.

Of even greater and more obvious bearing was what Malthus euphemistically called "bad nursing of children" and what in honesty must be termed disguised infanticide. It was certainly prevalent in the late eighteenth and nineteenth centuries and seems to have been constantly on the increase.

In the cities it was common practice to confide babies to old women nurses or caretakers. The least offense of these "Angelmakers," as they were called in Berlin, was to give the children gin to keep them quiet. For the rest we have the following testimony from Benjamin Disraeli's novel *Sybil* (1845), for which he drew on a large fund of sociological data: "Laudanum and treacle, administered in the shape of some popular elixir, affords these innocents a brief taste of the sweets of existence and, keeping them quiet, prepares them for the silence of their impending grave." "Infanticide," he adds, "is practised as extensively and as legally in England as it is on the banks of the Ganges; a circumstance which apparently has not yet engaged the attention of the Society for the Propagation of the Gospel in Foreign Parts."

It was also customary in these years to send babies into the country to be nursed by peasant women. The well-to-do made their own arrangements, while the lower classes turned their offspring over to charitable nursing bureaus or left them at the foundling hospitals or orphanages that existed in all large cities. Of the operation of these foundling hospitals a good deal is known, and from this knowledge it is possible to infer the fate of thousands of babies that were sent to the provinces for care.

The middle and late eighteenth century was marked by a startling rise in the rate of illegitimacy, the reasons for which have little bearing on the present argument. But so many of the unwanted babies were being abandoned, smothered, or otherwise disposed of that Napoleon in 1811 decreed that the foundling hospitals should be provided with a turntable device, so that babies could be left at these institutions without the parent being recognized or subjected to embarrassing questions. This convenient arrangement was imitated in many countries and was taken full advantage of by the mothers in question. In many cities the authorities complained that unmarried mothers from far and wide were coming to town to deposit their unwanted babies in the accommodating foundling hospitals. The statistics show that of the thousands of children thus abandoned, more than half were the off-spring of married couples.

There is good reason to suppose that those in charge of these institutions did the best they could with what soon became an unmanageable problem. Very few of the children could be cared for in the hospitals themselves. The great majority was sent to peasant nurses in the provinces. In any case, most of these children died within a short time, either of malnutrition or neglect or from the long, rough journey to the country.

The figures for this traffic, available for many cities, are truly shocking. In all of France fully 127,507 children were abandoned in the year 1833. Any-where from 20 to 30 per cent of all children born were left to their fate. The figures for Paris suggest that in the years 1817–1820 the "foundlings" com-prised fully 36 per cent of all births. In some of the Italian hospitals the mor-tality (under one year of age) ran to 80 or 90 per cent. In Paris the *Maison de la Couche* reported that of 4,779 babies admitted in 1818, 2,370 died in the first three months and another 956 within the first year. . . .

. . . In the light of the available data one is almost forced to admit that the proposal, seriously advanced at the time, that unwanted babies be pain-lessly asphyxiated in small gas chambers, was definitely humanitarian. Cer-tainly the entire problem of infanticide in the days before widespread practice of contraception deserves further attention and study. It was undoubtedly a major factor in holding down the population, strangely enough in the very period when the tide of population was so rapidly rising.

Summing up, it would seem that in the days of the initial population ex-plosion one can discern many forces working against a major increase and few if any operating in the opposite direction. It is obviously necessary, then, to discover one or more further factors to which a major influence can fairly be attributed.

If indeed the birth rate was rising, this was presumably due primarily to earlier marriage and to marriage on the part of a growing proportion of the adult population. Even slight variations would, in these matters, entail sig-nificant changes in the birth rate.

Unfortunately the marriage practices of this period have not been much investigated. Under the feudal system the seigneur frequently withheld his consent to the marriage of able-bodied and intelligent young people whom he had selected for domestic service in the manor house. Likewise under the guild system the master had authority to prevent or defer the marriage of apprentices and artisans. Whether for these reasons or for others of which we have no knowledge, there appears to have been a distinct decline in the number of marriages and a rise in the age of marriage in the late seventeenth and early eighteenth centuries. Some writers have even spoken of a "crise de nuptialité" in this period. But by the mid-eighteenth century the old regime was breaking down, soon to be given the *coup de grâce* by the French Revolution. With the personal emancipation of the peasantry and the liquidation of the guild system, the common people were freer to marry, and evidently did so at an early age. There is, in fact, some indication that the duration of marriages was extended by as much as three years, at least in some localities. . . .

Marriage practices, though obviously important, seem hardly to provide a complete explanation of the population growth. To discover a further, possibly decisive factor, it is necessary to return to consideration of the food supply, recalling the proposition advanced by the physiocrats and heavily underlined by Malthus, that the number of inhabitants depends on the means of subsistence—more food brings more mouths. That population tends to rise and absorb any new increment of the food supply is familiar to us from the history of underdeveloped societies. Historically it has been demonstrated by studies of the relationship between harvest conditions on the one hand and marriage and birth rates on the other. In Sweden, for example, where careful statistics were kept as long ago as the seventeenth century, the annual excess of births over deaths in the eighteenth century was only 2 per thousand after a poor crop, but 6.5 after an average harvest, and 8.4 after a bumper crop. Invariably, and as late as the mid-nineteenth century, high wheat prices have been reflected in a low marriage and to some extent in a low birth rate.

The addition of an important new item to the existing crops would necessarily have the same effect as a bumper crop. Such a new item—one of the greatest importance—was the common potato, a vegetable of exceptionally high food value, providing a palatable and satisfying, albeit a monotonous diet. Ten pounds of potatoes a day would give a man 3,400 calories—more than modern nutritionists consider necessary—plus a substantial amount of nonanimal protein and an abundant supply of vitamins. Furthermore, the potato could be grown on even minute patches of poor or marginal land, with the most primitive implements and with a minimum of effort. Its yield was usually abundant. The produce of a single acre (the equivalent in food value of two to four acres sown to grain) would support a family of six or even eight, as well as the traditional cow or pig, for a full year. The yield in terms of nutriment exceeded that of any other plant of the Temperate Zone.

The qualities of the potato were such as to arouse enthusiastic admiration among agronomists and government officials. It was spoken of as "the greatest blessing that the soil produces," "the miracle of agriculture," and "the greatest gift of the New World to the Old." The eminent Polish poet, Adam Mickiewicz, writing as a young man in the hard and hungry years following the Napoleonic Wars, composed a poem entitled *Kartofla*, celebrating this humble vegetable which, while other plants died in drought and frost, lay hidden in the ground and eventually saved mankind from starvation.

The history of the potato in Europe is most fully known as it touches Ireland, where in fact it became crucial in the diet of the people. It was introduced there about the year 1600 and before the end of the seventeenth century had been generally adopted by the peasantry. By the end of the eighteenth century the common man was eating little else:

> Day after day, three times a day, people ate salted, boiled potatoes, probably washing them down with milk, flavouring them, if they were fortunate, with an onion or a bit of lard, with boiled seaweed or a scrap of salted fish.

Because this was so, Ireland provides a simple, laboratory case. There were in Ireland no industrial revolution and no war, but also no fundamental change in the pattern of famine or disease. The unspeakable poverty of the country should, it would seem, have militated against any considerable population increase. Yet the population did increase from 3,200,000 in 1754 to 8,175,000 in 1846, not counting some 1,750,000 who emigrated before the great potato famine in 1845–1847.

It was perfectly obvious to contemporaries, as it is to modern scholars, that this Irish population could exist only because of the potato. Poverty-stricken though it might be, the Irish peasantry was noteworthy for its fine physique. Clearly people were doing very well physiologically on their potato fare. Young people rented an acre or less for a potato patch. On the strength of this they married young and had large families. . . .

Why should not the impact of the potato have been much the same in Britain and on the Continent as in Ireland? If it made possible the support of a family on a small parcel of indifferent soil, frequently on that part of the land that lay fallow, and thereby encouraged early marriage, why should it not in large part explain the unusual rise in the population anywhere?

A definitive answer is impossible partly because the history of potato culture has not been intensively studied, and partly because the situation in other countries was rarely if ever as simple or as parlous as that of Ireland. The most nearly comparable situation was that obtaining in the Scottish Highlands and the Hebrides, where the potato proved to be "the most beneficial and the most popular innovation in Scottish agriculture of the eighteenth century." By 1740 the potato had become a field crop in some sections, grown in poor soil and sand drift and soon becoming the principal food of the population, much as in Ireland. In these areas also the spread of potato culture ran parallel to a marked expansion of the population.

In the Scottish Lowlands, as in England, the potato met with greater resistance. Scottish peasants hesitated to make use of a plant not mentioned in the Bible, and it was feared in many places that the potato might bring on leprosy. In southern England in particular, the peasants suspected that the potato would tend to depress the standard of living to the level of that of the

Irish. Nonetheless the potato, having in the early seventeenth century been a delicacy grown in the gardens of the rich, was strongly urged in the 1670's as a food for the poor. In Lancashire it was grown as a field crop before 1700. During the ensuing century it established itself, even in the south, as an important item in the peasant's and worker's diet. The lower classes continued to prefer wheat bread, but growing distress forced the acceptance of the potato which was, in fact, the only important addition to the common man's limited diet in the course of centuries. Long before the end of the eighteenth century large quantities of potatoes were being grown around London and other large cities. By and large the spread of the potato culture everywhere corresponded with the rapid increase of the population.

Much less is known of the potato's history on the Continent. It was introduced in Spain from South America in the late sixteenth century and quickly taken to Italy, Germany, and the Low Countries. As in England, it was cultivated by the rich in the seventeenth century and gradually adopted by the common people in the eighteenth. It appears to have been grown quite commonly in some sections of Saxony even before the eighteenth century, while in some parts of southern Germany it became common in the period after the War of the Spanish Succession. In several instances soldiers campaigning in foreign lands came to know and appreciate its qualities.

One of the greatest champions of the potato was Frederick the Great, who throughout his reign kept urging its value as food for the poor, prodding his officials to see that it was planted by the peasants, and providing excellent instructions as to its culture and preparation. He met at first with much resistance, but after the crop failures of 1770 and 1772 even the most hidebound peasantry came to accept it. They were impressed by the fact that the potato thrived in wet seasons, when the wheat crop suffered, and that the potato did well in sandy soil. They also realized that it would make an excellent salad and that it went exceptionally well with herring. . . . Any conclusion to be drawn from these data must be tentative. The great upswing in the European population beginning around the middle of the eighteenth century can never be explained with any high degree of assurance or finality. It is extremely difficult to demonstrate whether it was due primarily to a decline in the death rate or to a rise in the birth rate. And beyond any such demonstration would lie the further question of the forces making for such demographic change. It is most unlikely that any single factor would account for it. Thus far the many explanations that have been advanced seem woefully inadequate. It seems altogether probable, therefore, that the introduction and general adoption of the potato played a major role.

A Sexual Revolution?

EDWARD SHORTER

One of the first decisive changes in the traditional outlook of the common man in Europe and North America may have concerned sex. A number of historians are now claiming that peasant society, at least in northern and western Europe, was quite prudish. Marriage occurred rather late, and premarital sex was frowned upon. (Here is another aspect of preindustrial family life that might raise important questions about the satisfactions it provided.) During the eighteenth century, however, a number of changes began to occur. The age at which puberty was attained gradually lowered. Choirboys, for example, found their voices changing at around the age of fifteen instead of the traditional eighteen—to the detriment of sacred music. Undoubtedly, improved food supplies were largely responsible for this change, but new sexual expectations may have played a role as well, for scientists have discovered that psychological factors as well as a better diet are involved in bringing about an earlier onset of puberty. Earlier marriages became more common. In addition, the conception cycle changed. Instead of bunching the conception of children at a few peak periods during the year, particularly during the late spring, as was traditional in rural society, villagers began to space the birth of children out through the year, which at least implies more regular sexual intercourse. And, as the following selection outlines, there were other important changes in sexual behavior that began in the eighteenth century and continued as the modernization process advanced.

Obviously, any judgment about sexual change must be in large part speculative. We know with a fair degree of certainty that the rate of illegitimate births increased; we can only surmise the extent to which this represented a change in values, a new sense of the individual ego.

Edward Shorter confirms the impression that a basic revision of outlook was at least beginning among the common people in the eighteenth century, before the full onslaught of industrialization and urbanization occurred. In seeking the causes of this revision, Shorter looks primarily to prior economic changes and the related extension of urban influences. These in turn altered family relationships by loosening traditional parental control and, perhaps, increasing the importance of sexual compatibility between husband and wife. (It must be remembered that the marriage age was dropping even as illegitimacy was on the rise.) This is a plausible explanation, but it leaves open the question of what caused the economic changes.

Even so, the recognition that lower-class attitudes began to "modernize" this early helps us approach the next question, the impact of the industrial revolution. For here the central issue is whether the lower classes could adapt positively, or whether they were completely confused and alienated, possibly for a long time. The fact that some adaptation had already begun in response to more limited changes may help us to answer the question. If the common people were becoming more individualistic, if indeed they found greater pleasure in sex, perhaps they were at least partially prepared to face still greater changes.

The following selection raises two final points. It clearly took two to tango in the sexual revolution, but did the revolution have the same meaning for women as for men? Certainly, for women burdened with illegitimate, or even legitimate, children, it could have distinctive consequences. We do not yet know if men and women engaged in sex for the same motives (women, for example, may more normally have expected marriage to result, often being disappointed in the outcome) or with the same sense of pleasure or liberation.

And what are the ongoing links between sexuality and modernization in Western society? We have faced further changes in sexual behavior since the onset of modernization; are they a part of a common association between sexual expression and the modern outlook? And how far will modernization take us in this area, and with what social and psychic results?

The central fact in the history of courtship over the last two centuries has been the enormous increase in sexual activity before marriage. Before 1800 it was unlikely that the typical young woman would have coitus with her partner—certainly not before an engagement had been sealed, and probably not as a fiancée, either. But after 1800 the percentage of young women who slept with their boyfriends or fiancés rose steadily, until in our own times it has become a majority. And recently there have been large increases especially among adolescents, in intercourse by unengaged women (if one can imagine such a thing).

Illegitimate births and premarital pregnancies give us the most reliable data for determining the incidence of sex before marriage. Of course, not all women who are sexually active before marriage bear children. Some practise contraception—at least to the extent of saying, as in France's Vendée, "Look out!" before their partners ejaculate. Others force an abortion or miscarry spontaneously, and still others are not yet entirely fecund. But assuming such factors remain more or less equal, there will be at least a general coincidence

Excerpted from *The Making of the Modern Family*, by Edward Shorter, pp. 80–84, 85, 95–96, 149–50, 165–67. © 1975 by Basic Books, Inc., New York.

between the level of coitus among unmarried women and the rate at which they become pregnant. Provided that the other "intervening" variables (such as contraception) remain unchanged, we should be able to infer from a long-term rise in premarital conceptions a similar rise in sexual activity before marriage. . . .

1550–1650   A brief, relatively insignificant rise and fall in out-of-wedlock pregnancies took place, most likely caused by a similar rise and fall in premarital intercourse. Of all periods, this is the most poorly documented; exactly what was going on in the *vie intime* of young Europeans in the late sixteenth century remains largely a mystery. Various charts of illegitimacy show an unmistakable peak in the 1590s, especially in England. Evidence is present that premarital pregnancy underwent the same uphill-downhill course. There is nothing to indicate that more sexual intercourse caused this increase. We have neither qualitative testimonies (other than the usual lamentations that the young were becoming more "immoral") nor sufficient data on such "intervening" variables as fetal mortality or female health (fecundability) to let us point to intercourse by process of elimination. As for the years that followed, the notion of the Counter-reformed, Puritanical seventeenth century as a time of sexual repression is so firmly entrenched that I shall give it a respectful nod here as the probable explanation for the charted decline between 1600 and 1650.

1750–1850   There was an enormous rise in illegitimacy and premarital pregnancy in the years of the French and Industrial revolutions. Late in the eighteenth century, the number of out-of-wedlock pregnancies began to skyrocket in virtually every community we know about, often reaching three or four times the previous levels. In case after case, from interior Massachusetts to the Alpine uplands of Oberbayern, the number of infants conceived before marriage increased markedly. Indeed this is one of the central phenomena of modern demographic history. In a moment I shall suggest that this huge upsurge in part reflected a decline in abortion and an improvement in female health and hence reproductive biology. Primarily, however, it was the result of increasing sexual activity. . . .

I prefer to see the giant rise in out-of-wedlock pregnancy in the late eighteenth century as the principal phenomenon to be explained. It changed the lives of more people than any fluctuation in premarital sex had previously or has since (before the 1960s, at least). And it accords perfectly with a larger notion of social change that I am advancing here: that there was, once upon a time, such a thing as traditional society, which endured relatively unaltered for a number of centuries but which was finally destroyed and replaced by something else we call "modern society." I see our own dear modern times as entirely different from this world we have lost, especially in everything touching intimate life, and I believe this huge one-time change in premarital sexual behavior to be part of the transition from one to the other. . . .

In point of fact, the years 1750–1850 witnessed a crescendo of complaints about immoral sexual activity among the young. This amount of lamentation was unprecedented since the Reformation—before that time my knowledge falters—and it was not again to be attained until the 1920s. Doctor after sober doctor, senior administrator upon administrator, would turn from their normal weighty concerns about infant hygiene or local self-government to comment upon the sad state of sexual morality. What could have been going on in their minds? Had all these observers been seized by some collective delusion, some secular millenarianism dormant since the fifteenth century? Or were they in fact picking up, even in their self-inflated, self-righteous ways, a shift in the fabric of intimate life about them? I believe the second.

Observe some German examples. Bavarian administrators early in the nineteenth century became alarmed about dancing because they thought the walk home customarily meant a stopover for sexual intercourse. Women would appear unescorted at dance locales and wait there until they had been asked to dance or had found a male partner to escort them home; nine months later the fruits of these casual couplings would appear. But the good Bavarians didn't need dancing as an excuse for coitus, as Joseph Hazzi discovered around 1800 in an administrative tour of Oberbayern. In the Seefeld district: "Both sexes are so inclined to debauchery that you scarcely find a girl of twenty who's not already a mother." Around Marquartstein County this interest in sex nestled within a larger rebelliousness. The proverb "We'll have no lords" was popular among people who "get married enthusiastically and very early, produce lots of children, among whom sufficient illegitimate ones that this is considered much more a beneficial than a sinful deed." Officials in Oberfranken testified in 1833 that communities full of deflowered maidens were commonplace. "In the countryside a girl who has preserved her virgin purity to the age of twenty counts as exceptional, and is not at all esteemed for it by her contemporaries." In Unterfranken even the "middle classes" in rural areas, and certainly the laborers in cities, had by 1839 concluded "that the natural satisfaction of the sex drive is neither legally forbidden nor morally very reprehensible." By 1854 premarital sex had apparently become so commonplace that provincial officials were hand-wringing: "Every time single boys and girls go out dancing or to some other public entertainment they end up in bed. In places where male and female servants work side by side, sexual intercourse is a daily phenomenon; and Altötting County reports that it's not seen as sinful at all to have produced children before marriage." These are droplets in a torrent. Literate observers were shaken in southern Germany during the first half of the nineteenth century by what they deemed a sexual revolution, first among the youth of the lower classes and then finally even among those of their own class. . . .

To begin with, what evidence do we have of the infusion of romance into courtship before 1900? For one thing, people either started to say they were in love or to act in ways consistent with no other interpretation. After 1730 there was a big jump in the use of such words as "amour" and "passion" in the explanations that unmarried women gave to municipal officials [in] Grenoble of why they were pregnant, and there was a decline in the use of such terms as "amitié" that suggests a limited commitment.

In a small town in western France, to take another example, a young journeyman cabinetmaker impregnated the daughter of his employer in 1787, a banal event and in every way "traditional"—save for the young man's remaining in contact with the girl after his flight to avoid prosecution (the traditional seducer would have vanished without a trace), and save for the tenderness of the love letters he wrote. "My dearest, I embrace you with all my heart. I am unable to forget you. Everyday I think of you and hope you do the same for me. Tell me how you feel, if you want to make me happy. I remain your close companion. . . ." Note that the young man was not a peasant but an artisan; for as we shall see, it was outside the agricultural middle class that the revolution begins.

Towards the mid-nineteenth century we learn the following of the coastal town of La Ciotat (Bouches-du-Rhône): "The young men are constantly letting partners with handsome dowries go begging. When they marry, it's ordinarily for inclination and not for advantage. They would be incapable of feigning sentiment they did not feel. Such is the case above all for the young lads who go to sea." So seafaring people, at least, were willing to sacrifice their pocketbooks for their affections. And if it wasn't love, how else may we explain that in a Gascon village, around 1911, "three mailmen became needed instead of two because the posts got so cluttered by all the magazines and post-cards the young men and women were in the habit of sending one another"? . . .

The uses of sex   In traditional society, sexuality mainly served instrumental objectives. That is, it helped the participants to achieve ulterior goals of a nonsexual nature rather than serving the exploration of the personality. For traditional unmarried women, especially, intercourse was a means to an end (such as having peace with the employer, or ratifying a marital alliance between two families) rather than an end in itself (sex as personal fulfillment). The testimony we have reviewed suggests that in Europe before 1800, people seldom had sexual intercourse before it was absolutely certain they would marry, and that sex served for them the larger ends of procreation and the continuation of the lineage, rather than being in itself an object of joy and delight. Otherwise the emotionless, passionless, affectionless courtship rituals we have observed would be incomprehensible.

With the first sexual revolution came a breakthrough in intimacy, a dismantling of the sex-role barriers that had hitherto kept men and women locked in watertight compartments with little hope of emotional exchange. The libido unfroze in the blast of the wish to be free. In the years after 1750, lower-class young men and women awakened to the fact that life involved more than just doing your duty in the eyes of the local social authorities and doing your work in the same way that your father had done it, and his father before him. People had personality needs that might conflict with the surrounding community's need for stability. Among these needs was "happiness," and among the cardinal ways of becoming happy was undertaking an emotional relationship with a person of the opposite sex. Such a relationship, of course, meant fooling around, for sex was an obvious extension of emotional intimacy. And so the first sexual revolution would be danced out in the stiff, awkward manner of people who had spent eons in immobility and who were just beginning to create for themselves a sympathetic world of symbols and signs, a culture congenial to romanticism.

The first sexual revolution of the late eighteenth century shifted supervision of courtship from the community as a whole to the peer groups of youth itself. Barriers to promiscuity there had to be—firewalls against the fulmination of all this erotic nitroglycerin that the onrush of sentiment had started agitating—but barriers within the context of a subculture generally sympathetic to self-discovery and intimacy. So there was a lot of sex, and because the youth organizations lacked much of the coercive power of the larger village networks, accidents happened, suitors jumped ship, and illegitimate children were born. Yet the coital partners were doubtless anxious to follow the standards of the larger peer groups of which they were a part.

The second sexual revolution of the 1960s seems to have removed even this feeble peer-group control over adolescent mating and dating. The wish to be free has frayed all the cables that used to tie the couple to surrounding social institutions. Self-realization—accomplished through sexual gratification—has taken command of courtship.

The New World of Children

J. H. PLUMB

Changes in attitudes and behavior toward children seem basic to the modernization process. This is not surprising, though historians are just uncovering the magnitude of the change; a new treatment of children would produce new personalities, and new personalities constitute the essence of modernization in its most encompassing form. The radical improvement in the outlook toward children, described in the following selection on eighteenth-century England, may seem surprising, for we constantly uncover in our own society signs of neglect and cruelty. In part, our continued derelictions reflect the fact that new principles of treatment were goals, not uniform practices. In part, they follow from the uneven social base for the "modernization" of child-rearing. In the eighteenth century the new standards were those of the upper and middle classes. The poor could not afford the new artifacts, such as toys and books. Indeed their changing sexual behavior suggests quite a different pattern for the young, involving greater freedom from parental control, a pattern which newly vigilant "proper" parents were eager to prevent in their own charges. Modernization, particularly in these early phases, was less a social than a class phenomenon.

Finally, our continued anguish over our failures toward children reflects the very attitudes that began to develop by the late eighteenth century. It is not farfetched to say that, just as the new methods of child-rearing were designed to produce new kinds of guilt in children, so they guaranteed parental guilt. The parent was now morally responsible for the child, an intrinsically good creature, so it was next to impossible to be a consistently satisfactory parent in one's own eyes. The task was awesome, and it still is.

What caused the new approach to raising children? J. H. Plumb suggests the inspiration of people like John Locke, themselves guided by the scientific revolution. With new knowledge available, teaching became a matter of greater importance. Children had to be prepared more to be taught than to be controlled. But is this intellectual impulse an entirely satisfactory explanation? Why did so many parents change their habits in what was, for such a private matter as child-rearing, a surprisingly brief time? (Compare the childhood outlined below to that of just a century earlier, detailed in the selection by David Hunt.) It is clearly easier to describe what was happening than to discover basic motivations. What we can be sure of is that the new methods of treating children guaranteed further social change in the future.

The modernization of childhood was of course double-edged. Nothing shows the mixture of gain and loss in the new social framework more clearly. Children had a better world in many respects but also a host of new restrictions, including the simple fact of more watchful parents. Play itself was altered when new toys were designed to improve the child. We are still working out what implications our attitudes toward children have for the quality of life and the ability of man to be free.

There had been, however, towards the end of the seventeenth century, a perceptible new attitude—John Evelyn, long before Locke, had practised many of the Lockeian ideas on education on his own son, preferring a system of rewards, provocations, emulation and self-discipline to physical punishment or verbal chastisement. His whimsical friend, Aubrey, was also strongly against corporal punishment, although he allowed the use of thumbscrews as a last resort! Indeed, Locke's book encapsulates what was clearly a new and growing attitude towards child-rearing and education which was to improve the lot of the child in the eighteenth century.

Locke, although not opposed to corporal punishment as a final sanction, nor indeed for very young children of an age too tender to be reasoned with, in order to instil the necessary fear and awe that a child should have for an adult, strongly disapproved of beating once formal education had begun, just as he was equally opposed to bribing the child to work through material rewards.

> The *Rewards* and *Punishments* then, whereby we should keep children in order, are quite of another kind; and of that force, that when we can get them once to work, the Business, I think, is done, and the Difficulty is over. *Esteem* and *Disgrace* are, of all others, the most powerful Incentives to the Mind, when once it is brought to relish them. If you can once get into Children a Love of Credit, and an Apprehension of Shame and Disgrace, you have put into them the true principle. . . .

As well as arguing for a more liberal attitude towards the child, Locke also pleaded for a broader curriculum. He believed education should fit man for society, as well as equipping him with learning, hence he pressed not only for lessons in drawing, but also in French. Indeed, he opposed rigid grounding in English grammar and urged that Latin be taught by the direct method, as it would have been had it been a living language. . . .

Not only did this new attitude towards children begin to emerge among educationalists in the middle decades of the eighteenth century, but we can deduce also from the success of small private academies, from the development of a new kind of children's literature, and from the vastly increased expenditure on the amusements and pleasures of children, that parents, too, were no longer regarding their children as sprigs of old Adam whose wills had to be broken. Many had come to look upon their children as vehicles of social emulation; hence they began to project their own social attitudes as the moral imperatives of childhood. And so education for society became paramount. Owing to the growth of economic opportunity and social mobility, it was now less necessary to make a child accept its calling as a dictate of God. Locke's attitudes were replacing those of the catechism.

The repercussions on the world of children were very great. Society required accomplishment, and accomplishment required expenditure. The children's new world became a market that could be exploited. Few desires will empty a pocket quicker than social aspiration—and the main route was, then as now, through education, which combined social adornment with the opportunity of a more financially rewarding career for children. . . .

Parents were commercial targets through their children—they could, through the best of motives, be made to spend money on schools which they could scarcely afford, but there were other ways to the parents' pocket-books, educational games and industrial toys, which became increasingly available as the century progressed.

Books by which children could be taught had existed from the first days of printing—alphabets, grammars, and the like, but few, if any, were designed specifically for children. Authors and publishers made very little attempt to entice the young mind. Fairy stories, ballads, riddles and fables were intended as much for adults as for children. Indeed, Aesop was not specifically adapted for children until 1692, when Roger l'Estrange produced his edition.

As with so many cultural developments, the late seventeenth and early eighteenth centuries saw the beginnings of a changed attitude towards children's literature and methods of learning to read. In 1694 "J.G." published "A Play-book for children to allure them to read as soon as possible. Composed of small pages on purpose not to tire children and printed with a fair and pleasant letter. The matter and method plain and easier than any yet extant," which was, for once, a true statement in a blurb. The book has wide margins, large type; its language simple and concrete and mostly within the compass of a child's experience. The author states in his preface that he wished "to decoy Children in to reading." It did well enough to be reprinted in 1703, by which time a few other authors—notably William Ronksley—were attempting to find methods and materials more suitable for very young children. He believed in teaching by verse according to the metre of the Psalms—first week, words of one syllable, the next week words of two syllables, and so on. And he used jokes, riddles and proverbs to sugar his pills. Even so, his and other innovative children's books of Queen Anne's reign were designed, quite obviously, to be chanted, to be learnt by the ear, rather than by the eye. They were more for teachers and parents to teach with than books meant for a child's own enjoyment. Similar books were slow to appear and it is not until the 1740s that the change in style of children's literature becomes very marked. The entrepreneurial noses of Thomas Boreman and John Newbery twitched and scented a market for books that would be simple in production, enticing to the eye, and written specifically for children. Of course, it was not quite as simple as that. Children do not buy books, adults do.

So the new children's literature was designed to attract adults, to project an image of those virtues which parents wished to inculcate in their offspring, as well as to beguile the child. These alphabet and reading books, by their simplicity, also strengthened the confidence of parents in their ability to teach their children to read in the home. The new children's literature was aimed at the young, but only through the refraction of the parental eye. . . .

Education was public as well as private, and there was far more entertainment designed both to amuse and instruct, to which parents were encouraged to take their children by sharply reduced prices for them. Children were expected to be companions of their parents in ways which would have been impossible in the seventeenth century, because the attractions did not then exist. Exhibitions of curiosities; museums; zoos; puppet shows; circuses; lectures on science; panoramas of European cities; automata; horseless carriages; even human and animal monstrosities were available in provincial cities as well as in London. Sir Ashton Levers's Museum of Natural History at Leicester House, a typical eighteenth-century hotch-potch, advertised family tickets. A yearly season ticket for the entire family was quite expensive at five guineas, but it included both the tutor and the governess, and so was aimed at the rich. In April 1773 families of Leeds were regaled by Mr. Manuel of Turin with his display of automata which, as well as having an Indian lady in her chariot moving around the table at ten miles an hour, also contained the "Grand Turk, in the Seraglio dress, who walks about the table smoking his pipe in a surprising manner. All, of course, to the accompaniment of mechanical musical instruments. The prices were cheap enough, 1s. front seats, 6d. back, and servants 3d. Mr. Manuel also sold fireworks as a sideline. After Mr. Manuel M. Utt arrived with his principal marvel, a self-moving phaeton which travelled at six miles an hour, climbed hills, and started and stopped with a touch of a finger. He also brought along an electrifying machine, his camera obscura, his miraculous door which to travel the Midland circuit, Nottingham, Coventry, and so on, but only with his scientific apparatus. Quite obviously he made a tolerable living.

On 10th August the attraction at Leeds was geographical rather than mechanical, when the model of the city and suburbs of Paris arrived at the Town Hall. It was extremely elaborate and eighteen feet square. Viewing started at 9:00 in the morning and closed at 8:00 in the evening, price, as usual, one shilling. In September a spectacular, double-column advertisement with woodcuts announced the arrival of Astley's circus, prices as usual a shilling for front seats, sixpence back, but Astley warned that boys trying to climb in would be taken care of by guards. He now also brought along with him his famous "Chronoscope": an apparatus for measuring the velocity of projectiles.

The emphasis was on marvels, curiosities that were new and remarkable, and usually mechanical or optical; hence many children were given a keen sense of a new and developing and changing world in which mechanical ingenuity, electricity and science in general played an active part—a totally different cultural atmosphere to that in which their grandfathers had lived. Their cultural horizons, too, were widened by the availability of music to listen to in festivals and concerts, the cheapness of musical instruments, and the plentiful supply of music teachers; the same is true of art. Art materials were to be found in every provincial town, and so were drawing masters, who taught in the home as well as in the school. Prints of old masters and modern artists were a commonplace of provincial as well as London life. Visually it was a far more exciting age for children than ever before. And they could travel. By the end of the century middle-class families were on the move, visiting country houses and ancient ruins, viewing the industrial wonders of Boulton and Watt, Wedgwood, Arkwright, and braving the dangers and dirt of coal-mines, sailing in splendid barges along the new canals, going off to the sea—to take the water externally and internally—an outburst of travel that is recorded in hundreds of illustrated books which depict children with their parents enjoying, as they themselves enjoyed, the wonders of their world. The intellectual and cultural horizons of the middle-class child, and indeed of the lower middle-class child, had broadened vastly between 1680 and 1780, and the change was gathering momentum. Parents, more often than not, wanted their children with them, not only in the home but on holidays.

However, through most of the amusements ran the theme of self-improvement and self-education. The same is true of indoor games, as well as outdoor excursions. Playing cards had long been used to inculcate knowledge—largely geographical, musical or classical. One of the earliest packs of about 1700 taught carving lessons—hearts for joints of meat, diamonds for poultry, clubs for fish and spades for meat pies. But more often than not these were instructions, usually from France. The eighteenth century witnessed a rapid growth of English educational playing cards, in almost every variety of knowledge or educational entertainment could be found imprinted on their faces. The majority of booksellers, provincial as well as metropolitan, stocked them. Some cards were designed for the education of adults, or at least adolescents, but there were packs, very simply designed, for young children to play with and learn at the same time. One pack taught the first steps in music. . . .

A hundred years had brought about a remarkable change in the lives of middle- and lower middle-class children, and indeed of the aristocracy as well. From Locke onwards there had been a greater preoccupation with educational ideas; indeed, in the second half of the eighteenth century, stimulated by Rousseau, the advanced radicals—the Burghs, the Days, the Edgeworths, and the rest—had been deeply concerned. Many, particularly the Edgeworths, disapproved of the growing indulgence of parents towards their children, particularly the waste of money on useless toys. Maria Edgeworth denounced dolls and dolls' houses, had no use for rocking-horses, and strongly disapproved of baa-lambs, squeaky pigs and cuckoos, and all simple action toys. She was for a pencil and plain paper, toys which led to physical exercise—hoops, tops, battledores and a pair of scissors and paper for a girl to cut out her fancies; later boys should be given models of instruments used by manufacturers— spinning-wheels, looms, paper-mills, water-mills which, as I have said, were readily available. Maria Edgeworth resonates with modernity, but the interest in her long discussion of toys lies in the huge variety which obviously abounded in the 1790s—a variety not as extensive, of course, as today, but reflecting our world rather than that of seventeenth-century England. Indeed, wherever we turn in the world of children—clothes, pets, toys, education, sport, music and art, their world was richer, more varied, more intellectually and emotionally exciting than it had been in earlier generations.

And yet all was not gain. One must not paint too radiant a picture, too exciting a world. Mrs. Trimmer was there, so was Hannah More. One must remember the Fairchild family trooping off to view the corpse decomposing on the gibbet, the frightful treatment of William Cowper at Westminster, the horrors of Harrow and Eton and Winchester that drew boys into violent rebellion. Nor should we forget the dangers to children in the growing sentimentality about the innocence of the child which needed to be protected at all costs, nor the dangerous intellectual concept that regards each human life as recapitulating that of the human race, which firmly placed the child in Eden, but surrounded by serpents and cluttered with apples.

As a richer life in material objects became available to children, so did their private lives, in some aspects, become more rigidly disciplined. The world of sex was to become, in the eighteenth century, a world of terror for children, and one which was to create appalling guilt and anxiety. We know little about the history of sexual attitudes. In eighteenth-century children's literature, adultery is mentioned, not approvingly, of course, but as a fact of

as their nicknames of "Doctor Johann" and "Doctor Hans" suggest. In February of 1811, the cantonal physician of Sarre-Union denounced to the prefect a "quack and famous ignoramus who is called Dr. Johann."

> I have been told that he is from around Bischwiller, arrondissement of Strasbourg, travels around the region, works terrible havoc, and swindles money from the credulous and superstitious inhabitants of the countryside. The people, who are gladly drawn to miracles and extraordinary things, chase after him in a mob in order to consult him. He gives prescriptions transcribed from an old German medical book, which he has others write down. . . ."

He required the assistance of others to record the prescriptions because, according to the mayor of Bergzabern, where Dr. Johann had his main practice, he could neither read nor write. The quack's background is obscure. The prosecutor at Wissembourg reported that his real name was Johann Propheter (significantly he gave the forename as "Jean"), and that he came from Switzerland originally and was already "getting on in years." Other accounts said that he was from Bergzabern (Wissembourg), or even from the environs of Strasbourg, although the subprefect of Wissembourg added that he had "long since lost his rights as a citizen and his domicile." The cantonal physician at Wissembourg at one point called him a baker; this is the only reference to a previous occupation. Propheter had travelled widely in the department, practicing medicine in the cantons of Sarre-Union and Wissembourg, as well as in the arrondissement of Strasbourg, and had previously been arrested several times at Deux-Ponts (Zweibrücken), just over the border in the department of Mont-Tonnerre. So well established was Dr. Johann's reputation that the local apothecaries filled the prescriptions he wrote for his patients. His practice in the Bas-Rhin continued at least two years; he appeared again in a census of illegal practitioners in 1813.

The career of Dr. Hans was both longer and more varied. Jean (Hans) Volk or Volck probably came from Freiburg in the Grand Duchy of Baden; originally a shoemaker, he sometimes went by the second sobriquet of "Schumacher Hans." The first mention of Dr. Hans comes in a report of January, 1811, by Hoffmann, a physician at Wissembourg, on an epidemic in the communes of Ober- and Niederbetschdorf. Volk was a "foreigner . . . who after being driven from his own country, came to seek refuge in ours, where he wanders with no fixed abode and works hard at making dupes. . . ." Volk's activities ranged so widely that he appeared in the reports of several different cantonal physicians in 1813. In the canton of Brumath, Dr. Hans had been "very much in vogue a year ago in and around Gambsheim," where he "kept hidden during the day and travelled at night to see his patients, who were sometimes very far away." Buchholtz, cantonal physician at Wissembourg, also denounced Volk, noting that he had already cited him in his regular report to the prefect in January, 1811. And at Woerth, the cantonal physician complained that the "vagabond who calls himself Doctor Hanz . . . works great havoc in my canton. . . ." In this report he was linked with a local cartwright as one who was "adept in magical arts and sorcery." Volk became a notorious recidivist, probably the best known illegal practitioner in the Bas-Rhin. He was subsequently convicted of illegal medical practice in 1818 and denounced still another time by the cantonal physician at Soultz-sous-Forêts two years later.

Sedentary Healers

The itinerants, with a few exceptions such as Dr. Hans, rarely succeeded in establishing a regular following in the regions where they worked; many, indeed, were careful not to visit the same place twice with the same bag of tricks. Some might establish themselves in or near a large town for as long as several months, like Albertine Dränkler, who settled at Bischheim-am-Saum near Strasbourg in 1801, boasting that she could cure more than twenty disorders using surgery or medication. But the resident healers belonged to the community in which they found a clientele, and if they were to practice any length of time they needed a permanent pool of patients. Even with a loyal following it was difficult to maintain a full-time practice outside of a city such as Strasbourg, although some local healers in France enjoyed at least a passing vogue which enabled them to draw patients from towns and villages as much as a hundred kilometers away. In most cases medicine could only be a sideline.

The majority of sedentary healers practiced routine empirical medicine or simply sold a few secret remedies. But a justice of the peace at Strasbourg dealt with one case in 1799 involving a pair of occult healers: Jean-Frédéric Küchel (or Kiechel), a former notary, and Barbe Richert, wife of a hemp grower. Barbe Richert was a "somnambulist"; on emerging from a hypnotic trance she recommended remedies to her patients, who purchased them from local pharmacies. Küchel was a magnetizer (mesmerist); he induced the trances and noted the responses of his partner, who did not know how to write. Küchel's mesmerist practice was not limited to hypnotism; he reappeared in 1808 as the discoverer of a "new infallible means to cure most of the external disorders of the body promptly and radically, whatever may have produced them, without the help of medication, by a light laying-on of the hand, or by a simple touch."

The Bas-Rhin seems to have had no well-known religious healers in the early 19th century, comparable to the "saint of Savières," near Troyes, who enjoyed a few years of notoriety in the 18th century. The clergy continued to exercise their traditional healing function, and some were indistinguishable from the quack doctors, at least in the eyes of the medical profession. In 1818 the cantonal physician at Niederbronn denounced "two scourges of human-ity": a Protestant minister at Barenthal (Sarre-Union) and the curé of Lich-tenberg (Petite-Pierre), both of whom administered remedies after inspecting the patient's urine and saw to it that they were "paid well." One inspired healer was seen as a deviant by the local communities as well as by the author-ities. The son of a blacksmith in the Haut-Rhin, he settled at Sélestat in the Bas-Rhin in 1841, calling himself "brother Martin." According to the prefect, he had already lived in various parts of the arrondissement as a hermit and most recently at "a pilgrimage near Dambach, where the inhabitants expelled him for laxity of conduct. . . . " He even went to Strasbourg, according to the report of the cantonal physician, "where he must be treating several per-sons." Marginals of this sort posed a ticklish problem for the authorities and for the new discipline of forensic psychiatry: were they madmen or impostors? Clearly they were beyond the pale of both official medicine and folk culture.

As for folk medicine itself, it rarely passed into the records of medical police; when no injury was done and no money changed hands, a case was unlikely to wind up in the courts. One zealous cantonal physician, Lion at Soultz-sous-Forêts, did complain about the "unfortunate accidents that have befallen Jewish children, as a result of the ineptitude of the person who per-forms the operation of circumcision on them." There was no mention, though, of the *schormer*, or mystical healer, who was consulted by Jewish and Gentile patients alike in Alsace. Folklore practices usually became visible to the authorities only when they constituted a threat to public order. One such incident occurred in 1820, when a girl at Lembach developed symptoms which the local population attributed to demonic possession. The cantonal physician offered the opinion that she was suffering from delirium and con-vulsions; he attributed her condition to worms. But the girl's father, deciding that the "assistance of medicine" was useless, ascribed the disease to a "super-natural cause." It therefore became "a question of exorcising his child, who said that the devil was waiting for her at the door, and who blasphemed when other persons prayed." Although charlatans played no role in this religious cure, the authorities expressed alarm at the presence around the patient's bed, day and night, of "some thirty weak and credulous persons," in a market town of about 1,800 inhabitants. The prefect intervened and transferred the girl to the local asylum, where the resident physician found his own positivist explanation for her behavior: "symptoms which indicate strong pains in the head and perhaps a case of hydrocephaly." Superstition, then, could become a police problem. Accusations of witchcraft and charges of swindling by local magicians could also provoke disturbances, and records of some of them turn up in the judicial archives. But of the world of witches and *devins-guérisseurs*, pilgrimages and healing saints, the medical bureaucracy of the early 19th century took little direct notice. . . .

The physicians' sense of impotence in their relations with the quacks contrasts with their apparent sense of confidence in dealing with the literal *fléau destructeur*, epidemic disease. In the case of the Protestant pastor, for example, two victims of the empiric were said to have been rescued by timely attention from medical doctors. To be sure the physicians' rhetoric owed something to political interest; they could not very well report to the administration that they were helpless to fight disease but all-powerful against charlatanism. Still, although many physicians may have adhered in principle to a doctrine of expectant medicine and in practice made little use of drastic treatment, they had a strong sense that their intervention was essential; the motif "if only a physician had been called in time" was a commonplace long before the age of scientific medicine. Physicians saved; quacks killed.

The quack, though, was more than a murderer; he was also—and in the eyes of the physicians this was an almost equal offense—an *escroc*, a swindler. Not only was his practice unauthorized, but in the Ancien Régime his *charlataneries* had run counter to the spirit of guild regulations on fair dealing; now he was guilty of a breach of what we would call professional ethics, which were intended to safeguard the rights of the practitioners as much as those of the patients. The great villain in the rhetoric of medical enlightenment was not the superstitious peasant but the schemer who knowingly exploited his "vulgar errors." The cantonal physician at Brumath reserved his severest censure for a woman healer who in his view did the most harm because she was "an old hypocrite." His counterpart at Geispolsheim (arrondissement of Strasbourg) developed this theme in a section of his 1813 report in which he added to his list of illegal practitioners "a few general considerations" on what "universally constitutes empiricism in the countryside":

> Bigotry and ignorance are indisputably an enormous source from which arise the swarm of prejudices that infect the countryside and resist even the most persuasive statements by enlightened men. Nevertheless, it is not the stubbornness of the people that must be blamed the most; let us rather point the finger at the audacity of the impostors who know how to take adroit advantage of its credulity and dupe its good faith. In what class of men, then, do we find most of these artists of deception, of these swindlers, I venture to say?
>
> Leaving aside abuses in matters of empiricism which prevail exclusively in the domestic economy and which consist in the fact that many heads of families are possessors of a few universal remedies, good against all ills, and whose secret is transmitted only from father to son (we often see similar remedies advised, obtained and administered by a man or woman neighbor, result in fatal consequences); there are besides a certain number of dreamers, magnetizers, makers of sympathetic magic and others, for whom I cannot give the names or places of residence, places where they are best able to conceal their activities and escape the pursuit of the police. Strasbourg, they generally say, is the center.

Although the comment treats domestic medicine as hazardous, the author singles out for blame the entrepreneurial activities of the city quacks, "artists of deception" and "swindlers." Medical charlatanism may be added to the long list of vices attributed to urban corruption. The wily empiric knew how to extract the peasant's small cash savings—better, indeed, than the physician did. His irruption in the countryside constituted a breach of the economic peace.

Without reducing all of the physicians' attacks on the quacks to a question of material interest, it can be argued that the charlatans affronted the official practitioners' sense of economic justice. Their profession had traditionally made a heavy investment in education and charges for membership in the medical corporations in the Ancien Régime; even under the new medical order costs were high, and they believed that the profession deserved an enforced monopoly of patients' fees. The history of illegal medical practice in the early 19th century suggests that medicine was given over (as some had wished to recognize explicitly during the Revolution) to "free enterprise" (libre commerce), just as much as other economic activities. The physicians, while hesitant to advocate reviving the old corporations in their earlier form, remained resolutely anticapitalist in their professional domain.

If the quacks appeared as economic deviants, so in their own way did the occasional healers who neglected or abandoned a regular trade. The physicians' comments are impregnated with a class morality which the French sometimes call la morale du bonhomme Richard, after Franklin's Poor Richard: indolence and vice explained a behavior which might well have resulted from economic necessity. Lion, cantonal physician at Soultz-sous-Forêts, remarked of "Weber Jackel": "laziness, mother of all the vices, has banished him from society; it is only through swindling that he supports himself." Material pressures may have forced Jacques Vern to abandon his "profession and trade"; he was possibly a victim of the economic crisis of 1810–11 in Alsace, which affected the textile industry. He may even have sought an "honest" supplementary occupation to help him sustain an adequate income when times were hard, since the general list of empirics for the arrondissement identified him as a shoemaker as well as a weaver. But in the physician's eyes he was unwilling to work. An even worse offender was the healer who had no recognized trade other than quackery, such as Justin Breit, known as "Justul." "Instead of working and earning his living honestly, he hurries from one village to another in order to carry out as many swindles as possible, using his poisoned remedies." The descriptions of the offending popular healers recall a conventional image of the social deviant: crafty and indolent, the empiric was the very type of the bad citizens.

Indeed physicians could often accuse popular rivals of multiple forms of deviance. In one case, for example, the informant charged that a healer mutilated conscripts to make them unfit for military service—a crime which particularly attracted the attention of the administration to popular healers. In another case, a barber practicing medicine at Huttenheim was said to be "under the influence of wine from the morning on." Two stereotypes of the fringe healer, however, are absent from the police reports of the Bas-Rhin, although they were common in the medical literature of the time. Quacks sometimes appeared to contemporary observers as lunatics, especially when they claimed to be religiously inspired; but only the case of "brother Martin" approaches the conventional image of the madman. The misogyny which sometimes led a physician to say that medicine was practiced in his district by the most ignorant peasants "and even by women" is muted here; the commentaries include no general denunciation of *femmelettes* who meddled in the healing art. . . .

Looking to the future of medical police, the physicians expressed only a guarded optimism. At best they expected a decline in classic charlatanism; the less visible forms of popular healing would be more difficult to attack. The strongest statement of this view came from Buchholtz, the one cantonal physician who (no doubt too sanguinely) reported no resident empirics in his jurisdiction in 1813:

> The extirpation of charlatanism is probably a difficult thing to attain in every country under an orderly government, as we learn from the example of other countries, and especially those of Germany, where for a long time the governments have dealt with it without having obtained a perfect result from their efforts up to now. Public quackery can be destroyed; the public displays of quacks can be forbidden; the very tendency of the age makes repressive laws on this matter almost superfluous, since these sorts of crude speculations can no longer find dupes; but empiricism that is domestic and, so to speak, legal, if I may express myself thus, is more difficult to strike a blow against, although it is the most dangerous of all where public health is concerned. . . .

In the early 19th century, the repression of medical folklore did not become a consistent objective of medical police; even the census of small-time healers never developed into a coherent program. The movement for reform produced only the jeremiads of official medicine, without the systematic surveillance that might have permitted effective repression. The means and motivation were lacking. Occasional practitioners were too difficult to distinguish from the rest of the population and constituted a slighter threat to public order than did the quacks. Although the prefects ritually denounced popular superstition in their departmental *Statistics*, folk healing did not constitute a regular target of the police and administration. Or rather, it was not simply a question of medical police in the usual sense where the "credulous and ignorant" people and their superstitions were concerned; there was no need to identify individual delinquents where deviance was, so to speak, the norm, where an entire culture was deviant. To suppress popular medicine nothing less was needed than a reform of the peasant mind; and the institution of socialization best suited to this task, however much the physicians may have wanted to have a hand in it, was the school.

Seen in the context of a local jurisdiction, the repression of popular medicine appears in the early part of the 19th century as an unrealized project. To be sure, medical power was not entirely a myth. A well-designed bureaucratic mechanism existed to combat illegal medical practice; individual healers did stand trial, and some of them went to jail. Yet the recidivism rate must in itself have suggested the inadequacy of what might have been called, to borrow an expression from the physicians, "heroic measures." If the Bas-Rhin, with its well-developed system of medical police, could not regulate medical practice effectively, then it is unlikely that any local administration could have done so in the first decades after 1803. It would be a mistake to equate a repressive program with the reality of social control.

On the local level, the representatives of official medicine found themselves obliged to compete for a space in medical practice occupied by a host of parttime medical entrepreneurs, as well as by the more conspicuous survivors of the traditional medical network of the Ancien Régime. In the medical literature of the 19th century, the contest between the physicians and their rivals sometimes appears as the heroic phase of professionalization, pitting medical enlightenment against popular superstition. But the protagonists in the local struggle were rarely the physician-scientist, on the one hand, and the witch-healer, rooted in folk culture, on the other. More often, highly insecure "professionals" confronted still more vulnerable marginals—vagrants, unsuccessful artisans, widows, people without a safe niche in a changing economy and society.

Some of the subsequent success of official medicine can be ascribed to the therapeutic advances of the late 19th and 20th centuries. Education and urbanization could be cited among the many forces which have broken down peasant resistance to official medicine; the regular medical network has become more accessible for most Frenchmen, and social security has provided a powerful financial incentive to consult licensed practitioners. Repression of illegal practice played a small role in this transformation. It is of course true that social control can be realized through other means than direct police action, and the factors just cited contributed indirectly to what has been called medical power. But this study suggests that in the early 19th century there was a critical disparity between the aspirations of a group which proposed to exercise hegemony over one professional domain and the reality of frustration and social inertia. To read the later developments which privileged professional medicine into the earlier period would be anachronistic. Like medicine itself, medical power had its limits.

The Foundations of Middle-Class Life

W. J. READER

The rise of middle-class values was a key development in nineteenth-century society. Indeed, modernization, insofar as is involves changes in mentality, is to a substantial degree coincident with middle classness. Almost everyone is familiar with aspects of middle-class gains, for they have touched our lives deeply, whether we are middle class, aspire to be, or wish we were not. We know about the virtues of the self-made man, the ethic of competitive achievement.

But where did the middle class come from? W. J. Reader, an expert on the history of the professions in nineteenth-century England, suggests that it has long been with us, simply a subordinate part of society until the modern era. Perhaps, there were hosts of venturesome misfits in the value systems of preindustrial Europe, waiting for a chance to burst out, a chance provided by the technological and political developments of the half century around 1800. But other observers find preindustrial merchants (though more on the continent than in England) a rather conservative lot and suggest that a jolt was needed even to create the values that men like Samuel Smiles so confidently preached to industrial audiences.

And the modern middle class was not composed of venturesome businessmen alone. Reader rightly points to the rise of professional groups, not all new but newly defined, who created a distinctive middle-class mix that allowed for social gain but at the same time continued contact with older standards of "gentility." And from the nineteenth century onward, society, including business, would become increasingly professionalized. Is the middle class, for all its trumpeting of competition, seen here as a class open to talent, or a group bent on insuring, through control of education and licensing procedures, its own monopoly of positions of power and prestige? Is middle-class society really new and open, or more a redefinition of the same old hierarchical show? Serious consideration of the process and motives of professionalization provides one important clue.

And on this in turn rests a good bit of the judgment of modernization. If the middle class really did recast the definitions of social success and the bases of attaining it, then modernization is likely to have real meaning. If, however, they used new rhetoric to grab old power (talking of merit while really hoping to promote their own children through advantages of birth), modern society may be less distinctive under the surface than the middle class believed.

Clearer still is the relationship between judgments of the middle class and an assessment of the quality of modernization. The middle class has had bad press from many historians and contemporary observers alike: Its values were too narrow, its criteria of success too exclusive and rigorous. Yet, in a society now worried lest the achievement ethic disappear, the nineteenth-century heyday of the middle class may look very appealing. In any event, the heritage lingers. Certainly a good bit of the history, and indeed the present situation, of groups in society, ranging from middle-class children to factory workers, must be viewed in terms of their interaction with the middle-class mentality. As Reader suggests, the workplace and the schoolroom were the locales where the mentality itself was expressed and honed.

"And in this spirit he addressed them on more than one occasion . . . pointing out that their happiness and well-being as individuals in after life, must necessarily depend mainly upon themselves—upon their own diligent self-culture, self-discipline, and self-control—and, above all, on that honest and upright performance of individual duty, which is the glory of manly character." Thus Samuel Smiles, in 1859, expressed the central creed of the middle classes: that individual effort, backed by austerity of life, would propel any man, no matter what his origins, to success in this world and (Smiles might have added) if reinforced by the right brand of piety, to salvation in the next.

This, of course, was thoroughly subversive doctrine, since it struck at the roots of the traditional social system in which every man "knew his place" and kept to it. But the sober, godfearing family men who lived by it were saved from being conscious revolutionaries by an intense respect for the old system and an ambition to thrust themselves and their families into it, provided that it could be suitably modified to accommodate them. They were quite ruthless about that—the old social order must be modified—but, once modified, they wanted to inhabit it, not to overthrow it, and the story of the middle classes in Victorian England is very much the story of a take-over bid for the established order of society.

Their central principle was competition. They found a society in which most of the best things in life—wealth, property, social position—were conventionally regarded as belonging to those who were "born to them." They wanted to substitute for it a society in which those who had the ability might seize the prizes—and then enjoy them under a system of law which would still protect the rights of property. This new, competitive society was not at all to the liking of supporters of the old order. A Tory writer, about 1850, spoke of "the system . . . of leaving men to practise for their own advancement all arts save actual violence," and in this opinion he would no doubt have been echoed by men otherwise of a diametrically opposed turn of mind such as the early Socialists. But it was an unfashionable view, and it was not the view which, in the long run, was to prevail. The competitive society was on its way in, and Samuel Smiles's *Self-Help* ran to sales of 20,000 copies in its first year.

There was nothing new about the middle-class outlook. It would have been perfectly familiar to a seventeenth-century tradesman. But the new industrial order of things put the middle classes in a position of unprecedented power and influence. They were able under Victoria to set the tone of the national life in a way that would have been inconceivable under George III.

The industrial world was run by the middle classes; as it grew, so did their opportunities. In the past the representative middle-class man—the shopkeeper, the merchant, the closely related banker—had been concerned with the sale of goods and the use of money, but not directly with manufacturing, which was the affair of craftsmen. There had been very little scope for middle-class technical or professional employment. There were the skilled artisans on the one hand, the lawyers on the other; that was about all. But as factories went up, factory owners began to appear alongside merchants and bankers at the top of the middle-class tree. The whole scale and scope of commercial activity expanded; clerks, commercial travellers and technicians multiplied.

New professions came into being. The mechanical engineer, often a Northerner or a Scot, emerged from amongst blacksmiths and millwrights; the civil engineer from the designers of fortifications and other military works. Between them (often combined in one man) the two sorts of engineer equipped the factories and built the railways. By the fifties the accountant was distinct from the clerk; as firms grew and their finances became more complex his profession flourished. . . .

With good solid schooling behind him the Victorian middle-class lad could confidently start looking for his livelihood. The prosperous tradesman's son might stay at school until he was sixteen or thereabouts and then set to learning the family business, which had been the middle-class way for generations. Without family interest or without capital his prospects in business would be poor, unless he was exceptionally enterprising, able or lucky, for salaried employment above the miserable level of the clerk or shop assistant was rare. Most firms were run by their owners who took care to keep the best jobs for themselves and their relations (including relations by marriage). Although the Victorian middle classes were against patronage when it lay in hands other than their own, especially aristocratic hands, it did not at all follow that they would apply the same principle to patronage which they themselves controlled. It was almost hopeless for an outsider to try to break into the higher management of, say, brewing, the London coal trade, banking, or virtually any other established and prosperous activity. When, from time to time, a new man did fight himself into a position of strength, the ring would open just wide enough to admit him (and his family) and then close again.

There was, however, an alternative, which the Victorian middle classes did a great deal to develop, and this was to seek a professional qualification which would make its holder as independent as he could reasonably hope to be of the need for influence or family connections, though both were extremely useful if you had them. It is not quite true to say that the Victorians invented the professions, but it is true that they extended them, provided them with a good deal of *mystique*, tradition and snobbery and left them altogether stronger and more venerated than they found them. The professions, along with the public schools, became part of the essential fabric of middle-class life, and to become a professional man represented the height of ambition for boys born a little too far down the middle-class scale for comfort.

The solidest reason for seeking a professional qualification, especially if it carried a legally entrenched right to practise, was that it gave the surest possible hope of a secure livelihood. Like the skilled artisan who had served his apprenticeship, the doctor, lawyer, clergyman or engineer "had a living in his hands" which nothing but villainous ill-luck, gross incompetence or crime was likely to take away. Moreover, once the framework of qualifying exams had been set up, a professional qualification depended on ability alone (even if only the ability to pass exams), and not on "influence," patronage or wealth. It was an essential weapon in the middle-class struggle to throw profitable careers open to talent. And the knowledge that one had the ability to "qualify" was a useful boost to a young man's self-confidence at the beginning, just as, later, the consciousness of being a skilled practitioner of some difficult art added to the established man's self-respect.

Almost equally important, professional status was a marriage between gentility and trade which the middle-class mind found highly congenial. The middle classes were built on trade and were loth to sacrifice its profits, but trade had a dubious social standing. The younger sons of the gentry had not, in the past, found it beneath their dignity to join some flourishing merchant firm, and the gentry—the nobility even—had never scorned rich merchants' daughters for their brides. But riches lent enchantment to the view; the great merchant had enough money to live like a gentleman and conceal his origins. Not so with your shopkeeper or petty trader who, besides, cultivated an undignified and ingratiating manner towards his customers. Not so with your rough northern manufacturer, newly sprung from the lower middle class or worse. "Trade" in general, unless profitable enough to provide an income comparable with that from a landed estate, was no occupation for a gentleman, and, in view of some trade practices, understandably so.

The professional man, though still inspired by the profit motive, undertook to observe rules of conduct which a tradesman might ignore, though exactly what the rules were it was not always easy to define. They certainly did not stand in the way of making money. A writer of 1850 quoted the income of a rising barrister at £5,000: of "a physician who is becoming popular" at £1,000 more. The professional man, at some sacrifice of his freedom of action, might rank as a gentleman without being a penny the worse off than if he had been "in trade"—indeed, he might do a great deal better—and that was exactly what the ambitious middle-class man wanted, if not for himself, then for his sons. Hence the energy put into the cultivation of old professions and the launching of new ones, and into setting up an educational system which would serve professional needs.

But what was a profession? Divinity, physic and law would have been an earlier generation's answer, but the matter was not so simple as that. Take "law," for example. Nobody doubted the dignity of bench and bar, but attorneys were a different matter. "They are of various grades," wrote a barrister of 1850, "from the low, rapacious pettifogger, who grasps at three-and-sixpenny fees, and is something between the common cur and bulldog of the law, up to the finished gentleman, who has in his hands the most important affairs, and is professionally acquainted with the most delicate secret histories of the first families of the land." Amongst newer occupations the engineers early made out a claim to professional standing, but again there was a cleavage, for the civil engineers considered themselves superior to the mechanical. Then there was teaching; what was one to say of that? No one doubted the social position of masters at the public schools. They were mostly, in any case, Anglican clergy. But teaching shaded away down, by imperceptible degrees, to wretched drunken ushers in back-street private schools; could they claim professional status? Most teachers, anyway, were women, which raised a very awkward problem: was the professional woman a possible animal?

Matters of status were seriously regarded. Escott, in his survey of England, devoted several pages to discussing it and concluded, amongst other things, that professions like the bar, where fees did not pass directly from client to practitioner, ranked higher than professions like medicine, where they did. It was also, in his view, a slight mark of inferiority if a professional man had the right to recover his fees by legal process. The whole thing ought rather to proceed on the fiction that the transaction—in law, medicine or whatever it might be—was simply an exercise of friendship by one gentleman on behalf of another, to be rewarded or not as the beneficiary might decide. This may have been a rarified view, but the marks of professional status, whatever they might be, were sought after by the practitioners of one occupation after another, until by the end of the century the ancient three had been multiplied many times over.

The professionalizers' greatest triumph, and one of their earliest, was in medicine. At the beginning of the century there were only three bodies in England—the Royal College of Physicians, the Royal College of Surgeons, and the Society of Apothecaries—who could claim anything like a systematic course of medical education, attested by examination. Membership of these exalted and rather stuffy bodies, especially of the Physicians, conferred some social standing, but the ordinary general practitioner did not belong to any of them. Such knowledge as he had he would have picked up as an apprentice and in practice, or by even sketchier methods. He was subject to no controlling body and was unrecognized in law. The surgeon's trade, before anaesthetics, was a rough one, and "sawbones" was not likely to be a gentleman.

Against the apathy or opposition of the Royal Colleges, a movement began for better medical training and for proper control of qualifications. Enterprising young doctors of the better sort went abroad and to Scotland for training; in the provinces of England medical schools were set up in defiance of the Colleges. By 1858 twenty-one authorities had rights of granting licenses to practise—some general, some specialized; some geographically restricted, some universal throughout the United Kingdom.

In 1858, after twenty years of effort, a Medical Act was passed. It did away with training by apprenticeship and called for "an elaborate series of lectures" instead. It set up the Medical Register and placed severe restrictions on unregistered practitioners. To enforce this newly established discipline it set up the General Medical Council, a body found from within the profession itself, which wielded as its principal weapon the right to "strike off."

The Census Report of 1871 recorded that in the ten years from 1861 "medical men remained nearly stationary [in numbers]: the qualification having been much raised," and that was undoubtedly a direct result of the Act. With the raising of qualifications the general standing of doctors in the community rose as well, and it came to be no longer a matter of wonder that a man of good family like Doctor Thorne in Trollope's novel should become a country practitioner. But the process was a slow one, for quacks did not disappear all at once, and even as late as Escott's time, twenty years or more after the passing of the Act, the general practitioner—"the lineal successor of the apothecary"—does not seem quite to have made good his position.

The 1858 Medical Act gave precise expression to the professional idea. It established three great principles—qualification by examination, a legally entrenched right to practise, and the right of a profession to internal self-government. It raised the whole standing of the medical profession by insisting on proper qualifications and at the same time it conferred on those who obtained them protection against unqualified competition. After it was passed, "professional status" had a legal form and others who desired it had a model to copy. They were many, for its advantages were great.

Proprietary schools were being founded in great numbers in the forties and fifties. The competitive examination for entry into the Indian Civil Service was established by law in 1853. In 1854 Sir Charles Trevelyan and Sir Stafford Northcote recommended a similar competition for entry into the Civil Service at home. The first Medical Act was passed in 1858. In the sixties the country's schools were very thoroughly investigated by Royal Commissions and important reforms followed. In 1870 the Northcote-Trevelyan recommendation for competitive entry into the Civil Service was put into effect, and in the same year the purchase of commissions in the Army was abolished, to be replaced by a system based on examinations.

In all these things the vigorous middle-class mind can be seen at work, moulding the life of Victorian England. Competition in a clear field is the great principle; patronage, privilege and "influence" are to be detested and got rid of. Ancient institutions must be examined, reshaped, brought up to date; new ones must be invented if nothing old will do. At the roots of it all lay the determination to give education a strong shove in the direction of the "useful arts" and to organize middle-class occupations on a basis of strength, efficiency and social recognition. By 1870 or thereabouts the foundations had been laid. The second generation of the Victorian middle class was about to enter on a world designed very much according to middle-class ideas.

The Changing Nature of Protest

CHARLES TILLY, LOUISE TILLY, and RICHARD TILLY

By the end of the Middle Ages the common people of western Europe had developed a standard form of protest—they rioted against deteriorating economic conditions and against more general encroachments on their rights. With the onset of modernization many groups stepped up their rate of protest but did not initially change its nature. Protest still largely took the form of riots in the name of past rights and standards, a reaction against changes imposed by the outside world. The protesters sought the restoration of a previous price level or of previous taxation rates or of previous rights to the land or to guild protection. Some of the most dramatic passages in nineteenth-century history, such as the revolutions of 1830 and 1848 in France, were based on the common people's reaction against change. Typically, the groups most involved were not new factory workers, but peasants or artisans, who still had a sense of traditional community and past values on which protest as a reaction could be based.

But protest did change, often suddenly for some groups, as people learned that the trends of modernization could not be confronted head on. Instead it was discovered that these trends might be used for compensatory gains such as a higher standard of living or new political rights. The following selection stresses the contrasts between the old and the new protest in form and duration; in basic orientation, seeking to master change rather than reacting to it; and above all in the scale of organization. New or modern protest becomes distinctively political in its attempt to use the state, though earlier protesters had manifested their own sense of politics.

The new kind of protest could be vigorous, bitter, and certainly violent, but for the most part it worked within the framework of a modernizing society rather than rebelling against it. Expanding rights—to vote, to demonstrate, to strike—encouraged more frequent protest than ever before. But in the advanced industrial nations, including France, it usually fell short of outright revolution, though with the rise of anarchism, socialism, and communism there were more avowed revolutionaries than ever before. There are many reasons for the decline of revolution; one of them may be that, although they had learned to ask for more within the modern scheme of values, protesters were no longer seeking a distinctive set of values of their own.

Yet we must ask if motivations changed as much as protest form did. In the following selection protest is labeled very neatly, but organization is stressed more than human content. Many people may have accepted large-scale organization as a necessity of modern life, while still harboring traditional sentiments. Others may have turned away from the most overt forms of protest because massive organization was itself unacceptable. It is not as easy to find the human meaning in modern as in traditional protest, which may caution us against accepting too simple a categorization, or too optimistic an assessment, of the ability of protest to express grievances in modern society.

[The] vast series of changes in French social structure reshaped the struggle for political power in three fundamental ways. First, position in the national structure of power came to matter far more than local for practically every purpose. Second, the struggle increasingly took the form of contention or coalition among formal organizations specialized in the pursuit of particular interests; communal groups virtually disappeared from politics. Third, new contenders for power emerged as the class structure and the organizational structure evolved. The rise of organizations speaking for segments of the industrial working class was the most important single movement. Other bids for power came from representatives of assorted groups of peasants, of youths, of schoolteachers, of Catholic employers, of government employees. Furthermore, as long-organized groups such as landholders and churchmen contended for power, they adopted the new associational style.

As in other western countries, the political parties which emerged to full activity in Third Republic France compounded diverse interests. The Radicals, the Socialists—and, for that matter, the Radical Socialists—long represented curious melanges of the French electorate. But, compared with her neighbors, France always had a remarkable susceptibility to party fragmentation, an exceptional openness to new parties representing new or old but separate political interests, a considerable tendency for parties to slim down to a single major interest. The Parti Ouvrier Français, the Parti Social Français, the Boulangists, the Christian Democrats, the Communists, the Poujadists represent different phases of this specialization.

Fragmentation was the normal condition of French parliaments, alliance among fragments the parliamentary game. Genuine threats to the parliamentary system came less from this kind of splintering than from the occasional appearance of an important political force acting outside the parliamentary arena: the Ligue des Patriotes, the Croix de Feu, Algerian nationalists, sometimes the Gaullists or the Communists. Inside or outside parliament, the twentieth-century political struggle pitted associations representing relatively narrow segments of the population against each other and aligned them with or against the regime. Interest-group politics emerged in France.

Our review of social change in France has pointed up spurts of industrialization, urbanization, and demographic transformation after 1850, after 1920 and—preeminently—after 1945; they contrast with crises and reversals at the times of the Franco-Prussian War, the two world wars, and the depression of the 1930s. These are but ripples in a fast-flowing stream. An urban-industrial class structure gradually emerged from a class structure based on land and locality. The new structure relied on control of capital and labor rather than on landed wealth. It separated owners and managers of large formal organizations (factories, governments, schools) from their employees. It emphasized position in the national labor market over local attachments, and gave exceptional rewards to technical expertise. Periods of urban-industrial growth accelerated this transformation of the class structure.

The centralization of politics through the growth of a massive and powerful state apparatus continued trends established centuries before, although the advent of Louis Napoleon after 1848 and the extension of controls over the economy in the 1940s speeded the process. The nationalization of politics through the shift of power and participation to an arena far larger than local went on more or less continuously, but the political mobilization of 1848, of the early Third Republic, of the Popular Front, and of the years just after World War II probably drew men into involvement in national politics faster than at other times. The shift of collective action—both political and nonpolitical—from communal to associational bases proceeded inexorably over the entire period, especially during those same periods of political mobilization. These changes transformed the struggle for power, and thus transformed the character of collective violence.

How? Most immediately by changing the collective actions characteristically producing violence. Group violence ordinarily grows out of collective actions which are not intrinsically violent—festivals, meetings, strikes, demonstrations, and so on. Without them the collective violence could hardly occur. People who do not take part in them can hardly get involved in the violence. The groups engaging in collective action with any regularity usually consist of populations perceiving and pursuing a common set of interests. And collective action on any considerable scale requires coordination, communication, and solidarity extending beyond the moment of action itself. The urbanization and industrialization and political rearrangement of France from the Revolution onward utterly transformed the composition of the groups capable of collective action, their internal organization, their interests, their occasions for collective action, the nature of their opponents, and the quality of collective action itself. The transformation of collective action transformed violence.

Again, how? It is easy to illustrate and hard to analyze. The classic

French tax rebellion, for example, took two forms, singly or in combination: first, a group of taxpayers attacked the matériel of tax collection, typically by smashing tollgates and burning assessment records; second, many of the residents of a community greeted the tax collector by blocking his way, by beating him, or by running him out of town; if he brought an armed force the villagers fought them. A typical small version of the tax rebellion occurred at St. Germain (Haute-Vienne) in August 1830. Local tax collectors stopped a carter to check his load and collect their toll. A crowd of men, women, and children "armed with picks and with stones" surrounded them, shouted against the tax, and led away man and wagon from the helpless revenue men. This elementary form of resistance sometimes compounded into widespread and grave rebellion, as in the years before the Fronde, during the early Revolution, and (for the last time) in 1849.

Although the sheer difficulty of paying when times were hard certainly had something to do with this common form of resistance to the state, it is important to see how regularly and directly it centered on the very legitimacy of the tax. Not long before the Revolution of 1830, the procureur général of the judicial district of Poitiers reported that "seditious posters" had been appearing in the city of Fontenay (Vendée); "the content of the posters is always to forbid the payment of taxes before the ministers who voted the budget are brought to trial." The same sort of campaign was gathering strength in other parts of France at that time, and continued through the Revolution; often it operated secretly and without violence, but now and then it showed up in a public confrontation. The tax rebellion developed in the sixteenth century, flourished in the seventeenth, recurred in 1789, 1830, or 1848 as new revolutionary officials sought to reimpose the state's authority; it vanished after 1849. Its history traced the government's long struggle to secure both obedience and income.

Gabriel Ardant has identified the general conditions for waves of fiscal revolts in France: a sharp increase in the central government's demands for cash; a sharp decrease in the market for products of rural industry or agriculture (hence in the ability of villagers to convert their surplus into cash); or, more serious, both at once. He has also pointed their clustering in areas of "closed economy"—not necessarily poor, but little involved in production for the market, typically composed of self-sufficient farms. As he sums it up for the Massif Central:

> The proportion of the population in agriculture remains relatively large. No doubt some industries have grown up in the Massif Central near the coalfields, but the coalfields themselves are less productive than those of the North and the East. Furthermore, the factories do not have the advantage of channels of communication comparable to the networks of rivers and canals in the North and the East. In any case, industries like agriculture are far from the important markets of the North, the East and the Parisian region.

From all this comes a larger tendency than elsewhere to live in a closed economy. Thus we can explain that the regions of the Massif Central have been perpetual zones of fiscal rebellion, that movements like those of the Croquans have periodically reappeared in Limousin, Perigord and Quercy, that in 1848 and 1849 the resistance to taxation developed in these same provinces. In our own time the Poujadist movement started out from Haut-Quercy (now the department of Lot), and the first departments affected were the adjacent ones, the locales of fiscal sedition under the old regime.

Tax revolts grouped together in time and space, primarily because the changes in national policy which incited them affected many localities sharing common characteristics at more or less the same time. The largest nineteenth-century bursts of tax revolts came in 1830, when the officials of the new monarchy sought to reimpose taxes on the provinces; in 1841, when the new Minister of Finances tried a special census as a step toward reorganizing the whole inequitable tax system; and in 1848 and 1849, when another revolutionary government tried to put its fiscal affairs in order.

The tax rebellion often succeeded in the short run. The tax man fled, the tollgates fell. Its success, its timing, its personnel, its very form, however, depended on the solidarity of small, local groups of taxpayers and on the vulnerability of a system of control which relied on agents dispatched from cities into treacherous hinterlands. While individual Frenchmen have shrewdly finagled and dissimulated to avoid taxes up to our own day, their capacity for collective resistance to the tax collector sank fast after the middle of the nineteenth century. When anti-tax movements revived with wine-growers after 1900, small distillers in the 1930s, or shopkeepers in the 1950s, the groups that joined the combat were no longer the taxpayers of a single commune, then of the next, but specialized regional and national associations responding to centralized direction. Marcelin Albert's Comité de Défense Viticole (in the first period), Henri Dorgères' Comités de Défense Paysanne (in the second), and Pierre Poujade's Union de Défense des Commerçants et Artisans (in the third) all adopted the defensive stance of earlier tax rebels, right down to their titles. All left violence aplenty in their wakes, but in these cases the defensive actions and the violence came after the deliberate, strenuous organization of protest groups through substantial sections of small-town France.

Changing Forms of Collective Action

Around the middle of the nineteenth century, both the scale and organizational complexity of the collective actions that normally produced violence—hence of violent action itself—increased rapidly and decisively. That happened for two related reasons: first, the scale and organizational complexity of the groups contending for power also increased rapidly and decisively, the expanding organization of industrial workers being the most notable; and second, communal groups dropped out of the struggle as the new associations, and new groups organized associationally, joined it. The organizational revolution reorganized violence.

There is something more, something the tax rebellion alone cannot reveal. Consider for a moment the point of view of the state. From that perspective the predominant forms of collective violence in France during the first half of the nineteenth century were *defensive*: tax rebellions fended off state employees; food riots beat back outside merchants; attacks on machines repelled technical innovations. The demonstrations, strikes, and rebellions which grew in importance over the century had a much larger offensive component; their participants reached for recognition, for a larger share, for greater power.

The crux of the contrast is the relation of the participants to organization at the national scale: the national market, the national culture, and, preeminently, the national state. In the earlier, defensive phase most of the participants were resisting the claims of national structures, especially the state. In the latter, offensive phase most of the participants were bidding for power over the operation of these national structures. In between the nation won out.

We can be more exact. Suppose by "violence" we mean damage or seizure of persons or objects. Suppose by "collective" we mean that a substantial number of people act together. (The minima may be arbitrary; later we will report what happens when we use as a threshold the participation of at least one group of fifty or more persons, plus at least one person or object damaged or seized over resistance.) In that case, "collective violence" will ordinarily grow out of some prior collective action which is not intrinsically violent: a meeting, a ceremony, a strike. A question about the causes of collective violence immediately breaks into two questions. Why do these forms of collective action occur? Why do they sometimes—but not always—end in violence?

The nationalization of politics and of economic life in France divided the major forms of collective action which commonly produced violence into three main categories. They waxed and waned successively. The first we will call *competitive* collective action. Competitive actions which once produced a good deal of violence include feuds, acts of rivalry between adjoining villages, recurrent ritual encounters of competing groups of artisans. Although each of these had a distinctive form, by the nineteenth century national observers tended to lump their violent forms together as *rixes*: brawls. The report of the Royal Gendarmerie for the Department of the Rhône in June 1830 expressed alarm that:

in the arrondissement of Villefranche the young men of its communes, having had some earlier conflicts, get together on holidays, Sundays, and days of fairs in groups of several communes, one against another, and fight tooth and nail; but if the Gendarmerie tries to intervene in those fights to restore good order, the combatants close ranks against the gendarmes, whom they often treat improperly, even making so bold as to attack them with stones, clubs, etc.

Such battles are the most visible form of a general phenomenon: the constant contention among communal groups within small-scale, local political systems. They predominated, statistically at least, in France before statemakers such as Mazarin and Colbert began pressing the claims of the national state and the national economy over local commitments and resources.

That bitter struggle of the statemakers for control over the general population and its resources promoted defensive, backward-looking conflicts between different groups of local people, on the one hand, and agents of the nation, on the other. . . . The word *reactive* describes them. The tax rebellion, the food riot, violent resistance to conscription, machine-breaking, and invasions of enclosed land rose and fell in their own rhythms. They often occurred in the course of transfers of power which our comfortable retrospect permits us to treat as progressive revolutions. Yet they had in common a tendency to involve communal groups jostled and outraged by the commotion of statemaking. This does not mean in the least that the actions of the groups involved were blind or incoherent. In October 1848 we find that the prefect of the Seine-Inférieure had first suspended exports of grains and potatoes because of a food shortage and then lifted the suspension:

> Strong opposition arose at once. Groups gathered on the quay d'Ile about 10 A.M., near some ships which were loading. One of these ships, le *Blé*, was boarded by fifty workers, who started to unload the sacks of potatoes which were its cargo. They had hardly gotten fifty sacks onto the quay when they went to another ship, the English sloop *The Brothers*, which was completely loaded and preparing to sail from the outer corner of the quay. The workers climbed onto the ship themselves, towed the ship toward the bridge, and moored it in the basin, without any resistance from the crew. But the English captains raised their flags to protest against the visits their ships were receiving.

The National Guard came to repossess the ships from the workers; after some scuffling they expelled the workers; then the ships sailed under armed guard. Only in the general pattern of such disturbances does their essential character emerge. They embodied resistance to the growth of a national market exercising priority over local needs and traditions. This was the pattern: the disturbances were clustered in areas torn between the needs of the local population and the demands of the national market; they followed a well-defined routine in which the actors assumed the places of the authorities but melted away when the authorities took the approved action, even if people remained hungry. Yet each incident, including the boarding of ships in Rouen, tended to display a kind of coherence and conscious intent which fits ill with the word usually applied: riot. From the point of view of the statemakers, such actions can only be ill-considered and disorderly; from the point of view of the participant, they are justice itself.

The state and the national market eventually triumphed. Their most difficult battles had been won by the time of our sketch of 1868; by 1968, they belonged to a fading historical memory. From the period of those eighteenth- and nineteenth-century victories by the state, proactive forms of collective action became the standard settings for collective violence. They are "proactive" rather than "reactive" because at least one group is making claims for rights, privileges, or resources not previously enjoyed. The deliberate attempt to seize control of the state is proactive. So are the majority of demonstrations and strikes. Daniel Guérin, a leftwing author, recollects a famous encounter between the far left and the far right. The setting is Paris, February 1934:

Toward 10 P.M., a column of marchers comes from the rue Royale, filling the whole width of the street, carrying tricolor flags. In the middle of the street gentlemen of mature and respectable appearance, with their ribbons of the Legion of Honor, shout the "Marseillaise." They don't look like rioters. Along the sidewalks, all around them, young workers in sweaters and caps sing the "Internationale." Neither of the two kinds of choristers seems inconvenienced by the presence of the other or bothered by the bizarre cacophony. Instead they give the impression of demonstrating together against the power and the police. Someone tells me they are veterans, some from the right, others from the extreme left. But most of the kids who are thundering the Red hymn aren't old enough to have been in the war.

The parade, not having been able to reach or cross the bridge, doesn't stay forever on the Place de la Concorde. And pretty soon the Place is taken over by scattered curiosity-seekers, come to see the damage left by the riot. But suddenly toward 11:30, the black curtain of demonstrators (which was still visible in the distance, on the bridge) rushes toward us in disorder. Under the influence, it seems, of a colonel of gendarmerie who, posing as History, roars "Follow me! Forward!," two columns of cops start to attack. One comes out of Cour-la-Reine toward the Champs-Elysées; the other passes between the horses of Marly where the demonstrators built a bit of barricade at the beginning of the evening, and tries to clean out the bushes of the Champs-Elysées in the direction of the Théâtre des Ambassadeurs. A crackle of gunfire breaks out. A mad panic comes over the bystanders. I have just enough time to put my bicycle on my shoulder, to run just like everyone else, as fast as my legs will carry me, to cross as best I can (given the weight of my machine) the half-barricade at the entrance to the Champs-Elysées, and at a full run try to make it to the avenue Gabriel. Bullets crash into the glass of the streetlights, which break into fragments. Next to me, people fall on their backs, all four limbs thrashing. Others crawl below the line of fire. A young man, a little farther along, complains about a burn on his ear; he touches it with his hand, which fills with blood.

On that February night thousands of individual experiences compounded into a grave conflict. Seventeen persons died and at least two thousand were wounded. As a more or less direct consequence, the Daladier government fell. Yet the events began with nonviolent, proactive demands for power.

This sort of collective action differs from the reactive varieties in important ways: in pivoting on attempts to control, rather than resist, different segments of the national structure; by involving relatively complex special-purpose associations rather than communal groups; through a great articulation of objectives, programs, and demands.

These characteristics imply further contrasts with reactive conflicts. One is a lesser dependency on natural congregations such as markets, church services, and festivals in favor of deliberate assemblies and shows of strength (since special-purpose associations rarely draw all their members from the same round of life but are often effective at calling together a diverse membership at crucial moments). Another is a tendency of the disturbances to be large and short. Communal groups, once committed to a conflict, rarely mobilize large numbers of men, rarely have leaders with the authority to negotiate quick compromise settlements, and rarely can call off the action rapidly and effectively; it may also be true (as it has often been argued) that communal groups have an exceptional capacity to hold out in the face of adversity. Associational groups, on the other hand, tend to become involved in violence as an outgrowth of brief, coordinated mass actions which are not intrinsically violent. Still another contrast between reactive and proactive movements is a prevalence of indignation about the loss of specific rights and privileges in the reactive cases, as compared with a greater emphasis in proactive cases on rights due as a consequence of general principles.

Two features of the shift from competitive to reactive to proactive forms of collective action as prime settings for violence stand out: the change in organization of the participants, and the change in locus of the conflict. First, the groups taking part in collective action become bigger, more complicated, more bureaucratized, more specifically committed to some public program or ideology, more open to new members prepared to support the group's special goals; earlier we called this a transfer from communal to associational bases for collective action. Second, the locus of the conflicts involved moves away from the purely local toward the national, even the international, scale; although by 1830 Frenchmen were making national revolutions and demonstrating in support of Poland, the bulk of violent conflict aligned local groups on essentially local issues; by the 1930s national issues and national antagonists took precedence. From a national perspective this change seemed to involve a "politicization" of conflict.

The trouble with that way of stating it is the fact that the competitive and reactive forms of collective action also grew out of well-developed struggles for power, out of political conflicts on a smaller scale. The tax rebellion, the food riot, the invasion of fields, and even the artisans' brawl pivoted on local questions of rights, duties, and power. For that reason, we would be better off speaking of a "nationalization" of conflict, integrally related to the nationalization of political life. In our own day we may have to speak of a further stage of "internationalization."

It is wrong to picture competitive, reactive, and proactive collective action as three distinct, exclusive stages. That image has two defects. First, some communal groups gradually acquire associational characteristics, yet retain their capacity for collective action throughout the process: a city's traditional elite joins a national pressure group; a religious community becomes a corporation. During the transformation their characteristic forms of collective action, and thus of collective violence, also change. Second, the proactive forms of collective action emerged early in those sectors of French social life in which the national structures emerged early: major cities, areas of advanced industry, the hinterland of Paris, and so on. At the center of the centralized French system, men had begun struggling for control of the state and the national market centuries before their brothers at the periphery stopped fighting the expansion of the state and the market. The rapid nineteenth-century transition from predominantly reactive to predominantly proactive forms of collective action resembled the movement from one terrain to another rather than the passage of a guarded frontier. We might visualize the statistical distribution of violence emerging from each of the major forms of collective action as that shown in Figure 1.

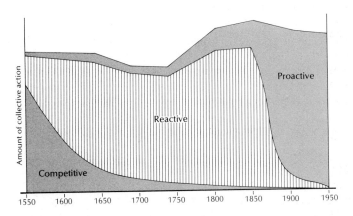

Figure 1. Hypothetical Evolution of Collective Action in France

In the absence of reasonable criteria for the "amount" of collective violence and of reasonable data for the period before the nineteenth century, the exact shapes of the curves represent no more than informed speculation. The biggest speculation is that the volume of reactive violence swelled rapidly during the heroic statemaking of Louis XIII and Louis XIV. We know that popular rebellions of a reactive form abounded at that time, but too little work has been done on conflicts well before and well after the Fronde to verify the general timing. The graph rests on a firmer factual footing in stating that reactive conflicts rose to a nineteenth-century peak, instead of gradually diminishing. The real point of the diagram, however, is to portray the slow displacement of competitive by reactive forms of collective action as the French state extended its claims, and the rapid displacement of reactive by proactive collective action during the nineteenth-century nationalization of the struggle for power.

Crime and Industrialization in Britain

J. J. TOBIAS

The history of crime has as yet only barely been sketched, so we cannot claim definite correlations between crime and modernization. Crime may go up as the strains of modernization increase—it seems to have risen generally in the twentieth century—but it also may go down, as it did in many areas in the nineteenth century. The nature of crime does change with modernization. Crimes of violence probably declined with urbanization in Europe. The tensions of life in small villages—tightly knit communities from which escape was not easy—and the absence of police were conducive to violence, particularly when supplemented by the pressures of population growth. The growth of more impersonal, better-policed cities reduced the rate of violent crimes, while encouraging new expectations that led to an increase in crimes against property. Thus the nature and motivations of criminals were changing. In this sense crime should be analyzed in the light of the broader modernization of lower-class outlook, for its motives may be seen as perverse expressions of more general new values.

This selection attempts a general survey of English crime patterns during the first stages of modernization. Tobias finds that crime reached a peak in the first half of the eighteenth century, just before the first signs of modernization emerged. Thereafter crime probably declined; violence certainly did. If these findings are accurate, they constitute an important contribution to our understanding of modernization, at least in Britain, for they suggest that urbanization and industrialization created more new constructive opportunities than they did tensions. They resolved more problems for the lower classes than they created.

The change in the nature of crime is also noteworthy. Not only did violence decrease—itself a development of major importance—but crimes became more subtle, and the old hero-criminal, the man of daring action, became a less common figure. Again, it does not seem far-fetched to suggest a major change in the outlook of criminals paralleling the broader process of modernization.

The passage also suggests the problem of public attitudes toward crime. In the early nineteenth century, when social unrest was severe and the strains of industrialization were particularly acute for upper-class traditionalists, crime was generally thought to be rising, whereas in fact it was probably declining.

Attractive as these judgments are, if only because they overturn any simplistic approach to crime in modern society, they must be subjected to critical scrutiny. The judgments bear on urban, not rural, society; yet the problem of crime may have been greater in the countryside. They derive almost solely from qualitative studies by contemporary observers; there are no hard statistics. Contemporary observers can be wrong, even when their impressions contradict more fashionable opinions by pointing to a decrease in crime.

One may wonder, then, if the crime pattern is as clear-cut as Tobias suggests. In particular, there must be some lingering uncertainty about the 1820s and 1830s, when material conditions in the cities seem to have been deteriorating. But the long-range trend Tobias projects seems hard to refute for Britain. By the second half of the nineteenth century crime was decreasing. The passage suggests a number of reasons for this, relating primarily to city organization and material conditions. One must ask if these are sufficient explanations. Broader changes in lower-class culture may have been involved as well. The decline of crime by children and the general drop in violence might, for example, point to new kinds of behavior in the family.

The lawlessness of London in the first half of the eighteenth century has often been described. Mrs. M. D. George, in her *London Life in the XVIIIth Century*, observes that at the beginning of the century "the forces of disorder and crime had the upper hand in London"; she quotes the City Marshal's remarks of 1718:

> Now it is the general complaint of the taverns, the coffee-houses, the shop-keepers and others, that their customers are afraid when it is dark to come to their houses and shops for fear that their hats and wigs should be snitched from their heads or their swords taken from their sides, or that they may be blinded, knocked down, cut or stabbed; nay, the coaches cannot secure them, but they are likewise cut and robbed in the public streets, &c. By which means the traffic of the City is much interrupted.

These remarks, moreover, apply to the area within the jurisdiction of the City, then better policed than the growing portion of the metropolis outside the City limits.

Over 30 years later, Henry Fielding, the pioneer Bow Street magistrate, took an equally gloomy view; his famous and often-quoted work, *An Enquiry into the Causes of the Late Increase of Robbers . . .* , leaves us in no doubt of his views about the crime of London in 1751, three years after his appointment. Fielding can be left to speak for himself:

. . . The Innocent are put in Terror, affronted and alarmed with Threats and Execrations, endangered with loaded Pistols, beat with Bludgeons and hacked with Cutlasses, of which the Loss of Health, of Limbs, and often of Life, is the Consequence; and all this without any Respect to Age, or Dignity, or Sex. . . .

Street Robberies are generally committed in the dark, the Persons on whom they are committed are often in Chairs and Coaches, and if on Foot, the Attack is usually begun by knocking the Party down, and for the Time depriving him of his Sense. But if the Thief should be less barbarous, he is seldom so incautious as to omit taking every Method to prevent his being known, by flapping the Party's Hat over his Face, and by every other Method which he can invent to avoid Discovery. . . .

How long have we known Highwaymen reign in this Kingdom after they have been publicly known for such? Have not some of these committed Robberies in open Day-light, in the Sight of many People, and have afterward rode solemnly and triumphantly through the neighbouring Towns without any Danger or Molestation. . . . Great and numerous Gangs . . . have for a long time committed the most open Outrages in Defiance of the Law. . . .

There are at this Time a great Gang of Rogues, whose Number falls little short of a Hundred, who are incorporated in one Body, have Officers and a Treasury; and have reduced Theft and Robbery into a regular System. There are [members] of this Society of Men who appear in all Disguises, and mix in most Companies. Nor are they better versed in every Art of cheating, thieving, and robbing, than they are armed with every Method of evading the Law. . . . If they fail in rescuing the Prisoner, or (which seldom happens) in bribing or deterring the Prosecutor, they have for their last Resource some rotten Members of the Law to forge a Defence for them, and a great Number of false Witnesses ready to support it. . . .

It is possible that one or two of Fielding's remarks would not stand up to investigation, but that the substance of them is correct is not in doubt. Jonas Hanway in 1775 wrote:

I sup with my friend; I cannot return to my home, not even in my chariot, without danger of a pistol being clapt to my breast. I build an elegant villa, ten or twenty miles distant from the capital: I am obliged to provide an armed force to convey me thither, lest I should be attacked on the road with fire and ball.

There is much similar evidence, which has been described by other authors.

Indeed, so powerful were the criminals that parts of the town were wholly given over to them: it was not until well into the eighteenth century that the Alsatia, or area of sanctuary, disappeared from London. Such places, by the end of the seventeenth century,

in theory . . . had no existence, or existed on sufferance only to secure
. . . the protection of the debtor against imprisonment for debt; in practice
they were criminal quarters where the officers of justice were set at defiance,
and where no man's life was safe unless he had the privilege of being an
inhabitant.

They were a survival of the medieval sanctuaries, where criminals could take
refuge prior to appearing before the coroner to admit their guilt and abjure
the realm. The comment that the sanctuaries had in theory ceased to exist
was justified . . . [but] sanctuaries continued to exist, and in the last decade
of the seventeenth century there were several in London. . . .

Mrs. George, after taking stock of the crime situation in London in the
early part of the eighteenth century, suggests that things were at their worst
in the 1740s and 50s, and that thereafter an improvement took place. Though
some contemporaries raised the "cry of national deterioratoin," she sides with
Francis Place, the Radical tailor of Charing Cross, who claimed that the
"crimes and vices" of the days of his youth greatly exceeded those of the
early nineteenth century. "By the end of the [eighteenth] century," she sums
up, "we are in a different world."

While Mrs. George quotes testimony to the good order in London at
the end of the eighteenth century—a guidebook of 1802 claimed that "no city
in proportion to its trade and luxury is more free from danger to those who
pass the streets at all hours, or from depredations, open or concealed, on
property"—other modern writers take a more pessimistic view. Dr. E. O'Brien
quotes the Solicitor-General in 1785—"nobody could feel himself unappre-
hensive of danger to his person or property if he walked in the street after
dark, nor could any man promise himself security in his bed." Professor
A. G. L. Shaw quotes advice of 1790 to visitors to London "never to stop in
a crowd or look at the windows of a print-shop, if you would not have your
pocket picked." Patrick Colquhoun's well-known *Treatise on the Police of the
Metropolis* . . . , which went through several editions between 1795 and
1806, has often been used to show the level of criminality that existed at the
time he wrote. He spoke of "the outrages and acts of violence continually
committed, more particularly in and near the Metropolis by lawless ravagers
of property, and destroyers of lives, in disturbing the peaceful mansion, *the
Castle of every Englishman*, and also in abridging the liberty of travelling
upon the Public Highways." In Cheapside, he said,

> a multitude of thieves and pickpockets, exhibiting often in their dress and
> exterior, the appearance of gentlemen and men of business, assemble every
> evening in gangs, watching at the corners of every street, ready to *hustle
> and rob*, or to *trip up the heels of the warehouseporters and the servants of
> shopkeepers carrying goods*; or at the doors of warehouses, at dusk and at the
> time they are locked, to be ready to seize loose parcels when unperceived;

by all which means, aided by a number of other tricks and fraudulent pretences, they are but too successful in obtaining considerable booty. In short, there is no device or artifice to which these vigilant plunderers do not resort: of which an example appeared in an instance, where almost in the twinkling of an eye, while the servants of an eminent silk-dyer had crossed a narrow street, his horse and cart, containing raw silk to the value of *twelve hundred pounds*, were driven clear off. Many of these atrocious villains, are also constantly waiting at the inns, disguised in different ways, personating *travellers, coach-office clerks, porters and coachmen*, for the purpose of plundering every thing that is portable; which, with the assistance of two or three associates if necessary, is carried to a coach called for the purpose, and immediately conveyed to the receiver.

He described in great detail the various river thieves who preyed on the shipping in the Port of London, though he had the satisfaction in the later editions of the work of recording that the Marine Police—of which he was the originator—"may truly be said to have worked wonders in reforming the shocking abuses which prevailed."

There is thus a conflict of views. Those who consider conditions around the end of the eighteenth century are struck with the level of crime and violence then prevalent, while Mrs. George, surveying the century as a whole, sees an improvement. Others indeed have shared her opinion. Crime of course still abounded, and criminals were often violent; but things, it seems, were probably better than they had been earlier.

The changes appear to be associated with the Industrial Revolution. . . . In the last half of the eighteenth century and the first half of the nineteenth century, . . . society was in violent transition. The towns were growing rapidly, and the facilities available to their rulers were very limited and their knowledge of how to use them even more limited. Their population, ever increasing, was predominantly a young one, and the young town-dwellers were faced with a whole host of unfamiliar problems, problems for which their background and training provided them with no answer. The towns, and especially London, had always had a criminal problem different from and larger than that of other areas, and there were groups of people, living in distinctive areas, who had evolved a way of life of their own based on crime. Many young town-dwellers, faced with these problems and receiving no assistance from their families or their employers (if they had families or employers) or from the municipal authorities, found solutions by adopting the techniques, the habits and the attitudes of the criminals. There was thus, in London and the other large towns in the latter part of the eighteenth century and the earlier part of the nineteenth century, an upsurge of crime which was the fruit of a society in rapid transition.

We now return to the question of the course of crime at the end of the eighteenth century. It was seen earlier that the weight of evidence is in favour of the view that the level of crime about the year 1800 was lower than it had been earlier in the century. However, if the analysis just made were correct it would be expected that crime should by then have increased somewhat as a result of the first decades of the Industrial Revolution. The contradiction can, it seems, be resolved. First, it is necessary to make a distinction between qualitative change and quantitative change. There seems no reason to doubt the view that crime was becoming less violent in its nature in the eighteenth century—there is considerable evidence that such a trend existed throughout the nineteenth century. Such a change can be ascribed to the more civilised way of life and the reduction in the violence of life in general which is attested by historians of the eighteenth century. Mrs. George, for example, speaks of the

> change in the attitude towards social questions which was the outcome of the new spirit of humanity, the new command of material resources, and the new belief in environment rather than Providence as the cause of many human ills. . . . There had been a number of obscure reforms, whose cumulative effect was very great . . . an increasing realisation of evils and a growing intolerance of hardships. . . . The improvements in medicine and sanitation had bettered conditions . . . in London.

It is perhaps not irrelevant to note here that by the end of the century a much lower proportion of those condemned to death was actually being executed than had been the case earlier. For example, in the period 1749–58 two in three of the offenders sentenced to death in London and Middlesex were executed, but by the end of the century the ratio had dropped to less than one in three. There are thus grounds for accepting that there was a reduction in the amount of violent crime. However, such a reduction could very well have accompanied an increase in the amount of non-violent crime. Indeed, as violent crimes are the spectacular and eye-catching crimes, a decrease in their number could well have blinded contemporaries to an increase in the total amount of crime. Some contemporary observers were in the early nineteenth century able to insist that crime was increasing in quantity at the same time that they agreed that it was decreasing in violence; but a lesser increase in non-violent crime might well be masked from view. However, it is not necessary to adopt this line of reasoning, for it seems probable that other special factors were operating at the end of the eighteenth century.

A number of changes had taken place in the latter part of the eighteenth century which may well have offset the effects of the movement to the towns. Mrs. George attributes the reduction of crime which she notices, in part at any rate, to the various improvements in the lighting and policing of London, and she regards Henry Fielding's magistracy at Bow Street (1748–54) as "a turning-point in the social history of London." The street-lighting of

London had indeed improved considerably during the eighteenth century. . . .

. . . The provision of better lighting would undoubtedly have made crime more difficult.

Equally certainly the life of the London criminals was made more difficult by improved machinery for enforcing the law. From the time of Henry Fielding's appointment, there was in London a magistrate who was both honest and zealous in the prosecution of crime. . . . One of Henry Fielding's achievements was the establishment of a small group of detectives, "Mr. Fielding's People," who eventually became the Bow Street Runners; and when the seven police offices were established in 1792 each of them had a group of detective police officers of its own. There was also, from about 1782, a Foot Patrole of 68 men attached to the Bow Street Office and patrolling the streets at night. The changes thus made in the policing of London were to prove inadequate before long; but their impact might well have been sufficient to account for the improvement in the crime situation detected by some observers. . . .

. . . It is of course necessary to be very cautious before making pronouncements about changes in the nature or level of crime over any period of time, let alone one so remote as the nineteenth century. However, there are two propositions on this topic that can be put forward with some assurance.

The first of these is that there was a continuing trend to less violence in crime over the century. Such a trend probably existed in the eighteenth century; the evidence for its existence in the nineteenth century is even stronger. Throughout the century contemporaries accepted that criminals were becoming less violent, each generation seeing an improvement over the previous one.

The evidence before the Select Committee on Police of 1816–18 sets the tone. "Daring, desperate things seem to be worn out, except daring forgeries," said one police officer, and the question put to John Nares, a police magistrate of over 20 years' experience, and his reply will serve as a summary of the rest of the evidence: "The Committee have had in evidence, and indeed the observation of every one must have given him the information without that evidence, that atrocious crimes have of late years considerably diminished?—I have no doubt of that."

Blackwood's Magazine did indeed in 1818 write that "one strong feature of the times is the prevalence of atrocious crime. This is the common remark of every day." However, the Select Committee's reports leave no doubt that many people in the post-Waterloo period took the more optimistic view.

Street robberies in London increased dramatically in the early 1820s, and one writer in 1829 spoke of gangs being ready to "hustle, rob, or knock down" anyone carrying valuables; but he also said that "there have been few instances lately of forcing houses in the old-fashioned way, at the front, and taking possession by *coup de main*." Francis Place in 1831 was sure that crimes had decreased "in atrocity"; Edwin Chadwick too had no doubt about the matter. In 1829 he wrote: "It is acknowledged on every side, that crimes attended with acts of violence have diminished," and in 1839 the Report of the Royal Commission on a Constabulary Force, drafted by him, said that "Crimes of violence committed for the sake of obtaining property have diminished. . . . In the towns, burglaries and depredations in the streets are now rarely accompanied by violence." In 1832 a writer in *Fraser's Magazine* attempted an explanation:

> The character and feelings of the public thief, as of all other classes of society, have undergone a visible and marked change within the last thirty years. . . . Formerly, the heroes of their party were fellows conspicuous and famed for open and daring acts of plunder, in whom the whole body had a pride, and whom they all felt ambitious to imitate; failing only to do so for lack of the same quantum of courage. The more desperate and numerous the instances of robbery, the more were the parties lauded and admired. . . . All this kind of heroism has subsided; their leaders now are men rendered famous for scheming, subtlety, and astuteness. Formerly, the passport to enrolment under their banners was a name for boldness and monstrous acts of outrage; now a certificate must be brought of the man never having committed an indiscreet act in his calling.

Opinion remained the same at mid-century. Thus, despite outbreaks of violent crime over the whole country between 1850 and 1853, Frederic Hill, a former Inspector of Prisons, could write in the latter year that crimes were "taking a milder and milder form." Violent crimes continued to attract public attention on various occasions during the 1850s and 60s, particularly of course during the famous garrotting attacks in London in 1862. They caused much public alarm—perhaps more acute because of the relative safety of recent years—but belief that there had been an improvement over earlier years persisted. In 1862 the *Cornhill Magazine* wrote that the criminals' "character in respect of violence and cruelty has been much ameliorated during the last fifteen or twenty years. They do not like resorting to violence if it can possibly be avoided. . . . The modern thief depends upon his skill."

In the closing years of the nineteenth century the story was unchanged. Looking back over his long life a few days before his death in 1890, Edwin Chadwick summed up his views on this point in a letter to the Editor of the *Daily Chronicle* prepared for his signature but never signed:

> When the Police were first instituted [presumably the reference is to the establishment of the Metropolitan Police in 1829], men who were mechanics in good position were asked why they did not have a watch to mark the

time. "Yes" was the reply "and get my head broken by thieves." They could hold in safety no personal property of any sort, and life would have been insecure. So with their families. They had no silver spoons, nor any other article of that kind. The possession of such property at that time endangered their lives.

It must be admitted that in 1891 the Rev. W. D. Morrison wrote that "offences against property with violence display a tendency to increase," but he was talking about the number of cases recorded in a particular statistical category rather than the quality of the acts themselves. Charles Booth in the 1890s found that violence was regarded by criminals and police alike as a breach of the "rules of the game, which provide the rough outlines of a code of what is regarded as fair or unfair." Thomas Holmes, surveying in 1908 his 21 years' experience as a police-court missionary, was satisfied that there were fewer crimes of violence.

Thus over the whole of the century there is evidence, much of it from sources entitled to our respect, that the use of violence in crime had decreased; and the conclusion that this is true seems irresistible.

A qualitative change in criminality can thus be established; what can we say about quantitative change? Here it is much more difficult to make definite statements. The difficulties of ascertaining changes in the level of crime are well known, and the people of the nineteenth century were not likely to have had any clearer idea of what was going on than we have of what is going on today. The evidence of what they thought was happening is, moreover, hard to interpret. What exactly do we understand when someone says that "the tranquility . . . of the whole town is miraculous . . . very different from what I remember, even within a few years," but adds "we have a vast number of pickpockets occasionally, and frauds in abundance"? How far is he being contradicted by a witness who affirms that "the petty offences" and "the juvenile depredators" have increased? Does either of them mean the same thing as the witness who thought that there had been an increase but only in "simple larcenys, burglaries and so on, nothing very enormous" or the witness who agrees that crime is on the increase "in numbers certainly, but not in depravity by any means; we have . . . less serious offences"? Despite these difficulties, however, it is worth surveying the evidence, and for this purpose it is convenient to divide the century into two parts, the division occurring in the middle 1850s.

The phrases quoted in the previous paragraph show that it is easy to produce testimony to an increase in non-violent crime in the first of these two periods. Other evidence can be quoted. The Under-Sheriff of London and Middlesex said in 1817:

As to the length of the Old Bailey sessions, it is within the memory of most persons who are now engaged in its business, that if a session continued from the Wednesday in one week to the Monday in the next (or five days) it was an extraordinary circumstance, whereas it has now become a common occurrence for a session to last a fortnight and three weeks. . . . I am persuaded that the actual increase of crime will alone explain the increased length of sessions and assizes.

The Rev. W. L. Clay, writing in 1861, had no doubt that in the early part of the century "the real increase of crime had been very serious, the apparent increase terrible," and though the comment quoted was made in relation to the 10 years from 1825 to 1834, it represents his view of the whole period from about 1810. Several witnesses before parliamentary committees of enquiry and others whose opinions are on record put forward similar views. On the other hand, the contrary view is well supported, and if the bulk of the evidence is for an increase, there are one or two powerful names in the opposing camp. Alderman Matthew Wood, m.p., who was a leading figure in the affairs of the City of London but who on this occasion can be regarded as a disinterested witness, as he was talking about London outside the City, said in 1828 that there were fewer offences but that more were being detected because of improved policing—"that is a fact I have no doubt about." Francis Place was of the same opinion.

Moreover, some observers of the criminal scene in the post-war years were not prepared to accept that any change had really taken place. In 1816 a witness had said that juvenile delinquencies had not increased "so much as is generally supposed; I apprehend that they are more known from being more investigated." He "hoped, and was inclined to think" that there had been an increase in police activity rather than a "real augmentation in the number of crimes." In 1828 the Superintendent of the Hulks said that "The increase of crime has not been much beyond the increased population of the country; I do not state that it has not increased, but not to that extent that seems to be the prevailing opinion." "Do not you think," he was asked, "that on the whole the general notion as to the great increase of crime is exaggerated, and not quite founded in fact?" and he replied: "Certainly." The Select Committee on Police before which he was speaking was the one which reversed the tenor of previous reports and recommended a change in the police of the metropolis, and thus gave Sir Robert Peel the opportunity to create the Metropolitan Police. However, even they did not go further than to say that they had obtained "no information which justifies them in reporting further, than that" the increase in commitments and convictions in the metropolis must be considered to emanate

> from a combination of causes. . . . A portion only of the accession to Criminal Commitments, is to be deemed indicative of a proportionate increase of Crime; and even of that portion, much may be accounted for in the more ready detection and trial of culprits, also in less disinclination to

prosecute, in consequence of improved facilities afforded at the courts to prosecutors and witnesses, and of the increased allowance of costs.

Edwin Chadwick observed in 1829 that for the previous 6–8 years there had been a general belief that crime in the metropolis had been steadily increasing since before 1815 but that there was no evidence for this belief; all that had happened was that crime was more prosecuted and more exposed to view.

This game of matching quotation to quotation could go on for a long time; until the early 1850s the argument between the three points of view continued. Enough has been said, however, to show the difficulty of reaching any conclusion. It seems probable that the level of crime after about 1810 was higher than that of the previous two decades. Professor Radzinowicz has recorded the view that crime in the early nineteenth century was on the increase, but despite this powerful authority it is difficult to reach any firm conclusion about changes in the amount of crime in the period from Waterloo to the middle 1850s.

When we turn to the second part of the century, from the middle 1850s to its end, we reach the second point about which a reasonable degree of certainty is attainable. There was a marked drop in juvenile crime and in the number of juvenile criminals in the 1850s and 60s. In the 1850s some writers were still speaking of an increase of juvenile crime, but already opinion was beginning to change. The Rev. John Clay, the Chaplain of Preston Gaol, in his report for 1855–6 wrote:

> Any doubts which may have been entertained as to the successful issue of reformatory schools, when the great movement in their favour took place a few years ago, ought now to be set at rest, for it has been sufficiently proved that wherever they have been earnestly and judiciously worked, there criminality has received a check.

In 1859, T. B. L. Baker, a Gloucestershire magistrate and a prominent writer on criminal matters, claimed that a reduction in juvenile crime had commenced, and he later gave details of what he thought had happened. He regarded 1856 as the year in which the decisive change took place, that being the year in which it became the general practice to commit all qualified offenders to reformatory school on a second conviction, almost regardless of the actual offence. He thought that the progress was maintained despite a minor increase of crime in 1860–3. It must be admitted that he was relying, in part at any rate, on the criminal statistics, as indeed other people may have been; but some of the names on the list of those who shared his opinions are impressive. The Rev. John Clay has already been quoted; the others include the Rev. S. Turner, the Inspector of Reformatory Schools, in his 1859–60 Report, the Rev. W. L. Clay in 1861 and Miss Carpenter in 1861 and 1864. These are powerful authorities.

The case for saying that there was a marked reduction of crime in the 1850s does not rest merely on the testimony of those active at the time. Looking back over the perspective of a decade or two, people could see that the change was not merely quantitative but qualitative as well. The hardened juvenile thief, the hordes of criminal youngsters, had disappeared from English towns. There were few children left as bad as those of twenty years before, wrote C. B. Adderley in 1874. "It is almost impossible in these days," wrote the *Gloucestershire Chronicle* in 1886, "to realise the extent to which juvenile crime prevailed forty years ago." The Royal Commission on the Reformatories and Industrial Schools of 1884 accepted that the gangs of young criminals had been broken up, and an end put to the training of boys as professional thieves.

There were dissenting voices, of course. W. Hoyle, an ardent advocate of temperance, used the criminal statistics to show that an increase of crime had taken place. Rather more weight should perhaps be given to the Rev. W. D. Morrison, who in 1892 argued that crime had increased during the previous 30 years, i.e., from a period just after the reformatory schools had begun to have an effect. In his view "whatever the prisons have lost," the reformatory schools and the industrial schools have "more than gained." His argument was in part based on the number of juveniles in these three types of establishment taken together but, as Captain Anson, the Chief Constable of Staffordshire, pointed out, the increase was mainly in the number of those in industrial schools, not all of whom were offenders. Moreover, Morrison himself had the previous year said that "crime in England is not making more rapid strides than the growth of the population"; this is at any rate an acceptance that there was no increase in crime relative to the population.

It thus seems certain that a marked decline in the level of juvenile crime took place in the 1850s and 60s, and that at the end of the century the general level of crime was lower than it had been during most of its course. The Rev. J. W. Horsley felt that the last 20 years of the century had seen a real decrease in crime and a steady improvement in conduct in general. Sidney and Beatrice Webb wrote that "It is clear that the proved criminality of the eighteenth century was enormously in excess, both absolutely and relatively, of that which prevails at the opening of the twentieth century." It may fairly be claimed that it is only in the decades indicated that there is any sign of this "enormous" decrease taking place. R. F. Quinton just before the First World War wrote of the steady decrease of crime, and especially of serious crime, in the past 30 years. He too spoke of an "enormous" decline, this time of the number of professional criminals; he was quite sure there was an "actual decrease in crime." Mr. B. D. White, in his survey of the history of Liverpool, notices a fall in crime from 1875 to the end of the nineteenth century (and an increase in the first 14 years of the twentieth). . . .

Crime and the Development
of Modern Society

HOWARD ZEHR

Here is a second effort at determining a direction to the history of modern crime, associating it more explicitly with a concept of modernization. Howard Zehr eschews an effort to use modernization to predict any definite trend in the rate of crime. Dealing with France and Germany instead of England, he finds a somewhat different pattern from that posited by Tobias. In this selection initial industrialization and accompanying urban turbulence, rather than preindustrial decades as for Tobias, stamp a particular character on crime for a few decades. But for Zehr, it is the relationship between crimes of violence and crimes against property (the Theft/Violence Ratio, or TVR) that attracts particular attention, suggesting again a major change in the motivations of criminals. Material problems increased as a focus of tension or frustration; comparatively, personal clashes declined. Changes in crime targets invite comparison with the modernization of protest goals, discussed in the Tilly selection.

Yet questions remain about any association between modernization and crime. The selection suggests a continuing relationship in the twentieth century. But if crimes of violence rise, how much does it matter that crimes against property rise faster? Historians like Zehr and Tobias warn against a facile assumption that crime in general automatically or uniformly increases with modernization. They also refute any idea that preindustrial or rural society was blissfully crime free. But whether there is a modernization of crime, applying to the twentieth century as well as to the nineteenth, and, if so, what its character is, are questions that continue to plague social analysts, even as some specifically nineteenth-century patterns become clearer. Modernization, if applicable, must also be flexible enough to account for national variations, as between England and the Continent or, even more blatantly, Europe and the United States.

. . . What then happened to crime during the nineteenth century? Can any general statement be made about patterns in crime during this period? By now the pitfalls in such a question are obvious. Statements about crime-in-general

From Howard Zehr, *Crime and the Development of Modern Society*. Reprinted by permission of Rowman and Littlefield, © 1976.

are often misleading because of substantial differences in the behaviour of various crime categories—although it is noteworthy that each crime category appears to have had its own characteristic pattern of behaviour which, in many cases, transcended regional or national boundaries. Similarly, the tenuous nature of many national averages and patterns of crime is clear; regional patterns or styles of crime obtained which often were rather independent of national boundaries. Nevertheless the question is legitimate and several conclusions about nineteenth-century criminal behaviour are indeed possible.

The most important general phenomenon which has been observed here was the change in the nature of criminal behaviour which took place during the century, especially in non-rural areas. The dimensions of this change were several. Crime rates in general, but especially property crime rates, rose during the nineteenth century; on the whole, then, crime was more frequent by 1913 than it had been in 1830. Against this must be balanced, however, the declining importance of violence—and especially serious violence—relative to theft in the long run. Concurrently, a change occurred in the economic determinants of crime: the relationship between basic subsistence costs and both violent and property crimes loosened as the century progressed due, seemingly, to rising standards of living. But neither of these developments occurred instantly. A transitional stage has been observed in which violence kept up with or even outstripped rising theft rates while the connection between crime and costs of basic staples loosened only gradually.

This transitional period, during which crime rates soared particularly rapidly, had a potential impact well beyond its own duration. The rapid rise in crime occurred as many social groups, including the new middle class, were being exposed to city life for the first time. It could give an empirical base to a sense that urban life was dangerous, even out of hand, and thus strengthen such important new trends as residential segregation, and ultimately suburbanisation, by class. And the resultant fear of the city could outlive the actual transitional period of crime itself. It has certainly stimulated impressions of a relationship between city and crime not only in the public mind but also among many scholarly analysts of crime as well.

But the long-term evolution in patterns of criminal behaviour, which includes a more modest tendency toward an increase in crime rates, is more significant in actuality. This alteration in patterns of criminal behaviour has been characterised here as a transition from pre-modern to modern forms of criminal behaviour, reflecting the eventual abandonment of rural traditions, rising standards of living and thus rising expectations, and in general adjustment to life in an urban, industrial society. What we have traced, in other words, is a modernisation of criminal behaviour paralleling and accompanying the modernisation of society in general. But a word of caution is in order. This investigation has stopped at the First World War, and thus cannot tell us whether the pre-war patterns which we have termed modern have in fact persisted since then. A spot check suggests that they may have—according to

French correctional court records, for example, the TVR in France continued its decline after the war so that in 1941–50 it was only 0.17, or less than half the level of a century earlier; but changes in the administration of justice since the First World War make comparisons between pre-war and present patterns difficult.

Data from the United States in the twentieth century are interesting in the context of this problem. Overall, the pattern here seems similar to that seen for Germany and France in the nineteenth century; violence is low relative to theft (TVR = 0.05 for the period 1960–73, with no apparent trend during these years) and, at least in the early 1950s, the TVR was significantly higher in rural areas (0.08) than in urban areas (0.04). But a closer examination of some U.S. statistics indicates an important difference (Table 1).

TABLE 1.   Theft-Violence Ratios in Urban and Rural Areas of the United States, 1966–7. Population Size Classes in Thousands.

All cities	.048
1,000+	.088
500–1,000	.053
250–500	.045
All, 250+	.060
100–250	.046
50–100	.034
25–50	.034
10–25	.050
under 10	.041
Suburbs	.037
Rural areas	.071

The expected urban-rural difference in the theft-violence ratio did hold true generally in 1966–7; the average TVR was significantly higher in the rural group than in the urban group. But unlike the nineteenth-century European pattern, violence rates in the very largest cities in the nation were much higher relative to theft than anywhere else, including rural areas, while the TVR in most small-town groups was significantly lower than in either the most urban or the most rural areas. This difference in patterns raises an interesting question: should these differences in criminal behaviour be attributed to national or to chronological differences? That national differences may obtain is reasonable, of course; it is highly likely that crime patterns in a mobile, frontier society would differ from those in a European context. But there are also numerous reasons why patterns may be expected to have changed during the past half century or so, and this would not necessarily be inconsistent with the interpretation which we have advanced here. The great wars of the twentieth century, for example, to some extent upset previous trends and patterns of behaviour. The "second" industrial revolution based on new sources of energy and a new cluster of technological achievements has brought new disruptions and has forced new adjustments upon European as well as American society. The emergence of the "post-industrial city" has changed the nature of urban life: with the rise of metropolitan communities and the increasing importance of suburban life, the city has become less centralised; the urban economy has become more service-centred; new patterns of immigration to—as well as emigration from—the city have emerged; and the spread of mass communication has broken down many rural-urban distinctions, resulting in the "urbanisation" of rural society. Hi-jackings, kidnappings and "rip-offs" in the 1970s suggest that crime is becoming increasingly politicised. What has been identified here as a modern pattern of crime thus may only be modern in the context of the nineteenth century, describing an intermediate pattern of crime characteristic of a specific historical period. The continuous, open-ended nature of the historical process must, that is, be affirmed.

But is the "modernisation" of criminal patterns, even if confined to the nineteenth century, applicable beyond the two countries studied? It is premature to speculate too fully without further research, but the congruence of patterns in the two countries might seem persuasive. Thus it is interesting to compare these findings to those of another recent historical study of crime, that by J. J. Tobias, which has related nineteenth-century crime patterns to modernisation in England.

Tobias' results are at variance with those found here for Germany and France at several points. Tobias claims to have discerned an actual long-term decline in crime during the century, for instance, and he found no recurrent connection with fluctuations in economic conditions. His study concerns England rather than the continent and of course it is possible that the English experience was distinctive. At the same time, Tobias' conclusions must be considered exceedingly tentative because he often does not distinguish between types of crimes and because, since he opted for literary rather than quantitative sources, his conclusions are necessarily impressionistic. Interestingly, however, at one very important point his findings are consistent with ours. Among juvenile offenders, at least, Tobias found very high and perhaps rising rates of crime in the initial stages of industrialisation but then a decrease after about 1850. As in Germany and France, in other words, a period of substantial urbanisation and industrialisation coincided with a period of high crime rates followed by some stabilisation or even a decline in criminality. The transitional stage in the modernisation of criminality is thus confirmed by his findings.

Tobias' explanations are traditional. High rates during the first half of the century are attributed to the lack of opportunities for "honest work," to poor educational facilities, to congested housing, to "the pernicious effects of a morally unhealthy urban environment." Most important, however, is his emphasis on social disorganisation: urbanisation meant the breakdown of the family, personal disorientation, a cultural shock which naturally led to crime. The eventual stabilisation or decrease in criminality, then, came about because of a "more settled social environment." By this time the number of immigrants to the city had fallen off and cities were taking steps to make urban life more pleasant. Also, the improvement of urban police forces, the increased certainty of punishment due to judicial reforms, improvements in education and, finally, the development of reform schools—an interesting argument, given what is known about the effects of reform schools today—all helped to reduce crime.

The inadequacies of this interpretation by now are basically familiar; there is no need to belabor them. However, the Tobias book and its popularity do illustrate the persistence of this sort of outlook, and it does provide a useful contrast to the interpretation outlined here. Crime is not, we argue, a symptom of social and moral disorganisation; the argument stressing these factors would be hard pressed to explain patterns of crime in any but the initial stages of nineteenth-century industrialisation, and even there it is inadequate. Changing patterns of crime do reflect and reveal changing value and social systems, but not "normlessness" or social disorganisation. Rising theft rates indicate rising expectations, the spread of "modern" economic values and, with some qualification, are characteristic of modern, urban society. In a sense, therefore, theft represents an adaptation to modern social goals, although it of course reflects a rejection of—or even a protest against—socially legitimate means of reaching such goals. Violence, on the other hand, represents a traditional form of criminal behaviour, and its rise in a situation of change reflects the retention rather than the breakdown of traditional behaviour. Interpersonal violence is an expression of frustration and tension, a form of social conflict. To some extent it might be viewed as a form of primitive, "unrealistic" protest against developments in society and the economy. Thus criminal violence might usefully be seen as an index of social tensions, with drops in violence indicating reductions in tension and, in the long run, the abandonment of traditional forms of behaviour. . . .

Because crime was normally an individual act, easier to mount than organised protest, it may have reflected new expectations earlier than the strikes and riots that have more commonly been the subject of historical attention. The relationship between banditry and other social unrest has been noted for groups on the verge of modernisation; the present study confirms this, in broad outline, for the period in which urban crime was in transition, expressing a new intensity of conflict but in rather traditional forms. We can add now the possibility that the modernisation of crime, after this dramatic period, was a vital part of more adaptive social change. Judging by the larger patterns of crime, modern offenders, however much they felt left out of modern society, wanted in and saw crime as a way to realise modern values.

Part 3

MATURE
INDUSTRIAL
SOCIETY

1850-1918

Working class scene, London, 1877

With industrialization well established in central and western Europe, some of the more dramatic social dislocations eased, if only because a smaller percentage of the population was moving from countryside to city—that is, from a traditional to a dynamic environment. Major problems of adaptation remained, however; the conversion of rural people to new values had just begun. Many workers were still new to the factory setting. Even some older workers, who had successfully preserved elements of a traditional approach to work during the early stages of industrialization, had major problems of adjustment as industrialization became more firmly entrenched.

And the nature of industrial society continued to change. For factory workers and artisans, the introduction of new techniques and the rise of big business organizations created obvious difficulties. Women in many social classes felt the impact of change more acutely in this period than ever before. In the early industrial revolution, middle-class women preserved many traditional goals. They worked closely with their husbands in business. They expected to have many children. Working-class women faced a less familiar situation, particularly when they worked outside the home, but again their outlook probably remained fairly traditional. They expected to marry, after which the vast majority would stop working outside the home, and service to their families would largely define their lives. In the later nineteenth century a declining birthrate gave women more free time, and as most women were now exposed to schooling, and a minority to advanced schooling, rising levels of education produced new expectations. In some cases expectations outstripped opportunity, for the definition of a woman's "place" changed only slowly. In the middle class particularly, problems of adjustment became increasingly obvious. By the 1900s, one result, in many countries, was an intense feminist movement.

The late nineteenth century, in which modern technological and organizational structures were well established (though still evolving), was probably the key period of change for women and workers. Before this—with some exceptions such as lower-class sexual behavior aside—

traditional values had been preserved, even in radically new settings. But was this new round of change really modernization, to be lumped with earlier alterations of mentality among, say, middle-class men? Here is a clear test for the frequent claim that modernization is a catchall, without a sufficient linkage among various kinds of change.

Many of the attitudes formed during this period of maturing industrialization proved quite durable. Although many workers were new to their situation, and the nature of industrial life continued to change, a recognizable working-class culture began to emerge—one major outgrowth of the general modernization process that endures in most respects to the present day. Many of the new ambiguities in women's lives also persisted. At the same time, the broader popular culture was changing in directions that seem quite familiar to us today. It was in the later nineteenth century that a new interest in sports arose, soon to become a consuming passion for many people.

The outlines of modern society were becoming clearer. Most people in western Europe were now accustomed to change, so questions arising from the sheer confrontation between tradition and innovation gave way to more subtle issues. Was the new interest in leisure, for example, an expression of modern man's alienation, his desire to escape monotonous labor and recover, if only vicariously, some of the aggression and passion of his primitive ancestors? Or was the rise of leisure a more positive sign, an indication of growing affluence and leisure time and an expression of the desire to develop new fields of individual achievement? The changing position of youth might be seen as an application of modern values to a new age group, or as an expression of stress caused by modern institutions and family life, forcing isolation of age segments that did not readily fit the mold. Similar questions apply to more familiar topics: Did the rise of socialism signify a growing belief in progress and an orderly political process on the part of working people, or the institutionalization of class warfare and periodic acts of violence? Was imperialism the product of a confident, dynamic society or of a society that translated its insecurity into aggression abroad? With change established as an inescapable part of modern life, the need to assess its meaning became paramount.

BIBLIOGRAPHY

The history of women is beginning to receive considerable attention, but completed work remains scanty. J. A. Banks has written *Prosperity and Parenthood: A Study of Family Planning among the Victorian Middle Classes* (New York, 1954), and with Oliver Banks, *Feminism and Family Planning* (Liverpool, 1964). Good general introductions to recent writing on the history of women are Martha Vicinus, ed., *Suffer and Be*

Still: Women in the Victorian Age (Bloomington, Ind., 1972), and *A Widening Sphere: Changing Roles of Victorian Women* (Bloomington, Ind., 1977). Other valuable collections are Lois Banner and Mary Hartman, *Clio's Consciousness Raised* (New York, 1974), and Renate Budenthal and Claudia Koonz, eds., *Becoming Visible: Women in European History* (New York, 1976). Another recent study is Duncan Crow, *The Victorian Woman* (London, 1971). Some key trends among working-class women are discussed in Margaret Hewitt, *Wives and Mothers in Victorian Industry* (New York, 1958). William L. O'Neill, *Woman Movement: Feminism in the United States and England* (Chicago, 1969), is a good brief survey of this important movement at the turn of the century. Two important surveys are Patricia Branca, *European Women since 1750* (London, 1978), and Joan Scott and Louise Tilly, *Women, Work and Family* (New York, 1978).

Studies that deal with workers, as opposed to formal protest movements by labor, are not overabundant. For Britain, E. P. Thompson, *The Making of the English Working Class* (New York, 1964), and Eric J. Hobsbawm, *Labouring Men: Studies in the History of Labour* (New York, 1964), are works of major importance. Daniel Wallkowitz and Peter N. Stearns, eds., *Workers in the Industrial Revolution* (New Brunswick, N.J., 1974), covers several countries. On Germany, Guenther Roth, *Social Democrats in Imperial Germany: A Study in Working-Class Isolation and National Integration* (Totowa, N.J., 1963), relates the rise of socialism to the situation of the working classes. See also Harvey Mitchell and Peter N. Stearns, *Workers and Protest: The European Labor Movement, the Working Classes, and the Origins of Social Democracy, 1890–1914* (Itasca, Ill., 1971), and Peter N. Stearns, *Lives of Labor: Work in Maturing Industrial Society* (New York, 1975). To follow continuities in working-class culture into our own time, see John H. Goldthorpe et al., *The Affluent Worker in the Class Structure* (New York, 1969). See also Robert Blauner, *Alienation and Freedom: The Factory Worker and His Industry* (Chicago, 1964).

Carlo M. Cipolla, *Literacy and Development in the West* (Baltimore, 1969), and Geoffrey H. Bantock, *Culture, Industrialization and Education* (New York, 1969), provide a general background for the modern history of education. There are no overall surveys in English on the development of the French educational systems. Michalina Vaughan and Margaret S. Archer, *Social Conflict and Educational Change in England and France, 1798–1848* (New York, 1971), is good on the early period. E. H. Reisner, *Nationalism and Education since 1789* (New York, 1923), deals with another important theme, the inculcation of nationalist values through the schools. F. Ponteil, *Histoire de l'enseignement en France* (Paris, 1966), is a fine French survey. On rural education, Roger Thabault, *Education and Change in a Village Community* (New York, 1971). English education has been extensively studied; see B. Simon, *Studies in the History of Education, 1780–1920* (London, 1960), and Howard C. Barnard, *A Short History of English Education* (New York, 1955). R. D. Altick,

The English Common Reader: A Social History of the Mass Reading Public, 1800–1900 (Chicago, 1957), deals with the uses of growing literacy.

The history of leisure is another of the important subjects that has not been given much attention by serious historians. For a brief general interpretation, see Michael Marrus, *The Rise of Leisure* (St. Louis, 1976), and *The Emergence of Leisure* (New York, 1974). Peter C. McIntosh, *Sport in Society* (New York, 1963), and *Physical Education in England since 1800* (London, 1969), are useful. Eugen Weber, "Gymnastics and Sports in Fin de Siècle France: Opium of the Classes?" *American Historical Review* (1971), pp. 70–98, see the rise of sports as an aid to political conservatism. See also Foster Dulles, *A History of Recreation* (New York, 1965). On drink, Brian Harrison, *Drink and the Victorians* (Pittsburgh, 1971).

Age groups are just beginning to catch historical interest. See, for the United States, Joseph Kett, *Rites of Passage: Adolescence in America, 1790 to the Present* (New York, 1977). Peter N. Stearns, *Old Age in European Society* (New York, 1977), deals with another important group.

Middle-Class Women

PATRICIA BRANCA

There has never been much question that the middle-class woman of the nineteenth century was in a novel position, but there has been great debate over what the novelty consisted of. Some historians see the woman trapped in an essentially idle domestic role, praised for her purity and lack of sexual desire, pampered as an ornament, but given no effective life functions other than having a few social graces and bearing children. They note that this woman was part of some positive changes. The middle class pioneered in birth control, though this can be seen as a decision by sexless women to limit their responsibilities still further or by harried husbands to reduce the drain on the family budget. From the middle class, unquestionably, came women reformers and ultimately feminists, but they are seen as rebels against the middle-class way of life, its vacuity and boredom, not as positive products of it. Indeed, the Victorian woman, in this view, has only negative impact on modernization, symbolizing values and constraints against which really modern women had to fight, and must fight still.

Patricia Branca takes a different view. Admitting the primacy of the household for women, she sees the middle-class wife and mother as a key agent of change. Far from functionless, she was burdened with huge responsibilities, many of which were newly defined. Motherhood, for example, became much more arduous with fathers at work and a new sense of concern for children's health and well-being. (Changes in the concept of the child here become central to the life of adult women.) As mothers and housewives, women worked in novel urban surroundings, amid intense criticism for failures ranging from sloppiness to inadequate child care. On the whole, despite great anxiety, women met the challenge by applying much the same mentality that their husbands were developing in the business and professional worlds. This meant, above all, a desire to gain new dominion over their lot. Birth control, stressed again as a middle-class innovation, here stems from women's modernized outlook, their openness to new techniques, and their desire for satisfactory self-expression.

Ending with the late nineteenth century, Branca leaves open the question of woman's future. Would they be able to apply their modernized mentality to a wider sphere, or did their horizons remain too purely domestic even to cope with the implications of birth control itself in reducing the domestic function? Was their modernization, in other words, part of the larger social process, or was it distinctly female, leaving women changed but still trapped in a set of gender roles that would find them ill prepared for the twentieth century.

The Victorian woman's life would never be quite the same with the birth of her first child. Most of her thoughts, her worries, and her energies would revolve around her child, and with each child the responsibilities grew more and more intense. She did not feel confident in the adequacy of her maternal instincts and so she worried continually about her child and its care. Her major concern was for the child's health. With every sickness of childhood, the mother's anxieties heightened. Even the most basic aspects of child care, for example, feeding and discipline, were to create serious problems for her. She continually sought advice on the best method of care for her child. But in the end, as was the case with her own health, there was very little she could do to improve the child's situation given the limited means available and the traditionalism which still maintained a strong hold on this part of her life.

With each new birth, the Victorian mother experienced many anxious moments wondering if the babe would live or die. The fate of thousands of infants dying prematurely every year was to become a burning issue in Victorian society. The outcry against the needless tragedy of infant mortality continued throughout the century. The sentiment expressed was similar to that concerning the state of maternal mortality, but more intense because of the greater numbers involved and the helplessness of the victim. A declining sense of fatalism and a growing determination that this tragedy need not be, were again much in evidence. A typical reaction was that of Dr. Alfred Fennings, author of *Every Mother's Book: or the Child's Best Doctor*, who noted that

> The OMNISCIENT GOD never intended that nearly half the babies born in this country should die as they now do, before they are five years old. Carelessness . . . and a general ignorance of simple and safe remedies to cure their peculiar diseases have been the fatal causes.

Dr. R. Hall Bakewell, who wrote a series of articles on "Infant Mortality, and Its Causes" for *The British Mothers' Journal*, was of the same belief.

> We cannot deny that there must be something wrong in the management of children during the early years. Children are not sent into the world to

die, they are sent to live to a natural term of man's life; and a system by which one-fifth of all who are born never see the first anniversary of their birth, must be radically wrong somewhere.

These are just two examples of the growing concern over infant care. There were hundreds of books published and articles written specifically on child care. The books were widely publicized: for example, Dr. Fennings' book was advertised regularly in *The Mothers' Friend*, a monthly magazine. One of the advertisements made the following claim:

Do not let your children die. Fennings' *Every Mother's Book* contains everything a mother ought to know about her child's Feeding, Teething, Sleeping, Weaning, also Hints, Cautions, Remedies for all diseases, and Secrets worth 500 Guineas. Mothers and Fathers, save your child's life by reading it. Its instructions have already saved thousands.

However, in spite of the intense concern, in spite of the sage advice, infant mortality remained a perplexing problem for the Victorian mother. The infant deathbed scene so popular with the religious writers, the grief of a bereaved mother at the loss of her child, which was a regular feature in many of the women's magazines, reflected grim reality. . . .

doctors, who gave it eight calomel powders, applied one leech to the chest, one blister to the chest, six mustard plasters, and gave it antimony wine and other medicines in abundance. Yet the poor thing died!' The friend in amazement replied, "Died! It would have been a miracle if it had lived."

It is difficult to say when women sought medical attention for a sick child. Judging from the mortality rates it would appear that it was not often enough or soon enough. Traditional ideas about childhood illnesses were still very strong, as indicated by Dr. Bakewell in his last article on infant mortality. His warning was that

I would caution my readers against the notion, too prevalent among mothers, that ailments will get well of themselves when the child has cut all its teeth. Very frequently we see children suffering from scrofulous and other constitutional diseases, who are undergoing no treatment, because their mothers 'fancy' it is nothing but the teeth.

He also noted that many children died of bronchitis because their mothers failed to take them to a physician soon enough. Mothers ignorant of the disease treated it as a cold, but even a delay of twenty-four hours could make the case hopeless because of the rapid progress of the disease in infants. But in many cases even when a doctor's advice was sought it was of little use, because of the lack of knowledge of pediatric care. Traditionalism and the state of medical practice supplemented each other.

Hence the growing concern about children's health enhanced anxieties on the mothers' part and at the same time, in public discussions, produced a barrage of criticisms of maternal care. Not yet would the concern produce the kind of knowledge about the infant's health and care that was needed. As with the advice on women's health, the advice for child care was too general, based in fact on the same three principles of general health: regulation of diet, proper clothing and plenty of fresh air and exercise. There was little concrete assistance for the mother faced with serious illness and the prospect of frequent infant death. The middle-class mother, no longer resigned to infant mortality, had to feel an acute sense of helplessness and frustration when she realized that despite her efforts and intentions the fate of her child was still so very precarious.

Along with the growing concern for the physical health of the child a profound interest developed in securing the child's mental and moral health. Here too a new attitude toward children was beginning to make strong inroads among the middle-class by mid-century and was to alter child-rearing methods significantly by the end of the century. The child was beginning to be viewed as an individual with very particular needs which only a loving mother could fulfill. The ramifications of this new concept of the child for the Victorian mother was indeed great, as they increased her responsibilities to the child even more. . . .

The deliberate limitation of family size was one of the principal contributions of middle-class women to the modernization process of women generally. This decision flowed not only from the new definitions of childhood and motherhood; it represented the only means available in the mid-nineteenth century of resolving several key problems arising from the new situation and new consciousness of women. As manager of the household the middle-class woman, confronted with limited means, was acutely aware of the expenses involved in maintaining her children in the new fashion. Also birth control was the most practical means of coping with the unresolved problems of maternal mortality.

The positive aspects of the decision to control births were perhaps the most compelling for the middle-class woman. As we will see, the middle-class woman's new image of self involved a new sexuality—one of more intense personal enjoyment. In order to maximize sexual enjoyment, it was necessary to prevent the traditional consequences of sex—pregnancy. Through the adoption of birth control the middle-class woman found the most important ingredient to liberation. . . .

It is probable that the most significant devices involved in the middle-class birth rate decline were the sponge, the douche, and the vaginal diaphragm. One cannot ignore the fact that all the other methods—abstinence, *coitus interruptus,* and the condom—were well-known before the nineteenth century, yet it was not until the introduction and development of the three new methods of birth control that the birth rate began to drop significantly. The fact that the newer methods were designed for the female at a time when she was beginning to exert more and more control over her body also cannot be ignored. Just as the woman rejected the fatalistic attitude related to pain in childbirth and sought chloroform, just as she rejected the fatalistic attitude toward the discomfort and burden of nursing and sought artificial feeding methods, so she rejected the fatalistic attitude to the inevitability of pregnancy and sought contraceptive devices. Is it mere coincidence that as the burdens and responsibilities of motherhood increased the demand for and production of birth control methods particularly for the woman also increased? Overall, the array of available contraceptive devices makes it abundantly clear that the woman was an important factor in the decision-making process. This is not to imply that the husband had no part to play, though the advertisement for the Check Pessary suggested that this might sometimes be the case. The mutuality of decision-making so commonly invoked by the marriage manuals may well have operated in this area. We can reasonably be sure that the woman was no passive partner and that her changing values and situation—even more than economic factors—heavily influenced the decision taken, whether by husband and wife together or, as was technically possible, by the wife alone.

The Victorian middle-class woman experienced dramatic changes in her role as mother. She challenged the traditional attitude toward infant mortality and maternal mortality by seeking advice on better care for herself and the child. Unfortunately, until very late in the nineteenth century, the challenge was successful only in so far as she was able to limit the number of children she had, and thereby lessen the risk of death for herself and her child. Here again, the development of birth control is a vital feature of the history of Victorian motherhood.

The Victorian woman took her role as mother seriously. She realized the importance of the new emphasis on the intimate relationship of mother to child, which added significantly not only to the physical work involved with child care, but also to the mental strain on the mother's part. She assumed complete responsibility for the future health and happiness of her child. The new birth control methods aided her in meeting her responsibilities as mother and helped eliminate an important threat to her life and health. . . .

After an examination of some of the more important aspects in the life of the middle-class woman, one begins seriously to question if the Victorian woman, as she has so long been depicted, ever really existed. Certainly, the woman whose life was characterized as leisurely, dependent, prudish, and boring was not the married middle-class woman of the nineteenth century. Whether or not the image applies to upper-class women remains to be investigated, and it is a task worth undertaking in nineteenth-century English social history. The woman portrayed in this study perhaps lacked some of the glamor and romantic flavor of the woman in the image. However her life, viewed in terms of realities, in terms of the problems she encountered, gives the Victorian woman more meaning and substance than ever before. Within the context of the family, her role was not only functional but central and crucial. One could not possibly understand anything about the Victorian family without understanding the woman in the family, who nurtured it, who managed it, who comforted it. In her role as mistress of the house, in her relationship with domestics and most importantly, in her role as mother, the middle-class woman of the nineteenth century defined herself.

Yet the middle-class woman's historical role transcended the boundaries of the family during the nineteenth century, for she was caught up in the broader transformation of English society. In her daily functions she began to develop attitudes and behavior patterns that form part of the process of modernization. The evolution was incomplete, even well after the 1880s, for the middle-class woman retained important links with traditional values. And assessment in these terms is complicated by the failure, heretofore, to apply any but economic criteria of modernization to the history of women. Nevertheless, the stresses and problems with which this study has been concerned cannot be understood without relating them to a more fundamental evolution, in which middle-class women led the way. If other women, many of them unmarried, seem as individuals closer to a modern set of values during the nineteenth century, the married middle-class women constituted the first large category to undergo the modernization process, precisely because they applied it within the context of the family.

Before proceeding with this discussion, it is necessary to elaborate the precise definition of modernization. Modernization involves industrialization and urbanization on a broad scale. Concentrated population centers replace isolated rural communities as the normal human environment. The nature of work obviously changes, and the bulk of the populace is removed from the land. And modernization brings about not only changes in work and style of living, but also a new attitude of mind, which in the long run is probably its more significant feature.

Modern man has conventionally been defined as possessing a mentality that, for the most part, is open to innovation and new experiences. This involves belief in planning and organization in every aspect of life, in the benefits of science and technology, and a conviction that one's environment was calculable, that it could be improved. The modern mind rejects fatalism, and it is present- and future-oriented rather than backward-looking. Characterization of modern man in many ways defines the new middle-class man of the nineteenth century, and in combination the modernization theme and progressive middle-class values are familiar enough. But what about modern woman? Since this study claimed from the outset that the Victorian middle-class woman was the first modern woman, it is necessary to apply the definition of modernization to her life. Did she follow the same pattern? Did she share the same outlook?

The process of modernization was never a voluntary process for women (nor was it for men). It was more a result of outside forces, the new pressures of urban industrial society coming together and making their impact in the nineteenth century, first on the values of the middle class. More than her upper-class sister or her working-class sister, the middle-class woman, in order to maintain herself in this period of great transition, had to adapt to new economic means and a new environment. The working- and upper-class woman long maintained more traditional life styles. For example, the upper-class woman never encountered the economic pressures which continually perplexed the middle-class woman in her effort to maintain an appropriate living standard. The upper-class woman could still afford her retinue of servants and enjoy the society and seasons of the fashionable world during most of the nineteenth century. While the working-class woman shared more of the experiences of the middle-class woman, on the whole, and was certainly deeply affected by industrialization, her life was restricted by a number of factors. Her material means were long insufficient to enable her to alter greatly her lot in life. Her education and outlook were not the same as that of the middle-class woman. Her attitudes toward ordering her home and children remained tradition-bound for the greater part of the nineteenth century. In some respects, in the initial reaction to industrialization the working-class woman developd a special function in preserving as many traditional familial values as possible, to cushion the shock of change. In contrast, the middle-class woman was ultimately able not only to react to change but to initiate some changes on her own. The primary impulse toward modernization stemmed from the middle-class woman's accession to a modest level of prosperity which ultimately brought about a new life style—a lifestyle defined by middle-class values and goals—which neither imitated the aristocracy or attempted to throw up purely traditional defenses against change within the family.

The impact of urban living was profound for the middle-class woman of the nineteenth century. The problems of urbanization—overcrowding, polluted waters and air—were not of great concern for upper-class women, who maintained control of the better sections of the city during most of the century. Also the upper-class woman was able to maintain her traditional rural ties by keeping a place in the country. However, urban society was the only life for the new middle-class woman and in this she shared many of the problems of urbanization with the working-class woman. But in contrast to the ability of many working-class wives to recreate a supportive family network, the middle-class woman was more on her own. Admittedly, until a serious investigation is made into the demographic changes of the middle class in the nineteenth century, we have to rely upon impressionistic evidence. It appears from the literature of the day that one of the special problems for the middle-class woman was the frequent changing of residence. The results of this constant state of flux was that the middle-class woman had no sense of roots, no sense of belonging to an established community, and often lacked strong extended family ties. It is interesting to note that in all the various sources used for this study, there is no mention of any type of family relationship beyond the nuclear family. Never once was there a reference to the role of grandparents, aunts, uncles, or cousins. This lack of relationships beyond the immediate family was particularly striking in the discussions on pregnancy. It would seem likely that at this very important event in a woman's life she would have her mother or sister or some other close relative assist her. However, the middle-class woman was advised to seek the aid of a friendly neighbor. The absence of guidance from experienced kin could have accounted for the middle-class woman's need for such fundamental advice on child care. Also the middle-class woman would be able to innovate in child-rearing more easily without the more tradition-bound influence of her mother. She was certainly freer to adopt artificial feeding methods and contraceptive techniques.

Another important aspect of the modernization process in the lives of married middle-class woman, which must be viewed as both cause and result, was the declining influence of religion in their lives. Historians have generally accepted and documented the overall decline of religion in the nineteenth century. It is well known that the returns of the Religious Census of 1851 indicated severe limitations in the numbers attending church, for approximately half the population was not present at religious services. Contemporaries claimed that widespread absenteeism was due mainly to a waning of religion among the working class, and subsequent historians have generally accepted this position. However, more recently, it has been noted that "there was proportionately as much conscious unbelief, if not indifference, in the Victorian middle-class as amongst the workers . . ." Yet even if this point is accepted it is tempting to assume that indifference was confined to men only; and the image of the Victorian middle-class woman as extremely pious and religious continues to persist. However, there were some indications of changes in women's outlook during the nineteenth century which suggest, at least, a growing modification of traditional religious beliefs. There is no need to claim complete separation or a defined anti-religious sentiment; but religion lost some of its meaning for middle-class women.

One indication of the declining influence of religion was the increasing secularism of the material read by women. In the early years of the century, the printed matter for women was primarily of a religious nature. By the second half of the century, the literature was almost completely lacking in religious inspiration. The few religious magazines, such as *The British*

Mothers' Magazine, constantly bemoaned the decline of religion among the fairer sex. One example of the new trend of secularism was found in the editorial policy of the very popular *EDM* [Englishwoman's Domestic Magazine], which stated that it was the policy of the magazine to exclude all religious composition from its pages. It would not answer any theological questions, or even publish poetry of a religious nature. Looking through the hundreds of magazines printed in the nineteenth century for women, one is left with the impression that women were more concerned with the condition of their wash or the nature of their complexions than the state of their souls.

In sum, middle-class women shared with other groups many of the general pressures of urbanization. They shared also a decline of religious interest, and this may have had a distinctive impact on them because of their exposure to secular reading materials. Their ability to modernize was particularly enhanced by an unusually nucleated family structure and by the ability to forge a standard of living above the subsistence level. Other causes may have been involved, for we are in a better position to describe the modernization process than to assess the reasons for its special applicability to middle-class women, but even this short list suffices to explain why middle-class women were able to innovate in response to new pressures.

But not all middle-class women could adapt. Even for most, as we shall see, modernization should not be regarded as a triumphant conquest of progress over tradition but as a painful, often confusing, reaction to change. Some women could not manage even this, especially given the real physical burdens that still defined their lot. As with most social groups, middle-class women divided between adapters and nonadapters, although we are not yet in a position to suggest the size of the latter group and the boundary line is admittedly unclear.

The rapidity and vastness of change could cause a sense of bewilderment, which was especially difficult for many women to cope with because they had very little outlet for their tensions. The growing sense of insecurity seen in the many letters asking for advice is one sign of the tensions modern society produced in the life of the middle-class woman. Forced into the mainstream of a new style of living, the middle-class woman developed anxieties, as we have suggested in the study of her various roles in the family. The changing concept of motherhood is a case in point. The middle-class woman believed that she could be a better mother so she ventured new methods of child-rearing. However, she was still very insecure about the new ways; hence the continual seeking of advice, perhaps as a source of reassurance. In some respects aspirations changed more rapidly than reality, as in the desire for better health or for an orderly improvement in the standard of living, which added frustrations to anxieties.

Not surprisingly, given the tensions of initial modernization, some symptoms of disturbance emerged among some middle-class women. There is evidence that some women sought refuge in alcohol and drugs. The subject of alcoholism among women was discussed a number of times, indicating that it was a serious problem for some. In 1870, a letter appeared in the *EDM* from "A Sufferer of Low Spirits," asking advice from other women on her problem with depression and alcohol. Especially in the health manuals, women were often warned about the ill effects of alcohol. In the manual, *The New Home; Or Wedded Life*, the story was told of a young girl who came to realize the folly of taking a little gin, or brandy, or beer every time she was low, overworked, or simply out of sorts. The relief it offered was very brief, but the destruction it wrought upon her health was lasting. Another indication that women might have resorted to alcohol is suggested by the article, "Intemperance in Women, with Special Reference to its Effects on the Reproductive System," which appeared in *The British Medical Journal*. The author noted that one of the principal causes of alcoholism among women was domestic problems.

Drugs were commonly used in the nineteenth century and were readily available, as was seen in the discussion of infant mortality. There is, again, no direct evidence about the use of drugs by women, but some contemporary observers noted a problem here too. For example, Dr. Robert Dick, in his health manual, made the following observation on the need of drugs by women:

> Many women would pass the most indifferent night; many would be inadequate to the task or duty of entertaining their guests or meeting their friends; in others the chagrins of life would prey too severely; regrets and disappointments and painful reminiscents would visit them too acutely did they not deaden the poignancy of suffering, actual or remembered, by the 'drowsy syrups'; . . . or by something analogous.

He remarked that many women, because of the pressures of society, needed artificial sedatives or stimulants, such as opium, morphia, hyoscyamus, prussic acid, camphor, musk and valerian. Further indication of the probability of considerable drug use comes in the many home remedies found in the manuals and periodicals for headaches or sleeplessness which included strong dosages of drugs. The following is a preparation recommended for use as a sedative: orange flower water—2 oz., laurel water—1 oz., syrup of poppies—½ oz., acetate of morphia—½ grain. A teaspoon of the above was to be taken every hour.

All of this, obviously, involves impressionistic evidence. There is no reason to suggest that alcoholism or abuse of drugs were the normal lot of middle-class women or even that they necessarily followed from the tensions of modernization in every case. The extent of the phenomena cannot presently be determined, but they must be taken into account both because they suggest an interesting group of women who could not cope with their lot and because they emphasize some of the pressures that women more generally encountered during the period.

The more durable impact of modernization on the life of the middle-class woman can be seen more directly by looking back upon the discussion of mistress of the house. It was shown that the middle-class woman's most important considerations here were time and money. She never seemed to have enough of either, so they required of her careful planning and organization. Admittedly, she was not totally successful in meeting these requirements, but she did display a willingness to accept and try the new concepts. She was the major purchaser of the proliferating manuals that proclaimed the new science of domestic economy. She seemed to realize that she had novel problems which required new solutions.

One of the clearest illustrations of the middle-class woman's willingness to participate in the mainstream of modern society was her acceptance of innovation and technology into her home. The sewing machine is one very important example. Objections were voiced concerning the sewing machine, similar in many ways to the objections roused early in the century over the introduction of machines into industry. There was a lament that the sewing machines would destroy the long-valued skill of hand sewing—that element of personal touch associated with the craft and womanhood. However, the criticism was never persuasive enough to deter the middle-class woman as she readily adopted this new invention and eagerly sought information on it. No doubt the primary reason women welcomed this advance in technology was necessity. There were just so many hours in the day, and so much time to spend on sewing. With the sewing machine, the middle-class woman was able efficiently and economically to come to terms with both problems. However, one cannot neglect the fact that she was willing to give up, almost overnight, a long tradition of hand sewing in favor of a machine which did take away much of the personal touch. One could further suggest that the sewing machine was, in some ways, an expression of the woman's growing sense of individualism within the household. In buying the machine she acquired a new piece of property that was hers, as well as one that worked primarily to her own benefit. This does not mean that she was the heroine of passive consumerism as depicted in the conventional image—the manifestation of the paraphernalia of gentility—but in her own sphere she was trying to define herself, as well as make her life easier, in new ways.

Viewed in the light of modernization, the familiar list of other household innovations that gained ground in the later nineteenth century assumes new importance. One could argue that if the middle-class woman had not been so receptive to innovation, the process of modernization, which depended on mechanization, could not have progressed as rapidly as it did. As was noted in the earlier discussion of the mistress of the house, the middle-class woman was the prime consumer of many of the new products of industrialization. She was the only woman who both needed and could afford the advances in technology. The upper-class woman with her retinue of servants did not necessarily need the innovations, while the working-class women could not afford them. Other major industries, such as advertising and women's magazines, depended heavily on the middle-class woman as consumer. In other words, because of her new attitudes and her decision-making power, the middle-class woman emerged as a significant force for consumer-related economic development.

There are other aspects of the process of modernization in the life of the middle-class woman which are not as easy to recognize but equally significant. In the discussion on health it was shown that the middle-class woman was intimately involved with many of the changing attitudes now associated with modernization, such as sanitation. Also, the middle-class woman more and more rejected the traditional, fatalistic attitude toward death, especially where infant and maternal mortality were concerned. By seeking advice about her health and that of her children, she demonstrated the belief that her world could be ordered and improved. She expressed a growing reliance on science; first through her purchase of health manuals which were generally written by doctors, and second by her increasing use of doctors to tend to her health problems. There was some evidence that she clung more to traditional ways in this particular aspect of her life than as mistress of the house. The reliance on quack medicines was certainly based to a great extent on tradition, but we have noted that the key to success for many of the patent medicines in the nineteenth century was the claim to innovation and scientific expertise, most often in the forms of bogus testimonials from doctors. It was also pointed out that one major reason for apparently traditionalist behavior lay with the reluctance of the medical profession to implement available innovations rather than with the woman.

The Victorian woman's personal life was profoundly altered by modernization. This was seen very clearly in her receptiveness to chloroform, artificial feeding and contraceptive devices. In all three cases, especially the last, there was evidence of the middle-class woman's growing desire to order her own personal comfort, thereby demonstrating a sense of strong personal autonomy. In the discussion of contraception the development of a modern mentality was most evident. Women accepted contraceptive devices for selfish reasons in part, to insure their own physical well-being by limiting the number of children they bore, and to increase their opportunities for sexual pleasure and gratification.

There were, of course, ambiguities in "modern" attitudes themselves. For example, the woman's desire for greater personal autonomy was juxtaposed with the equally modern notion that as mother she should devote herself intensively to the care and attention of her child. This is a dilemma in the modernization of women that has even yet to be resolved. And these and other modern attitudes did not win complete acceptance by the 1870s, for the hold of traditional values was still strong. The period covered in this study emerges as an important transitional stage. The advent of birth control is perhaps the most obvious sign of the development of new attitudes, and by releasing some energies from traditional functions it sets the stage for other developments. But we can now see that this change was part of a larger modernization package, which saw the middle-class woman seeking to define herself, albeit within the family, as an individual and to gain new control over her body.

The changes in behavior and outlook that did occur in this transitional period were both marked and confused by the constant carping from contemporary publicists, which has in turn tended to mislead historians dealing with Victorian women. Contemporary observers found the middle-class woman a convenient vehicle for criticism of modernity generally. They sensed her desire for new things and therefore exaggerated her indulgence in luxuries. Many critics, some of the strongest of which came from among the religious spokesmen, found an audience among middle-class women themselves. This undoubtedly reflected an uncertainty among many of these women about the new ways, even as they largely persisted in them. There was also some unintended coincidence involved: reading matter that was sought primarily for recipes or patterns often contained a lament over the decline of true womanhood. And this raises again the question of the impact of the criticism in heightening the middle-class woman's sense of insecurity and anxiety. Victorian society, in terms of its official culture, was very demanding of its women. It expected them to be perfect ladies, perfect wives, and perfect mothers. The Victorian woman was to have an observing eye, a calculating head, a skilful hand, concise speech, a gentle step, external tidiness and internal purity. She was expected to exercise constant patience and forebearance, in spite of narrow means, inconvenient houses, crying children and preoccupied husbands. Her responsibilities were indeed overwhelming, and if she failed she had only herself to blame:

> . . . on you *fair* and amiable creature who was born to assuage our sufferings, dispel care, wipe away the tears of grief, and to exalt all our enjoyments, much more depends than you commonly imagine. For, if we so frequently remark that marriages of attachment end in anything but cordiality and happiness,—if it be obvious that indifference has crept in where all was once love and respect,—it is (we are sorry to state) but too probable that the lady has originated this fearful change. The angel has become a demon of domestic strife.

To be sure, middle-class men encountered some criticism of their life style as well, but it was never as intense as that directed against women. For women, the adverse public culture could not only cause feelings of guilt about new patterns of behavior but could inhibit a consciousness of the significance of this behavior. Women were seeking more autonomy and control but they may not fully have realized their own goals, because they lacked public sanction. Here is another complicating factor that requires consideration in an understanding of the modernization of women.

Clearly, the middle class needs renewed attention if we are to grasp the dynamics of change in nineteenth-century Britain, and indeed elsewhere. The study of Victorian women suggests that the middle class had not only its own life style but a complex series of problems that have rarely been appreciated in the cursory treatment the class has received from historians. Its men have been too often dismissed as exploiters or conquerors; its women as useless ornaments barely deserving a serious history. In fact, while the social historian cannot point to the stark misery that has lent drama to many of the treatments of the working class, the problems with which the middle class was grappling have at least as much enduring significance. Aspirations were often unmet in a life that remained rigorous in many ways. The class did advance, and Victorian women did benefit from the modernization process. But the changes were hard-won, for new ideas were the product neither of leisure nor of luxury. Most middle-class women had enough margin to avoid taking refuge in traditional family functions alone, but they suffered considerable anxiety as they tried to develop a new life style. That many of the behavior patterns they developed ultimately became part of the modernization of women more generally is a tribute to their ingenuity as well as their influence. But the complexities of the transitional period have enduring significance as well, for they have by no means been shaken off. Here is where middle-class women, like the middle class as a whole, deserve a careful historical assessment, and not merely a characterization.

The Adaptation of Workers

PETER N. STEARNS

      This essay examines various forms of adaptation or alienation found among German workers in the late nineteenth century. Despite the fact that industrialization had begun many decades before, many German workers were still in an early stage of adjustment. A significant minority maintained traditionalist views. Another group had picked up almost middle-class values with regard to individualism and mobility aspirations. A large group stood in between. These workers found traditional goals inappropriate and were groping toward new values, but they found the transition exceedingly painful.

      In broad outline, the values that developed among German workers prevailed among workers elsewhere, and they have shown great durability. Workers in Britain in the 1960s, although far more affluent and less often fervently socialistic, maintained a similar culture. They too expressed expectations for themselves and for their children that they could not really follow up; they too found factory work distasteful; they too had difficulty planning rationally for the future. They had, of course, made a more complete transition to a consumer ethic, so that they were willing to endure boring labor for the rising wages that resulted; this trade-off was only beginning to develop among German workers around 1900. And there have been changes in family structure and residence patterns that reflect new trends in adaptation to modern life. But many elements of the culture that workers developed in response to industrialization have persisted, and they continue to set workers off from other social groups in modern society. Given a distinctive class reaction of this sort, does modernization continue to have any meaning? Does it primarily describe an idealized middle-class stance rather than the development of the whole society?

      This selection raises another vital question toward understanding the modernization process: Has modern society progressively eliminated pleasure in work? A modern mentality may find compensations (a concrete translation of the idea of progress), but direct job satisfaction may decline, most obviously for manufacturing workers but also for office staff. Here is potentially a huge qualification to any equation of modernization and progress. It involves, however, an assumption that the quality of work was once higher (which Laslett, for example, does suggest). German workers around 1900 faced enormous work adjustments, and workers to the present day may still be paying the costs of the varied adaptations to the modern job.

German industrialization was about fifty years old in 1900. The modern working class was still quite new. Thanks to the sociologists and the socialists we have qualitative information about the workers that does not exist for, say, English workers at a comparable stage. We can answer some questions about adaptation to industry using the German materials, or at least phrase the questions far more precisely.

I am not, then, interested in what is distinctively German about the German working class between 1890 and 1914. I recognize of course that points about Germany cannot automatically be transferred to other countries in comparable stages of industrialization. German socialism was certainly an un-usual phenomenon compared to patterns either to the west or to the east; it influenced workers' adaptation, though not too greatly. German industry was more advanced in organization and mechanization than industry had been in Britain at an otherwise comparable stage; this would tend, I think, to make adaptation more difficult. German peasants were traditionally far poorer, German artisans far more guild-oriented than their western counterparts as they came into the factories. This too would leave a distinctive mark on adaptation. Admitting all this, I nevertheless believe that information about German workers at least suggests lines of inquiry that can be applied to other instances of industrialization.

The issue that has dominated historical consideration of working classes—material conditions and their trend—need not delay the student of German workers too long. Real wages rose fairly steadily for factory workers from the beginning of industrialization. They certainly were rising between 1890 and 1914, despite rapid inflation, though the rate of their increase diminished. Conditions were still bad, far worse than in France or Britain. Housing was cramped, diet still rather meager. Yet there was improvement in most con-sumption items. This being reasonably well established for the 1890–1914 period, we can more readily turn to questions of adaptation to industrial life which many historians, in their preoccupation with material conditions, have only touched in passing. We must in fact broaden the scope of "material conditions" to include pace of work or transportation time from home to job. For material conditions were obviously part and parcel of adaptation. German workers' adaptation may have been facilitated, vis-à-vis Britain at least, by the improvement in living standards over accustomed levels; but we must be sure that the quality of material life did in fact improve, that modest gains in con-sumption do in fact allow us to judge this quality.

Many aspects of German manufacturing suggest the transitional character of the labor force even after 1900. Of course, given the constant change which industrialization imposes, a social group is always in transition. And a com-

From Peter N. Stearns, "Adaptation to Industrialization: German Workers as a Test Case," reprinted, with permission, from *Central European History*, III, No. 4 (December 1970), pp. 303–31.

parative framework for the German economy needs to be more carefully worked out than has been done heretofore. Nevertheless, it can be suggested that from the standpoint of the working class the German economy was not so uniformly advanced as national production figures imply and that some categories of workers were touched by traditions that had long been forgotten not only in Britain but also in France. . . .

The majority of factory workers were first- or second-generation even in 1914. Census figures reveal this clearly. Between 1895 and 1907 the mining labor force almost doubled, as did that in metallurgy. Textiles grew more slowly and chemicals advanced only 60 per cent, but the machine-building industry almost tripled its employment. More specific studies confirm this pattern. In the wool hat industry in Luckewalde, where the industry began in the 1870's and grew only modestly, only 30 per cent of the workers had had fathers in the textile industry and only 24 per cent had had grandfathers who were factory workers of any sort. Of the fathers 23 per cent had been artisans, 9 per cent peasants, 11 per cent members of the higher professions; of the grandfathers 38 per cent had been peasants. In the Ruhr mines in the mid-nineties only 37 per cent of the workers were children of miners, and a few years later only 40 per cent of the miners' children of working age were in the mines—and this in an industry where stability was usually high aside from outright increments to the labor force. In one Mönchen-Gladbach textile firm only 14 per cent of the workers had peasant fathers, though in the city as a whole large numbers of the new semiskilled workers came directly from the countryside. In clearer contrast, a Berlin machine-building giant had only a small core of workers whose fathers had been in the industry; a large number of the new workers were from East Prussia while many of the unskilled had previously been handworkers in textile or shoe manufacturing, many of the skilled former smiths. Everywhere machine building, including automobile production, drew in massive numbers of locksmiths from the villages and small towns.

Despite Germany's ranking as an industrial power, industrialization in the literal sense was new to most of its workers around the turn of the century. It was drawing in peasants. It attracted servant girls, following a common pattern in relatively early industrialization in which servant status constituted a transition from rural life to factory life. It attracted many small-town artisans, even though none of the large artisanal groupings was declining in size. This, too, reminds us of an important aspect of early industrialization which had largely ceased in Britain.

We can, then, learn something about the nature of adaptation to new artisanal forms and to factory industry by studying German workers. Adaptation to new residence and to new work is a massive subject, and I cannot pretend that what follows is an exhaustive treatment. The role of religion, for example, is not directly examined. Some questions that are germane to earlier industrial situations cannot be followed up for Germany at this point. There was little overt resistance to machines. When a Bremen shipbuilding company introduced riveting machines, manned by semiskilled labor, older workers angrily curtailed their production, but in general the reaction to machines was subtle. Obviously machines were too well entrenched for Luddism to be conceivable, nor was this the truly brand-new industrial labor force from which Luddism stems.

The most basic subject to raise is whether the work itself was found pleasant or unpleasant. A study of the modern British working class bases its claim that a distinctive class exists primarily on workers' distaste for their jobs. Can this be applied to an earlier industrial situation? Immediately after this we must ask what the wage meant and the extent to which consumption was viewed as a compensation for unpleasant work. The big question here is the extent to which a traditional view of both work and the wage gave way to a market or progressive view that related production to wage incentives and insisted on steady improvements in living standards off the job. Changes in family structure were naturally forced by industrialization; what did they mean to workers? What was the workers' general outlook? Insofar as adaptation involved stress, what remedies did they seek? Finally, in all these questions, to what extent were workers united in their reaction? Were they developing, as E. P. Thompson suggests for British workers as early as 1832, not only common institutions but a common structure of feeling and a collective culture?

Unskilled workers who came into the factories from the countryside worked hard without complaint. There is overwhelming evidence on this point. Silesian miners who came to the Ruhr thought it was evil to miss a shift. Amazed at the laxness of the Ruhr miners, they thought, "We Silesians are better than this crummy crew." In metallurgical factories in Hanover Poles and Germans of rural origin were noted as zealous workers. In a Mönchen-Gladbach textile plant workers from small towns and the countryside earned up to 12 per cent above the company's average because of their high production. Key groups of workers were loath to strike for a reduction of hours. Dockers did not mount the pressure for a limitation of their long workday that their counterparts in French ports began in the 1890's. Many were proud of the ability to work around the clock periodically, if only because their extra earnings contributed to their family's well-being. German miners rarely raised questions of hours of work in their strikes, though their working day was two hours longer than that in France and Britain. Their docility in this matter was due to the fact that over half of them were freshly in from the countryside.

There were several reasons for the new arrivals' zeal for work. They were grateful for regular employment. German unemployment rates were quite low for unskilled workers according to official figures, but there was substantial seasonal unemployment, at the least, in the countryside and the small towns. Satisfaction with what seemed to them high pay was another obvious factor. Miners from eastern Germany thought that pay in the Ruhr was splendid. They delighted in daily meat and butter and were happy to be allowed to work hard, accepting overtime on top of their long shifts. Accustomed to hard work anyway, many of them found nonmaterial satisfactions in working with machines. Some were entranced by the sheer power of machines. Others were lured by the prestige of a big company; a worker took pride when it could be said of him. "He is with Daimler." Perhaps most important, they found factory work exciting or at least not boring. Women were particularly pleased with the bustle and camaraderie of factory work, when contrasted to their rural traditions or their work as servants.

How much did the ardor for work mean beyond the willingness to put in long hours? In the one study of the Mönchen-Gladbach textile factory, the above average production of workers from the countryside contrasted with the up to 30 per cent below average production of city-bred workers. Rural masons and bricklayers also seem to have outproduced their urban counterparts. But in general it seems likely that the rural workers accepted long hours in part because their pace was rather leisurely. They were not usually highly skilled and therefore were not subjected to the most intense pressure to produce at maximum. Comparative studies revealed that German workers despite their longer hours were less productive than British; textile workers, for example, handled only a half to two-thirds the machinery per worker that their British counterparts managed. There is some indication that German workers took more breaks during the day than workers in France and Britain. The unusually high ratio of foremen to workers in Germany reflects the leisurely pace that many workers sought to adopt. Production fluctuated more during the week in Germany than was common elsewhere, with productivity on Mondays particularly low. And workers, including some of rural origin, had habits of job-changing that reduced both their productivity and the work they actually put in during a given year. Much of this evidence admittedly is hard to apply to the newly arrived workers specifically. But it does suggest that the zeal for work had yet to be harnessed to an industrial pace, that it consisted mainly of plodding through a long day.

German workers generally had a different view. Some of the contrast has already been suggested. Big-city workers and miners established in the Ruhr did not seem to work as hard as the new arrivals. Skilled workers found the Arbeitsfreude of the unskilled proof of their unintelligence. Adolf Levenstein's survey gives us a statistical picture of sorts. In textiles, 75 per cent of the workers found no joy in their work; 60 per cent of the miners agreed, while 15 per cent enjoyed the work if the pay was good, and 18 per cent professed indifference. Of the metal workers surveyed, 57 per cent found no pleasure in their work. Levenstein probably had a biased sample, for he elicited responses from an unusual number of convinced socialists. A survey of workers in Mönchen-Gladbach textile plants, while not focusing on attitudes toward work specifically, revealed that 44 to 50 per cent of the workers were "satisfied" with their position, though only 29 per cent said that they really wanted to be textile workers.

There were workers, then, who enjoyed their work. A weaver wrote that he could get through the day quite pleasantly thinking about other things, particularly astronomy. A miner said, "There is no work so interesting as that of the miner." Many skilled workers remained proud of their work, even when new machines were introduced. Printers who switched to the new composing machines resisted any return to manual labor, partly because this involved longer hours but partly because, though the skill required on the machines was reduced, they were able to read more manuscripts. Still other workers took pleasure in working for a piece rate, because it increased their freedom and made the job more interesting. This was particularly true of the highly skilled, including some who had been artisanally trained in small towns.

But majority sentiment was against these positions, even if some groups of workers, in metals particularly, had to surrender their opposition to piece work. Textile workers complained of exhaustion: "My eyes burn so—if I could only sleep." Metal workers worried more explicitly about their health. Both complained of noise and boredom, one noting that his work was so dull that "wild longings" tormented him. A miner in the Ruhr, Max Lotz, wrote an impassioned lament about the dangers and hardships of his work, which he found beneath human dignity. Even in the mines he found that "The work is becoming increasingly mechanical. No more incentive, no more haste, we muddle along wearily, we are worn out and mindless."

The outlook of the majority of German workers, particularly among the skilled, was revealed in strikes and in the trends of per capita productivity. Construction workers cut their production dramatically as more and more construction shifted to the big cities, perhaps by as much as 50 per cent. In 1913 Berlin masons set 300 stones a day, compared to 600 in Göttingen. Their production had begun to drop in the 1890's and by 1912 had reached British levels—suggesting that urban construction workers could catch up to the patterns of advanced industrial countries rather quickly, a point to which we shall return. In mining, productivity which had more than doubled in the second half of the nineteenth century fell slightly between 1900 and 1913; in one Silesian company it dropped from 368 tons per worker in the 1890's to 340 tons between 1901 and 1910. Technical factors undoubtedly contributed to these developments, particularly in mining as shafts deepened, but there is evidence here of genuine worker reaction. Both mining and construction were of course loosely supervised industries in which workers could indulge their resistance to hard work with some freedom.

Thirty-two per cent of all German strikes between 1899 and 1914 raised demands concerning hours of work. This contrasts vividly with the situation in France, where only 15 per cent of the strikes involved hours of work. To this should be added many of the 21 per cent of German strikes directed against foremen or other workers, though this rate was not so unusual. Many German strikes that seemed to stem from other issues actually concerned the intensity of work. Miners in Barsinghausen, for example, struck for a raise because this seemed a safe demand, but the real cause of their strike was a new foreman who was driving them to work harder. Construction workers and metal workers pushed hard for an eight-hour day—far harder than their counterparts in France or even in Britain. And the strikes for hours reduction were justified in different ways in Germany. In France, workers who struck for shorter hours generally talked of the desirability of cutting unemployment; some also wanted to seize the opportunity for more overtime pay. These factors were present in Germany. Unemployment rates among skilled workers ranged around 5 per cent in normal years—much higher than the rates among urban unskilled, ironically—and this undoubtedly encouraged strikes for shorter hours. But workers also talked directly about the need to curtail their fatigue and the dangers to their health. The key grievance in the great Crimmitschau strike was chronic fatigue. Shoemakers in Pirmasens struck for nine hours because new machines had made the work more intensive. Doubtless socialist influence helped workers articulate their resistance to intense work, but labor movements in France and Britain tried the same arguments with far less success among their constituents. Finally, skilled workers in Germany began to seek annual vacations. Far more strikes—though still only a handful —involved this issue than was true in other countries, and far more workers won the point. In 1908, 75,591 metal workers (particularly in machine building) had gained regular vacations; in 1912 the figure had risen to 233,029.

The German strike movement was not, as a whole, nearly as sophisticated as that in France or Britain. Strikes were smaller, longer, and for the most part raised less advanced demands. So the attention to relieving the intensity of work stands out strongly.

The reaction to factory work was unquestionably intensified by the speed-up devices manufacturers everywhere were introducing around 1900— such as the Kalkulationsbüros which appraised piece rates—and by the relatively advanced technology. Even so, the German workers' reaction may tell us something of the difficulties new workers experienced in comparable stages of industrialization elsewhere. We can speculate about English workers' first exposure to the din and pace of factory labor, but we know that many German workers were appalled. It took a generation for unskilled workers to shake off their rural-bred resignation, but the workers born in the cities and the large contingent of artisans entering factories or large craft units for the first time had real problems of adjustment. Their vigorous resistance may have alleviated the problems, of course, as hours of work declined and in some cases as productivity itself leveled off. At the same time it can be suggested that this stage in the adjustment to industrialization was just that, that contentment with work might grow as experience increased and job conditions improved. A survey of German workers in the 1920's revealed that 67 per cent of the skilled workers and 44 per cent of the unskilled felt more pleasure than distaste for work. . . .

For general purposes, three sets of reactions to industrial labor can be marked off. The first is of course the traditionalist approach brought in by the unskilled, to work long hours but not usually very intensely; traditionalism was sometimes abetted, particularly among women, by a sense that the factory was a diverting place. The second reaction was one of shock and resistance, as with male textile workers. The third embraced workers who found some genuine interest in their job, or whose resistance paid off sufficiently, in shorter hours for example, to remove any fundamental grievance, or who learned to compensate for unpleasant work by other enjoyments. The second group set much of the tone for the period, as was reflected in the polls that were taken. But we cannot determine the importance of each group by reaction to work alone. The outlook toward wages varied widely also, exacerbating the despair of some of those who detested their work—like Max Lotz, who could scarcely imagine being paid enough to compensate for his arduous labor—but aiding the adjustment of others to new methods and a new pace.

The outlook of the new, unskilled workers toward the wage has already been suggested. They seemed content, even delighted with the pay and living standards they won in the factories. As a skilled worker noted scornfully, they were "satisfied when they are able to buy cigarettes." They concentrated particularly on improving their diets, recalling a rural childhood of potatoes and milk. Silesian workers in the Ruhr, particularly the women, adopted local styles, but in most factories a hierarchy of dress persisted in that the unskilled wore simple garb. In Stuttgart factories the unskilled wore no overcoats and professed to find this appropriate. Perhaps the key was the attitude of the women, who were used to plain clothes and did much of the family sewing. Housing—which was quite exiguous in the cities—seemed satisfactory. The unskilled complained of rents but not of housing directly. Here, obviously, the bad quality of rural housing set low expectations. The unskilled were generally satisfied with two rooms. They were not the ones who pressed out to surrounding villages to seek their housing; what they found in the cities sufficed. There was little interest in other items of expense. Medical care was feared. As one East Prussian woman said, "God is the best doctor. If he wishes, I'm healthy; otherwise not . . . I would rather die than let them cut." It is, I admit, always presumptuous to talk of satisfaction among poor people, but this seems to be accurate here. Traditionally low standards which factory work exceeded in terms both of pay and of regularity of work, plus the hope of some that factory life was only temporary, a basis for a return to the countryside with enough money to buy land, make this outlook understandable.

The traditionalists were a large group, but probably not a majority of the labor force. What of the rest: the textile workers and others who hated their work, the skilled workers in factories and shops who faced changing conditions on the job?

To what extent were German workers eager to improve their wages? As the outlook of the traditionalists indicates, such eagerness cannot automatically be assumed. The question can be further refined. To what extent did workers become aware of the wage as a market item, as an incentive which should be increased when production increased? Did they transfer some of their dissatisfaction with their work to the wage? Or did they view the wage more as consumers, in which case the question is less involved in the work situation, more in the degree to which improvements in the standard of living were sought? Both of these approaches are useful, but I find the latter more applicable to the situation of most German workers in this period.

Again, even aside from the traditionalists, German workers were divided in wage matters, but let us begin with some general points. Compared to workers in older industrial countries, German workers were not avid for wage gains. It is true that their real wages continued to increase, though slowly, in contrast to trends in Britain and France after 1900. It is also true that one must not exaggerate French and British eagerness for material progress. But there is a difference, clearly related to the stage of industrialization. . . .

In many of their wage strikes, German workers argued simply in terms of poverty. Masons in Gelsenkirchen asked for a raise so that they could earn enough "that we can regularly feed our families." Arguments of this sort almost never appeared among workers in older industrial countries. They suggest that many German wage strikes and the high rate of wage strikes overall reflected no new attitude toward the wage but rather the marginal conditions in which many German workers lived. . . .

Working-class budgets confirm the judgment that German workers found it difficult to envisage major improvements in their living standards. Overall, German workers spent a low percentage of their income on rents and recreation—the two items most revealing of rapidly rising material expectations. This, of course, is partly a statement of their relative poverty. More important for our purposes is the fact that when incomes went up, workers did not alter their budget allocations greatly. Metal workers earning under 1200 marks a year spent 56 per cent of their budget on food and drink; those with incomes of 1200 to 1600 marks dropped this only to 55 per cent; those with incomes of 1600 to 2000 marks dropped it yet another two percentage points; those with incomes of 2000 to 2500 marks dropped it to 52 per cent. Conversely the percentage spent on rent rose from 12 to 14 to 15 per cent in both the higher income groups. All this suggests a desire to use higher earnings mainly to improve existing levels slightly, with particular stress on a better diet including more meat; yet metal workers had more advanced expectations than most German workers. Textile workers actually increased their percentage expenditure on food with higher earnings, while cutting the rent percentage. Recreation and health expenditures were very low generally.

Only in clothing were there signs of hopes for rather rapid improvement, as Ruhr miners and others awakened to possibilities of new fashions. Correspondingly this was the only nonfood budget category where German workers led those of the older industrial countries. The interest in clothing is characteristic of workers in many early industrial situations. Possession of respectable clothing for walking about the city on Sundays was extremely important. Along with some improvements in diet it seems to be the first new consumption interest to emerge. Why? Obviously clothes are cheap; perhaps an interest in them is naturally human, an extension of the skin as Marshall McLuhan would have it. But students of consumption habits can beware of calling anything "natural." Only by indirection were many workers led to want better housing; as we shall see, changes in family life rather than a virgin birth of the modern economic man were often involved. The early interest in clothing was a reaction to change, a desire to prove one's place in fairly well known terms, for even in the countryside differences in dress were known marks of status. For some of the small-town artisans and others who had status anxieties as well as a general sense of uneasiness in the factories stylish clothes may have been particularly important. By the same token the interest in clothes was not immediately part of a desire for more material goods generally. Workers could be satisfied with better dress. And clothing was cheap enough that it did not prompt elaborate wage demands.

Three factors add to this impression of limited expectations; at least two of them, like the limited expectations themselves, flowed naturally from the early industrial setting. German workers were filled with a longing for the countryside. "I believe that every city resident, as soon as time permits, should go to the countryside, go to nature, and fill his lungs with pure, unspoiled air." Workers acted on this sentiment. An overwhelming majority listed walks in the country and gardening as their favorite recreations; pastimes that cost more money and might have induced higher expectations—including books and education—could not compete. Miners and then textile workers particularly relied on nature and gardening, but the interest was general. Longing for nature reflected the rural origins of many workers and the grievances about work that many felt. One may speculate that the walks and gardening not only inhibited material expectations but also, for the millions of workers who still could enjoy them, provided some genuine satisfaction.

Drink was another carry-over from tradition that was also fed by discontent with work while inhibiting higher expectations. Many German workers were frequently drunk. They spent 6 to 11 per cent of their budget on alcohol—an allocation that was not matched by higher segments of German society until the level of university professors. Articulate miners deplored their fellows' penchant for drink, which retarded their education and limited their goals. When polled, a fifth of the miners admitted their dependence on drink. Less than a tenth of textile and metal workers made a similar admission, but their budgets too revealed high rates of spending on alcohol which tended to rise as incomes went up.

Skilled German workers showed a marked interest in cleanliness. (The unskilled did not, so I think we can dismiss sheer Germanness as a cause of the characteristic.) They carefully washed and changed clothes before leaving the worksite and they often struck for improved wash facilities. Their concern stands out among workers of other industrial countries. It suggests some of the tension and status anxieties of workers from small-town and craft environments. It is related, obviously, to the interest in clothing. It may also have distracted workers from more elaborate consumption expectations because so many German companies provided excellent wash facilities and because agitation for further improvements took up energies that might otherwise have been used for wage gains. As one group of Ruhr workers noted when they won new rules on bathroom conditions in their factory, "These rules are worth much more to us than a pay raise."

In contrast to the general hesitancy about advancing wages, a minority of workers were committed to expanding prosperity. Some were in factories, like the metallurgical workers who shunned company housing and moved into towns distant from concentrations of lower-paid workers. Far more were still in the crafts. At an extreme, artisans like printers adopted an essentially bourgeois consumption pattern, even though their wages might be in the middling range. They cut the percentage they devoted to food—down to 39 per cent in one case. They drank little and sometimes had their wives make their clothes. But they valued housing, spending up to 28 per cent on rent, and they saved for the education of their children. Still more workers kept a rather proletarian expenditure pattern but strove for steadily advancing wages. Skilled construction workers led the way. Their wage strikes resembled those in France and Britain in frequency and in the arguments used, which means they sharply departed from the norm in Germany. They conducted 32 per cent of all strikes between 1899 and 1914, though they numbered only 18 per cent of the manufacturing labor force, and their offensive wage strikes were almost 30 per cent more frequent among all their strikes than the rate for strikes in general with construction strikes excepted. They led the way also in wage movements that did not result in strikes; in 1905, for example, masons conducted 507 such movements affecting 106,761 workers. These workers, along with printers, brewers, and others, had a "modern" idea of the wage and of advancing living standards. They were not for the most part new to their trade. Though many of them faced radical changes in business organization and substantial changes in working methods in this period, they could adjust through the wage. And, minority though they were, their numbers were not small.

Examination of adjustment to work and the wage yields three groups of workers—an assortment that is not surprising but one that is decidedly hard to unify. At one end were the traditionalists in work habits and consumption expectations. At the other end craftsmen and metallurgical workers either found enjoyment in their work—remember the printers on the composing machines—or compensated by seeking higher wages, or, most commonly, both. This leaves the group in the middle, the reasonably skilled factory workers, many from small-town craft backgrounds. Most of them had not made a full transition to a progressive view of the wage and consumption. Some of them were content with their work—the middle group of the work-aggrieved was smaller than the middle group of consumption-conservatives. But there was a mass of workers, in textiles, mining, machine building, and shoe manufacture, who disliked their work without finding full compensation in a new view of the wage. These workers were not yet capable of making the basic bargain that industrialization required, to admit new work methods, sometimes unpleasant ones, in return for advancing earnings.

Were these workers bereft of hope? Did they find other compensations? Some undoubtedly were extremely unhappy. Some of the most convinced socialists whose voices have reached us, apart from formal socialist leaders, fit this category. Hear Max Lotz: "What is my meaning in this great world plan where brutal physical and psychological forces feast themselves in orgies? Nothing! . . . Only Social Democratic activities could give me goals and offer me economic security too, so that I may attempt my plans. I therefore adhere to socialism with every fiber of courage and idealism." Moritz Bromme was perhaps even more typical of the ardent socialist. Self-taught like Lotz, he desperately wanted to be an artisan but was blocked by his lack of money for apprenticeship. His life became increasingly hard, if only because his lack of knowledge of birth control methods burdened himself with too many children and an increasingly shrewish wife. Socialism may have had its deepest meaning for men like this who were still close to traditional ways of doing things but with frustrated hopes for a better lot. There is evidence for this on a broader scale. Levenstein's polls showed that textile workers—those archetypically discontented workers in this transitional period—rated socialism as a goal over earning more money. For metal workers the situation was reversed. Eighteen per cent of textile workers thought about politics and union matters while at work, like the man who said, "I build a new world while I work."

Here, I think, is the key to the special hold socialism had in Germany at this point. It fit exactly the mood of those workers who hated their work but could not easily find personal compensations. These workers were in a minority except among male textile workers. Most socialist workers took their doctrines less seriously—as witness the fact that over 80 per cent of the books taken out of party libraries had nothing to do with social issues. A socialist machine builder stated the more normal qualified position:

> You know, I never read a Social Democratic book and rarely a newspaper. I used not to occupy myself with politics at all. But since I got married and have five eaters at home I have to do it. But I think my own thoughts. I do not go in for red ties, big round hats, and other similar things. All that does not amount to much. We really do not want to become like the rich and refined people. There will always have to be rich and poor. We would not think of altering that. But we want better and more organization at the factory and in the state. I openly express what I think about that, even though it might not be pleasant. But I do nothing illegal.

Still, there was a large enough minority of desperate workers to give German socialism an unusual role. Did socialism in the long run help allay the desperation of these workers or did it perpetuate their alienation? Did it tend to delay their conversion to new personal expectations?

Well-organized socialism had not been present in a comparable stage of workers' developments in France or Britain, of course. A second aspect of the German workers' survival effort, oddly but closely related to socialism, has more general applicability. The workers formed elaborate expectations for themselves and, to a degree, for their children. Some, the unskilled particularly, could not answer questions about what they would most like to be; their goal was simply to get through life. The wool hat makers in Luckewalde, of heavily peasant origin, could not articulate goals. Most simply said they wanted a happy old age, though the young males talked of hopes for their own business or land. In general textile workers had more trouble forming a personal dream world than metal workers, partly because such hopes were far less realistic. But in a Mönchen-Gladbach textile factory, where only 29 per cent of the workers said they wanted to be in textiles, 27 per cent wanted to be artisans and 22 per cent yearned for the higher professions. Skilled automobile workers in Stuttgart—many trained in small-town crafts—talked of wanting to be artisan masters or, with almost equal frequency, state officials. In a Berlin precision-tool factory, the order of popularity of major goals was as follows: 1. a secure old age; 2. one's own business; 3. foreman; 4. freedom from capitalism; 5. possession of savings; 6. obtaining postal or railroad work. Here, I think is a common mixture: some sheer traditionalism (secure old age), a bit of socialism, and a good bit of longing for independent business or the dignity and security of state employment.

Obviously these latter goals were realistic for some workers. We must again refer to a minority, particularly in the crafts, who were decidedly upwardly mobile. Some skilled metal workers or their children did get their own bicycle repair shops. Many metallurgical workers advanced steadily from unskilled to skilled in a generational process; this was the clear pattern at Krupp, where even the unskilled planned their families with care to assure future advance. Printers were generally upwardly mobile. In one large survey only 7 per cent of all printers were children of printers, while 40 per cent came from the ranks of journeymen and the unskilled; in contrast 30 per cent of their children of job age were printers while 35 per cent were teachers, booksellers, technicians, bureaucrats, or professional people. This mobility is exceptionally important, but it does not describe the majority of workers who harbored hopes for their future. The workers themselves sensed that their goals were hopeless. They talked almost in the same breath of God's will determining what would happen or of ending "where the wind blows me." Did such goals nonetheless offer occasional comfort, as pleasant dreams, or was their hopelessness a nightmare that exacerbated despair? There is evidence that the trait continues among workers, who talk of bright futures for their children while doing little to further them.

Workers were able to make some adjustments to their lot, apart from their dreams and apart from work and the wage. They altered their family relationships. Again, we cannot talk of workers as a whole. The unskilled from the countryside tried to preserve the traditional family pattern. Many of them delayed the marriage age until twenty-eight or so. Many got their wives pregnant before marriage, peasant fashion, to be sure they were not "buying a pig in the poke." They let their wives work only if severely pressed; in Berlin they brought their wives back home as soon as their income reached 1200 marks a year. Many of them had large families and were ignorant of contraceptive devices. Bromme describes how experienced factory workers increasingly talked of contraception, many claiming that *coitus interruptus* was best, others swearing by "Parisian articles" (condoms); but it took time to get new arrivals in the plant to adopt any "artificial" method. At the other extreme craftsmen, who also had traditions of late marriage age, maintained essentially middle-class family size, a key element in their generational mobility. They, too, were loath to have their wives work, though the wives often took care of boarders (which could add 300 marks a year to the family income).

But what of the workers in between? They were limiting their birth rates rapidly, particularly in the textile cities (compared to mining and metallurgy) where incomes were low. The birth rate among these groups of workers dropped 25 per cent between 1900 and 1913. Relatedly, their wives were working in increasing numbers. Again, textiles led the way, but metal workers and others followed close behind. In Berlin 17 per cent of the skilled factory workers' wives were employed, compared to 23 per cent of the much poorer unskilled workers; the cutoff income for the skilled was about 1500 marks a year. What does this mean? Obviously, a taste for a higher living standard. Perhaps the desire to raise the living standard by these means preceded (in part by necessity) a coherent effort to improve the wage by collective action. Obviously also, since the women's work (aside from some of it in textiles) was not a strict economic necessity, it meant a recognition of greater independence for the woman. Women often wanted to work. Furthermore, the reason behind the hope for higher income is intriguing, at least in the case of the Berlin machine builders: they wanted a two-bedroom apartment so that their children would sleep apart from them.

Add all this up: reduced birth rate by "artificial" means, new attitude toward wives, separate bedroom for the children. There is suggested here a new sentiment within the family, the possibility of greater affection for the children, who were not underfoot all the time, and greater sensuality and equality in the relationship between man and wife. All this, I admit, is tentative. It certainly reflects the absence, in Germany, of some of the worst pressures on the family that prevailed in early English industrialization. It suggests the beginnings of working-class family relationships that have been examined by contemporary sociologists. I think these relationships may have begun to develop rather early in industrialization, even before decisively new attitudes to the wage can be found. They were at once the product of earnings above the subsistence level and the need for an emotional balm for increasing tension at work. They may have been an important solace indeed.

I can be far more definite about the last reaction to industrialization, though here too it is not easy to interpret the role it played for workers. Workers changed jobs with incredible frequency. Not all workers. The unskilled tended to be much more stable, in their gratitude for regular employment. Many firms, particularly the big ones, had a nucleus of old-time skilled workers who did not quit; a few paternalistic firms, like Krupp, managed to stabilize most of their workers. But this was not the norm. In Upper Silesia 76 per cent of the workers left the company in the first year, though those who did not quit the first two years were unlikely to and so 40 per cent of workers in the average firm had been there over five years. Many Ruhr miners shunned company housing so that they could switch jobs easily, and their shifts were frequent. In one company for each one hundred workers 63 were in, 51 out in 1899; by 1907 these rates were up to 63 and 58; by 1911 to 69 and 61. This was the common pattern. In textiles the rate was lower, but still up to a third of the workers changed companies each year. Many changed professions as well; several studies revealed that over half the male textile workers had had two to four different professions. Metallurgical workers stayed in their profession, but they changed jobs more frequently even than miners; in 1906 163 per cent of Düsseldorf blast-furnace workers changed jobs—that is, a large number changed jobs more than once.

What does this extraordinary fluctuation mean, aside from a reduction of worker efficiency? We have one precise poll, of skilled precision mechanics in Berlin who had changed jobs. Twenty-five per cent of them did so to better themselves; an almost equal number did so because of lack of work; 18 per cent left because of a pay cut; 15 per cent because of a clash with the foreman; 8 per cent because of a speedup of work; 6 per cent because of wanderlust; the remainder for more scattered reasons. Motivations varied with the industry. Metallurgical workers changed jobs above all to seek higher pay. Machine-shop workers changed jobs much less often than foundry workers, because the latter were subjected to a much more rigorous pace of work. We obviously have to see job-changing as a direct reaction to discontent with the work—it must often have given workers a needed brief vacation. There is a correlation also between job-changing and workers' vague dreams for a better lot. Male spinners had much higher personal goals than weavers; they could not realize these goals but they could change jobs, which they did far more frequently than weavers did. Workers from the small-town craft background were particularly prone to job-changing in all industries. How many felt like the turner who said, "I didn't feel really at home in the big hall," or like the slightly more industrialized type who changed jobs until he felt able to "feel with the machine"?

Massive job-changing was common in the early stages of other industrializations, as in France. It reflected motives that were more common still. There was a stable group in the factories, composed partly of the traditionalist-unskilled but partly also of those skilled workers who found their work pleasant. The two groups together were near a majority, as in Silesian mining. In the unstable group was an important minority of upwardly mobile workers or workers who sought steadily advancing pay—this was actually a majority in metallurgy. These workers had made a full adjustment to industrialization. Another minority changed jobs because of lack of work or out of the traditional reaction to a cut in pay. This leaves the largest group, who changed jobs to seek relief from work or work situations they did not like, and to prove their independence, and to make some vague gesture at fulfilling their thwarted aspirations. The question remains: how much did job-changing provide at least temporary solace and make factory life endurable? My guess is, quite a bit. I think it did give workers a sense of freedom, a chance to thumb their noses at their supervisors. Certainly it inhibited collective protest. But possibly it too proved just a delusion, particularly as workers grew older and could not afford to indulge in it so frequently.

Workers did have some sense of choosing their occupation, even if they did not like it. This was possibly the most concrete result of job-changing. Even in textiles only 40 per cent of the workers polled said they did not know why they were textile workers or that they had simply obeyed their parents' wishes. Again, we cannot say whether the sense of making a decision was of much comfort. But it does demonstrate how far these workers had moved from peasant traditionalism, in their ability to think of themselves as individual agents in the economy.

I need not belabor the point, in conclusion, that I find no unified working class in this mixture of traditionalists (really peasants as heart), artisans, skilled factory workers who could adjust to the new work and wage, and skilled factory workers who could not. All, it might be added, except the traditionalists, could be loyal socialists. For if we find the greatest fervor among the maladjusted factory workers, we find large numbers of socialist voters among all the nontraditionalists.

Nor do I need more than mention the implications of this study for the history of protest. Artisans aside, workers in this stage of their development were not likely sources of massive direct-action protest unless material conditions were deteriorating or the rural milieu from which many came was already troubled. Neither of these factors applied to German workers at this point. German workers were also spared major disruption of their family life by outside forces, which further differentiates them from British workers earlier in the nineteenth century. The grievances workers felt most keenly were hard to articulate. Even the high rate of strikes for reduction of hours of work only palely reflects the anxiety that the pace and strain of factory labor produced. The traditions of lower-class protest—in Germany as elsewhere—directed attention to problems faced as consumers, to the prices of goods. They were of little help in expressing problems in the work situation itself. Well after 1914, and not only in Germany, workers had trouble translating work grievances into protest. Before 1914 in Germany, as in western Europe earlier, too few workers had been converted to new material expectations to produce massive protest on this basis. Some of their efforts at adjustment actively inhibited collective protest; individualistic job-changing was a more important inhibition than that familiar villain, drink.

For what must be stressed above all in this stage of industrialization is the extent to which workers other than traditionalists had been won to individualism (which is not meant to be incompatible with being a convinced socialist). We know that much loneliness was forced upon early industrial workers, as they encountered strangers and impersonality—like the German workers' wives who endlessly wrangled in their crowded tenements or the metallurgical workers who, conscious of others' opinions and the complex hierarchy in their own ranks, carefully ate lunch in separate corners so that no one would see what they ate. Much violent protest was individual as well. Many workers in Germany fought among themselves, particularly when foreign workers were present, and general crime rates in the industrial areas rose rapidly. More important was the adjustment which even most discontented workers made to their situation. They formed dreams of individual advancement. They changed jobs according to their individual needs, more often psychic than material. A majority had some sense of consciously choosing their occupation even if it fell short of their hopes. They developed new ties—more individualistic but probably more intense as well—with their

immediate families. This was the first step in the modernization of their outlook. It was in part forced upon them. It was often small comfort for the
hardships industrial work imposed. But it did reflect a positive adjustment
by people who were not simply cogs in an industrial machine. It suggests that
—not surprisingly—immense changes in popular outlook accompanied the
first generations of industrialization. Some of the changes have been overlooked in the historian's search for protest movements and some of them have
proved much more durable.

Popular Education:
Peasants into Frenchmen

EUGEN WEBER

Many of the dramas associated with modernization occurred during the intriguing, difficult, and ambiguous process by which education was forced on the rural population. At one level, the state served as the compelling agent, breaking local traditions, from language to religion, in favor of the very essence of a modernized mentality: belief in progress, in science, in a new idea of work and personal advancement. At another level peasants opened a new interest in education in response to broad structural pressures around them, such as the rise of market agriculture with concomitant need for new technical knowledge. In between was a host of mediating factors, including changing concepts of the child (over which state and peasant long warred) and that curious new creature, the schoolteacher. The spread of education came largely from the top of society downward—which is why the process in America has been dubbed a matter of "social control" by many recent historians. But it was also colored by new and old interests of the constituents, who could see some value in certain kinds of change, and by the intermediary groups involved.

It is not surprising that peasants adapted to modern values and institutions more slowly than any other social group. Peasants maintained contact with many traditions, including religion. Their adaptability was further limited by the exodus of many younger, enterprising peasants to the cities. Yet peasants were pressed to change their outlook and way of life, and the national education systems that developed in the later nineteenth century played a major role in this change. Many peasants who long refused to send their children to school finally did yield. Their understanding of the possible vaule of education reflected their changing circumstances. Small-town artisans had quickly seized on education as a means of social mobility, often seeking new skills to compensate for the diminishing utility of traditional craft training. Peasants, however, had to undergo a more fundamental shift in values to make a similar transition. The intense economic problems in agriculture from the 1870s onward helped expedite this shift.

As education was accepted, further changes were inevitable. Everywhere, the state and the upper classes sought to use education to shape the lower classes into obedient and productive citizens. They preached national loyalty. They also emphasized the value of science and technology, and in France after the 1870s, they actively attacked religion.

Most schoolteachers eagerly supported these positions, for their own prestige was enhanced by associating themselves with progressive forces. So peasants were exposed to many new ideas. In a real sense education brought them, at least in France, into contact with the concepts of the Enlightenment. Although they did not necessarily accept all they learned, they could hardly avoid questioning traditional ideas, and for some, education did prove to be a truly radical force.

The following passage surveys the major facets of the establishment of mass education in the French countryside under the Third Republic. It clearly delineates the destructive power of education; old ways of thinking and speaking were rooted out, though not without difficulty. Yet the result was not a clear victory for modernization in the most simple sense. Peasants were not uniformly transformed into secular, progressive, individualistic citizens. Rather they were encouraged to transfer loyalty and blind faith from religion to the nation, a process with immense political and diplomatic consequences but suggesting a more qualified change in the thinking of the peasantry itself. Modernization has entailed unprecedented involvement of the masses with the broader society, but is this because the outlook of the masses has really changed or because the state and the ruling classes have found new ways to manipulate it?

The school, notably the village school, compulsory and free, has been credited with the ultimate acculturation process that made the French people French—finally civilized them, as many nineteenth-century educators liked to say. The schoolteachers, in their worn, dark suits, appear as the militia of the new age, harbingers of enlightenment and of the Republican message that reconciled the benighted masses with a new world, superior in wellbeing and democracy. Observers have pointed out that there were schools before the 1880's, and have quarreled with implicit assumptions or explicit statements that there was no popular education under the Ancien Régime. But we shall see that the now-classic image of a profound change of pace, tone, and impact under the Third Republic is roughly correct if it is placed in the proper context.

The context matters because schools did in fact exist before Jules Ferry, indeed were numerous; and so, to a large extent, did free education. What made the Republic's laws so effective was not just that they required all children to attend school and granted them the right to do so free. It was the attendant circumstances that made adequate facilities and teachers more accessible; that provided roads on which children could get to school; that,

Excerpted from *Peasants into Frenchmen: The Modernization of Rural France, 1870–1914*, by Eugen Weber, with the permission of the publishers, Stanford University Press. © 1976 by the Board of Trustees of the Leland Stanford Junior University.

above all, made school meaningful and profitable, once what the school offered made sense in terms of altered values and perceptions. . . .

The schools that priests or laymen ran for the poorer classes before the last quarter of the nineteenth century tended, in the nature of things, to put first things first. First things were those the masters thought important: the ability to gabble the catechism or a part of the Latin service. The teaching of even elementary reading, writing, and arithmetic was rare before the Revolution, reflected the prefect of Yonne in 1810, and teachers were little interested in "broad public education, I mean the sort concerning the greatest number of people." In any case, a great many teachers taught whatever they taught with limited competence. Until 1816, no title or proof of competence was required from a teacher. . . .

It takes a real effort today to conceive such an educational system, one in which both teacher and taught were ignorant of the material they were dealing with, and in which the capacity to draw letters or pronounce them completely outweighed any capacity to comprehend. Letters, words, and sentences were formulas and spells. "No child understands what he reads," reported a school inspector from Var in 1864. And in Brittany the inspectors noted that, though the children read along with fair fluency, "no child can give account of what he has read or translate it into Breton; hence there is no proof that anything is understood." In such circumstances, Latin was no more difficult, no more incomprehensible than French, and many a bright village child "learned" Latin in this fashion and left school full of bits of scripture, canticles, and the catechism, "rattling along in Latin like a phonograph, without understanding a word of it," and capable of writing in four different hands, accomplishments most impressive to his illiterate parents. . . .

From 1833 onward the government, supported by a steadily growing vested interest, bent itself to advance and develop public education. Nationally, the conscripts affected by the law of 1833 showed a much smaller measure of illiteracy than their forebears. And in an illiterate department like Corrèze, the change was equally evident. The proportion of conscripts who knew the elements of reading rose from 14.3 percent in 1829 to 31.9 percent in 1855, 34.8 percent in 1860, 41 percent in 1865, 50 percent in 1868, and 62 percent in 1875. By 1863 only about one-fifth of the children between seven and thirteen received no instruction whatever. What we want to know is the kind of instruction that was given and who got it. The evidence suggests, and so does common sense, that urban areas had more schools than rural areas, that these schools were more regularly attended by more of the local children, and that the quality of the teaching in them was better. By 1876 nearly 800,000 of 4.5 million school-age children were still not registered in any school. Most of these belonged to rural communes; and many who were registered hardly ever attended class. This was the enduring problem.

The next great change came in the 1880's. It would have come earlier had the Minister of Education Victor Duruy had the chance to develop the plans he elaborated in 1867. But he did not, and most of his initiatives remained in the project stage. Hence the importance of the reforms introduced by Jules Ferry. In 1881 all fees and tuition charges in public elementary schools were abolished. In 1882 enrollment in a public or private school was made compulsory. In 1883 every village or hamlet with more than 20 school-age children was required to maintain a public elementary school. In 1885 subsidies were allotted for the building and maintenance of schools and for the pay of teachers. In 1886 an elementary teaching program was instituted, along with elaborate provisions for inspection and control. . . .

One reason for the slow progress in eliminating illiteracy, strangely ignored by even the best accounts of education in France, was the fact that so many adults—and consequently children—did not speak French. As we have seen in 1863 by official tally some 7.5 million people, a fifth of the population, did not know the language. And as we have also seen, even that figure is questionable. The actual number was probably much larger, particularly if one includes those whose notions of the language were extremely vague.

The greatest problem faced by the public schools in the 8,381 non-French-speaking communes, and in a good few of the other 29,129 where French was said to be in general use, was how to teach the language to children who never or hardly ever heard it. The oft-repeated claim that they were learning their mother tongue could hardly have rung true to those whose mothers did not understand a word of it. "The children [of Lauragais] don't have to learn simply how to read and write," commented M. F. Pariset in 1867. "They have to learn how to do so in French, that is, in another language than the one they know." The result was that, for a lot of them, the instruction received in school "leaves no more trace than Latin leaves on most of those who graduate from secondary school. The child . . . returns to patois when he gets home. French is for him an erudite language, which he forgets quickly, never speaking it." Officially, the problem was faced by denying its existence and forcing even those who could scarcely master a few words to proclaim, as in a catechism, that what *should* be true was true and what they *knew* to be true was not: "(1) We call mother tongue the tongue that is spoken by our parents, and in particular by our mothers; spoken also by our fellow citizens and by the persons who inhabit the same *pays* as us. (2) Our mother tongue is French." So read an army examination manual in 1875. Unofficially, the schools continued to struggle to make the slogan true. Teaching French, "our beautiful and noble mother tongue," asserted Ferdinand Buisson, the leading light of Republican education in the 1880's, "is the chief work of the elementary school—a labor of patriotic character." The labor proved long and hard. . . .

French was gaining ground. But not so much through persecution as

through the peasants' growing appreciation of the usefulness of a less parochial language and of the skills learned in the schools. Universal military service both spread the use of French and made at least a smattering of it
important to more people. The introduction and spread of kindergartens—
salles d'asile—to relieve teachers of the care of three- and four-year-olds given
into their charge familiarized very young children with authority figures who
spoke French rather than the mother's language.

Most important of all, perhaps, more girls were being schooled, more
girls and women learned French, more mothers could speak French to their
children if they chose to do so. Women had willy-nilly perpetuated local
speech. Girls had been left untaught at the village level much longer than in
bourgs and towns, a fact that the available statistics hardly mirror at all. Only
in 1867 were communes over 500 souls required to provide a girls school (they
had been required to provide schools for boys in 1833), and it took some time
before the results of this law were felt. In any case, girls schools were generally
run by members of religious orders, and their standards remained quite low
until the 1880's. Nor did the girls have the benefit of military service as a
refresher course in French and "civilization." It follows that the school laws
of the 1880's had the broadest impact on the literacy and schooling of girls,
both of which had lagged far behind. And that when the results came to be
felt in the 1890's, the women's cultural role in the family would suddenly
change and, with it, attitudes to schooling and to the use of French.

There was another great problem that had to be mastered before French
could truly be made the national language: the teacher's own poor knowledge
of the language that he had to teach. "Most teachers don't know French,"
complained a report of 1803 in Ardèche. Half a century later things had hardly
improved. A special summer refresher course for teachers held in 1839 at
Privas reported great success: when it ended those who began with 60 to 80
mistakes in a page of dictation made only 25 to 40 errors when the exercise
was repeated. Through the 1840's and 1850's many teachers still found it
difficult to spell or to form a proper sentence. . . .

Neither students nor teachers read enough to be familiar with, let alone
teach, French literature. In Basses-Pyrénées we hear that cultivated people
knew French (1874). But what kind of French? A year later the normal
school at Lescar reported having problems with the language because "even
the cultivated who speak it don't speak it very well, and that's all the students
have heard when they have heard it." In Dordogne in the same year, 1875,
examiners for the teaching diploma were warned to make sure that every
teacher "*knows at least how to write his language correctly.*" (To be certain
the point got across, the warning was underlined.) In the Landes in 1876
student teachers and their mentors had mastered the language only shakily.

"Many masters read no better than their students," and in explaining a reading both sides offered plain absurdities. At the Avignon normal school, also in 1876, "the master himself knows French badly." At Perpignan in 1878 student teachers read and understood French badly; they were used to Catalan and only great efforts could "familiarize them with French." Much the same thing in Puy-de-Dôme in 1877: "Detestable local accent," and patois hindering everyone. The reports of 1881 carry similar criticisms. The teachers don't do very well in French because they have been insufficiently prepared to handle it (Lot-et-Garonne). The teachers are insecure in their use of French; they lack solid training in using it on their own account (Basses-Pyrénées). Even many of the normal school teachers are local men who have never left the department; they retain the local accent and habits, and pass them on to their students (Aveyron).

In short, with few exceptions teachers were merely peasant lads who hoped to improve their condition or wanted to escape military service. Only in extraordinary circumstances would a man who expected to inherit property have wasted his time on something that until the 1880's brought little profit or prestige. The reports amassed in the government's survey of the state of primary instruction in 1864 show that student teachers came from the "working class" and from families of small farmers chiefly interested in getting an exemption from military service for their sons (Dordogne, Eure, Savoy); that they were recruited from the poor families of the countryside (Lot-et-Garonne); that they had the defective pronunciation and habits of the peasants (Calvados). A motion of the governing board of the normal school of Montpellier encapsulates the problem in blunt terms: "Whereas the department's . . . wealth offers young men of intelligence and a little money careers much more profitable than that of elementary teaching and which they in fact prefer; whereas the students of the normal school are recruited only among the poor inhabitants of the mountain areas in the department's north and west . . ." Even as late as 1881 we hear that recruitment came easily in the poorer regions; but that in wealthy ones, where families had few children, only those who were useless in the fields were sent to normal schools. Many must have gone off with the greatest reluctance to what we could generously describe as miserable holes, far worse than barracks. "A sorry, mean, and shabby dump materially and morally" was how one report described the normal school at Parthenay (Deux-Sèvres) in 1882. "Intellectually nonexistent, depressing on all counts, it forms or deforms poor young peasants to become poor old teachers."

Also, we may add, acolytes of the priest. "Elementary education properly understood . . . is the fraternal union of presbytery and school," pronounced Rector Denain at an awards ceremony in 1862. Just how fraternal, the readers of Flaubert's Bouvard and Pécuchet could learn. "The teacher is no more than a mnemotechnical auxiliary of the priest," complained Félix Pécaut, less mellifluously than the rector. Yet by then things had improved since the day when the teacher's first duty was to assist the priest, sing all the offices, sweep the church once a week, dust and polish the ornaments, see that the bells were rung and the clock was wound, and finally keep school and instruct the children according to the true faith. But inspectors in the day of Marshal Mac-Mahon still checked to make sure that "teachers show themselves useful auxiliaries of the priests." The peasants greatly appreciated teachers when it came to practical matters such as surveying land and measuring properties, remembered a beginner of those days; but their subjection to the priests was horrid. One need not wonder at the consistent devotion of teachers after the 16th of May to a Republic that emancipated them from their humiliating bondage. One need not wonder either that it should take something of a revolution—in training and consequently in outlook—for the village schoolteacher to blossom into the dynamic missionary illustrated in our books.

But before teachers could take on the role of missionaries, they had to learn to live the part. Too many teachers "dress like peasants, think like peasants. They are peasants who have a slightly different trade." They mixed with the villagers, went off to fairs with them; there was no distance here and certainly no respect. "One has a lot of trouble to make them give up such habits." The 1880's saw a campaign to turn these browbeaten peasants into models of the new enlightened style. Above all, they were not to go around "dressed in smocks, caps, and sabots, keeping their heads covered in class like their students . . . as uncivilized as the populations in whose midst they live." In their persons and in their actions teachers were expected to maintain standards that would reflect their elevated functions and their representative role.

Though pay improved somewhat, such standards were difficult to maintain. Beginning teachers earned 700 francs a year in 1881, 800 ten years later, and 900 between 1897 and 1905, when the starting salary was raised to 1,100 francs. The highest pay doubled in the same period. By the turn of the century, after withholdings for pensions and other things, country teachers at last earned as much as a miner and more than a Paris laundress or a textile worker. But they had to "dress suitably," and to keep up at least outwardly a style of living that went with their position as *fonctionnaires d'Etat* (1889) and aspiring notables. That they were willing and able to make the attempt was due to the training inculcated by the reformed normal schools. . . .

As early as 1865 the teachers' growing influence rated an official warning. Teachers were running the affairs of negligent, often illiterate mayors. They had become legal advisers to the villagers; lent farmers money, wrote their letters, and surveyed their fields; had "become occult powers." Their prestige was great, their status in the community almost "sacerdotal." Most alarming of all, warned the sub-prefect of Joigny (Yonne), teachers were even beginning to go into politics. Hardly the browbeaten figure that Flaubert etched.

Such forebodings became serious fact when village teachers, trained to greater competence and new self-respect, became the licensed representatives of the Republic. By the 1890's they not only ran the administration in almost all the communes, but also in some instances worked as correspondents for the local newspapers, earning a useful increment in salary and prestige. A theme that recurs frequently in political accounts is the observation that the local schoolteacher "had turned the commune round politically by his influence on the young." The teacher was the municipal lamppost, the *bec de gaz municipal*, a half-friendly but suggestive nickname. The political influence attributed to him was probably a reflection of shifts that we have seen to have had more complex roots. But even if exaggerated, such reports attest to the growing role of the man whose light, however dim, glowed strongly on his parish.

This could not have happened as long as schools remained irrelevant to a great many people; and this they did into the last quarter of the century. Most peasants wanted their children to work and contribute to the family budget. If they sent them to school at all, it was usually for the sole purpose of getting them past their first communion, a crucial rite of passage. Once that was accomplished, the child was withdrawn. Parents send their children to school for a few winter months before their communion, grumbled a Breton teacher in 1861, and that short time was almost exclusively devoted to learning the catechism, an awkward business since the children could not read. For this reason communions were made as early as possible, between the ages of ten and twelve. As a result school enrollments of children past that age diminished sharply, and children soon forgot the little they had learned, mostly by rote, lapsing once again into a "state of complete ignorance."

In any case the country school provided little stimulus to learning for its pupils, not even the challenge of exposure to more motivated students. Parents in comfortable circumstances who were willing and able to keep their children in school for a time preferred to send them to the bourg or to a boarding school. More important, the offspring of wealthier parents, aware that schooling would play a part in their later activities, assimilated more and retained more of what they learned. The parents took more interest in their work. Thus the children of the poor had access to poorer schools, less time to attend them, and far less reason to make the most of such opportunity than their better-off mates.

Some poorer families kept their children out of school under the pressure of local landowners who did not want their future work force to be subverted or diminished by even a modicum of book-learning. More were discouraged by the distance the children had to cover to get to school and by the state of the roads. Where the peasants lived in small, dispersed settlements or in isolated houses the problem was twice as difficult. One village in Finistère refused to build a school because "the distance from the hamlets to the center does not permit farmers to send their children there. In summer they need them to watch the cattle; in winter they could not get to school because of the bad state of the roads." Another, in Ille-et-Vilaine, pointed out that though the present school seemed to have cramped quarters, the space was adequate because no child could make his way to school before the age of eight or nine, which cut the potential attendance by half. In Sarthe the rural roads were too bad for children to negotiate in the winter months; in Maurienne, Tarentaise, and Savoy generally, only the twelve- or thirteen-year-old child had the stamina to get to school regularly. At that point they left! Not especially surprising, considering that they might have had to cover three to five miles on foot each way or use a boat to get there. In the Lannion district of Côtes-du-Nord where, in 1877, one child in three was not enrolled in a school though nearly every parish had one, the figures show that distance from isolated farms and hamlets made a significant difference, with the loneliest cantons averaging only half the enrollment of the others. . . .

Where and when children were registered in school, what matters, after all, is not their enrollment as such, but their attendance. This varied with the region and its ways, but tended generally to be restricted to the winter months. As actual or potential workers, children were free for school only when there was no work. In the Limousin they did not say that a child had been in school for three years but that he had three winters in school. He entered it in December, after the chestnuts had been gathered and the migrants he had helped replace had returned home, and left in late March or early April when the migrants set off again. Similarly, in Côte-d'Or and the Jura, which had more elementary schools for their outlying villages and hamlets than most departments, children usually had to work much of the year, and attended class for only a few months in the winter, forgetting in the interval whatever they had learned. The only ones who benefited from schooling were the sons of those with sufficient means to do without their help. In the Doubs, on the other hand, winter is hard and long. This kept the children in school longer, and they picked up more. Yet even children who did not help their parents left school in March or April. In Lozère children attended school four months a year at most. After Easter, only infants were left; schools were either closed down or turned into day nurseries (1877). In Manche parents were happy to leave children in school during the years when they would only get underfoot around the house, but wanted to withdraw them as soon as they were able-bodied, precisely when they would be at their most teachable (1892). Alain Corbin concludes that child labor disappeared only slowly, between the 1870's and the late 1880's. By the end of the century, at any rate, inspectors could note a greater regularity in school attendance in the winter. Continued complaints of irregularity now referred to the rest of the year. Grumbles were bitter, but standards had been raised. . . .

We hear of a large Périgord village, with a quota of 20 scholarships, whose school in mid-century was attended by only three paying and three non-paying pupils. It was not enough to admit the needy free. In 1884 Georges Clemenceau met a peasant in a field with his son, and asked him why the child was not in school. "Will you give him a private income?," the peasant answered. The child who went to school had to bring a log for the fire, or a few sous instead. He had to provide his own ink, pen, and paper for writing—and though a slate could be used, the results were less than satisfactory. "A great number of children admitted to schools free get no benefit because they cannot acquire the indispensable books and class materials," read a report of 1875. "The well-off send their children away to school," reported a teacher from Tarn in the 1860's. "The poor don't send them to the elementary schools, because it costs 18–24 francs a year plus books, paper, etc., which can raise the cost to 30 francs." So, even if tuition was free, the child attending school, a useless mouth around the household board, was an expense. The "inexplicable inertia," the "indifference" that perplexed and annoyed apostles of the school, was in good part due to poverty—a lack of cash so great that, as a pastor in the Pyrenees explained in 1861, "even if the school fees were only 50 cents, they would still be a painful subject of anxiety and concern for the farmer." We must conclude, with a correspondent from Gironde, that "it is not enough for schooling to be free; the child's work must bring in some revenue to cover his keep or simply because the family needs it."

But the same report held out the hope of change: "The remedy to this state of things lies in public opinion. Even the most ignorant portion of the masses begins to understand that instruction is useful to all [and not just to their betters]. Country people know now that reading, writing, and arithmetic are means of rising in the world." Let us say at least that they began to know it. Free education had been gratuitous, that is, seemingly useless, to the children of the poor because it did not serve any needs that their parents could discern. The remitting of fees did not prove a critical factor in rural school attendance. There is no good evidence that the poor children who were admitted as free students attended school more diligently as a result; indeed, often they attended less regularly than the paying students. The crux of school attendance lay in the social practice: when going to school was the thing to do, all would do it. It also lay in the dawning comprehension, related to changing circumstances, that instruction was useful. With this realization, even lack of means would not deter many from sending their children to school.

We have arrived at the fundamental cause of that "indifference" to book learning that Philippe Ariès, like Destutt de Tracy before him, finds indigenous to the countryside. The urban poor had occasion to use the skills picked up in parish schools and to observe the opportunities of improving their position with that learning. In the countryside, such skills brought little profit, their absence small disadvantage, and there were fewer chinks in the armor of misery through which curiosity or enterprise could find escape. The *Statistique* of Vendée, regretting in 1844 that the department's inhabitants "showed little inclination for the study of sciences and polite literature, or for the culture of fine arts," sounds ridiculous until it shows that it understands why this was not surprising: "Far from the sources of inspiration and taste, they were rarely in a position to know their value or [to find] any object of emulation." Objects of emulation were scarce in the countryside, sources of inspiration even scarcer.

School was perceived as useless and what it taught had little relation to local life and needs. The teacher taught the metric system when *toises, cordes,* and *pouces* were in current use; counted money in francs when prices were in *louis* and *écus.* French was of little use when everyone spoke patois and official announcements were made by a public crier in the local speech. Anyway, the school did not teach *French,* but arid rules of grammar. In short, school had no practical application. It was a luxury at best, a form of more or less conspicuous consumption. Corbin has pointed out the significant role that all this played in the lack of interest displayed by parents and children. When Martin Nadaud's father wanted to send him to school, neighbors and relatives argued that for a country child school learning was useless, enabling him merely to make a few letters and carry books at mass. Teachers and school inspectors failed to persuade the peasants that reading and writing had any value in themselves. And parents found their reticence justified by the slight difference in the situation of those who attended school and of those who did not. When Ferdinand Buisson linked poor school attendance to a lack of concern for the moral benefits that children could derive, he was in the great (abstract) tradition. Yet show people a practical benefit that they could understand, and the problem would shrink to manageable proportions. Rural inhabitants, explained a village mayor, were "only very vaguely conscious of an intellectual or moral culture that has no immediate or tangible relation to pecuniary profit." That seemed to make sense. Before a man could want his child to go to school, he would have to abandon "the gross material interests" that were all he understood. Not so. It was when the school mobilized those interests that men began to care.

In darkest Finistère, while the other local councils squirmed uncomfortably before the requirements imposed by Guizot's education law of 1833, the council of Audierne alone voiced a positive response. Since most children in the little port "belong to families of sailors and soldiers, and are destined, like their fathers, to defend the fatherland [on] sea or land, where they can expect no advancement if they lack basic instruction and cannot read, write, or reckon sums," the council decided that "a school appears necessary." Not all municipalities enjoyed such enlightened majorities and many, we have seen, placed the personal interests of men who could fend for their children's schooling above the training of potential competitors or social rebels. But the connection between practical interest and school, when it became apparent, was a potent force.

A number of individuals had overcome the disadvantage of illiteracy by self-education. Others, faced with the need to keep accounts, devised private systems of notation. By their nature, such records were not likely to survive; but we do know about a Loire mariner who, around 1830, kept track of his expenses by drawing the objects of his outlays or figures of little men accompanied by ciphers to show francs and sous. Clearly, mariners were involved in trade and in commercial transactions long before the peasants of the isolated countryside had reason to engage in such activities. Yet by the 1870's even sharecroppers in Brittany were being pressed to keep accounts. Manuscripts of the accounts maintained by two illiterate sharecroppers in Finistère have survived to show the new need for records. Each man separately seems to have devised a system of figurative notation to identify purchases (rope, horseshoe, horse collar), hired help (a man with a spade to dig up a field or an expensive sawyer), the number of horses or cattle sold, and coins (*sol, réal, écu*). These rough records, with their crude, ingenious shapes reminiscent of children's drawings, were preserved by offspring who went to school. The very treasuring of them as artifacts suggests the reasoning that led to that decision.

My point is that it needed personal experience to persuade people of the usefulness of education. Certain migrants had learned this, and we have seen how they and their children recognized at an early date "the value of instruction and the profit one can derive from it in the great centers." Through the second half of the century, school attendance in migrant Creuse was far better than in neighboring Haute-Vienne and Corrèze—higher by 7 percent and 12 percent, respectively, in 1876. Another spur to schooling came from the military law of 1872, not only because it abolished the purchase of substitutes, but also because it provided advantages for men who could read and write and threatened illiterate conscripts with an additional year of service. The school authorities made haste to refer to these facets of the law to persuade parents to send their children to school. In Isère a poster was even displayed in every schoolroom, and teachers were required to read and discuss it at least every two weeks, presumably arguing that the fulfillment of one patriotic duty could help lighten the burden of another.

But another army was growing, as important as the regular one—the body of public and private employees, access to which was opened by the school certificate, the certificate of elementary studies. The little school of Roger Thabault's Mazières put its graduates into the numerous jobs that opened up there (and elsewhere), with economic, social, and political development: the town's 15 civil servants in 1876 had become 25 in 1886, and there were seven railway employees as well. Ambition was encouraged by propaganda. "A good primary education allows one to secure a post in several state services," the student was told in a first-year civics text published in 1880. "The government servant has a secure position. That is why government posts are in great demand." They were. Given the chance, many peasants wanted to stop being peasants, to change to something else. In 1899, 40 former natives of the little village of Soye in Doubs, population 444, worked as functionaries elsewhere, and 14 inhabitants worked as domestics in town. The prefecture of Seine received 50,000 applications for 400 openings in its departments.

Other times had seen the growth of a state bureaucracy that triggered the expansion of education to fill the available posts. Such educational booms, however, had been restricted to relatively high social groups. Under the Third Republic the means for those too humble to have gotten their share of the educational pie were made available just when the ends (i.e., the jobs) emerged to reinforce and justify their use. Around the 1880's even rural laborers began to lend attention to the schools. As the number of jobs expanded and getting one became more than an idle dream, the education that would help secure such prestigious jobs became important. Even more so the certificate to which it led. Scattered encomiums to its practical uses appear in the late 1870's. By 1880 Pécaut could report that the school certificate "is slowly being accepted. Families realize that this small diploma can be of use for several kinds of jobs; hence they consent ever more frequently to leave their children in school for a longer time." Schools were still badly housed, still far from home, but children now were made to attend even when they lived six km away, because "the idea of the utility and the necessity of elementary schooling" had caught on so well.

The recognition of new possibilities and of the school as a key to their exploitation was in full evidence by the 1890's. By 1894 practically every child in a village of Lower Provence that had been almost totally illiterate a generation earlier was attending school, even those who lived one and a half hours' walk away. In the southwest the image of little boys doing their homework of an evening by the light of the dying embers became a reality. Municipal councils voted rewards for teachers whose pupils won the coveted certificate. Families became avid for it; they celebrated when a child got one; too many failures could become issues raised at council meetings. In a natural evolution, the school certificate, significant because of the material advantages it could help secure, became an end in itself. "It is an honor to get it," wrote a little girl (and wrote it very badly: "être ademise s'est un honneur d'avoir son certificat d'étude"), about what popular parlance dubbed the "Santificat." The passing of the examination became an eminent occasion, competing in importance with the first communion. Men who had taken it in the 1880's remembered the questions that they had to answer, had every detail of their examination day graven in their memories. To take one example among many, here is Charles Moureu, member of the Academy of Medicine and professor at the Collège de France, speaking at the graduation ceremony of his native village in the Pyrenees in 1911: "I could if I wanted to recite by heart the exact details of the problem that turned on the things Peter and Nicholas bought and sold."

There were of course more immediate gains: there would be no more need to go to the nearest town to consult a solicitor or a notary when one wanted to draw up a simple bill or promissory note, make out a receipt, settle an account in arrears, or merely write a letter, explained a thirteen-year-old schoolboy in the Aube. The literate man did not have to reveal his friendships, his secrets, his affairs to some third party. And he could better himself—in local politics, or teaching, or the army (whence he returned with a pension and decorations, achieving a position "that places him above the vulgar crowd").

The vulgar crowd was full of the sort of peasants whose stereotyped image filled current literature: they spoke ungrammatically, used characteristic locutions, mishandled the small vocabulary at their command, and "do not look more intelligent than other peasant farmers around them." The only escape from this was education, which taught order, cleanliness, efficiency, success, and *civilization*. Official reports coupled poor education with rude, brutal ways. Where schooling did not take hold, "ways are coarse, characters are violent, excitable, and hotheaded, troubles and brawls are frequent." The school was supposed to improve manners and customs, and soothe the savage breast. The polite forms it inculcated "softened the savagery and harshness natural to peasants." Improved behavior and morality would be attributed to the effects of schooling. Schools set out "to modify the habits of bodily hygiene and cleanliness, social and domestic manners, and the way of looking at things and judging them." Savage children were taught new manners: how to greet strangers, how to knock on doors, how to behave in decent company. "A bourgeois farts when his belly is empty; a Breton [peasant] burps when his belly is full," declared a proverb that seems to confuse urban and rural differences with race. Children were taught that propriety prohibited either manifestation; and also that cleanliness was an essential part of wisdom.

The schools played a crucial role in forcing children to keep clean(er), but the teachers had to struggle mightily to that end. Hair, nails, and ears were subject to regular review; the waterpump was pressed into frequent use; the state of clothes, like the standards of the child's behavior out of school, received critical attention and constant reproof. Study, ran the text of one exercise, "fills the mind, corrects false prejudices, helps us order speech and writing, teaches love of work and improves capacity for business and for jobs." What does study tell us? Among other things: cold baths are dangerous; the observance of festivals is a religious duty; labor abuses the body less than pleasure; justice protects the good and punishes the wicked; tobacco is a poison, a useless expenditure that destroys one's memory, and those who use it to excess live in a sort of dream, their eye dead, incapable of paying attention to anything, indifferent and selfish. And then there was the lesson of

Jules and Julie, who are rich and therefore do not work at school; and who, having learned nothing, are embarrassed later by their ignorance, blushing with shame when people laugh at them for the mistakes they make when speaking. Only the schools could "change primitive conditions," declared Ardouin-Dumazet. The primitive conditions themselves were changing, and schools helped their charges to adapt to this.

Of course they did more—or they did it more broadly. If we are prepared to set up categories with well-drawn limits, society educates and school instructs. The school imparts particular kinds of learned knowledge, society inculcates the conclusions of experience assimilated over a span of time. But such a view, applicable to specific skills and subjects, has to be altered when the instruction offered by the school directs itself to realms that are at variance with social education (as in the case of language or measures), or that social education ignores (as in the case of patriotism). In other words, the schools provide a complementary, even a counter-education, because the education of the local society does not coincide with that needed to create a national one. This is where schooling becomes a major agent of acculturation: shaping individuals to fit into societies and cultures broader than their own, and persuading them that these broader realms are their own, as much as the pays they really know and more so.

The great problem of modern societies, or so François Guizot considered in his *Memoirs*, is the governance of minds. Guizot had done his best to make elementary education "a guarantee of order and social stability." In its first article, his law of 1833 defined the instruction it was intended to provide: the teaching of reading, writing, and arithmetic would furnish essential skills; the teaching of French and of the metric system would implant or increase the sense of unity under French nationhood; moral and religious instruction would serve social and spiritual needs.

What these social needs were is laid out clearly in various writings, both official and unofficial. "Instructing the people," explained an anonymous writer of 1861, "is to condition them to understand and appreciate the beneficence of the government." Eight years later, the inspecteur d'Académie of Montauban concurred: "The people must learn from education all the reasons they have for appreciating their condition." A first-year civics textbook set out to perform this task:

> *Society* (summary): (1) French society is ruled by just laws, because it is a democratic society. (2) All the French are equal in their rights; but there are inequalities between us that stem from nature or from wealth. (3) These inequalities cannot disappear. (4) Man works to become rich; if he lacked this hope, work would cease and France would decline. It is therefore necessary that each of us should be able to keep the money he has earned.

The ideals of the educators were to be fulfilled at least in part.

Schools taught potent lessons of morality focused on duty, effort, and seriousness of purpose. Hard work and rectitude were bound to bring improvements, internal and external. You must be just and honest. The Roman Camillus refuses to take a town by treachery: the people of the town become the allies of Rome. Never forget that no end, however useful, can justify injustice. Progress is good, routine is bad. "Routine consists in refusing to make any improvement and in following the methods of our ancestors." Progress was new schools, fire companies, municipal bands. It was Monsieur Tardieu, mayor of Brive, who built a bridge that permitted people to sell their goods in the market on the other side of the river, and thus increased the prosperity of his town: "The Brivois perceived the possibilities of gain, and the more they worked, the richer they got." A Vosges village teacher's report of 1889 echoes what he taught and what his students learned: "The farmers are better educated and understand that they have to break with their routine, if they want to earn more. In 1870 they only did what they had seen their forebears doing."

"Believe in progress with a sincere and ardent faith. . . . Never forget that the history of all civilization is a perpetual glorification of work." Perhaps it is true that men are seldom so harmlessly employed as when their energies are bent on making money. "Work draws men together and prepares the reign of peace." "Work is the instrument of all progress." Francinet and his little friends are told the story of the sago tree, which feeds a man during a whole year in return for only a few hours' work, but in so doing, destroys his moral values. Conclusion: "Work is moralizing and instructive par excellence. But man only resigns himself to constant and regular labor under the pressure of need." One rises in the world by work, order, thrift: "Not all at once, of course. My father had nothing, I have something; my children, if they do like me, will double, triple what I leave behind. My grandchildren will be gentlemen. This is how one rises in the world." The speaker is the shoemaker Grégoire, hero of several little moral tales in a collection published by Ernest Lavisse in 1887. They warn against idleness, indolence, and thriftlessness, and make their point with lots of solid detail ("his charming wife brought a dowry of 5,000 francs; he had 3,000 . . ."), with useful explanations of things like bankruptcy law and fraud, and not least, with a profoundly realistic sense of values.

Such is the tale of Pierre, who, called to serve in the 1870 war, escapes death when a German bullet is deflected by two five-franc pieces sent him by his father and his brother as tokens of their affection. Decorated with the military medal, which the proud father frames and garnishes with flowers, Pierre "will go every year to draw the 100 francs to which his medal entitles him until his death, and place the money in the savings bank." Both family affection and heroism are expressed and rewarded not only in elevated feelings but in concrete terms: a thoroughly sensible view. No wonder that patriotism was advocated in similar terms. The fatherland was a source of funds for road repairs, subsidies, school scholarships, and police protection against thieves—"one great family of which we are all a part, and which we must defend always."

We come here to the greatest function of the modern school: to teach not so much useful skills as a new patriotism beyond the limits naturally acknowledged by its charges. The revolutionaries of 1789 had replaced old terms like schoolmaster, regent, and rector, with *instituteur*, because the teacher was intended to *institute* the nation. But the desired effect, that elusive unity of spirit, was recognized as lacking in the 1860's and 1870's as it had been four score years before.

School was a great socializing agent, wrote a village teacher from Gard in 1861. It had to teach children national and patriotic sentiments, explain what the state did for them and why it exacted taxes and military service, and show them their true interest in the fatherland. It seems that there was a great deal to do. The theme remained a constant preoccupation of eminent educators. Twenty years after this, student teachers "must above all be told . . . that their first duty is to make [their charges] love and understand the fatherland." Another ten years, and the high aim is again repeated, that a "national pedagogy" might yet become the soul of popular education. The school is "an instrument of unity," an "answer to dangerous centrifugal tendencies," and of course the "keystone of national defense."

First, the national pedagogy. "The fatherland is not your village, your province, it is all of France. The fatherland is like a great family." This was not learned without some telescoping. "Your fatherland is you," wrote a thirteen-year-old schoolboy dutifully in 1878. "It is your family, it is your people [*les tiens*], in a word it is France, your country." "The fatherland is the *pays* where we are born," wrote another, "where our parents are born and our dearest thoughts lie; it is not only the *pays* we live in, but the region [*contrée*] we inhabit; our fatherland is France." The exercise was a sort of catechism designed to teach the child that it was his duty to defend the fatherland, to shed his blood or die for the commonweal ("When France is threatened, your duty is to take up arms and fly to her rescue"), to obey the government, to perform military service, to work, learn, pay taxes, and so on.

At the very start of school, children were taught that their first duty was to defend their country as soldiers. The army—and this was important, considering the past and enduring hostility to soldiers and soldiering—"is composed of our brothers or parents" or relatives. Commencement speeches recalled this sacred duty in ritual terms—our boys will defend the soil of the fatherland. The whole school program turned on expanding the theme. Gymnastics were meant "to develop in the child the idea of discipline, and prepare him . . . to be a good soldier and a good Frenchman." Children sang stirring songs like the "Flag of France," the "Lost Sentry," and "La Marseillaise." Compositions on the theme were ordered up, with title and content provided: "Letter of a Young Soldier to His Parents. He tells them that he has fought against the enemies of the fatherland, has been wounded . . . and is proud (as they must be too) that he has shed his blood for the fatherland." And teachers reported with satisfaction how they implanted the love of the fatherland by evoking "those memories that attach our hearts to the fatherland" from history, and then "develop[ed] this sentiment by showing France strong and powerful *when united.*" . . .

But the effects of school went further. In the first place, the literary or written language children learned in schools was as alien to the spoken tongue as spoken French itself was to their native dialect. In other words, schools began their work by propagating an artificial language, and this was true even for French-speakers. They did this largely through the discipline of dictations, "the instrument of a learned and universal language" beyond the local ken. As a result, many students learned to express themselves freely and easily in speech, but had difficulty when it came to writing or to expressing thought in an idiom close to that of the written word. We can glimpse this best in the surviving files of gendarmerie reports, which are often drawn up in a stilted administrative style and relate even simple events in an awkward and convoluted manner.

A striking result of this (much worse in areas estranged by dialect) was that "for months or years [the children] give no sign of intelligence, merely imitate what they see done." Just as legislation can create crime by fiat, so education created stupidity by setting up standards of communication that many found difficult to attain. "Our children cannot find, and indeed have no way to find, enough French words to express their thoughts," reported a Cantal teacher. The result was a divorce between school learning, often acquired by rote, and assimilation, which helped slow down the progress of the schools. Memorization saved the trouble of "having to translate one's thoughts into correct French." It also divorced word from reality. Many children "can spell, but syllables have no meaning for them; can read, but fail to understand what they read, or to recognize in writing some words they know but whose orthography is alien," or to identify words learned in French with the objects around them. "You will learn it, this language of well-bred people, and you will speak it some day," promised a prize-giver in Dordogne in 1897. The future tense used in such improbable circumstances suggests a possible reason why, by 1907, the number of illiterate conscripts seems to have been slightly higher than in the immediate past. The absolute banning of the native tongue, which had been helpful in teaching French as a second language, inhibited the learning of idiomatic French and impeded its full assimilation.

This is not to say that French did not make great strides forward. It did. But writing remained a socially privileged form of expression, and the French of the schools and of the dictations was an alienating as well as an integrative force. Perhaps that was what a school inspector meant when, looking back from 1897, he declared: "Ignorance used to precede school; today on the contrary it follows schooling."

Of course there were (from the school's point of view) positive results;

and these two went beyond the immediately obvious. The symbolism of images learned at school created a whole new language and provided common points of reference that straddled regional boundaries exactly as national patriotism was meant to do. Where local dialect and locutions insulated and preserved, the lessons of the school, standardized throughout France, taught a unifying idiom. In Ain, the Ardennes, Vendée, all children became familiar with references or identities that could thereafter be used by the authorities, the press, and the politicians to appeal to them as a single body. Lessons emphasizing certain associations bound generations together. The Kings of France were the older sons of the Church, time was the river that carried all in its waters, a poet was a favorite of the muses, Touraine was the garden of France, and Joan of Arc the shepherdess of Lorraine. Local saws and proverbs were replaced by nationally valid ones, regional locutions by others learned in books: castles in Spain rose above local ruins, and golden calves bleated more loudly than the stabled ones. The very mythology of ambition was now illustrated by landscapes that education had suggested, more stirring than the humbler ones at hand and by this time no less familiar. These are only aspects of the wide-ranging process of standardization that helped create and reinforce French unity, while contributing to the disintegration of rival allegiances.

The cultural underpinnings of rural society, already battered by material changes, were further weakened by shifting values. First of all, manual labor was devalued—or better still, the natural aversion to its drudgery was reinforced. The elementary schools, designed to form citizens, neglected producers. The school glorified labor as a moral value, but ignored work as an everyday form of culture. The well-established contrast between the plucky, mettlesome spirit of the *courageux* and the idle *fainéant*—the one hardworking, especially or only with his hands, the other avoiding manual labor—was translated into scholastic terms. Soon, the idle boy was the one likely to be the most pressed into hard physical labor, the plucky boy the one most enterprising with his books. It made good sense, for the rewards of work now came to those not doing what had once been recognized as work. But it opened a crack—one more—in age-old solidarities.

In a great many homes, illiterate adults depended on small children to carry out what were becoming essential tasks—accounting, correspondence, taking notes, reading aloud pertinent documents or newspaper items. And new literacies at whatever level made new ideas accessible, especially to the young, to whom certain profound changes in the political climate of country districts were now attributed. In any case, the relationship between school and social claims was not ignored in their own time: "The Republic has founded schools," sang Montéhus, the revolutionary chansonnier, "so that now the people have learned how to count. The people have had enough of the pauper's mite; they want an accounting, and not charity!" More important, where, as in Brittany, a determined campaign taught new generations French, "children and parents form two worlds apart, so separated in spirit, so estranged by speech, that there is no more community of ideas and feelings, hence no intimacy. Often, as a matter of fact, any kind of relationship becomes impossible." This is both exaggerated and suggestive of a generation gap more easily discerned in modern societies than in traditional ones. But even granting the exaggeration, the corrosive effects of one sort of education on a society based on another kind are undeniable.

Like migration, politics, and economic development, schools brought suggestions of alternative values and hierarchies; and of commitments to other bodies than the local group. They eased individuals out of the latter's grip and shattered the hold of unchallenged cultural and political creeds—but only to train their votaries for another faith.

New Leisure: Social Drinking

MICHAEL MARRUS

Popular patterns of recreation were severely disrupted during the first phase of the industrial revolution. The confusion of movement from countryside to city and a concerted middle-class attack on leisure forms that wasted time or fostered violence or immorality are the most obvious causes of the decline of many familiar games and dances. New, individualistic recreations, such as heightened sexual activity, may have played a role as well. In any event, the later nineteenth century, when the masses of working people enjoyed some increase in income and above all some time free from work, saw diverse efforts to develop a new leisure style. Sports served as one expression of this; popular theater and, soon, the movies another; and social drinking yet a third.

In this period around the turn of the century, the meaning of the new strivings toward entertainment raises many questions still applicable to leisure in modern society. Were people trying to escape from the tragic reality of existence? Were they seeking to revive, in new forms and with new affluence, pleasures that had been common in preindustrial life? (Has leisure modernized or does it demonstrate a basic desire for continuity?) Have the leisure forms in fact produced enjoyment, and, if so, of what sort?

Drinking, by no means a new pastime in Western society, undoubtedly received unusual attention. Bars served as meeting places amid the crowded housing of the cities, and drinking easily took on attributes beyond the ingestion of alcohol. Without question, freed from customary community and family controls, drinking could get out of hand, a problem that has by no means ended with the further development of modern society. This kind of leisure can prove to be not just an escape from reality but a tragic way of life of its own. But social drinking is seen in the following selection to be more commonly an important first step in the development of new leisure interests, separate from work and from home alike. If it was hardly a glorious inaugural to a new age of leisure, it touched base with popular means and popular need, and, in somewhat different forms, has become a fixture in contemporary society. The novelty of modern leisure opportunities suggests some caution in condemning the avenues explored in the recent past; we are still having trouble defining and justifying what we do when we are not working, though most of us are bent on doing something.

When was the time that Frenchmen drank the most? For societies, even more than for individuals, inebriation in times past becomes quickly blurred in the collective memory; time itself has a way of obscuring the good old days, and the order in which things happened becomes lost in a mixture of nostalgia and uncertainty. In a country like France, however, the faded images of a long past of heavy drinking can at least be partially brought into focus with the aid of the long columns of statistics assembled in the *Annuaire statistique de la France.* How characteristic of this country, where administrative surveillance of social life has always been so important, that the painstaking surveys of the Ministry of Finance should cast light where the human memory fails! With the aid of this data, and with the perspective provided by a wealth of literature (mostly coming from the end of the nineteenth century), we can approach a subject which historians have tended to neglect. Looking closely at this material, it is possible to link changes in drinking patterns to larger changes in the nature of French society. The purpose of this paper is to open the question of social drinking in France during the century before 1914 by examining the great collective binge which took place as the period drew to a close. For this is the time, it turns out, in the era sometimes known as *la belle époque,* that Frenchmen drank the most.

Traditionally, it would appear, historians have discussed the subject of drink from the perspective of social pathology. More often than not, this is where they have begun and ended their consideration of the matter. Perhaps under the influence of middle-class commentary which has frequently been the basis for historical description, or perhaps through exposure to a particular line of temperance argumentation, historians frequently assume that periods of heavy drinking, especially among the lower classes, were also periods of severe social dislocation and unusual popular suffering. "The massive and habitual use of alcohol," it has been said recently, "just as with the abuse of narcotics, is a defense against anxiety, a means of coping with inner stress and tension. The appropriate historical question is: what were people so anxious about that they drank so much?" Some writers have reversed the terms and have assigned to drink a powerful and independent causal force. Thus Dorothy George's famous discussion of gin drinking in eighteenth-century London related what she felt as a remarkably high level of consumption in the first part of the century to various indices of social breakdown, especially mortality rates. With government action against spirits and the public's turning to a considerably less lethal beverage around 1750—good English beer—things were said to have improved. Whatever their views on these issues of historical causation, however, scholars commonly associate drink and social distress in describing a particular society. This approach is a familiar one in surveys of popular life during the first half of the nineteenth century, when

From Michael Marrus, "Social Drinking in the Belle Epoque," *Journal of Social History* (1974), pp. 115–41. Reprinted by permission.

the severe changes forced upon society by the beginnings of industrialization are thought to have provided a conjuncture of excessive drinking and popular distress more unhealthy than at any time before or since. William L. Langer, for instance, in his excellent volume on the first half of that century, considers the bleak years of the 1830s and 1840s to have been "the golden age of inebriation" in the industrializing north of Europe. Various other writers, impressed with the wretched conditions of many workers in such periods of rapid social change, have linked the propensity to drink with hard times. Thus, the first part of the century in Europe has a vague reputation for popular drunkenness and high levels of alcoholic consumption unmatched by any other era.

But these analyses both lack statistical underpinning and leave some important questions unanswered. There is, after all, the factor of cost. Can hard times be so easily linked with excessive drinking if people were living at subsistence or below subsistence levels? Is there any evidence that levels of drinking fell off as social and economic conditions improved? Was drink seen by the lower orders themselves as being associated with hard times? Or was drink rather seen as a luxury, an indulgence, as something which an improving society might provide in ever increasing volume? Questions such as these require two approaches to the subject which, because they have been only secondarily interested in studying drink, historians have tended not follow. First, it is important to look at the matter over a very extended period of time. An examination of drinking during the 1840s alone, for example, clearly does not give an adequate basis for evaluating the significance of drink during that period or, for that matter, in hard times generally. What kind of drinking, one is immediately inclined to ask, went on in better times? Second, the historian must try to see the question of drink from the perspective of the popular classes who were doing the drinking. If one shifts attention away from the reformers and towards those who were supposed to be reformed, a new understanding may emerge. To be sure, this is especially difficult when treating intimate or private levels of experience. Information on such matters is inevitably scarce, for neither contemporaries nor historians until fairly recently have thought them worthy of much attention. In particular, as we shall see, there are special difficulties in examining the overwhelming majority of the drinking population—the popular classes at the lower end of the social scale. But such an examination is worth attempting. Eventually, it can tell us not only what men thought about drink, but what drinking they actually did and what significance it had in their lives. . . .

These remarkable increases in consumption suggest, to my mind, that a major extension of social drinking emerged some time in the late 1870s and 1880s. People were drinking more from this time, but they were also drinking more socially; in later decades, following the First World War, by contrast, increased consumption did not necessarily point in the same direction. For the sorts of drinks which principally inflated the general consumption levels during the former period—spirits and especially *apéritifs*—were pre-eminently social drinks, consumed in cabarets and wine shops rather than at home or with meals. Drinking was (and to a lesser degree still is) largely a public activity in France, and the kind of drinking which activated the temperance forces in the early 1890s, and which brought a consciousness of the dangers of alcohol to the public's attention in France at that time, was social drinking, and on a scale which was unmatched in the country's history.

One of the hints of this change was the fact that by the 1880s public drinking was beginning to involve women with some claim to gentility. The world of the cabaret had hitherto been an almost exclusively male sanctuary, except, perhaps, among elements of the working class in a few very large cities. And even there women were a rarity in most drinking places. But all of this began to break down during the decades of intense social drinking before the First World War. . . . Absinthe, the bell-wether alcoholic drink of the *belle époque*, comes down to us today in advertising posters showing women actually enjoying themselves with glass in hand. Times had changed. . . .

What made the growth in the numbers of *débits de boissons* [drinking places] so important was the place which they had come to occupy in the lives of those who patronized them. In many ways, especially for lower-class Frenchmen, the *débit* was the principal if not the sole place in which popular sociability could take place. Living in cramped and insalubrious quarters which were often ill-lit and poorly heated, people felt a powerful attraction to the bright, warm and crowded world of cabarets and bistros. Here (and often only here) the working man could feel *chez lui*. According to the testimony of several observers, the *débitant* became an important figure in his neighbourhood, a *personnage* who was respected often as a kind of "social confessor," from whom one asked advice and revealed confidences. Just at the outskirts of most large cities, moreover, just beyond the city limits within which alcohol was often subject to special taxes, there were frequently cabarets or inns to which working men would walk on Sundays in order to pass the day drinking away from the urban core. In time, cities grew out to embrace these *guinguettes*, but their popularity remained high throughout the nineteenth century. Contemporaries noted that the habit of going to the cabaret was spreading to the countryside in the latter part of the nineteenth century, moving even into fairly isolated regions and replacing the family *foyer* or the *veillées* as the focus of leisure activity for men.

The *débit* performed a wide variety of functions in addition to serving the basic needs of sociability. It was a place where newspapers and periodicals were frequently available to be read, where writing material could be borrowed and where games of all sorts were organized, both indoors and out. Many employers preferred to pay their workers at the *marchand de vins*, much to the dismay of temperance activists who were unsuccessful at the turn of the century in attempting to have a law passed against this practice. Because the *débits* were used in this manner, it was not uncommon for the *patron* to undertake primitive banking responsibilities, taking charge of workers' or soldiers' pay, accepting deposits and withdrawals, providing credit or cashing money orders with less red tape than the postal authorities. Similarly, drinking places often served as employment agencies where subcontractors assembled gangs of workmen in specific trades, especially those involving heavy manual work. Sometimes too the *débit* became a much more formal placement bureau, in which individual workmen would be directed to specific jobs. Although the government formally suppressed this practice in 1904, many cabarets apparently continued to evade the spirit of the law. *Débits* provided places for their customers to sleep and were frequently accused of being centres for prostitution in large cities. They were the places where ordinary people celebrated a birth or a wedding, and they were the places to which mourners would repair after a funeral.

But most of all the *débit de boissons* was a place to meet. In the 40,000 or so *débits* in Paris at the end of the nineteenth century there were frequently two rooms—one for regular business and another for the gatherings of political groups, trade union locals, popular societies or whatever. Large public assemblies took place in schools or theatres, but virtually all small meetings were held at the local *marchand de vins*. In this respect the *débit* had changed little, at the turn of the century, from the time of Balzac; it was the latter who had once referred to the cabaret as "the parliament of the people." These parliaments, of course, did not abide by the same rules of order. An anarchist cell plotting in the back room could not have had much in common with a group of neighbours discussing the bicycle champions of the *Tour de France*. Nor was the traditional camaraderie of the *parti républicain*, (so solidly based in the cafés of France), of the same character as the working-class radicalism which habitually affected some bars in the mining country. In each case, however, the most congenial environment for sociability was invariably provided by the local *débit de boissons*. There was virtually no other place to go.

Much of what has just been said could be applied to the *débits de boissons* at any time throughout the nineteenth century. There were some developments, however, which were peculiar to the period we have estimated to be one of particularly extensive social drinking. As we have noted, the number of *débits* increased impressively beginning in the mid-1870s, moving far ahead of the general population growth and eventually tapering off about 1909. But not only did the numbers increase; so also did the attractiveness of the *débits* and the range of facilities which they offered. Modeling themselves on the sumptuous mirrored palaces which were the upper-class cafés of the Second Empire, many cabarets began to take on an elegant, posh appearance in the 1880s and 1890s. While the old *marchand de vins* with sawdust on the floor continued in operation for those with less extravagant tastes, a new "*cabaret de luxe*" developed for common people. In the capital these remained open throughout the night in certain quarters; "bars" which were considered in the American style appeared about the same time in Paris, Bordeaux and elsewhere, with their counters made of zinc and their wide variety of alcoholic drinks. Some of the new *débits* provided a special atmosphere to draw customers; waiters dressed up in special costumes or—an added attraction—women were hired to serve the drinks. In the "Café-Brasserie du Divorce" in Paris, set up after a statute permitting divorce was passed by the French parliament in 1884, waitresses wore legal gowns, buckle shoes and lots of ribbon. Even for more ordinary folk, the cabarets at the end of the century had new attractions. Mechanical games first made their appearance at the time, exercising their fascination for customers as they have done ever since; a less successful enterprise, but one which was apparently popular then was the automatic dispenser of alcoholic drinks. Telephones, indoor plumbing and electric lights also helped make the "salon of the working man" more congenial. By all appearances the period from the 1880s until the First World War was the golden age of the cabaret in France. . . .

Did people drink more because they had more free time? One of the most eloquent socialist spokesmen on the subject, the Belgian deputy Emile Vandervelde, believed that in some sense they did. Of course, he argued, the question of excessive drinking related in a fundamental way to conditions of inequity in a capitalist society. But it was his general observation that the workers who drank the most were not the most miserable, not those who were drowning their socioeconomic sorrows, but rather those with the time and money to spend. What happened was that as working conditions began to improve, and as wages slowly went up, workers naturally turned to drink during a transitional period because they were still adjusting to a more affluent state of affairs. What was new to them was the prospect of having any pleasure at all which was not furtively snatched from the grip of necessity. Workers could hardly be blamed, therefore, if they failed at first to act with prudence, for circumstances had not permitted them to develop morally and intellectually to the point where they could do much else with their leisure time. Paradoxically, Vandervelde was able to argue, the rise of alcoholism among the working classes was a sign that they were making rapid social progress. He felt that in time, this progress would work to reduce the high levels of working-class consumption. Others suggested in a similar vein that society provided virtually no alternative to drink when it came to a newly won leisure for the working masses of Frenchmen. Theirs were not the pleasures of the race track, the resort, the theatre or even the numerous associations and *cercles* that members of high society had indulged in for so long. Theirs were rather the simple pleasures of sociability, and sociability in France, as we have seen, meant drink.

Such, at least, was the argument. At times it has a patronizing ring, at least to our ears. But it suggests an alternative to the conventional wisdom of drink-as-despair which has seldom been criticized. Until the general question of leisure has received much more attention than it has by historians, it is impossible to go very far in evaluating this alternative approach. It is possible here only to suggest some general considerations which may be useful in relating drink to leisure time.

It is sometimes pointed out that work and leisure were not nearly so sharply differentiated in pre-industrial, as opposed to industrial societies. For our purposes it may be useful to draw attention to the obvious point that during much of the nineteenth century the drinking of alcoholic beverages was also less neatly relegated to a time of non-work as it generally is now. There is a wealth of testimony to the fact that many manual labourers and even some artisans—especially those who worked in warm places and needed to replace bodily fluids—drank regularly on the job. Building workers in Paris, for example, were not accustomed to spending more than two hours aloft without descending their ladders for a drink. Dock workers in Rouen were paid several times a day in the local bistro, and drank constantly while at work; so did bakers, metal workers, washerwomen and many others. In a good deal of their consumption, these workers drank for reasons of physiology, not pleasure. An elaborate folk mythology about the beneficial effects of alcohol on the worker usually accompanied this drinking. Now all of this, it is probably fair to say, was on the decline as the nineteenth century wore on. While workers in traditional crafts could sometimes escape the exigencies of a strictly disciplined work rhythm, factory workers were much too restrictively regulated and their jobs were frequently too exacting to permit such an indulgence. Employers proved less and less tolerant of what they deemed an unreasonable mixture of alcohol and toil. Instead, drinking was concentrated in the times when workers were off the job; more and more their drinking was to be done in the drinking place rather than in the work place. Similarly, the growing tendency of many workers to live at some distance from their employment brought them more frequently to the cabaret. Passing the *débit* on the way to and from work, sometimes eating a meal there rather than at home, spending more of the day away from their families, they were thus drawn into the ambiance of social drinking. One can speculate, at least, that drinking there was somewhat less restrained than the drinking on the job which was loosely disciplined by the need to continue working. The concentration of the time allotted to social drinking is at any rate a factor which must be weighed in the general balance.

Whatever future research in the area of lower-class leisure patterns might show, it seems plain that social drinking loomed large in the customs of the late nineteenth and early twentieth centuries. These were the years when the amount of time spent at work was beginning to shrink for a large proportion of workers; and this was also the period when the general standard of living began to improve for the working masses of the country. Eventually, of course, leisure and the image of the good life were to become commercialized, with sporting events, the cinema and other activities being taken up by ordinary people. But this was still in the future in 1914. What seems to be characteristic of the period before the First World War, rather, is the impoverishment of leisure, the sheer lack of things for ordinary people to do with the time in which they were not working. It even seems possible that matters had grown worse in this regard over the nineteenth century. Not only was there more time to spend, but there was also a thinner basis for communally organized leisure which had been such an important part of traditional social life. Two writers whose memoirs recounted working-class life at the turn of the nineteenth century described the way in which time had eroded the old artisanal festivals associated with specific trades. In both cases, however, where a rich tradition laden with religious and corporative significance had fallen away, one element alone remained and had become the exclusive preoccupation of the particular workers involved—getting drunk together.

Youth and History

JOHN R. GILLIS

Adolescence as a precise concept was one of the many social discoveries of the nineteenth century. John Gillis, in the following selection, details the reasons for the discovery of adolescence and the framework for life which it set. The definition of adolescence, a middle-class concern, relates closely to new attitudes toward children and toward the new importance of education. It had a demographic base in the massive new numbers of young people, the product of previous population upheaval. The potentially looser framework of urban life, and the visibility of the sexual and other behavior among young working-class people, provided an impetus to this new interest. The middle class would use its heightened sensitivity to adolescence to try to discipline young people, not only its own young but workers, whose activities increasingly fell into rigorous categories of juvenile delinquency. The discovery of adolescence, then, should not be confused with gains for actual adolescents; in many ways, Gillis suggests that the lot of actual youth had been freer before adolescence was invented. He stresses, particularly, changes in the role of leisure for young people, leading to more structured activities and away from the outlets of preindustrial society. These changes could affect even the broader society; the rise of sport, following from the new school experience, is a key example.

Was the new attitude toward adolescence a permanent feature of modernization or a brief reaction to the first impact of industrial life? The twentieth century has seen some relaxation of sexual strictures, certainly, and possibly a diminution of the concern with preparing adolescents to be men, apart from the world of women. And the numerical importance of adolescence declines steadily as the population becomes older. But adolescent rebellion has been a recurrent feature of twentieth-century life. Some of the confusions the nineteenth century developed about adolescence are now visible for a slightly younger age group. The tendency of modern society to define groups by age and to encourage an age-stratified, even age-segregated, pattern of life seems unabated. So, it might be argued, is a tendency to see each stage of life as one in which distinctive controls and institutional structures are necessary. The significance of adolescence in the modernization process, and in judging the goodness or badness of this process, has continued validity.

The failed revolutions of 1848 marked a turning point in the political history of youth, effectively terminating Europe's first period of student unrest and ending the independent role of the young within the working-class movements as well. Not until 1900 would youth again take to the public stage, and then in very different forms and in support of new causes. The traditions of radicalism and bohemianism survived to renew themselves in the socialist youth movements and the artistic avant-garde of the turn of the century, but at that point they were joined, and even overshadowed, by a new set of youth movements that tended to be focused on the narrower spectrum of youth we now call "adolescence." Not only were the new organizations younger in constituency, but their sense of fraternity was both more nationalistic and socially conservative. By 1900 the symbol of youth as a regenerative force was shifting from left to right, revealing the changed status of the young in European society.

In England we can detect this process beginning in the 1850s, starting with the upper and middle classes and then gradually trickling down to the lower orders. During the Crimean War one of the traditional festivals of Misrule, Guy Fawkes Night, became the occasion for outbursts of patriotic venom. The effigy of Czar Nicholas replaced that of Guy on the November bonfires, and although such substitutions were not new—Napoleon, too, had been burned at the beginning of the century—the accompanying enthusiasm for juvenile marching and drilling in the name of Queen and Country was unprecedented. . . .

In England, traditional dancing, mumming, and hunt festivals had been in decline since the 1850s. Manning found that by 1900 not only were the occasions once presided over by young men and women being abandoned to children of a much younger age, but that the class composition of the participants was also changing. This was true of the First of May in Oxford itself, where the crowning of a king and queen, once entered into by youth of all social ranks, had become the rite of the very lowest of youths, the poor chimney sweeps, who managed to keep the tradition only with difficulty in the face of harassment by city officials. The profane version of the hymns sung on May Morning from the top of the Magdalen College tower had long since been expurgated, making the whole occasion more the quaint tourist attraction it is today than the boisterous revel it had been earlier in the nineteenth century. Festivals like the Whit Hunt in Oxfordshire's Wychwood Forest were also a thing of the past, perpetuated at the turn of the century by gypsies and other "undesirables," but no longer respectable as far as the mass of the rural population was concerned. Morris dancing and the mumming associated with it had fallen into such decline that it took the attentions of urban folklorists to revive them. From photographs taken in the 1860s, Percy Manning had been able to identify two former dancers, whom he encouraged to teach songs and steps to younger men. But even Manning's desire for authenticity was not strong enough to displace his Victorian sense of decorum and when his dancers made their first appearance in Oxford in 1899, not only were their lyrics clean of the good-humored profanity, but the antics of the traditional Lord of Misrule were missing.

The tendency for youth to lose its autonomy and become an instrument of adult interests was resisted most strongly among the laboring poor. Yet, by 1900, traditions of Misrule were dying in the better sorts of working-class neighborhoods, revealing changes there that paralleled what was happening to middle- and upper-class youth. Behind both the decline of the journeymen's movements and the disappearance of student radicalism lay deeper transformations that not only eased the demographic and economic strains that had been a cause of troubled youth earlier in the century, but altered the life-cycle itself in such a way as to bring forth new forms of fraternity in the place of old. Youth's loss of political and social independence reflected the fact that a significant segment of that life-phase, the adolescent years 14–18, was becoming increasingly dependent. While older youth retained much of its earlier autonomy, becoming even more identified with the status of adulthood, this younger age-group was losing access to the economy and society of adults as it became increasingly subject to parental and other institutional controls. The moral autonomy attributed to youth by earlier generations was giving way to new kinds of conformity associated with a more mindless kind of physical vitality. In turn, this was reflected in the public image of the young, changing from Delacroix's rebels on the barricades, youth at war with society, to the late-nineteenth-century recruiting posters, glorifying youth at war for their society.

The discovery of adolescence belonged essentially to the middle classes, the first group, apart from the aristocracy, to experience a drop in child mortality and the consequences this entailed. The nobility was able to absorb larger numbers of surviving children, because of both its greater wealth and the firm tradition of primogeniture that allocated subordinate roles to younger sons. The middle classes, particularly their professional elements, having no comparable resources and not wishing to penalize the last born, turned to family limitation as the only way to relieve their burden. Although the actuality of the two-child family was still some way off, the English middle classes, and other groups claimant to that social status, were beginning to adapt it as an ideal in the 1860s and 1870s as a means of bringing into line with their incomes the growing expense of raising and educating children. Among this group, the situation of the early nineteenth century, with its superfluity of sons and daughters, was thereby gradually ameliorated; and instead of each successive generation being larger than the next, each was now smaller among those groups practicing family limitation.

Family strategy had changed from one of high to one of low fertility, altering parental attitudes toward the children in the process. Increasingly, each individual child was treated (according to sex) without prejudice to his or her place in the birth order. "Give the boys a good education and a start in life," wrote J. E. Panton in 1889, "and provide the girls with £150 a year, either when they marry or at your own death, and you have done your duty by your children. The girls cannot starve on that income, and neither would they be prey of any fortune hunter; but no one has a right to bring children into the world in the ranks of the upper middle class and do less." The consuming concern that had previously been reserved for the very young child appears to have been extended to older youth as well, not simply out of sentimentality but with the realization that the investment in long, expensive education should be carefully planned and conscientiously protected, rather than left to chance as had so often been the case in the first half of the century.

One aspect of this new care and concern for older children was the longer period of dependence that youth was now subjected to. Girls of the middle classes were kept at home until marriage, tightly supervised by their parents until they passed safely into the bosom of another family. An interest in female education was growing in the second half of the nineteenth century, partly as a result of surplus young women for whom marriage did not beckon; but this was still suspect among a group who believed that "love of home, of children, and of domestic duties are the only passions they [women] feel." Boys had greater autonomy, but their careers were also being carefully supervised by the parents, who, recognizing the decline in traditional kinds of apprenticeship, were taking a much greater interest in secondary education. Even businessmen, for whom classical education had previously held little attraction, were increasingly concerned to gain for their sons the benefits of schooling to 16 or 17, even when they expected the lads to join theirs or some other business. James Templeton, master of the Mission House School in Exeter, told the English Schools Commission of 1868: "Instead of what I heard in my younger days, a parent saying, 'I have done very well in the world. I was only six or twelve months at school,' the acknowledgment of such a man will now be, 'I had no such advantages or opportunities in my early life; I should like my son to be something of an educated man, and to have far greater advantages than I have had.'" A similar trend was noticeable on the Continent, where the decline of apprenticeship was also the product of parental desires to see their children have not only the intellectual but the social benefits of elite schooling.

The *Edinburgh Review* wrote in 1876 of an upper middle class which was "conscious that its retention of the advantages which it enjoys is still dependent on the mental activity by which they were gained; and keenly alive to the aesthetic and intellectual pleasures, the upper middle class seems the least likely of all to neglect its own educational concerns." The Schools Commission found them likely to keep their children in school the longest, to 18 or 19, and then to send them on to the university. But even the less well-to-do of the middle classes showed a similar concern, motivated by a desire to attain a similar privileged status. An ironmonger, Edmund Edmundson, testified in 1868 that because the traditions of apprenticeship had recently decayed, tradesmen's traditional prejudice against Latin education was diminishing. "The fact is, if a boy is not well educated he cannot keep his position in society. Society twenty years ago, as I recollect it, was a totally different thing to what it is now." The bias of the self-made man, never so strong to begin with on the Continent, was giving way all over Europe as the middle classes became increasingly dependent on the schools to guarantee a future for their progeny.

Smaller numbers of children encouraged longer coresidency, particularly on the Continent, where secondary education was organized around the day school. The growth of secondary education in the second half of the nineteenth century had made secondary schools locally available even in moderately-sized towns, making the need for boarding out while going to school much less prevalent than it had been earlier. Improved transportation facilitated the movement of pupils within urban areas where neighborhoods were not served by their own schools, and thus, by 1900, most French and German secondary students were living with their parents, leaving home only when they went on to the university or entered careers. Even in England, where the boarding tradition was continued and expanded during the second half of the century, longer vacations and better transportation were making contact between parents and their children much more frequent.

Whether a child was sent away to school or not, parents were assuming a much greater role in the supervision of the entire training process of each of their sons and daughters. German fathers were notorious for the strictness with which they oversaw their sons' training. They cloistered both boys and girls within the narrow confines of the home, allowing them only limited contact with the world outside, and then only for the purposes of formal training and education. The age of the patriarchal household, with its multiple economic and civil functions, was past by 1870, many of the prerogatives of the father having been usurped by factory, state, and school. Yet, the authority of the fathers persisted in what often seemed an outdated, tyrannical manner. Hans Heinrich Muchow has perceived a cultural lag operating in the fathers' slowness to adjust to the transition from the large multifunctional household to the small nuclear family unit: "Out of habit, he held onto the role, however, and thus pressed down on the nuclear family as a superfather [Übervater], especially on the growing children, who from the nursery onwards were subject to every impulse of their paternal master." Little wonder that the sons of the German middle class looked back on the earlier semi-dependent traditions of youth, especially the Wanderjahr, with a certain nostalgia. Trapped during their teen years between the tyranny of the home and the demands of the rigorous German academic school, the Gymnasium, they had lost contact with the sustaining force of the old peer-group structure and the autonomy which that represented.

In England, parental concern was no less intense or comprehensive, but, there, an alternative to fatherly tyranny offered itself. On the Continent, boarding schools and military academies remained the monopoly of the aristocracy, while in England this tradition was broadened to include a growing part of the middle class. The reform and expansion of the boarding (public) schools was a key instrument of the compromise between middle-class aspirations and aristocratic values that took place in the mid-Victorian period. The attractions to the social climbers were obvious: "In the great schools, which possess famous traditions, and in which the pupils come for the most part from the houses of gentlemen, there is a tone of manners and a sentiment of honour which goes far to neutralize the disadvantages of too early withdrawal from the shelter of home." For parents who were worried about sending their children away at an age that demanded care and protection, there was the assurance that "the master in this case stands in the parent's place, and to do his work properly ought to be clothed with all the parent's authority." Whether a boy remained at home for his schooling or was sent away to a boarding institution was obviously less important to the European middle classes than were the social controls associated with that education. The universal result was a state of dependence longer than that experienced by the previous generation: in effect, the creation of a new stage of life corresponding to what we now call "adolescence." . . .

Low mortality and low fertility made adolescence possible, but the real crucible of the age-group's social and psychological qualities was the elite secondary school. In England, the invention of adolescence was the unintended product of the reform of the public schools, whose beginnings are usually associated with the era of Thomas Arnold's tenure as headmaster at Rugby, 1827–1839. Arnold and the other reformers of his generation were the products of that earlier era of troubled youth, whose own training had been precocious and who themselves had known nothing like the adolescent stage of life that was to ensue from their reforms. . . .

Arnold proclaimed his calling as educator to be that of the keeper of the whole person: "He must adjust the respective claims of bodily and mental exercise, of different kinds of intellectual labour; he must consider every part of his pupil's nature, physical, intellectual, and moral; regarding the cultivation of the last, however, as paramount to that of either of the others." Arnold wished to turn out young men characterized by intellectual toughness, moral earnestness, and deep spiritual conviction. The feelings he wished to develop were not those of childish emotion but noble idealism. His own upbringing accustomed him to thinking in terms of precocious behavior and when he asked himself the question "Can the change from childhood to manhood be hastened in the case of boys and young men without exhausting prematurely the faculties either of body or mind?" his answer was staunchly affirmative. The object of a Rugby education was, he wrote, "if possible to form Christian men, for Christian boys I can scarcely make."

The philosophy of "boys will be boys" had no place in Arnold's world, one still so close to the conditions that encouraged precocity among the young earlier in the century. "If the change from childhood to manhood can be hastened safely, it ought to be hastened; and it is a sin in everyone not to hasten it," remained his educational philosophy to the end. As an admirer of tradition, Arnold did not attempt to destroy the structure of peer group. Instead, he turned the traditional hegemony of the older over the younger boys to his own advantage, purging the prefectorial system and the fagging of their violence, modifying both to fit the new, more paternal discipline of the schools. It will be remembered that in the early-nineteenth-century school, boys had virtually governed themselves, controlling their members through group pressure that tolerated an excess of bullying. When masters tampered with these rights of self-rule, they did so at their own risk, often provoking the kind of rebellion that was a frequent event in school histories throughout the first half of the nineteenth century. Nineteenth-century schoolmasters were infamous for their use of the whip, and reign by corporal punishment certainly did not end with the beginnings of reform. Nevertheless, the relationship between students and masters was both milder and more intimate. Repressive force was reduced by a system of almost fatherly supervision, aimed at preventing abuses rather than punishing them. And so it could be reported in 1864 that "the relationship between Masters and boys is closer and more friendly than it used to be. . . . Flogging, which twenty years ago was resorted to as a matter of course for the most trifling offenses, is now in general used sparingly, and applied only to serious ones. More attention is paid to religious teaching . . . and more reliance is placed on a sense of duty." . . .

Sport was taking over many of the functions of the rite of passage once reserved to Latin language study, for it, too, ensured the separation of boys from the world of women during the critical transition from childhood to adulthood. There was an important social change involved in this substitution, however. The model of the earlier Latin school was the monastery; the ideal of the public school was increasingly military. Women were to be avoided by adolescents because femininity was now associated with weakness, emotion, and unreliability. So strong was the avoidance of female traits by 1860 that men no longer dared embrace in public and tears were shed only in private. A whole series of male clubs sprang up to shield men from women. Some, like the Young Men's Christian Association, founded in 1844, drew their inspiration from the temperate evangelical fellowships of the late eighteenth and early nineteenth centuries; but, for the upper classes it was more likely to be hard-drinking, hard-riding organizations that attracted them. Despite their Victorian exteriors, these upper-class fraternal groups tended to uphold a double standard with respect to social morality, including sexuality. As males, they reserved for themselves the right of access to drink, gambling, and prostitution, rationalizing these things as "natural" to men and "unnatural" to women.

"God made man in His image, not in an imaginatory Virgin Mary's image," explained Charles Kingsley, one of the so-called "muscular Christians" for whom traits of sensitivity or domesticity in a man were a kind of sin against nature and society. And, of course, what could better preserve the differences between the sexes than the military?—thus a partial explanation for the popularity of the rifle clubs and cadet corps in the second half of the century. Here male and national chauvinism blended neatly in a spartan model of boyhood that permitted no deviation. Boys who did not play the game or march in step were looked upon as misfits. Uniforms, whether athletic or military, underlined the growing intolerance of individuality that characterized late-nineteenth-century schooling in both England and Germany. Max Weber, looking back on the enormous impact of student fraternities on German life, wrote of the false understanding of freedom that these engendered:

> The "academic freedom" of dueling, drinking, and class cutting stems from a time when other kinds of freedom did not exist in Germany and when only the stratum of literati and candidates for office was privileged in such liberties. The inroad, however, which these conventions have made upon the bearing of the "academically certified man" of Germany cannot be eliminated even today.

He praised the English for educating their sons to a broader definition of rights, but he might well have listened to those in England who warned of the trend toward mindless conformity that was the product of the philosophy, "boys will be boys." To George Trevelyan the results were clear:

> What else can be expected, when a young man at the age his grandfather was fighting in the Peninsula or preparing to stand for a borough, is still hanging on at school, with his mind half taken up with Latin verses, and the other half divided between his score in the cricket field and his score at the pastry-cook's?

Increasing concern with the physical elements of boyhood brought parents and educators face to face with sexuality, the taboo subject of the earlier generation. By the 1870s the subject of "puberty" was being discussed openly in both medical books and parents' manuals; and a decade later, even the conservative Oxford Clerical Association declared for "frankness" in the catechising of its young confirmees. Recognition of the sexuality of adolescence did not mean, however, a liberalization of Victorian attitudes. On the contrary, the tendency of writers was to blame parents for being too careless, allowing their sons to pick up bad habits from both peers and servants. Warned Elizabeth Blackwell: "The physical growth of youth, the new powers, the various symptoms which make the transition from childhood into young man- and womanhood are often alarming to the individual. Yet this important period of life is entered upon, strange to say, as a general rule, without parental guidance." If parents could not deal with it, then other institutions would. The cloistered sex-segregated schools were the best guarantee against sexual deviation, but Dr. William Acton also praised the efforts of the Young Men's Christian Association and the Volunteer Movement to impose continence: "I am convinced that much of the incontinence of the present day could be avoided by finding amusement, instruction, and recreation for the young men of large towns."

Contemporaries recognized that the high age of marriage among the middle classes (29.9 years for English professional males in the period 1840–1870) represented an enormous challenge to supervision and control, not just of relations with the opposite sex but of those between boys and boys. It was admitted by Acton and others that "a schoolmaster should be alive to the excessive danger of platonic attachments that sometimes become fashionable in a school, especially between boys of very different ages." As Robert Graves was to experience later, social attributes that were normal in the outside world were forfeited in favor of loyalty to the male group. Boys were forced even to abandon normal sex roles. "In English preparatory and public schools romance is necessarily homosexual," Graves noted. "The opposite sex is despised and treated as something obscene. . . . For every one born homosexual, at least ten permanent pseudo-homosexuals were made by the public school system; nine of these ten as honourable chaste and sentimental as I was."

For most, the regression to this form of innocent affection was but a temporary detour on the way to adult heterosexuality. Headmaster G. H. Rendall was probably accurate in his assessment that "my boys are amorous, but seldom erotic." Yet, while it is unclear whether the schools produced more than their share of adult homosexuals, almost complete isolation from the opposite sex had the effect of transforming the facts of genitality into a forbidden secret world, exposure to which had a traumatic effect on young asexuals like Graves. Confrontation with the effects of puberty was more unexpected and, therefore, more traumatic than today. At 17 Graves had his first real introduction to love play: "An Irish girl staying at the same pension made love to me in a way that, I see now, was really very sweet. It frightened me so much, I could have killed her."

Headmasters looked upon the peer group as a means of controlling sexual delinquency, both because it was the least expensive way of extending their own control and because they, like Arnold, sensed the power of "public opinion" among the boys themselves. Problems arose from the fact that group pressures became so strongly organized that any kind of individualism was immediately taken as a sign of sexual vice. A sure sign of "self abuse" (masturbation) was physical weakness: "Muscles underdeveloped, the eye is sunken and heavy, the complexion is sallow and pusty, or covered with spots of acne, the hands are damp and cold, the skin moist." How many innocents undergoing the physical change associated with adolescence, a growth spurt that was now coming earlier and more rapidly among the middle classes, must have been terrified by these symptoms of normal development? But even more telling was any failure to play the game or to march in step with the group, a sure sign of secret sin.

> The boy shuns the society of others, creeps about alone, joins with repugnance in the amusements of his schoolfellows. He cannot look anyone in the face, and becomes careless in dress and uncleanly in person. His intellect becomes sluggish and enfeebled, and if his evil habits are persisted in he may end in become a drivelling idiot or a peevish valetudinarian.

Thus, what were historically-evolved social norms of a particular class became enshrined in medical and psychological literature as the "natural" attributes of adolescence. The transmutation, through institutional imperatives, of social values into natural laws suited the new materialist outlook of the middle classes in the second half of the nineteenth century. One of William Acton's correspondents, writing to him concerning ways of convincing the younger generation of the dangers of incontinence, expressed the universal desire to find in science a new legitimation of old social controls: "It would be the greatest encouragement to know that physical science confirms the dictates of revelation." Conformity, self-denial, and dependence— all essentially functions of the kind of upbringing that was peculiar to a particular class—had become positivistic standards of human behavior by which an upper class could assure itself of its inherent superiority to the lower orders. The fact that children of the working class were independent and resistant to institutional controls was now proof of their inferiority.

However pleased the middle classes were with their invention, they were also aware of its difficulties, particularly the emotional deficits that arose out of so much investment in the artificial world of the school. "Left entirely to themselves they [adolescents] tend to disorder and triviality, and controlled too much by adults they tend to lose zest and spontaneity," wrote G. Stanley Hall. His conclusions were not unlike those Stephen Spender arrived at some 50 years later, when, reviewing English adolescence, he wrote that the schools taught "boys to take themselves seriously as functions of an institution, before they take themselves seriously as persons or individuals." England's schoolboys possessed a composure and polish that surprised and delighted most foreign visitors, but beneath this surface lay considerable turmoil and self-doubt, the product of an education that gave little attention to personality and emotional development. Robert Graves, who was particularly sensitive to this deficit in his own training, wrote of how the total institution was arranged so that boys came to view themselves as possessed of no personal rights as such, but only of statuses granted to them as privileges. "A new boy had no privileges at all; a boy in his second term might wear a knitted tie instead of a plain one; and a boy in his second year might wear coloured socks." A sturdy individualist like Graves was able to subvert the rules of Charterhouse School and develop a personal identity apart from its hierarchy, but most of his fellow students were not so fortunate. "School life becomes reality, and home life the illusion"; and boys whose whole lives had been built around team sports and fraternity life were naturally insecure in the company of the opposite sex. Moving on to university, the army, or the professions—all still exclusively male institutions—it was understandable that they should seek to allay their anxiety about this aspect of adulthood by perpetuating schoolboy comradery well past their own years of adolescence.

The most famous fictional schoolboy of the mid-century, Tom Brown, had been eager to get on with life. "If I can't be at Rugby, I want to be at work in the world, and not dawdling away three years at Oxford," he told his tutor. But in the end he accepted advice of the kind that was to become conventional by 1900: "Don't be in a hurry about finding your work in the world for yourself. You are not old enough to judge for yourself yet, but just look about you in the place you find yourself in, and try to make things a little better and honester there." The gap between Arnold's generation and that of the schoolmasters who followed them can be measured here. David Newsome has summarized it best: "The worst educational feature of the earlier ideal was the tendency to make boys into men too soon; the worst feature of the other, paradoxically, was that in its efforts to achieve manliness by stressing the cardinal importance of playing games, it fell into the opposite error of failing to make boys into men at all."

By century's end, schoolmasters all over Europe could congratulate themselves on the good order of their pupils. Never had the schoolboy been so at peace with the world, so accepting of his social deprivation, so apathetic toward his civil status. Although young fools might still play their pranks on a November night or dance on May mornings, middle-class boys did not ordinarily don the masks of Misrule except in a patriotic or conservative cause. Yet, beneath this surface calm many thought they detected an inner storm. The association of emotional turmoil with transition from childhood, which can be traced back at least to the writings of Rousseau, had by 1900 found a prominent place in medical and psychological literature. The image of the schoolboy had shifted from trouble-maker to troubled, particularly in Germany, where the relationship of the school to the home only increased the problems of prolonged dependence.

The day-*Gymnasium* lacked those features of a total institution which distinguished the English public school. In Germany, the middle-class family retained control of social learning, the school monopolized intellectual training, and both civic and sexual education were left at dispute between them. This uneasy allocation was the subject of increasing controversy at century's end. The demographic and economic situation of the German bourgeoisie was much like that of its English counterpart, except that it placed greater emphasis on academic success because of the greater prestige conferred on formal educational attainment in that society. There appears to have been the same growing pressure on adolescents to meet parental expectations and thus justify the growing investment in education. In contrast to the English public school, however, the German *Gymnasium* was less well-equipped to deal with the phenomenon of "boyhood" that this produced. Lacking the characteristics of a total institution, it had greater difficulty in shaping youth to conform to its elite goals. There were no sports or extracurricular activities to cope with the social and emotional side-effects of prolonged dependence; and thus the school appeared to many of its inmates as an arid brain-factory, unable to meet the needs of the young. A rash of student suicides in the 1890s caused Ludwig Gurlitt to ask: "Can there be any graver charge against a school system than these frequent student suicides? Is it not grisly and horrible if a child voluntarily renounces seeing the light of the sun, voluntarily separates himself from his parents and brothers and sisters, from all the joys, hopes, and desires of his young life, because he doubts himself and no longer can bear the compulsions of school?"

The family, on the other hand, was organized in an authoritarian way around its own private affairs and was also poorly equipped to deal with the larger tasks of youthful development. Sexual learning remained in a kind of no-man's land, attended to by neither parents nor schoolmasters, despite the growing anxiety about the onset of puberty. Deprived of youth's traditional agency of sexual education, the peer group, German middle-class boys and girls found their stage of dependency an extraordinarily lonely, disturbing experience. By 1900 this social experience was translating itself into literary expression, with the novels of Thomas Mann, Hermann Hesse, and Robert Musil exploring the inner turmoil of adolescence. Similar concerns were reflected in the work of the German and Austrian psychological schools, including, of course, Freud and his followers. And their definition of the "problematic" character of adolescence was then influencing views in both England and the United States, particularly in the latter, where G. Stanley Hall published his massive *Adolescence, Its Psychology and Its Relation to Physiology, Anthropology, Sociology, Sex, Crime, Religion, and Education* in 1904. Adolescence, wrote Hall, was one of the most important blessings that civilization had bestowed; and yet its promise was also its danger. A stage of life withdrawn from adult pursuits was desirable, but it also exposed the young to idleness and depravity. "Modern life is hard, and in many respects increasingly so, on youth. Home, school, church, fail to recognize its nature and needs and, perhaps most of all, its perils."

Part 4

THE
TWENTIETH
CENTURY

1918–Present

Steel worker, Brittany, 1974

Contemporary Europe began to emerge during the horror of the First World War. The war severely damaged Europe's morale. Its staggering death tolls distorted the population structure. The economic dislocations that resulted from it induced, or at least intensified, two decades of economic insecurity, culminating in the Great Depression. It set other disturbing trends in motion. For example, crime rates in Great Britain began to rise in the early 1920s and have continued to mount to the present day, although they have not reached the levels of the late eighteenth century. It is not hard to portray twentieth-century European history in gloomy terms, compared with the nineteenth century. Certainly any history that focuses on the two decades between the world wars must stress the extreme social and political chaos that prevailed throughout most of the continent.

But Europe recovered after the Second World War, and entered a new stage of affluence and industrial growth. Some observers believe that the society that has emerged since the 1940s is a radically new one, and they call it "postindustrial" or "postmodern." Has the basic process of modernization given way to some new set of values and institutions? My own belief is that the modernization process is still continuing, despite admittedly great changes in many areas ranging from technology to the world's diplomatic structure. But the question deserves serious consideration, particularly with regard to the lives and outlooks of the major segments of European society. The status of the family, for example, suggests that, while nineteenth-century patterns differed from traditional ones (as in the "modernization" of childhood), the society today is heading in a different direction. And, in general, the increasingly common references to "postindustrial" society raise the question of whether we have entered a new period *within* the modernization process or whether we are developing, so soon after modernization began, yet another social framework.

What is certain is that Europe continues to change rapidly and that, within a recognizably common range, it is developing a blend of the old and the new that in some cases differs from other advanced industrial countries. Compared with the United States, Europe is less violent. European family life is more stable, despite important changes in family values. At the same time, Europeans are much less religious, expressing less religious belief and engaging less commonly in religious practice. Politics in Europe tend toward greater diversity and extremes. Social mobility is about as common in Europe as it is in the United States, but Europeans tend to place less emphasis on it, so that European society at least appears to be more stratified. Similarly, the position of women may seem more rigidly controlled, and in some countries it is demonstrably inferior in law; but how great are the real differences between Europe and the United States in this area?

It is not easy to determine major trends in the very recent past, and the essays that follow cover only a few of many possible topics. We do, however, have something of a head start in interpreting key features in the development of contemporary European society. We know some of the basic responses to earlier modernization. We can compare recent patterns with these responses, to see if ordinary Europeans are reinforcing values established earlier or creating new ones. We can even try to assess the strengths and weaknesses of the society Europeans have developed.

BIBLIOGRAPHY

There are many studies of Nazism, but most deal purely with the movement itself. Alan L. Bullock, *Hitler, a Study in Tyranny*, rev. ed. (New York, 1964), goes well beyond the confines of biography and is an excellent survey. Karl D. Bracher, *The German Dictatorship: The Origins, Structure and Effects of National Socialism*, trans. Jean Steinberg (New York, 1970), deals extensively with the bases of Nazi strength. Ernst Nolte, *The Three Faces of Fascism* (New York, 1966), is an ambitious interpretation, but it is written mainly from the standpoint of intellectual history. A valuable specific study of Nazism's causes and impact in a small German town is W. L. Allen, *The Nazi Seizure of Power* (Chicago, 1955). See also Herman Lebovics, *Social Conservatism and the Middle Classes in Germany* (Princeton, 1969), and Peter Pulzer, *Anti-Semitism in Germany and Austria* (New York, 1964). For a recent interpretation of Nazism's effect on German society, see Ralf Dahrendorf, *Society and Democracy in Germany* (New York, 1969). Hannah Arendt, *The Origins of Totalitarianism* (New York, 1973), is an important general interpretive statement.

Seymour Lipset, *Political Man, the Social Bases of Politics* (New York, 1959), studies the variety of modern political attitudes from a liberal point of view. John E. Goldthorpe et al., *The Affluent Worker: Political Attitudes and Behavior* (New York, 1968), based on data from a recent study of the British working class, offers important interpretations of workers' political values. On French communism, see Robert Wohl, *French Communism in the Making* (Stanford, 1966).

Recent studies of sports include Richard Mandell, *The Nazi Olympics* (New York, 1971), and R. L. Quercetani, *A World History of Track and Field Athletics, 1864–1964* (New York, 1964). Robert Daly, *The Bizarre World of European Sports* (New York, 1963), is a stimulating interpretation.

Probably the most sensitive study of modern women, with careful attention to historical background, is Simone de Beauvoir, *The Second Sex*, trans. H. M. Parshley (New York, 1953). See also Betty Friedan, *The Feminine Mystique* (New York, 1963). A vigorous recent survey is Evelyne Sullerot, *Woman, Society and Change* (New York, 1971).

On the twentieth-century family, Colin Rosser and Christopher Harris, *The Family and Social Change* (New York, 1965), is an excellent detailed survey, based on a study of a Welsh city. See also P. Willmott and M. Young, *Family and Class in a London Suburb* (New York, 1960). *The Symmetrical Family* (London, 1976), by the same authors, is an interesting larger interpretation in historical context. Michael Anderson, *Family Structure in Nineteenth-Century Lancashire* (New York, 1971), offers valuable background material. Richard Sennett, *Families Against the City* (Cambridge, Mass., 1970), presents a pessimistic view of modern family trends, based on a study of a Chicago neighborhood, that deserves comparison with the European studies. Kent H. Geiger, "The Family and Social Change," in Cyril E. Black, ed., *The Transformation of Russian Society: Aspects of Social Change since 1861* (Cambridge, Mass., 1960), surveys recent developments in Russian family structure and offers something of a model of the modernization of the family. J. R. Pitts, "Continuity and Change in Bourgeois France," in Stanley Hoffman, ed., *In Search of France* (Cambridge, Mass., 1963), and John Ardagh, *The New French Revolution* (New York, 1969), comment on changes in the middle-class family. J. H. Goldthorpe et al., *The Affluent Worker in the Class Structure* (New York, 1969), specifically contests Ferdynand Zweig's thesis of growing working-class contentment, but the study barely touches on family relationships.

On health and medicine, see Ivan Illich, *Medical Nemesis: The Expropriation of Health* (New York, 1976). David Riesman, *The Lonely Crowd* (New Haven, 1969), offers an interpretation of the contemporary popular mentality that should be compared to a modernization model, and that is enjoying new vogue. Discussions of postindustrial society (mainly structural) are Alvin Toffler, *Future Shock* (New York, 1971), and Daniel Bell, *The Coming of Post-Industrial Society* (New York, 1973).

The Social Bases of Nazism

DAVID SCHOENBAUM

The rise of Nazism in Germany, and of similar movements in other countries, is the outstanding characteristic of the two decades between the world wars. How could such a movement take shape and win substantial support? Social scientists have developed a number of approaches in trying to deal with the phenomenon. Some see Nazism and other totalitarian movements as endemic in the condition of modern man. Robbed of traditional values, such as religion, and close community ties, modern man stands alone and fearful; he easily yields to the solidarity and discipline of movements such as Nazism. Others view Nazism as a specifically German phenomenon, seeking in the German past an acceptance of authority and militarism. Still others emphasize more temporary factors, maintaining that Nazism was the product of a massive and unexpected defeat in war and of a variety of severe economic presures, all of which had much greater impact in Germany than elsewhere. Even amid unprecedented social and political stress Nazism did not really gain popularity until the Great Depression.

Interpretation of support for Nazism is further complicated by the sheer opportunism of the movement, which tried to appeal to almost all groups and was quite capable of switching stands to win support. Relatedly, the reasons Nazism won popularity differ considerably from the results of Nazism in practice. No one has yet clearly assessed the extent to which Nazi anti-Semitism and aggressive nationalism won support; all we know for sure is that they did not deter the Nazi voters. But Nazism's promises of support for small business and small farmers and its suggestion of a return to a more traditional Germany were directly contradicted by the actions of the regime once in power. It has even been argued that, horrible as it was, the Nazi movement ultimately helped make Germany more genuinely modern and thus less susceptible to similar movements—after Nazism itself was defeated in war.

The following selection seeks to explain the varied social bases of Nazism, dealing both with the immediate problems and the longer-range grievances that led people to embrace the movement. It emphasizes the persistence of anxieties about modernization. Were these anxieties, or at least the intensity with which they were experienced, peculiarly German? Are war and depression sufficient explanations for the way in which these anxieties were expressed? Questions like these must be faced, for in understanding Nazism's appeal we must try to estimate the chances of its recurrence, in Germany or elsewhere. This in turn leads us to ask what has happened to the social groups and values that supported Nazism. Have they changed or disappeared with further modernization? The passage stresses not only social but also generational tension during the period of Nazism's rise. Young people were disproportionately enthusiastic about the Nazi movement. Again we must try to determine whether this is because of peculiar circumstances in the period, or German characteristics, or perhaps more enduring problems of youth in modern society.

The concept of a sick society causes problems if only because no one knows exactly what constitutes social health. But to the extent that the concept has meaning, Germany after 1918 was an appropriate place for its application. The most spectacular symptoms—the propensity to physical violence, the hyperbolic inflation of 1923, and the near-overnight disintegration of the economy in 1929–30—had their equivalents elsewhere. But elsewhere they led to crises and convalescence recognizably within the limits of previous historical experience and the status quo. In Germany, however, the permanent disaffection of major social groups, the alienation of those groups who presumably support a liberal republic, was reflected in the progressive and total collapse of all liberal parties, and in the discrepancy between social reality and its political interpretation. They testify to a latent malaise whose consequences, even without Adolf Hitler, would have led to major social and political transformation. This need not have led to war and Auschwitz. But with high probability, it would have been fatal to the Weimar Republic in the form envisaged by the authors of its constitution.

National Socialism was not the cause of the malaise, nor was its ultimate totalitarian, imperialist form the inevitable consequence. Its programmatic demands were neither original nor peculiar to Hitler's Party. The Nazis came to power by miscalculation rather than by some exclusive popular demand focusing on the person of Hitler or his Party. The mandate with which Hitler took office was a conglomerate of disparities and contradictions long apparent to anyone interested in politics, both outside the party and in it. The common denominator of Nazi appeal was as remote as the smile of the Cheshire cat. In its negative form, it was a promise to make things different, in its positive form, a promise to make things better. But as far removed as it was from the unitary political will Hitler claimed to see in the uniform columns of the SA (Sturmabteilung—Storm Troopers, "brown shirts") or the ecstatic acclamation of a mass audience, there was in it nonetheless a homogeneity great enough to cover the yawning cracks in the Party program with ballot papers. This was the homogeneity of common disaffection.

The disaffection was structural, endemic in all Western industrial societies, but intensified in Germany by special historical factors: a non-competitive, highly concentrated, high-priced industrial economy, the disproportionate influence of a small class of large landowners, a high birthrate until World War I, too many rural smallholders, an inflated urban petite bourgeoisie. All of these had been built into Bismarck's Reich. Carried along on the winds of economic expansion, they formed a fair-weather constellation whose stability was virtually identical with the success of its political leadership in balancing the conflicting demands and requirements of industry and agriculture, labor and capital, West and East, centralism and particularism, Catholic and Protestant, rich and poor. Success created a clientele that included even the nominal enemies of the established order. Their own vested interest in this order was certainly an important factor in the SPD (Social Democrat) decision to vote war credits in 1914. But the compromises of the old order failed to solve, even precluded solving, the problems of an industrial society. The collapse of the monarchy in 1918 with its chaotic "return to normalcy" only reintroduced the problems of the prewar era after four uneasy years of civil truce. But they were now complicated by the by-products of defeat: a "lost generation" of demobilized soldiers; a floating population of eastern refugees, many of them aristocrats; the liquidation of millions of war loans floated with middle-class savings; and a large disproportion in the demographic relationship of women to men. Finally, there were the economic consequences of the war: reparations, loss of export markets, exhaustion of both plant and raw materials, and inflation. The latent social problems of the prewar era were further complicated by a crisis of legitimacy in the political order coinciding with economic disintegration. The results were paradoxical; on the one hand, consistent and uninterrupted extension of the social tendencies of the prewar era, on the other, an ideologized misinterpretation of these tendencies that effectively prevented the solution of the maladjustments they caused.

A statistical résumé leaves no doubt about the unambiguous course of social development (see Table 1).

TABLE 1. German Occupational Distribution in % of Population

Year	Agriculture	Industry and handicrafts	Services
1882	42	36	22
1895	36	39	25
1907	34	40	26
1925	30	42	28
1933	29	41	30

This was the classical pattern of industrialization, urban growth, industrial rationalization, and the development of distribution and service industries. While only 5 per cent of the German population had lived in cities of over 100,000 in 1871, the proportion had grown by 1925 to 27 per cent. Equally striking was the relative redistribution of ownership and economic status (see Table 2).

TABLE 2.   German Occupational Status in % of Population

In %	1882	1895	1907	1925	1933
Independent	38	35	27	21	20
Their employed dependents	4	4	8	10	11
White collar including civil service	8	11	14	19	18
Workers	50	50	51	50	52

While the figures were neutral as economic indicators—pointing only to advancing industrialization and relative only to success in feeding, housing, and clothing an industrial population—they were full of implications as a reflection of social and political tendencies. The loss of economic independence, the employment of family members, the ballooning white-collar population characteristic both of the big city and the bureaucratic state and economy all affected the self-respect of the people they touched—or at least were capable of doing so as soon as they seemed to coincide with a decline in the standard of living. If the processes themselves were characteristic of capitalism, it stood to reason that those affected by them would come to consider themselves anti-capitalistic, without, however, accepting the theoretical Marxian implications of their misery and disappearing in the traditional proletariat. Theodor Geiger estimated, on the basis of the 1925 census, that 25,000,000 Germans could be classed, socially, as proletarians. But 45,000,000, roughly three quarters of the population, were living—during a period of increasing prosperity nearly five years before the depression—on proletarian incomes.

Particularly characteristic of this tendency were the retail traders, a bumper crop sown by the imperial order and in constant fear of being mowed down by the economics of the Republic. Between 1882 and 1907, the number of small retail traders had grown faster than both population and the national product as people sought to exploit urban growth and a rising living standard in tobacco shops, groceries, drugstores (Drogerien), and delicatessens (Feinkosgeschäfte). Even before the war, existing statistics pointed to a decline in professional quality. A survey of Brunswick grocers (Kolonialwarenhändler) in 1901 established that only 34 per cent had had any vocational training compared with 67 per cent in 1887. Even before the depression, the economic consequences of the peace had revealed the weaknesses of the small shop-keeper, exposed to the business cycle, unresponsive to shifting population, and inadequately trained for either successful competition or other employment. Added to his problem on the one hand were the price-sinking creations of advancing technology and concentrated capital, the chain and department stores, and on the other, the vast overaccumulation of non-competitive man-power in retail trade. Between 1907 and 1925, the number of retail outlets rose from 695,800 to 847,900, an increase of about 21 per cent. Between 1924 and 1929 it increased another 3 per cent. Geiger estimated that in 1925 nearly 45 per cent of those engaged in retail trade were already living on pro-letarian incomes.

Meanwhile the number of department store subsidiaries rose from 101 in 1925 to 176 in 1929. While their absolute share of retail turnover was still small enough, their relative share by 1928 was growing 22 per cent faster than the total volume of retail trade. Between 1925 and 1931 so-called "specialty" shops lost 5 per cent of their share of retail volume, a relatively small figure but one magnified by higher operating costs, lively imaginations, and then by the depression. A 1929 tax study showed that the department stores had, in fact, taken over only 4 per cent, the chain stores at most 1.1 per cent of retail trade. This included, however up to 6 per cent of the turnover in cloth-ing and 20 per cent in household goods and furniture. By 1928 retail pressure groups were pressing for increased taxes on department stores, a goal achieved by 1929 in Munich and Frankfurt, Main. In 1932, the Brüning government declared a limit on further department store expansion, followed before the year was out by a similar ban on chain stores. Whether his misery was caused by his own inefficiency, his aversion to co-operatives, to the methods, eco-nomics, or good advertising of larger units within his own line, or by the department stores was a matter of indifference to the retail merchant whose effective desire was a self-contradiction: free enterprise minus its attendant risks.

But while the economic implications of retail trade seemed to point in the direction of the Marxist prognosis, toward concentration, intensified com-petition, and the strangulation of the small, independent proprietor, another development pointed in the opposite direction. This was the rapid growth of the white-collar population, "sociologically perhaps the most significant de-velopment of the last decades," as Ferdinand Fried called it in 1931. It was indeed characteristic of the period that the white-collar workers formed one of the best-observed of all social groups, their origins, attitudes, and habits becoming a subject of considerable public interest. Siegfried Kracauer's Marxist phenomenology of the white-collar worker ran for weeks in a daily news-paper in 1929 while the white-collar "little-man" became in 1932 the hero of a fictional best seller, Hans Fallada's Little Man, What Now?

Coming as they did both from the ranks of the traditional bourgeoisie and from the proletariat, it was nonetheless clear that the white-collar workers were neither workers nor middle class in the traditional sense. Contemporary social science begged the problem of categorization rather than solved it by calling the entire group, from shop clerks to graduate engineers, "the new middle class." But this was hardly a guide to their behavior, which was, from the Marxist point of view from which they were most often observed, a collection of anomalies.

The white-collar worker was usually employed in a big city and by a big employer. He—or still more likely, she—was often of working-class origins, even before the war. Hans Speier quoted a number of surveys (see Table 3).

TABLE 3.   Survey of White-Collar Worker Origins

Year	Job classification	Working class origins
1906	Berlin saleswomen	33.6%
1909–11	Young Munich saleswomen	66.9
1932	Cologne saleswomen	51.5
1929	Apprentices of Gewerkschaft der Angestellten (clerical union):	
	Male	33.6
	Female	42.9

White-collar workers showed a progressive tendency to organize, and in a relatively militant organization from which employers were excluded. But both the form and the objectives differed from the traditional union pattern, corresponding in part to the different social origins of the membership, in part to the nature of their employment. While Geiger estimated that less than 4 per cent of the working-class population was skilled (qualifiziert), he estimated that 70 per cent of the white-collar population had some professional qualifications. This alone might have led them away from the traditional union demands. While 80 per cent of the workers were organized in the so-called "free" socialist unions in 1931, only 25 per cent of the white-collar workers were organized in the socialist Gewerkschaft der Angestellten (clerical union), while 22.6 per cent were in the national-liberal Hirsch-Duncker unions and 34.1 per cent in the so-called "Christian-National" organizations like the Deutschnationaler-Handlungsgehilfenverband (German National Sales Clerks Association) (DHGV), perhaps the only economic-interest organization in Weimar Germany that combined a racist-nationalist (völkisch) program with mass membership. It is also of interest that 39 per cent of the DHGV membership came from working-class origins.

While the white-collar union was a tough negotiator and the pressure of economic circumstances could bring about a professional solidarity great enough to overcome the ideological divisions separating the white-collar groups, white-collar consciousness made itself felt in a preoccupation with salaries instead of wages, long-term contracts, and pensions; reflections of a concern with security—including the security of social status—that distinguished it from the blue-collar unions. Weimar legislation continued to distinguish white collar (Angestellten) from blue collar (Arbeiter), granting the former special job security, separate status in wage contracts, and a separate insurance fund.

Both Schumpeter and Lederer-Marschak claimed to see the line between blue collar and white collar fading, Schumpeter because the workers were coming to live like petits bourgeois, Lederer and Marschak because the white-collar workers were coming to behave like other workers. The depression proved the contrary. Unemployment hit blue collar and white collar alike, but psychologically it hit the white-collar worker harder. Speier quotes an unemployed white-collar worker: ". . . one is immediately ostracized, one is déclassé, without means of support, unemployed—that's equal to being a Communist." Déclassé is clearly the important word, reflecting a sensitivity of self-esteem different from that of the traditional working class. The increased employment of women—between 1913 and 1921 the proportion of women in the white-collar organizations had grown from 7.7 to 23.8 per cent—tended to increase the tension by making higher paid male jobs more vulnerable and compounding class war with sex war.

A key group in the white-collar population was an academically trained class, multiplied by postwar circumstances beyond its prewar numbers and increasingly absorbed in salaried employment in an economy that placed growing demands on technically trained manpower. The economic crises of the first Weimar years fell with particular weight on them, a group already sensitive to its exclusion, in part real, in part apparent, from traditional careers in the Army and civil service. While the social structure of Germany's political leadership changed significantly, the structure of the university population changed little except to the extent to which it grew and suffered. The 1922 Who's Who revealed that 20.3 per cent of the political entries came from the working class and 30.8 per cent from lower-income groups while only 40.8 per cent came from the old upper classes (Oberschicht). But the universities were peopled by the sons of the groups most conscious of the loss this revolution had caused them. The relative frequency of sons from the families of professional men went up in proportion to the restrictions imposed on business and the military. But while the sons of lawyers cautiously chose to make their ways in other areas, considerable numbers in medicine, pharmacy, and the natural sciences, the law faculties were filled with the sons of the petite bourgeoisie seeking the traditional prewar way to the top. In 1929, 23.4 per cent of all students were from the families of university graduates, 11.5 per cent from the homes of the rich—big landowners, company directors, etc. But 64.2 per cent came from the middle class intent on making their way in a world whose political direction was increasingly dominated, as they would tend to see it, either by the discredited representatives of the old order or by their social and cultural inferiors.

"The age of the self-made man is past," Robert Michels claimed. The only career open to the talented working-class boy was political. At the same time there was every evidence of dissatisfaction in a university graduate population of 840,000 while the student population tended to grow by 10 per cent a year. Since the routes to the top narrowed, and the traffic increased, the result appeared to be fewer and fewer rewards for higher and higher qualifications. Fried, who clearly felt himself a victim of the process, was eloquent in his description of its consequences: four to six years of university study, costing from five to nine thousand marks, rewarded with starting salaries ranging from two to four hundred marks monthly and advancing to a level commensurate with family obligations and social status only when its recipient reached the age of forty or fifty. The university graduate, Fried declared, felt as he had once felt during his first weeks of military service: spiritually and physically exploited. But while he might once have become a reserve officer for his pains, his civilian occupation under present circumstances offered him the chance of one day becoming—with the best of luck—a prokurist, a kind of economic sergeant. "The way to the top is blocked off," he concluded, including among the obstacles the oligarchy of age. Reichstag deputies were, on the average, fifty-six years old, the two hundred leading economic figures, sixty-one years old—"rigid, dead, outdated and reactionary like the SPD."

One other major social group, the farmers, shared the general disaffection. Geiger estimated that nearly 60 per cent of them were living on proletarian incomes. The intensity and quality of their disaffection varied according to region and market conditions but was ultimately reducible to the classic problem of agriculture in an industrial society: the farmer's inability to control prices and production in an otherwise manipulable economy. The result was a curious dilemma. Massive economic disintegration might bring him short-term advantages, as it did during the 1923 inflation which liquidated his debts and brought him the short-term benefits of a barter economy and a sellers' market. But in the long run, the farmer suffered as the general economy suffered. On the other hand, prosperity, even as it brought him higher prices, tended to increase the lag between farm and industrial income on one side and farm and industrial prices on the other. His efforts to overcome this gap resulted in overproduction with a consequent decline in prices. . . .

None of these problems was new or unique to Germany. In one form or another they had been, since the middle of the nineteenth century, not only the raw material of German politics but in varying degrees of the politics of all industrial and industrializing countries. In America similar phenomena had fueled political controversy since at least the election of Jackson in 1828 and formed the bases of the mass Populist and Progressive movements before World War I and later the basis of the New Deal.

What complicated solution in Germany was not a failure to recognize the structural inadequacies of industrial society, but rather a failure to find an alternative social model adequate to correct them. Advancing literacy, urbanization, industrialization, and the development of overseas agriculture all pointed to the liberal society envisaged by the Weimar Convention. But the main currents of social thought since at least the constitution of the Reich pointed away from it. They aimed instead at what René König calls "the two revolutions that didn't occur." One of these was Marxist. The other was what Fritz Stern has called "the politics of cultural despair," a kind of Peter Pan ideology for a society that didn't want to grow up. As aware as the Marxists of the evils of industrialization, the cultural pessimists saw their correction not so much in a redistribution of ownership as in the elimination of industrial society itself. They waged war against the city, turned rural emigration into the pejorative "Landflucht" as though it were a form of desertion, created a distinction between Gemeinschaft, the Arcadian community of the rural village, and Gesellschaft, the soulless rat race of urban society, and turned the sociological discussion of the period into an exhaustive analysis of "class" and "estate." The homestead act of 1919 and the economic parliament foreseen by the Weimar Constitution were testimony to their influence even during the brief honeymoon of popular support for the liberal Republic. In the form of land reform and conventions of estates (Ständekammern) and supplemented with demands for industrial profit sharing, nationalization of trusts, and redistribution of department store properties to small business, both measures found their echo only a few months later in the "inalterable" Nazi program of 24 February 1920.

This was less evidence of Nazi originality than of the Zeitgeist. The infant Party was obliged to climb on the bandwagon to remain in the race. What subsequently turned the NSDAP into a mass organization with a voter potential of fourteen million, and finally into Germany's governing Party, was at no point its programmatic command of the issues or pseudo-issues, but its manipulation of them. It was the mobilization of disaffection.

A form of this general disaffection had created National Socialism even before Hitler discovered it. In its original form, National Socialism was a phenomenon of the South German border areas, an organization of "little men," frequently handicraftsmen, frequently of small-town origin, all of them hungry for the respect of their German-National social betters. An outline of its general premises can be found in the unassuming autobiographical essay of Anton Drexler, the chairman of the little German Workers Party Hitler discovered in Munich in 1919. Drexler described with horror his youthful experiences in Berlin, his ostracism for unstated reasons by Socialist unionists, and the humiliation of having to play the zither in a restaurant. With the querulousness of the born crank, he was quick to find a Jewish-capitalist-Masonic conspiracy at the root of all problems, to appreciate its diabolical exploitation of existing class differences to plunge Germany unprepared into World War I and then to secure its defeat. While addressing himself to the working class, he was careful to avoid offense, to declare the worker a Bürger, and the officer and civil servant non-bourgeois. He declared himself in favor of capitalism but "healthy" capitalism, and drew a line between the Bürger, the farmer, the worker, and the soldier, on one side, and their common enemy, the capitalist Jew, on the other.

In industrially underdeveloped Munich at the end of the war and after the left-wing putsch that followed it, this was an ideology with a certain appeal. The following it attracted was not limited as Hitler later tried to suggest. Hitler, who joined with membership card No. 555, found both a rudimentary party program and a potentially expansive membership. The ideology was the work of a kind of Central European William Jennings Bryan, the engineer Gottfried Feder, whose specialty was inflationary fiscal policy and who had previously tried without success to sell his schemes to Kurt Eisner, the Socialist leader of the 1918 Bavarian revolution. The membership was mixed, in part a combination of desperate small shopkeepers, professional men, and workers like the machinist Drexler and his friends from the railroad, in part of demobilized soldiers like Hitler himself, at loose ends and unable to find their way back into civilian life. There being potentially large reserves in both the "civilian" and the "military" groups, this was a combination with a political future, provided that it found leadership capable of holding it together, and that economic and political stabilization did not undermine its attractiveness. . . .

While the Nazi vote for the Reichstag fell in 1928 to 810,000, or ninth in order of representation, the creation and combination of ideological clienteles—Feder's petite bourgeoisie, Rosenberg's cultural pessimists, Goebbels' and the Strassers' young activists—and, above all, the charisma of Hitler, sustained both a base and an image. Radical, youthful, anti-Communist, sympathetic to small business, not necessarily hostile to big business, and ferociously nationalistic, the Party, like its program, was potentially acceptable in one way or another to nearly every large social group. Even while the vote fell, membership rose steadily—from 27,000 in 1925 to 178,000 in 1929. National Socialism had its hard core, a sociological base more diversified than that of any other party except the Catholic Center (Zentrum), variously maintained by fear of the department store, fear of communism, fear of the Poles, fear of further decline in the price of farm commodities, and "the politics of cultural despair." The numbers were small but tenacious; the cadres were there.

On the eve of its first great election victory on 14 September 1930, the Party consisted of:

workers	26.3%
white collar	24.0
independent	18.9
civil servants	7.7
farmers	13.2
miscellaneous	9.9

Still more revealing of its sources of support was its age distribution:

18–20	0.4%
21–30	36.4
31–40	31.4
41–50	17.6
51–60	9.7
61–	4.5

youth

In the Party groups in Berlin, Halle-Merseburg, Mecklenburg-Lübeck, the Palatinate, and Württemberg-Hohenzollern, the 21 to 30 year-olds were more than 40 per cent of the total membership. In comparison to the average for the Reich, the underdeveloped areas of South Germany, Lower Bavaria, Franconia, the Palatinate, and Schleswig-Holstein with its chronic agricultural crisis were overrepresented.

The Nazi deputies elected to the Reichstag in September 1930—who, under Weimar's proportional electoral system, were men who had distinguished themselves in the Party apparatus rather than men with direct public appeal—included, by their own identification, 16 in crafts, trade, or industry; 25 employees, both blue- and white-collar workers; 13 teachers; 12 career civil servants; 9 editors and 6 Party employees, together 15 full-time Party functionaries; 8 military officers; a Protestant clergyman; and a druggist, Gregor Strasser; as well as 12 engaged in agriculture. Of the 107, 12 were under 30 (compared with 8 of the 77 KPD deputies), 59 between 30 and 40 (compared with 45 of the 77 KPD deputies, 17 of the 143 SPD deputies). Roughly 60 per cent of the Nazi (and KPD) deputies were under 40, compared with scarcely more than 10 per cent from the SPD.

Hitler's course from here to the Machtergreifung (seizure of power) was, even more than before, tactically rather than ideologically defined. As Weimar's social and political supports collapsed under the impact of the depression, his object, as before, was effectively negative: to do nothing that might antagonize potential support. This went so far, as Theodor Heuss noted, as to exclude Jews as the favored target. Hitler had nothing against "decent" Jews, he is supposed to have told a foreign visitor after the September election, and Heuss had the impression that Goebbels' characterization of bourgeois opponents as a "stinking dung heap" caused him genuine embarrassment. Even before the election, Otto Strasser—a "utopian socialist," as he considered himself—left the Party, antagonized by a series of what he felt to be officially sanctioned harassments and outraged, he reported, by Hitler's evident opportunism. There was no such thing as social or economic revolution, Hitler is supposed to have told him, redistribution of ownership was a Marxist chimera, the economy in its existing form was inviolable, and socialism meant nothing more than State intervention to assure the prevention of conflict. He even rejected autarky. "Do you think we can isolate ourselves from the world economy?" he asked. Nazis were forbidden to join a strike in Saxony in April 1930, another of Strasser's sore points. In October 1930 when the dimensions of a metalworkers' strike in Berlin made this impossible, the Party dispatched its economic advisor, the retired major Otto Wagener, to persuade Saxon industrialists that the alternative was a mass migration to the SPD. Officially Hitler announced in the *Völkische Beobachter* that participation in the strike was intended to teach German industry a lesson in the consequences of observing the conditions of the Versailles Treaty.

At the same time, the Party permitted itself occasional displays of its old radicalism. On 14 October 1930, the newly elected Reichstag deputation presented a bill demanding confiscation of all bank and brokerage fortunes, of the property of all East European Jews who had arrived in Germany since 1914 and of all profits accruing from the war or speculation, as well as nationalization of the larger banks and a maximum interest rate of 4 per cent. But they withdrew it in the face of the SPD and KPD who threatened to support it, knowing this would frighten Hitler's financial supporters, and equally in the face of Germany's economists who bought newspaper space to testify to the bill's impracticability. In early 1931 a bill in the budget committee of the Reichstag forbidding the acquisition of any further public debts and the financing of all public works with interest-free Reich credit bills testified to the survival of Feder's influence and the old populist spirit. So, in May 1932, did Strasser's famous proclamation of the antikapitalistische Sehnsucht (anticapitalist yearning), with its demands that Germany go off the gold standard, increase its farm productivity, break up its urban concentrations, create a rural labor service, control farm prices and wages, finance cheap credits, and lower interest rates.

But Hitler's course led away from specific demands rather than toward them, even at the risk of offending potential radical support like the SA, which was already susceptible to mutiny, or like the young Reichswehr lieutenant Richard Scheringer whose indignation about the Party's apparently anti-revolutionary course led him in 1931 to make a public switch to the KPD. The Party was becoming respectable, and Hitler, concerned very much with votes and financial support and very little with ideological consistency, did his best to ease and hasten the process. Fritz Thyssen reported later that Hitler had given him the impression that he intended to clear the way for a restoration of the monarchy, while the young and foolish Prince of Schaumburg-Lippe told of Hitler's assurance that his movement had room for monarchists and republicans alike. Thyssen agreed to underwrite the Party. Schaumburg-Lippe volunteered to campaign actively in its support and noted by 1931–32 that his relatives—one of the Kaiser's sons among them—already had not only accepted "high and highest" positions in the party and SA but had been sent ahead as Landtag and Reichstag deputies. Krebs, at the same time, noted that the later Hamburg Gauleiter Karl Kaufmann, then close to the Strasserite wing of the Hamburg Party, had been censured from Munich for his critique of Hitler's "Harzburg Front" with Alfred Hugenberg and the Stahlhelm, and that he himself was being edged out of his position as press secretary of the Party by a man with the "best connections" to the Hamburg merchant bourgeoisie.

Still presented in their "inviolability," the twenty-five points of the Party program were meanwhile subjected to a creeping violation intended to reduce any remaining resistance in yet untapped electoral reservoirs. As early as 1928 Hitler had replied to a challenge from the farmers' organizations by declaring that the land reform envisaged in the Party program would not lead to expropriations. The phrase "uncompensated expropriation," he stated, referred only to Jewish speculators. The Party stood firmly in support of private property. In its practical activity, the Party went still further. When the SPD in Brunswick presented a bill granting the state automatic priority of purchase right in sales of land, a bill whose language was copied directly from Rosenberg's official exposition of the land-reform paragraph in the Party program, eight of the nine Nazi deputies voted against it. As early as 1928, this combination of tactical accommodation with falling prices resulted in a steep climb in rural support, particularly in hitherto untapped North and East German Protestant areas.

Appealing to the middle class, Feder confined the problem of profit-sharing to the very largest industrial concentrations like the I. G. Farben, then redefined it as simple price-reduction, which would bring its benefits to everyone, rather than confining it to employees of the firm concerned. He also distinguished between "moral" industrialists and "anonymous, depersonalized" corporations. Rosenberg left the problem to the future. Still more important than ideological concessions was political organization in the form of the Kampfbund für den gewerblichen Mittelstand (Small Business Action League), another fellow-traveler group, under the leadership of Theodor

Ardian von Renteln, earlier the Party's first youth leader. The organizing of fellow travelers was meanwhile extended to every other possible interest group—to lawyers, doctors, teachers, schoolboys, and to women whose organizers were instructed to avoid titles, uniforms, and class appeals, and to concentrate instead on Christianity, motherhood, and the family as the basis of the future Reich. Hung above each subappeal—fixed prices for the farmers, jobs for the unemployed, liberation from competition with big competitors for small business, and careers open to talent for the young—was the general appeal of "Rescue Germany," an idealized form of "sauve qui peut," as Geiger said, directed at a population that had lost the selfconfidence of 1848 and 1870 and was now prepared to throw itself into the arms of its own desperation. Underpinning it was a style composed equally of radical activism, military hierarchy, and the grandiose hocus-pocus of a fraternal lodge, embellished with stars, stripes, oak leaves, medals, and badges. Hitler's Party had become a revolutionary mass organization whose members addressed one another with the formal, plural "Sie" rather than the familiar "Du." . . .

Seen against its social background, National Socialism is far too complicated a phenomenon to be derived from any single source or reduce to any single common denominator, whether it be the depression or the course of German history. Its very dynamism precluded easy generalizations. If, before 1930, the NSDAP tended to be a Party of völkisch true believers, like the Göttingen Nazis who saw their mission in the compilation of a directory of Jews in German academic life, it tended after 1930 to be an organization of the economically desperate with a considerable admixture of opportunism. "When I joined the NSDAP," Fritzsche testified at Nuremberg, "I did not have the impression of joining a Party in the conventional sense since this was a Party without a theory. . . . All the Party theoreticians were under fire. . . . There were already whole groups of former DNVP members in the NSDAP or of former Communists. . . ."

"The formula, 'National Socialism is exclusively that which So-and-so says or does,' whereby the particular proponent was referring to himself, replaced the Party program . . . ," Hans Frank declared in his memoirs. "Any number of names filled the formula at the start: Hitler, Goering, Strasser, Röhm, Goebbels, Hess, Rosenberg, and more. There were as many National Socialisms as there were leaders."

The most general theory—that National Socialism was a revolution of the lower middle class—is defensible but inadequate. National Socialism had a striking appeal for the Auslandsdeutsche, Germans who had spent the impressionable years of their lives in a German community abroad. Whether at the microcosmic level of the Göttingen Party or in important positions in Munich, like Rosenberg or Darré, there was an impressive number of them. National Socialism was no less a revolt of the young against the old. While a theory of National Socialism as a lower middle-class phenomenon applies very well to voter behavior, it fails to account for important sectors of Party leadership with their violent animosity toward the social forms for which their voters yearned. Himmler's contempt for the bourgeois self-indulgence of railway dining cars was no more a lower middle-class attitude than the longing for action, power, nights of the long knives, or a radical reorganization of society, shared by the Party's leaders. National Socialism drew unmistakably on the historical reserves of liberal support, but its leaders were unequivocally sworn to the destruction of liberal values and liberal society.

This hard core of revolutionary destructiveness existed before the depression in quantities too great to be dismissed as simple personal idiosyncrasy. The longing for security that it exploited existed before the depression as well, but sought its objectives elsewhere in unrevolutionary places. What brought them together, leaders and followers, was a common hostility to the status quo at a moment of unique desperation, a desperation only two parties, the KPD and the NSDAP were fully prepared to exploit. In promising everything to everybody, the Nazis promised nothing to anybody. The tactical pursuit of power obviated any immediate urgency in the discussion of what was to be done once it was attained. As it was to Frank and Fritzsche this was clear to the farmer who told Heberle ". . . we believe that in the Third Reich, we, the farmers, will be so strong a power that we can shape it as we desire." From a contemporary standpoint, National Socialism was wide open, its disparity not a handicap but a positive advantage. What united it ultimately was not a mandate for war and Auschwitz, but a universal desire for change.

Modern Politics: The French Communists

ANNIE KRIEGEL

Politicization is one of the leading features of modernization. Before modernization, the common people had a political system of their own. Peasant assemblies, for example, were often lively gatherings, making decisions on a variety of issues important to the village. Peasants were aware of wider political relationships, notably those that bound them to a manorial lord. But peasant politics were highly personalized. Peasants lacked an ability to grapple with abstract issues, and there is no doubt that the attitude of the common people toward the central government was not politicized in the modern sense. Peasants and city dwellers might have expected the central government to do some things for them—help out in famines, for example. They had a loyalty to the traditional monarch, but they did not see government as something in which they could or should participate. When they rioted they did not do so to challenge a political structure that excluded them. Indeed, they often explicitly declared their allegiance to the king, even as he sent his troops against them, because they believed he was misled by bad advisers.

We have already seen stages of the transition to a modern political outlook. The nature of modern protest, as Charles Tilly sees it emerging in the mid-nineteenth century, was in large measure based on political demands. Socialism served as a vehicle for voicing political as well as economic grievances. Socialist politics became central to the lives of many workers, in Germany and elsewhere. Nazism was politicization of another sort, drawing some types of people into the political process for the first time. These examples alone show how complex politicization has been and how difficult it is to predict the results.

Furthermore, each nation has something of its own political style. In England, where the politicization of the lower classes began early (in the eighteenth century), the ultimate political movement of the workers has been rather moderate. France continues to fascinate because of an addiction to political extremes, and as the following selection suggests, tradition itself is one explanation for the existence of a powerful Communist movement.

Yet even within a single country, the complexity of politics as a phenomenon of modernization remains great. Politics is no neat expression of class. Not all French workers are Communists, and vice versa. If communism is primarily a factory movement, and therefore a rather new one in France, it touches base also with the skilled elite of workers who have led working-class protest since the glory days of the French Revolution. Correspondingly, the poorest are not the leaders of Communist protest, as was also true in age-old protest tradition. In other words, the "politicization of protest," which has such a modern ring to it, should not conceal serious contact with attributes of nineteenth-century unrest or even preindustrial protest characteristics.

The nature of the protest commitment requires assessment along with the social base. Annie Kriegel, one of the leading analysts of the French labor movement, takes pains to discuss not only the different kinds of people but also the different degrees of commitment that go into French communism. The Communist movement has been a major force in France for over fifty years, and never more than at the present time. But how seriously is it an expression of worker interests? Is politicization really important to most workers, or is it just an overlay—however important to the political process itself—on traditional views, including a large dose of apathy? Are workers indeed in control of the political movement that claims to express them, given the number of nonworkers involved and the immensely important bureaucratic apparatus that is required to mobilize and channel any large groups of people? And finally, of course, has politicization made worker protest more effective? The workers whose votes swell the Communist totals but whose commitment is lacking may well be wondering if the state can ever be made to serve their ends. Again, beneath the surface of politicization, one must ask how much has changed in popular attitudes. French communism is of course particularly fascinating, since a strong Communist movement has proved unusual in western Europe. But it poses, in a sense, a particular form of a general question about the nature of highly organized mass politics and its significance for the masses themselves.

. . . My second observation has to do with the size of another category, that of the nonactive members [of the Communist party]. There is no heading marked "miscellaneous" in the statistics for 1966. We can only deduce from this that retired workers have been tabulated by their original occupations and "housewives" by their husbands' occupations. Since the over-sixty group (comprising a large number of retired people) amounts to 17.3 percent of the total membership, and since housewives represent 46 percent of all female members (25.5 percent of the total membership), we may assume that the sector which consists of those who are not part of the "active population" represents approximately 25 to 30 percent of the total membership. One member out of three or four is not or is no longer "in production."

These two observations correct the excessively flattering impression that

From Annie Kriegel, *The French Communists: Profile of a People*, trans. by Elaine Halperin. Copyright © 1972 by The University of Chicago Press.

the 1966 figures tend to give. But, having made these reservations, I should also point out that the French Communist party is really a party that springs from the *working-class world*—a designation that is perhaps more precise than "workers' party." This of course does not mean that *all* French workers or even a majority of them are communists. On the other hand, even if one figures, for example, that 981 out of every 1,000 workers are not party members, this does not mean that the Communist party is not a workers' party. It merely signifies that in France, as in other countries where social classes are averse to politics, only a small proportion of the working class is organized into a political party. The French Communist party as such is not noteworthy for its large proportion of factory workers—actually, the number of dues-paying communists in the Simca, Citroen, or even Renault factories is incredibly small. Moreover, it should also be pointed out that the official party figures for the percentage of "workers" in its ranks are somewhat contrived since there are included under this heading many thousands of party functionaries who are *former* workers. Nevertheless, even if they are no longer "in production," these militants, some of whom have not been workers for at least five years, continue to be steeped in a working-class ambiance through their contacts with relatives, young people, and neighbors. . . .

Although at present the party unquestionably has a socially more diversified membership than it had in the past, it has nonetheless maintained solid ties with its working-class nucleus. But it would be a mistake to believe that this happens naturally, spontaneously, or that a policy inspired by the interests of the industrial masses is enough to account for the continued existence of such ties. Constant vigilance and a variety of technical approaches are required to insure an adequate flow of new recruits.

Thus constant scrutiny accompanies the selection of candidates for the various communist schools and yields an accurate picture not only of the social composition of administrative bodies at all levels of the apparatus but also of the multiform institutions that enable the party to function in opposition to established society. Whenever necessary, the party does of course seek the help of qualified technicians, but directors or collaborators from the workers' world are assigned to these technicians—a system perfected by the Soviet republic during the early years of its existence.

The organizational measure most effective in preserving the preponderance of working-class people within the party was implemented in 1924–25. It is known as "Bolshevization." At that time the Communist International stipulated that all its sections must radically change the nature of their primary electoral districts upon which the party's structure was henceforward to be based. In the earlier type of socialist parties, the primary electoral district was the *commune*, the traditional scene of electoral battles; in the young "Bolshevized" communist parties, it was replaced by the factory, a privileged terrain "where the two basic classes confront one another."

It is from the factory, the mine, the shipyard, the office, that the outcry arises which unites in a single struggle all those subject to capitalist rule and to man's exploitation of man. It is in the factory, the mine, the office, the shipyard that thousands and tens of thousands of workers are brought together by the capitalists. The factory is the nerve center of modern society, the very threshold of the class struggle. That is why for you, as communists, the factory should be the center of all your efforts, of all your activities.

This reorganization resulted in an impressive upheaval that constitutes a highly significant episode in the history of French communism. Moreover, this revolution in organizational procedures was remarkable for its durability. Despite winds and storms the principle is still respected and the regulations still observed.

But the winds and storms were violent ones. The structure of a profession (in the building industry, for example, where mobile work-teams are temporarily tied to the existence of a shipyard or some other place of work), the way working time was organized (with day and night shifts, or "brigades" replacing one another), the nature of the labor force (of relevance here was the practice of giving bus service to those who worked in textile mills, mines, and certain steel plants, to say nothing of the presence of large contingents of foreign, non-French-speaking workers)—all these caused endless complications. Only protracted experience could provide solutions to the problem of how to gather communist workers together in companies as complex as the railways or the merchant marine, or how to reach migrant agricultural workers who are employed only seasonally. In every instance there had to be some precise indication of the unit that constituted the "territory" of the cell: workshop, office, shipyard. All things considered, the problem that proved to be the most difficult and also the one that was the most inadequately resolved was invariably that of organizing the unemployed.

Without even taking into account the factors that naturally contribute to instability—restrictive actions by the employers, above all the mergers that forced the less adaptable plants to shut down, labor's growing mobility—one can easily understand why, given the circumstances, the factory cells turned out to be quite fragile. Occasionally the mere departure of a few militant propagandists sufficed to cause the cells' demise.

Subjective factors proved no less powerful. A good many militants in charge of the sale of l'Humanité-dimanche arrive at their posts each Sunday with remarkable punctuality. But they are most reluctant to draw attention at their places of work. "The sector," Pierre Sémard conceded, "is at some distance from the employers, from capitalism, but the cell is much closer." Concern for one's career—the humbler it is, the more precious it may seem; a recurring anxiety whenever the labor market shrinks, or when advancing age lessens the chances of being reclassified; complications in time schedules wherever collective transportation is available only at the end of the day's work; preoccupation about output—these represent arguments that can be adduced against the pursuit of political activities in the shipyard or the factory. Such activities are not only quite unprotected by law; employers as well as most trade unions regard them with suspicion, sharing as they do a concern that is constant, equivocal, and characteristically French—a profound anxiety to make sure that the company does not become a political battlefield. . . .

Then there is another complication: factory cells, even in the "freest" sector, fail to attract representatives from all categories of workers. Although the party is largely indebted to the cells for its deep roots in the workers' movement generally, it is likewise indebted to them for its initial spread within one specific segment of the working class.

To regard the world of the factory as one that is entirely homogeneous and equal, without structure or hierarchy, is to hold a very superficial and false notion of the actual situation. On the contrary, the existence of hierarchies in the professions and trades, the conflicting ethnic and linguistic loyalties, the length of time people have lived in the city—all these create serious areas of friction. Yet the general image of the worker remains almost immutable: the typical proletarian continues to be thought of as a highly qualified French steelworker, or at least as someone born in France whose rural ancestry is already growing dim.

A Highly Qualified Steelworker   The professional competence of militant workers is well known. Apparently this is due not only to the moral qualities usually associated with skilled workers but also to the actual historical circumstances that prevailed in France when trade unionism first appeared. In effect, trade unionism was at first a defensive reaction on the part of the best-educated journeymen in the old building and steel trades. The priority and predominance of skilled workers represent a fact that has obtained throughout our history. The reasons for this are complex, indeed so much so that the whole subject of the existence of a working-class aristocracy will require considerable investigation. We merely note here that at the Eighteenth Congress of the French Communist party (1967), 349 delegates out of 409 were qualified professionals, compared to sixty unskilled and manual workers.

It would probably be just as profitable to ascertain the extent to which the occupational composition of the party (and of the trade unions) gives rise to the theoretical and practical uncertainties which mark the attitude of communists on the question of wage hierarchies. Curiously enough, the accusations of rigidity in regard to wage scales—including both temporary and regular remuneration—and the proposals for raising the wages of the most poorly paid come from the CFDT (Confédération française démocratique du travail, the Catholic trade unions).

This is a far cry from the egalitarian (utopian? of anarchist origin?) preoccupations which in 1939, under the aegis of the international trade-union federation of teachers, the FISE (*Fédération internationale syndicale de l'Enseignement*, an outgrowth of the *Profintern*), pushed the communist minority of the teachers' federation to insist publicly on uniform treatment for all teaching personnel. Besides, the really poor, in the strictly economic sense, who, as we know, do not provide a high proportion of communist electors, also do not furnish many militants, despite periodic appeals to them to do so.

We have said "highly qualified," but why "steelworkers"? The pre-1914 Socialist party was a peoples' party or, to put it better, a plebeian party. The little people felt comfortable in it. The Communist party for its part is made up of factory workers. This does not mean, of course, that you never find in it any village artisans or representatives of the city's little people, those who constituted the nucleus of Jaurès' following. But the worker predominates; and his political development probably coincided with the formation of the French Communist party. Just as the workers' movement during the first decade of the twentieth century was marked by the traditions of building trade employees, so the successful dissemination of communism in working-class circles during the twenties was the particular accomplishment of two groups: railway workers and steelworkers. . . .

The sociology of religion lists indicators that make it possible to measure the degree of loyalty of the faithful. Similarly, political sociology measures loyalty by participation in various kinds of cultic ceremonies. For communists, attendance at cell meetings corresponds, roughly, to attendance at Mass for Catholics. The average number of evenings devoted each week to militant activity probably constitutes a valid criterion that enables us to distinguish between the "active militant" and the ordinary member. The latter, like the "Easter Catholic," can be distinguished by his participation in two major ceremonies: renewal of his membership card in January of each year and attendance at the annual "Fête de *l'Humanité*" in September.

This procedure, however, has one drawback: distinctions between members are made solely on the basis of their outward behavior, which is not the most important issue. The real question is how much change for the better each person undergoes as a result of belonging to the communist movement.

Political Allegiance

There is, to be sure, one initial way of being a communist, a way we might call "Cartesian." This applies to every militant who fulfills his political duties rigorously.

To conceive of one's allegiance to communism as an allegiance to a political party, as the choice of one political policy among many, is in no way proof of intellectual honesty or clarity of vision. It merely signifies that certain communists are to be found at the plebeian levels of society, people who have joined the Communist party because it was the most "radical" of the leftist parties, the most "republican" of groups within the republican camp, the legitimate heir of Jacobin radicalism, of Guesdist socialism. Communists south of the Loire, of the red Midi, and especially those who live in the southwest, often belong to this category. This explains why the communist peasants of Corrèze and the Dordogne never felt guilty because they failed to give fervent support to any program for the collectivization of farms, even in the most modest and modern form of agricultural cooperatives. Communists of this kind would be extremely astonished if one deduced from the mere fact of membership that the party had anything to say or even an opinion about all those things in life that have nothing to do with politics. On the other hand, they like "politics" and they are active in it. But, as we shall see, orthodox communists "do not like politics" and are not active in it—I am using the word *politics* here, not in a strict electoral and parliamentary sense but in a far broader one: public affairs, world affairs.

Speculations at the café; political discussions among friends; the concrete "political dimensions" of local or national life, more rarely those of international affairs: these are some of the things that communists of this stripe like to indulge in. They are the sons of an open-air civilization where attendance at the forum is proof of the dignity of free men. Isn't it to such communists that we owe the widespread idea—one that is well founded—that communists have a feeling for the State? Or, to be more precise, a feeling for the City? To be sure, they have substituted the grimmer, more somber word, "comrade," for the plain one, "citizen," with its consciously intended juridical and "political" resonance. But at the very first appeal from a leftist union, full-bodied republican conceptions of discipline and public welfare spring up in their minds.

Existential Allegiance

There is another, broader, less selective, but no less relaxed way of being a communist: an existential way. This applies to those who equate membership in the Communist party with a state of nature—who belong to the party "from birth." Their attitude is not necessarily attributable to the fact that they were born into communist families. Rather, for them the communist option is of a piece with their national, social, occupational, cultural inclinations. Less a political party than a milieu in which one lives, the Communist party is for them the hospitable structure that is in harmony with and attuned to their initial potentialities; allegiance to it is felt to be something logical, rational, *normal*. This explains why, for such persons, membership in the party rarely takes place in the youthful years. Indeed, unless something exceptional should come along to hasten his evolution—a strike, a period of political agitation, occasionally a political campaign—the young worker is in no hurry. To become a militant is somewhat like becoming a father. It means the assumption of new responsibilities, the kind that are natural enough but that also imply that one is growing older. Unlike the student, who often becomes a party member quite young because membership for him means a break with his family, or at least an attempt to break with it, the worker who joins the party because he is seeking a means of self-expression is usually around twenty-four or twenty-five—when he returns from military service. Often he joins the party after a rather long interval during which he acquires the habits of his trade and a measure of occupational competence. The decision to join the party often stems from an internal debate that centers on whether a person should engage in the political struggle or improve his professional skills. He asks himself: should I become a militant or a technician, maybe an engineer?

One cannot ignore the fact that this pattern, while it indicates choices and implies sacrifices, is nonetheless dominated by the idea of conformity. This explains why such militants—the favorite protagonists of proletarian novelists as well as the leaders of cadres—are solid individuals, entirely mature, having totally internalized their options: serene, convinced, deep-rooted, representative. But they are also men threatened with sclerosis; their consciences tend to wane and they feel too much at home in their environments.

Here we touch upon one of the elements that have caused the party to slip away bit by bit from its revolutionary sphere. Many of its militants are extremely "well adjusted," by which we do not mean that they have become bourgeois, an accusation too readily made, but rather that they have accustomed themselves to a party that has become for them a way of life, part of the air they breathe.

Ideological Allegiance

Finally, there is a third way of being a communist, one that might be called ideological. As a general rule, this is the road traveled by students and intellectuals.

It is quite true that we find many intellectuals who can be classified as belonging to the first of our three categories. These men continue the tradition of the pre-1914 university, of these "flesh and blood socialists": Jacobins, patriots, Freemasons, Cartesians (because they were mechanistic), Kantians (if they had the nerve for it). They scorned a dialectic that a rigorous mind could only condemn; their vision was somewhat narrow; on occasion they were petty, childishly ashamed of human weaknesses whose mysteries offended them, discreetly ambitious but timorous, and ultimately indifferent; not always as naive as they wished to appear, they loved mystification if its object was our Greco-Latin past. All in all, they were scrupulous, erudite, affable; they believed in goodness, progress, justice, work, and truth.

Actually, such intellectuals—professors, physicians, scientists—are quite numerous in the Communist party, and they are highly prized. Care is taken not to trouble them with matters unrelated to their clear conception of the world and to their delicate sensitivity—this last, needless to say, being somewhat arid and devoid of imagination. The party does not bother them, for example, with problems that concern the intelligentsia in the socialist countries. Their penchant for abstraction, their capacity to reduce the complexities of the real and the concrete to notions, essences, blueprints, principles, makes them skeptical and consequently rather easy to handle. In short, never having had to make themselves over in the image of the party, they are quite willing to accept the fact that the party is not necessarily fashioned according to their image. This imperceptible distance between them and the party constitutes that mixture of a little contempt and a good deal of mutual indulgence that makes for good relations. . . .

The communist intellectuals who matter are part of an entirely different heritage; they are motivated by very different dynamics, the dynamics of a *spiritual conversion*. . . .

Tired of the arguments and the excessive logic of our scientists, the French intelligentsia of the 1890s was captivated by anarchism. It was a fire that spread, scorching the edges and cracks of organized society. Having smoldered for a while, it blazed high and clear, with all the suddenness and gratuitousness of cosmic catastrophes. By *intelligentsia* I don't mean intellectuals or professors, those who regard life as a long career in which truth is captured gradually, one point at a time. Nor do I mean the many solid writers and artists who have all the self-assurance that talent bestows. I mean the very young, the marginal people, the lazy, the foolish, the geniuses, the down-and-outers, the dreamers, the restless, those who are incurably ill with an unknown malady, the doctors, the tired heroes, the "outsiders," the "refractory ones," the "black sheep"—these are the sobriquets bestowed upon them by anarchist newspapers—in short, all those who for professional, social, intellectual, or personal reasons are a headache to computer programmers because they are unpredictable, unclassifiable. . . .

But to be an anarchist means something more than breaking with established society. It is a more intimate, more demanding kind of rupture: a break with the established self in an established society. The biography of any anarchist contains evidence of such a split, of such a death and resurrection. This kind of conversion represents an alteration of one's entire person. To change life, one must first change one's own life.

To be a communist, according to a certain interpretation of the phrase, involves this same internal wrench, entails this same process of condemnation, expiation, and rebirth. In accordance with German Social Democracy's orthodox interpretation of Marxism, Bolshevism and its offshoots have assumed the absurd and pathetic task of establishing the theoretical foundations of the party, invoking the socialism of the future, declaring right now what is true and promulgating this truth. Hence the perpetually recurring crises that take place in the relations between the Communist party and its intellectuals. By their very existence, and in any case by the nature of their specific activity, the intellectuals belie the contention that the party—the sole precursor of the world to come—is the source of all science. Herein lies the true originality of the communist intellectuals—and the challenge they address to themselves. A communist intellectual is not only a man who "honors" his party, a militant who contributes to the political life of the organization of which he is a member. He is also a man who dares to initiate within himself a complicated experiment. Or at least he could be such a man; everybody does not move at an identical pace along the path, and sometimes people do not move at all. Membership in the party marks the beginning of a long and hazardous process at the end of which, the individual having "placed himself in the position of the working class," according to the traditional formula, a "new type of intellectual" must appear.

Sports: The People's Game

JAMES WALVIN

Sports clearly constitute a prime form of modern recreation. The following selection sums up the present situation of English football (soccer), places it in its historical context, and deals with various interpretations of it. The character of sports has changed immensely, as games like soccer have moved from unorganized village contests toward clearer rules, wider spectatorship, and commercial control. Yet it is argued in this selection that the continuities override the changes. Violence, in the game and among the spectators, is not in this view a sign of modern social decay but an expression of a longstanding human need. But, if this is so, has the modernization of popular mentality gone as far as some observers would have us believe? Has it, indeed, gone far enough? For even if a propensity to violence is not new, structural modernization gives it far more dangerous outlets for expression than ever before. Consequently, by providing outlets for violence, leisure may take on a greater importance than it had in preindustrial society.

Yet the sports world is itself subject to change in modern society. Again, it is not easy to apply a clear modernization model to predict the future direction of leisure forms. What is the significance of a decline in direct spectatorship in favor of more remote television watching? And what is the role of the professional athlete in modern society? Will greater affluence and, perhaps, a continued change in personal values lead toward more individualized (and expensive) sports, and more participation as opposed to spectatorship? If so, one must ask how the needs served by modern versions of old games, such as football, will be met in the future. Distinctions of social class, in the leisure area, must also be considered. And so must regional and geographical differences. It has been suggested, for example, that spectators in the United States take greater pleasure in violent team sports than do spectators in Europe, where individual performance (such as bicycle riding in France) is more highly valued. Modern leisure, including sports preferences, clearly involves unprecedented choice and at least surface variety, as changes in fads over time are added to regional and individual diversity. The larger patterns of social significance are not easy to discern, but it would be misleading to dismiss sports simply as fun, without further analysis.

In an age when a great deal of discussion about football concentrates solely on the problems of violence on and off the field, it is salutary to remember the game's past. For centuries football was a by-word for violence. In 1829 a Frenchman who saw a football match in Derby asked, "If this is what they call football, what do they call fighting?" When, in the course of a game in 1583, three weavers, a fuller and a tailor attacked another man they declared, "We are making work for the surgeon." Nine days later the man died. Two years later a constable in Great Dunmore was attacked by a man he had ordered to stop playing. Twenty years earlier, in 1567 in Essex, Henry Ingoldge died after a particularly nasty tackle. These and countless other tales could be offered as an insight into the violence of pre-industrial football.

Now too, commentators are concerned with violence, though of a qualitatively different order. But football has won a social respectability which is a relatively modern phenomenon. Throughout most of its history football was respectable only among the lower orders who played it, and was consequently frowned upon by the upper classes, who had their own sports, and who saw in football merely an unlovely and almost inevitable outburst of lower-class turbulence.

For centuries much of our knowledge is dependent upon sources which, by definition, are bound to emphasize violence and illegality. As English society changed from its late medieval shape into one recognizably modern, the historical evidence about football is drawn from legal records; litigation and laws, proclamations banning football, accidents and death, illegal footballing encroachments on the Sabbath. To a very large extent then, the image of football in late medieval and early modern England is largely a result of the surviving sources, and we have reason to believe (following the lead of diarists and foreign observers) that many games were injury-free, and were played peacefully and without resulting prosecutions. But beneath the accident of surviving evidence there run a number of basic assumptions and attitudes, both implicit and explicit, on the part of the governing class towards the game of football and towards the people who traditionally played it. The pre-industrial game of football reveals as much about the frame of mind of the governing orders, as it does about the distinctive qualities of lower-class life.

This is also true of the history of football in the nineteenth and twentieth centuries. Reactions to football have inevitably varied and depended largely upon the respective social positions of player and commentator. For instance, many men who warmly approved of public-school football were proportionately unhappy when they saw the same game played by men and boys of a lower social station with the consequent undermining of industrial and work discipline. An exception was the way pre-industrial football on

Shrove Tuesday was tolerated as a safety valve for lower-class tensions which might otherwise prove dangerous. Such tolerance, in sharp contrast to the usual resistance to the game, clearly pin-points the great variety of reactions towards football. It also suggests the dangers involved in attempting to make historical generalizations over such an enormously long time-span. We clearly need to place each reference to the game in its historical context. Having done that, certain clear general trends emerge. It was traditionally a popular game played by ordinary people and frowned upon by their betters; it was a nationwide phenomenon and was frequently the cause of violence and unrest.

This book contends that football could only develop as a mass spectator sport on a regular, nationwide and commercial basis when enough time and money became accessible to the mass of potential fans. However, the argument presents a serious problem of historical interpretation. Since football has been strongest, has in fact thrived, in poorer areas and in times of general hardship, the thesis has been advanced, particularly in certain sociological analyses of the game, that the game functions as an "opium of the masses," or as an analogue to the Roman "bread and circuses." A German sociologist of the game, for example, argues that football is a device of the capitalist order which uses the aggression of players and fans as a safety valve to maintain the stability of bourgeois capitalism. A number of objections to this thesis arise: first, the turbulence of the game clearly predates the emergence of bourgeois capitalism; second, such trials of collective strength and controlled aggression are common to many games; and third, the non-capitalist footballers of Russia, East Germany, Poland, Hungary, North Korea and China seem no less aggressive and violent than those in the West. This book has avoided certain areas of recent interest in football (mass psychology, concepts of aggression and sociological theories of games and play) because the author is not competent to deal with them. But the "bread and circuses," or "opium of the masses" interpretations of the game find no place here simply because they are not consistent with historical analysis.

Closer inspection suggests a quite opposite situation, namely that working men could play the game when they were healthy enough or watch it when they had the time and money to do so; therefore the modern game is contingent upon improvements in working-class life. Also, much of the "opiate" thesis rests on an analysis of football as a spectator sport, into which thousands of working men channelled their resentments and aggressions and, so the argument runs, misdirected their desire for change. But the fact remains that football was not simply a spectator sport but was played by generations of young men, and it was at this level that working men moulded the game to suit their own interests.

Moreover, if we are to believe the repeated complaints of men in authority in business and commerce about the roughness and industrially disruptive impact of football from the 1880s to the 1940s, the game clearly did not work as an opiate, and did little to channel working-class aggression into acceptable paths. At the time in English history when such an opiate might have been needed (roughly the years 1789 to the 1860s, when a new industrial work force had to be beaten into shape), football had ceased to be effective or important as a lower-class game.

It has been argued by Ian Taylor, a sociologist of the game, that football was once a "participatory democracy" in working class communities. The present author considers that if the term is relevant, the game might profitably be viewed in that light. Football remains primarily a working-class game; played and used by working men to their own particular ends. The stars of today's professional game may well be out of reach of the rank and file fans, unlike the period up to the 1960s, but it has to be stressed that the great majority of professional footballers do not fall into this category; they remain within the social experience, geographical reach and sympathy of their supporters. To suggest that the prosperity of the few has produced an unbridgeable gulf between footballers and their fans (and then to suggest, by an unprovable assertion, that this gulf produces an alienation which leads to hooliganism) is to do an injustice both to the nature and history of English football, by suggesting that the well-paid élite are typical. Nor is it valid to view the commercial exploitation of football as a new phenomenon; a glance at the bitter complaints about commercialism between 1880 and 1914 will reveal the same syndrome, if not the same degree of money-making in and around the game. Footballers today remain overwhelmingly working class in origin, even though some now find themselves in the super-tax bracket. The link between boy street-footballer and professional is direct and unmarked by any sense of alienation of one from the other.

It would be pointless to seek the causes of football's contemporary problems (be they attendance, or hooliganism) solely within the game itself, and to isolate the game from its determining social pressures. Since the modern game was largely a function of rising prosperity, it would be unusual if the new wave of prosperity since the 1950s did not affect the game. Those who seek an explanation for falling attendances, in football itself miss the fundamental point which is writ large through the game's history over the past century. Similarly to believe that the introduction of more competitive football will bring back the missing crowds is simply to invite the fans to spread their attendance more thinly. Whatever crisis the game is in (and this is only true of the professional game), that crisis is a result of dramatically changing leisure patterns. Proposals which do not recognize this central fact are mere shadow boxing. T.V. for instance is clearly a permanent fact of modern life and its impact on football will not be arrested simply by refusing to allow transmission of matches. Football authorities must reconcile themselves to this, and to a host of new changes. This will inevitably involve painful reappraisals by men who, if their past histories are any guide, will find such leaps of the imagination difficult.

There are quite simply too many professional football clubs for the shrinking pool of spectators, and yet those clubs most in need of reorganization into less ambitious divisions form the core of voting power within the Football League and can hardly be expected to vote themselves into oblivion. Given such understandable resistance to much-needed changes, the only remaining way of pruning the game is by allowing the free market economic forces to operate; unless the game is drastically re-organized more clubs will go the way of Accrington Stanley. Whether the emergence of super clubs and the decline of the smaller ones is a good or bad thing is not at issue here; but it is a cruel fact of life which has to be recognized and acted on.

Even were the number of professional clubs reduced, the health of the modern game would remain largely unaffected because, as this book has reiterated, that strength has never been defined purely in professional terms (except by some prominent observers of the game). Football as the people's game is healthier than ever and the provision of football fields, changing rooms and training facilities cannot keep pace with the demand. Of course the rise of football at the grass roots of society was most marked between 1880 and 1914, but since World War II the game has, if anything, become more significant, thanks to the modern concern with leisure and the widely accepted benefits of vigorous recreation in an urban environment. It is of course from this national nursery that professional players emerge and at this level the professional game and the popular, amateur substratum are indissolubly linked.

The social context of football has naturally changed, and at no time more rapidly than in the years since the early 1950s. Today the game is arguably more fashionable than at any time since the dominance of Old Boy teams in the 1870s. But football's social acceptability is largely an armchair phenomenon; the game is discussed in abstract and often intellectual terms by people who rarely see a live game. In this, the fate of football has been remarkably similar to that of the cinema where, despite the collapse of the cinema boom, festivals and T.V. replays enable many non-cinema goers to talk learnedly about the cinema. Football's respectability in England came about quite suddenly and can be dated from the 1966 World Cup. But the subsequent nationwide T.V. audience, drawn from all social classes, ought not to mask the basic class nature of the English game.

The commercialism of football, another continuing theme, has developed in two directions. On the one hand, the development of the pools put the gambling always inherent in the game onto a new level: on the other hand, the game has spawned a large number of ancillary commercial enterprises, established as separate industries but entirely dependent on football. Since the 1960s this commercial side of football has grown in size and complexity and the players, for once, have learned to benefit from it.

The fortunes of professional footballers have undergone a revolution in the past twenty years. Until the 1960s they were exploited in a rather crude economic sense. Since 1963 despite the astronomical earnings of the top few, footballers are quite simply worked too hard. The result can be measured in the premature end of playing careers and the staleness which pervades top professional football towards the end of each season. This more than any other factor is responsible for the admitted failure of top professionals to enjoy the game as much as they did when schoolboys. Today it is difficult to conceive of the working conditions under which footballers were employed until the early 1960s. Beginning as an illegal institution, professional football slowly progressed to the point where, by mid century, it offered adequate wages for a few players and low wages for the majority. The players were consistently denied many fundamental industrial rights; their own union (more so the union leaders) was discriminated against. It was only the greater strength and militancy of the union in the late 1950s and 1960s which forced the authorities to pass on some financial benefits to the players. Unless we remember this backwardness of industrial relations in the professional game (and the exceptional appeal of those clubs who treated their players decently) it is easy to overlook a fundamental malaise which for long bedevilled the English game.

When austerity gave way to prosperity, English football entered the new era hag-ridden by an organization and outlook which had been forged in the 1920s. Football, surrounded by dramatic changes in leisure patterns, would have faced problems enough without the added burdens of unimaginative leadership, outdated direction and almost pre-industrial labour relations. The slow movement towards European football and a more realistic acceptance of footballers' rights was the work of a small number of players and managers, to whom present-day players owe a debt of gratitude. But the super-stars also owe their fame to the impact of T.V. which has simultaneously helped to undermine the spectator appeal of football and brought the game its largest ever audiences.

The halcyon days of professional football, most notably in the late 1940s, are not likely to return, in the light of people's widening material ambitions. Changing tastes and rising incomes may push people towards totally different forms of sport. There has been a pronounced drift for example away from team games towards individual sports—climbing, tennis, squash, golf and others—another clear sign of the embourgeoisement of western society. Despite these changes, however, the basic character of English football remains remarkably similar to its century-old pattern. It remains the game of ordinary people; watched and played by more people than any other spectator and team game. With the minor, though crucial interlude of the mid nineteenth century, this has always been true of English football—the people's game.

Modern Women

HELGE PROSS

The following survey of the situation of women in West Germany, written in the 1960s, raises above all the question of how much has changed during the last seventy-five years. The inferior position of women in jobs and in the family may have diminished, but the problem remains acute. Indeed the selection supports the desirability of measuring many of the large trends of modernization in terms of women: Have changes in the family, for example, kept pace with those in the economy? The frustration of women, caught between an abandonment of traditional resignation and resultant new expectations on the one hand, and a denial of full equality on the other, has been a familiar aspect of life in western Europe and North America at least since the later nineteenth century.

Hence the selection should obviously be compared with Branca's discussion of Victorian women. Branca claims some rather substantial changes for women, in mentality and function, within the home. But women in contemporary society are moving out into a larger world, most notably through taking or maintaining jobs after marriage. Did the previous changes in their outlook prepare them for this? Will they seek occupational levels and behavior comparable to those of men or find their own job definition? Did the special nineteenth-century characterization of women's nature and functions prepare society at large for new roles?

Helge Pross is, of course, discussing a variety of social classes, not the middle class alone. It is probable that the transition to more modern values occurred later in worker, and especially peasant, households than in the middle class. This created some unsurprising similarities between the nineteenth-century middle class and the twentieth-century working class. It may be that women are too large a group for precise social analysis. The author's viewpoint must be assessed, as in any study of human society; in this case the author has rather clear notions of what women's position should be. But with all the qualifications, the special problems of interpreting the impact of modernization on women remain. Although women's lives in all major social classes may have changed more than those of men, their frustrations may be no greater, but simply different. Yet women do seem peculiarly caught between the pull of tradition and new needs and opportunities, victims or beneficiaries of a tension that men faced much earlier in the modernization process. It does seem certain, also, that the full implications of the modernization of women have yet to be worked out. Can an understanding of the changes in women's lives over the last century and a half allow prediction of women's future roles?

West Germany today is a modern society indeed. Highly industrialized, about 85 per cent of her population of 53 million live in smaller or larger towns, and only 15 per cent reside in villages and semirural communities. Little more than one tenth of all gainfully employed do agricultural work while approximately nine tenths are occupied in industry, private and public administration, handicraft, commerce, cultural institutions, or other non-agricultural jobs. During the last three or four decades the German social structure has undergone fundamental changes resulting in a society chiefly middle class in character. After World War II, the landed aristocracy, powerful for many a century, disappeared, while the industrial proletariat, exploited and underprivileged in the past, achieved a greatly improved economic position. Since the turn of the century a large and still growing new middle class of white-collar workers and civil servants emerged. To be sure, class distinctions have not been leveled out. They are marked, as far as property, income, social prestige, and educational opportunities are concerned. There is a small upper stratum consisting of a few extremely wealthy capitalists, the top executives of large industrial firms, high government officials, and the decision makers in the major political parties and pressure groups. However, this upper class, strong as its influence may be, has ceased to be a homogeneous ruling caste. On the other hand, no class of paupers is left at the bottom of the social pyramid. Working in an economy which for nearly a decade and a half has known no unemployment; enjoying a large measure of leisure (the work-week has been reduced to forty to forty-two hours); protected by an elaborate system of social security against the financial pitfalls of illness and age; and supplied with numerous opportunities for education and amusement, most Germans are citizens of quite an "affluent society" indeed.

Modern as the Federal Republic may be in her economic and social structure, she has not as yet broken with all traditions of an authoritarian and patriarchal past. The democratization of the state after World War II has not made for an egalitarian society. Although all men are equal before the law, society does not offer all of them equal opportunities. Some groups are still underprivileged in various ways. This holds true particularly for women. Remnants of age-old traditions regarding them as the intellectually weaker sex, less able to shoulder responsibilities in politics or the professions, stand in the way of true equality. Although the struggle for emancipation has been won, women are still discriminated against in the world outside the family and the home. Generally speaking, women in West Germany are confronted with social and psychological problems that, to a large degree, arise out of the disharmony between a demanding present and an unmastered past, and the conflict between preindustrial roles and the demands of modern life.

The Legal Position

Women in West Germany have nothing to complain about in regard to their legal position. The Basic Law, the Federal Republic's constitution, adopted in 1949, endows both sexes with equal rights. Women have the franchise, and enjoy the right of equal pay for equal performance. In 1957, the Federal Parliament took the last and decisive step towards the implementation of full legal equality. By a special bill all civil law was adapted to the constitutional principle. Among the many provisions of the new law, most important are those revising property and inheritance rights of husband and wife.

Under the old civil law, formulated at the end of the nineteenth century, the husband had remarkable privileges: he had the usufruct of his wife's estate and acted as her trustee. He managed their common property, and could dispose of it even against her will. At his death, the wife inherited only one quarter of his estate unless the couple had concluded a special contract in her favor.

All this has now been changed. The management and disposition of the wife's property is solely her affair. The husband is no longer allowed to handle their common estate without her consent. All decisions about common goods must be made by both. If the husband dies, the wife inherits one half of the property. In case of divorce, regardless of which of them is the guilty party, she not only retains what she brought into marriage, but receives in addition half of the possessions acquired by the couple while married. Even if the husband accumulated a fortune from his earnings, while the wife had no income of her own, she gets 50 per cent. This provision is meant to protect the housewife whose work the law considers indispensable for the creation and preservation of the estate. Formerly, if divorced, she had no legal claim to her husband's savings, [but] she now suffers no financial loss if, instead of seeking gainful employment, she devotes herself to the family and the home.

In addition to the provisions mentioned, the new law parts in all other respects as well from the old principle of the husband's right to decide in controversial family affairs. Formerly the decision about the children's education—whether they should or should not be sent to a *gymnasium* (academic high school), or to a university—was left to him, now both parents must agree. Also, the wife now has legal claim to regular payment of household expenses and pocket money for her personal needs. . . .

Town and Country

In many respects West German agriculture lags behind the urban and industrial sectors of society. While some villages have taken great steps toward the modernization of their economic and social life, in others people still cling to more traditional patterns. Generally speaking, the rural population is also passing through a period of transition. Struggling to adapt to the requirements of a market economy, a large number of farmers surrendered and took up industrial jobs. In fact, from 1949 to 1959 about 50 per cent of the agricultural laborers, and one third (1.5 million) of the independent peasants quit agriculture. Many, if not most, of those who stayed cannot keep up economically with the urban population. Though all of them, male and female alike, work harder than the average city dweller, their standard of living is lower. So is their level of education. Of course, there are no illiterates in the rural regions, and much is being done to improve the farmers' general and vocational training. Many villages have centers for adult education or community houses offering regular lectures on agricultural techniques, home economics, baby care and sociopolitical subjects. Since these community houses frequently provide certain facilities, such as washing machines or deep freezers, for common use, they act as agencies of modernization also for those who could not be reached by mere theoretical instruction. In addition, radio and television, popular all over the country, are links to the non-rural world. Nevertheless, the average villager still seems to be less informed on national events. Nor is information about modern child-rearing techniques disseminated among them. In many places, children are looked after only until they are four years old. Afterwards, mothers leave them to themselves, rarely having the time to supervise and to guide them. Child labor is widespread, almost all village youngsters being obliged to help in the home, to look after cattle and poultry, or assist their parents in the fields.

Within the last two or three decades the rural family too has undergone some change. As to size, it does not differ much from its urban counterpart. Since the end of World War II the nuclear family has emerged as the representative and most widespread rural type. The number of children is small, almost never larger than two. This change indicates that the rural population has also turned to a more rational, calculating attitude toward life. The internal family structure is, however, somewhat different from the urban one. With respect to the position of mother and wife, roughly three types can be

distinguished, each representing a different stage of adaptation to more democratic ways.

First, there is the traditional patriarchal family, dominated by the father,
with wife and children still subordinates rather than partners. In these families, practically all decisions are left to the oldest male. He manages the
family budget, decides matters concerning the farm, and has the final word
in controversies about the children. It is interesting that the patriarchal
family's economic behavior also follows more traditional lines. Rarely are
economic ends and means linked in a rational way. Neither do such families
adopt a sensible scheme of division of labor, nor are there conscious efforts at
better management. One result is an overload of work for the women. Responsible for the house, the poultry and the garden, they also work in the fields
and have to step in wherever and whenever additional hands are needed.

In general, the working hours of peasant women in all types of families
are long, from 60 to 80 hours per week. In spite of this heavy contribution,
women are little respected. Most villagers show only a modest appreciation
of female work, and the women themselves are too much resigned to their
lot to object. Being overworked, they often are in a poor state of health and
thus lack the physical energy as well as the time to search for improvements.

While according to the estimates of some sociologists a decade ago this
traditional patriarchal family was the most widespread type in rural regions,
more recently a different type has developed, the so-called partnership family
(Partnerschaftsfamilie). In it, economic and personal matters are discussed
between husband and wife, and decisions reached by mutual agreement.
Again, family pattern and economic behavior are intimately linked, both
evincing a certain open-mindedness and a more enlightened philosophy of
life. On the whole, the partnership family seems to be quite efficient, oriented
toward the market, and eager to introduce modern methods in production,
work, organization and financial administration.

Finally, there is the family in transition, apparently the most unhappy
one. Wives in such families, though they no longer unquestioningly accept
the authority of the males, have not yet entirely emancipated themselves
from their traditional role of subordination. Being the dominated party, they
resent their responsibilities, and are as unable to collaborate reasonably as
are the husbands. In these families (but not only in these) the conflict between traditional and modern norms makes itself felt also in the relation
between older and younger generation. Regular pay and regular leisure, and
even the claim to both, being denied to them, the hard-working boys and
girls often leave family and village, though they may be heirs to the farm.
Girls in particular want to get away so that they need not lead the miserable
life of their mothers.

On the whole, the lot of rural women is difficult, particularly on
medium-size and small farms (that is, in the majority of all farms): too much
work, bad health, insufficient education, and too little help from outside.

What is needed is a large-scale effort of government and private groups to educate both husband and wife, and teach the women how to better organize their work, recognize and defend their rights. (Further mechanization, still badly needed in the household, will not lead to the expected results unless rural women become more efficient in the organization and planning of their jobs.) However, the improvement of village life depends not only on education and individual intelligence. In the long run education, even when coupled with much needed mechanization, can bear fruit only if also the property structure of the entire rural sector is thoroughly reorganized.

Working Women

As in most industrial countries, the life of women in West Germany is influenced above all by the necessity to combine what is usually referred to as "women's two roles." One role is that of wife and mother, and the other that of the working woman employed outside of her home. A young girl who leaves school or finishes her vocational training has to find a job, but most girls also want to get married and a good many of them do. However, in the older age groups there are some exceptions to this general rule. There are those women who devote their lives solely to the traditional female tasks. They belong exclusively to the older generation (from fifty-five years upward), in which there are still quite a few, particularly among the bourgeois women, who have never been anything but housewives and mothers. On the other hand, there is a large group of about two million women, now roughly between thirty-eight and fifty years of age, who never have been and never will be anything but working women. They too would certainly like to marry, but have no chance to do so as a result of the fact that their potential husbands were slain during the war or died in Nazi concentration camps. In 1965 there were 27.9 million men and 30.9 million women in the Federal Republic, a surplus of 3 million women.

While many women give up their jobs after getting married, or, more frequently, after the birth of their first child, quite a number of wives and mothers continue to work. To do so has become more popular in recent years, particularly among young wives. Although in 1950 only 28 per cent of all married women from twenty to twenty-five years retained their jobs, the percentage rose to approximately 50 in 1957. In 1962 nearly one third (4.7 million) of all married women, and a little less than one third of those married mothers who lived together with husband and children (mothers in complete families) were working. In addition, there were in 1957 nearly 1.8 million working mothers of incomplete families, that is wives separated from their husbands, widows, divorced women, and mothers of illegitimate children, all with children living with them in the same house.

Large as the number of working mothers was, of all mothers who lived

(1957) in complete families only a minority of 12 per cent (or one million) worked outside of the home. The majority, about 18 per cent (1.45 million) were occupied mostly in small family enterprises in or next to the home. These women, the wives of peasants, independent artisans or small business men, did not need to leave their children alone while at work. Though frequently overburdened, they can move freely between workshop and home. Neither of the two worlds these mothers live in, the family and their business world, is antagonistic to the other, and rarely do the tasks in the first conflict heavily with the duties in the second.

As compared with this group (the so-called *Mithelfende Familienange-hörige*), the 1.2 million married and unmarried mothers who worked (1957) in factory or office, and whose children (under eighteen years) lived with them, had a more difficult time. These constituted 16 per cent of all mothers (married and unmarried) with children under eighteen years. It is these women who have to leave the children alone or under the supervision of somebody else, usually a relative and very rarely a neighbor.

The demands on working mothers being high, why do they consent to the twofold task? The motives vary chiefly according to social class, and change with time. A decade ago almost any German family still suffered from the damages of war, having lost home, furniture and clothing, or being refugees from the eastern provinces of the former German Reich. Very often, families could be founded and the household rebuilt only with supplementary income produced by the mother and wife. Once this emergency passed, the motives changed. Today, it is primarily, though not solely, the desire to improve the household equipment, to buy an apartment, or to build a house which makes mothers seek employment. This is true particularly of women in the lower-income classes. While the wages of industrial workers and of the rank and file in civil service and private offices are usually sufficient to cover current expenses, they very often do not allow for additional expenditure. If the family wants to maintain what is nowadays considered a decent standard of living, the mother must step in.

It would be too simple to call these women (as is often done) materialistic. Normally, it is not for luxury that they work. Of course, the definition of luxury varies. According to present standards in West Germany, a private car, an electric refrigerator, perhaps also a television set, but certainly not a radio, are deemed by many families to be luxuries. On the other hand, the working women, like practically everybody else, are victims of the "hidden persuaders" of advertising. In this context, moral criticism is not only useless but unjust as well. It usually overlooks the fact that many industrial workers and small business men can rise above the level of mere subsistence only by the additional labor of the wife. For the first time in German history these classes have a chance to keep up with the bourgeois families, and thus become more self-assured. They believe that it is more important to get ahead and to secure for their children a materially better life than for the mother to be present in the home all day during the early phases of her child's life. Psychoanalytic theory not being popular with Germans, and practically unknown among workers and in the lower-middle class, mothers think it more essential to stay at home when the children reach school age than to be available for the babies.

There is a small fraction of mothers who go on working primarily for the sake of personal independence or because they just love their jobs. Almost exclusively they are wives who went to college, women physicians, lawyers, economists, high school and university teachers. While the majority of working mothers would prefer to remain at home, and while many are likely to do so as soon as the family can afford it, quite a number of the women university graduates would not voluntarily withdraw.

The German public, being conservative in many respects, is ambiguous about working mothers. Among their most ardent opponents are the women themselves: two thirds advocate a law forbidding mothers with children under ten years to accept gainful employment. In general, however, the agitation against working mothers is of no avail. Manpower being in extremely short supply in Germany, wives and mothers are the only labor reserve left. Barring a recession in the near future, more and more mothers will be absorbed in the productive process. Society could and should help the mothers and their children in counteracting this trend not by outlawing work for them, but by a revision of the tax and wage system in favor of low-income groups. If special rebates were given to large families, making it more attractive for mothers to stay at home, probably quite a number would do so. It was the working mothers and their families who, by shouldering additional burdens, made a large contribution to the so-called "economic miracle" in West Germany. The country having been rebuilt, with the wealth of the nation greater than ever before, it is now time for society to repay them in such a manner that no mother with small children need seek employment solely because otherwise the family could not rise above the level of mere subsistence.

The Women in the Family

Surprisingly little is known about family structure in the Federal Republic. Aside from some sociological studies carried out soon after the war, almost no empirical research was done in the field. Relevant questions as to the internal structure of the family, the balance of power between husband and wife, the relations of parents and children, and the emotional climate of the group, have not yet found satisfactory answers.

Even without adequate research it is evident that the authoritarian family, long representative in Germany, has vanished. No longer is the urban family ruled by a powerful father, and no longer are wife and children willing just to obey. Although it is clear that the traditional structure is broken, and that especially in families of the younger generation hardly any trace of it is left, there is no reliable information as to what has taken its place. While according to some authors the relationship between husband and wife is now more that of partners who arrive at decisions by discussion and compromise, others insist that no such democratic family pattern has evolved, and that an atmosphere of indifference prevails in which neither authoritarianism nor individualistic attitudes can thrive.

Generally speaking, the family in Germany shows all the traits characteristic of fully developed industrial societies. Girls and boys decide themselves, almost without exception, whom they are going to marry and get married at the average age of 23.7 and 26 years respectively. Arranged marriages are entirely unknown. The future partners meet on the job, in the youth groups, or at parties. They want to marry chiefly for love. There are other motives, too, for instance, to escape the sense of loneliness and to gain security. Also, quite a number of them feel obliged to legalize an actual relationship because the first child is on its way.

To what degree women are content in marriage is generally unknown. A study carried out as far back as 1949 does not give too rosy a picture. At that time only half of a representative sample of wives thought it necessary for a woman's happiness for her to be married, thus pointing indirectly to some sort of dissatisfaction with their own marriages. One in six confessed frankly to being unhappy, and one in four did not believe their sex life harmonious. On the other hand, men gave the impression of being emotionally and sexually more contented, thinking marriage more rewarding than did the wives.

The habit of having but two children is a novelty, and to some degree an amazing one. This is not so much because in the past children used to be numerous, particularly in the lower social strata, and now it is exactly these strata which adhere to the new pattern (while in the upper classes there is a slight tendency towards larger numbers of children). Rather, the almost universal adoption of planned parenthood and of having few children is surprising for another reason. From its advent to power until its collapse in 1945, the Nazi government strongly favored a population increase. By propaganda, by prohibiting the sale of contraceptives, and by making special allowances for large families, it tried to induce parents to have many children. The result was a relatively high birth rate in the 1930's. However, after the war a change set in without ever having been publicly recommended. On the contrary, since 1949 all national governments have been formed by the Christian Democratic Union, the majority party which was strongly influenced by Catholics. Also Protestants had, until very recently, reservations about birth control. Nor were there powerful private agencies spreading information. In fact, the Planned Parenthood Association is little known, and the subject of family planning is seldom discussed in public. Yet people do plan—primarily for economic reasons. Realizing that at present they cannot have both large families and a high standard of living, they cut down on the number of off-spring. This might change again, if material conditions continue to improve. Then Germany may witness a baby boom. Whether this would be desirable for women is open to question. It could easily lead to a revival of concepts defining the family as the only legitimate domain of women, and to public agitation to confine them to it once again.

How stable marriages are in this country is difficult to assess. Figures on divorce—83 per 1000 marriages in 1960 as against 75 in 1938—reveal little as long as other data, such as the number of couples living separately, remains unknown. It may well be that under the strain of war, and in the misery of the postwar period, families proved more stable than might have been expected. However, with the return to normality since the 1950's, this may have changed. Whatever the case may be, German experiences of the last three decades allow for the hypothesis that a national crisis does not necessarily become also a familial crisis, while, on the other hand, stability of broader social structures does not inevitably make for the internal stability of the family. Rather, it can be suspected that in the present relatively stable social order destructive impulses of the individual, having few outlets, turn against the family, upsetting its peace, without, however, destroying the unit.

Sex Mores

Aside from the few data about marital happiness and unhappiness, there is practically no reliable information available on sex mores, and one can only speculate. Casual observations seem to indicate that German young people follow liberal patterns, though not in excess. Nearly half of all first-born children were conceived before their parents were married. Furthermore, abortion seems to be resorted to very frequently, in spite of the Catholic-inspired laws prohibiting it.

While these facts indicate the prevalence of premarital sexual experience among young people, they do not reveal how frequently boys and girls change partners before they settle down to marriage. We may safely conclude that girls tend to disregard the traditional rules which insist on premarital virginity and to experiment sexually with their fiancés and probably with other men as well. The men accept this practice readily, no longer demanding chastity of their future wives.

Although nowadays young men as well as young women are strongly inclined to idealize the family and marriage as an escape from loneliness and lack of parental understanding, there is no doubt that adultery has become rather a common practice, particularly for men after several years of marriage. For men over thirty or so, there are abundant opportunities, since many women between thirty-five and forty-five are unmarried and quite willing to consent to a love affair with a married man. Prostitution is well established in all of the larger cities. Thus, the conditions prevailing since the end of World War II invite adultery and extramarital relations on the part of men, while women, both married and unmarried, are in a vulnerable position, and must compete with each other because of their larger numbers.

The Home Routine

From mere observation it seems that young wives with children are not too satisfied. Though probably all of them wanted to get married and to have babies, some find it difficult to adjust to the traditional roles. In the first place, they are frequently overburdened. Maids and cleaning women are in extremely short supply, and usually there are no relatives around so that housework is entirely left to them. Of course, technical facilities ease the job. However, many of the labor-saving devices, like dishwashers, washing machines, automatic electric stoves, and so forth, are still too expensive to afford. So far the average German household is far from being as well equipped with major and minor appliances as is the American one. Furthermore, German husbands are not yet quite used to helping their wives in the home. Thus, mothers are continuously busy, and do not always like their work. Some of them feel lonely, too. Used to working in the company of adults, to having more leisure and money of their own, they resent their isolation during the day.

This dissatisfaction, evinced especially by young women, has its roots not just in individual failure or simply in egotism. It is the result partly of the necessity to combine women's two roles, partly of inadequate preparation. The conflict between the new demands and the traditional attitude makes for trouble also among those who need not take a job after marriage.

Education

However, many of those who resent matrimonial life could easily spare more time for activities linking them closer to the outer world if they only knew better how to organize their work. Lacking adequate training either for the homemaking job or for her other tasks, the average woman is unable to find her way out of drudgery and isolation.

A definite deficiency in the principles of education makes itself felt here. While schools at all levels provide rather thorough training in many fields, they fail as far as social and psychological preparation for the future task of women is concerned. First, schools do not supply the information about women's position in modern society needed to make girls more aware of what lies ahead. Discussions in class about the changes in family structure and the female role in the family are rare indeed. Also, instruction in child psychology is entirely neglected. Consequently, many young women, not properly prepared by their parents either, underrate the importance of their duties as the prime socializing agent of their children and of their responsibility for the home. Such misapprehension might be one cause of frustration, of the woman feeling cut off from the stream of life. Obviously, abstract ideological tribute which is abundantly paid to mothers by the public at large will not do. Rather, the future mothers need to be prepared more realistically for their job, gain more self-confidence and pride in it.

Moreover, while at school girls are not sufficiently made aware that they themselves will be responsible for their lives, and that they have to take the initiative in introducing desired changes. Thus after marriage they rarely seize the opportunities to improve their condition. Neither the school nor the average parent imparts that rational attitude toward everyday problems which is a precondition of mastering them. The capacity to plan and to organize one's work is also insufficiently developed, as is the ability to grasp the limits of such endeavors. What women ought to learn, and schools to teach, is, therefore, a better awareness of ends, and the faculty to select means accordingly.

Once again it is evident that women in Germany are in a state of transition, confronted with new tasks while still searching more or less unsuccessfully for exemplars to guide them. For those married women who could manage to find spare time it would be helpful if some of their energies were channeled into voluntary work with political and social associations. More active participation of such women in local government, school administration, adult education and the like would certainly be to great advantage. However, such activities have so far gained little popularity, partly because the public is not used to them, and partly because the women themselves either do not recognize the opportunities or shy away from responsibility. This reluctance is not confined to women. Rather, it is a consequence of the specifically German political atmosphere. In contrast to the British and American tradition, the participation of individual citizens in local affairs and private initiative in public matters were never encouraged. Getting away from such patterns is more difficult for women. However, most men too still have to learn that lesson.

Women's Occupations

In 1962, West Germany had a female labor force of 9.4 million, roughly one third of all gainfully employed. Seventy per cent (6.7 million) were salary and wage earners, the remaining 2.7 million either independent business women, themselves owners and managers of small or medium-size firms, or assistants in some family enterprise. Two fifths of the wage and salary earners work in industry; one fifth in commerce, banking, and insurance companies; the rest in agriculture, traffic, and construction. Female labor is of course nothing new in Germany. Common among farmers, and in the handicrafts of preindustrial times, modern industry made use of it almost from its very beginning. Since the 1840's, proletarian women have entered the shops, and later on, also, bourgeois women came to the fore, chiefly in lower clerical and teaching posts. Ever since, a large army of females has been on paid jobs—some 15 million during World War I, and somewhat fewer during World War II. After 1945 many withdrew, only to return in the 1950's. Under the pressure of an extreme shortage of labor, the trend is towards further increase, which, however, may have reached its natural limits by now.

In West Germany, as in any industrial country, female labor is no transitory phenomenon. Women have entered the productive process to stay. Even the most conservative minds realize that without female cooperation practically no branch of the economy could function efficiently. If all working women went on strike, a national catastrophe would result. Thus the public debate about women's rights to gainful employment, carried on for many a decade, has come to an end.

Though entirely indispensable, working women are somewhat under-privileged in several ways. Subtle discrimination begins early with the selection of future training and job. In 1960, twice as many boys as girls of the lower and lower-middle classes, upon leaving school at the age of fourteen or fifteen, began vocational training. Young girls of the same strata have a narrower choice as far as training and vocation are concerned. In industry, there are some three hundred categories of skilled jobs, yet most girls, on the advice of parents or teachers, stick to only half a dozen, which are traditionally considered better suited for them. Others take a job without special training, attending, in addition, schools for home economics until they are eighteen. These unskilled or semiskilled women make up 90 per cent of all the female labor in industry as against 10 per cent who went through apprenticeships. On the other hand, among men, the ratio of skilled to unskilled or semiskilled workers is 50:50.

To be sure, the majority of girls would prefer to receive further education after high school. Formerly, almost all unskilled women hoped to enter a qualified trade, yet were refused the opportunity by their parents. Many parents, particularly in the lower strata, consider additional schooling for daughters a mere luxury. Trusting the girl will marry, they want her to earn money immediately after finishing school and to acquire a trousseau. Rarely are they aware that additional training would open better jobs to her, let alone that she has the right to have her talents awakened and developed. The girls themselves, being too young to stand up against parents and relatives, after a brief period on the job become indifferent, and profoundly resigned. Realizing that without additional training they have no chance to get ahead, they now cherish the dream of marriage, expecting it to bring salvation from factory life. In recent years, however, there has been some improvement. In 1960 twice as many girls became apprentices in qualified trades as in 1950. Also, the number of lower-class girl students in vocational schools has increased.

Girls of the upper-middle and upper classes who want to attend a university are also confronted with special problems unknown to boys. However, their number has risen too. While in 1951 girls constituted only one fifth of the student body, the percentage rose to 23 in 1964. Nevertheless, the fact remains that in universities and *Hochschulen* women cluster in the so-called typically female disciplines such as teaching and medicine. Only a few dare enter the fields traditionally reserved for men. In law only 5.5 per cent, and in economics and social sciences only 7.8 per cent of the students are girls.

Adult women too, are at a disadvantage in several respects. First, some of them still do not get equal pay for equal performance. While this situation might change in the near future under the pressure of the (not too energetic) trade unions and some sections of the general public, optimism is less justified with regard to women's careers and their chances of promotion in industry, public administration, and the professions. Among top executives of private corporations there are almost no women, with the exception of those whose inherited property gave them access to positions of control. Nor can they easily rise to the middle-managerial level. According to sociological studies carried out in recent years, the vast majority of female white-collar workers in business concerns is employed in the lowest ranks. Thus, in the administrative sector of corporations, women are, so to speak, privates led by an almost exclusively male officer corps. Or, as a group of sociologists has put it: "With regard to norms and stereotypes, the entire white-collar sector is dominated by conservative attitudes. To have a woman in a leading or otherwise highly qualified position seems in many places to be as revolutionary a thought as it was decades ago."

Also in the academic ranks of public or semi-public bureaucracies it is difficult for women to get ahead. While studying in the universities girls enjoy practically full equality with men, but upon graduation their situation becomes different. In the higher echelons of the German civil service, exclusively manned by university graduates, the proportion of women is between 2 and 3 per cent. Of all judges in the Federal Republic somewhat less than 3 per cent are females. One woman is a member of the Federal Supreme Court. The percentage of female university teachers is also low, not more than three. In the academic year of 1958–1959, of 2,328 full professors in the universities and technical universities of West Germany and Berlin, only eight were women. In the lower faculty ranks there were 3,558 men as against 111 women. There are almost no women among engineers, only a few in the diplomatic service (none of whom has achieved ambassadorial rank), and certainly not many in the legal profession. On the other hand, women are numerous in professions traditionally considered female. Thus they constitute roughly one third of the teachers in high schools (*Gymnasium*), two thirds of the teachers in elementary and secondary schools, and slightly less than one fifth of the physicians.

In politics, the picture is not much different. Of all adults entitled to vote some 55 per cent are women, and about one quarter of all members of political parties; but in state assemblies they are represented by only 6 to 8 per cent, and in the Federal Parliament by no more than 9 to 10. In 1961, for the first time in German history, a woman became the head of a national ministry, that of health.

Several factors explain why the number of women in higher and highest ranks is, and perhaps always will be, smaller than that of men. Many women do not really seek a career. Some of them, particularly young girls and married women, prefer to stay in lower positions with little or no responsibility involved. Many quit the job after marriage or after the birth of the first child. A further explanation is to be found in the fact, already mentioned, that on all levels the number of trained females is comparatively low. Some women work only temporarily to help out in a family emergency or to earn money for some other purpose. Finally, in a number of jobs such as civil service and teaching, it is difficult to promote married women, because promotion would demand that they move to another city. Since their husbands are usually tied to the place by their jobs, wives often turn down offers of promotion. It follows that even if they enjoyed fully equal opportunities, women would not be as numerous in the advanced positions as men.

All these factors, however, do not explain why the percentage of women in responsible ranks is so extremely small. The ultimate reason must be sought, not in the women themselves, but in the resistance of the environment. In conformity with the general ideological and intellectual conditions prevailing in Germany today, employers' attitudes and thinking are frequently dominated by old-fashioned prejudice, a general dislike of change, and possibly also by some fear of disturbance. Therefore, with rare exceptions, they hesitate to promote women. Many men in positions of authority are convinced that to remain in subordinate posts is to the good of the women themselves and of the community at large.

Generally speaking, the female role in Germany is still defined along traditional lines. The majority of men, and many women as well, hold with the old concept according to which the nature of women disqualifies them from shouldering responsibility outside of the home, acting as superiors, or performing intellectual tasks, let alone scholarly work. All the elements of the traditional definition of female character are still there: women are believed to be passive and emotional, and, due to their innate and unalterable disposition, incapable of abstract thinking. Nature, it can still be heard over and over again, has created them to serve in the family and the home, not in the world of men. Such arguments serve a twofold purpose: on the one hand, they restrain female ambition, on the other, they provide men with a justification for acting as they do.

When questioned as to their opinion about the promotion of women in business firms, employers usually point to these so-called innate deficiencies of women and to what they believe is woman's natural lack of technical interest, stamina, and psychological stability. On the other hand, they are believed to have an inborn talent for monotonous, dependent work, and should therefore be kept in dependence. It is interesting to note that those entrepreneurs who, in spite of widespread disapproval, promoted their women employees, gave excellent reports. Also, those women who did make their way up did not confirm the stereotyped expectation that they would not be accepted by subordinates.

To deem women principally incapable of qualified work is, however, not confined to businessmen. Leaders of institutions of higher learning cling to the same belief. University professors, usually considered more enlightened, would not like to have women on the faculties, either. First, so the learned men argue, women can have no authority with students, and second, they are mentally and physically unsuited for scholarly work. As one of them put it: "Intellectual creativity is a privilege of men," meaning that it should remain a male privilege. Ironically enough, none of those who were strongly opposed to having women on the teaching staff—and such is the attitude of the vast majority of those questioned—deemed the performance of girl students inferior to that of the men. The fact remains that the overwhelming majority of the men who hold the power of decision either hesitate or altogether refuse to let women get ahead. At best they do not encourage them.

The question arises why the considerable minority of women who want a career do not fight more energetically for it, and why in general women in and out of jobs do not strive more energetically for their rights. In many instances, such endeavors are likely to succeed, since the shortage of labor on all levels, including schools and universities, compels employers to hire even those deemed less fit. Although in recent years there may have been some progress, the number of women making use of such opportunities is still small. Obviously, the vast majority is not actively engaged in the strife. As mentioned above, there are some two million women now in their thirties and forties who realize that they have no chance to marry, simply because of lack of men. The self-respect of these women depends primarily on the appreciation of their work by superiors, colleagues and friends. However, even they do not rebel. Rather, they believe that the situation is unalterable. Why should this be so?

Again the answer must be sought mainly in the force of tradition which influences women no less than men. Growing up in a world which directly and even more indirectly tells women that they are unsuited for intellectual and technical work, for executive or other superior jobs, and for political activity, many actually become incapable. They have no chance to develop that kind of self-confidence which is a precondition of success. Further, they fear being considered unfeminine. If political activity, interest in a career, and professional ambition are considered unfeminine, then, of course, many women will behave "femininely" and avoid deviating from the commonly-accepted pattern. Instead of emancipating themselves from the outdated concepts, they adjust. Being afraid of society's criticism, and of becoming outsiders to their reference groups, they surrender, suppressing whatever fighting spirit might once have been in them.

One more cause for the resignation of many German women should be mentioned. Many accept things as they are from sheer physical and psychic exhaustion. The women of this country have for decades known no stability of national life, and hence none in their personal existence. Brought up in the misery of wars, thwarted by the experience of the vast unemployment in the late 1920's, witnesses to a totalitarian dictatorship, intimately acquainted with the horrors of refugee life—no wonder that they are exhausted, drained. Also, too many have lost their husbands, and devoted themselves entirely to bringing up the children without help. How could there be much energy left in them?

There are undoubtedly exceptions. It is on them, their activity, stamina and work performance that the future position of working women in Germany depends, to a considerable extent.

Outlook

Modern society grants many privileges to all its members, male and female alike. It gives them freedom from poverty and from ruinous physical labor; it prolongs the average individual's life; it makes free education available to all. In the democracies, each citizen enjoys a measure of political and personal freedom which was formerly unknown even to the ruling classes.

At the same time, society puts high demands on everyone, above all on women. They must act responsibly, not only in the family but also in the business world. More than ever before, the functioning and efficiency of the productive process depend on their cooperation; but, again more than ever before, also the functioning of the family depends on them. Whether the family will be able to realize its new possibilities: to be a humanizing agency, a haven for the individual where he can relax from, and shake off, the regimentation and discipline of his work, all this, almost entirely, depends on women. It is they who, more than men, will determine the future personalities of their children.

Moreover, women have to fill a third role as well, that of a citizen capable of forming judgments of her own and arriving at rational political decisions. In the political sphere, too, women have become indispensable. Western society, with all the economic well-being and social security it grants its members, is in constant danger not only from threats of war, but from domestic perils. The dangers of rightist or leftist totalitarianisms, with their tendency to transform men into masses, to deprive the individual of his own identity, to dehumanize the human being, threaten women no less than men. Thus, the political fight against them is of concern to both sexes. If women want to preserve their privileges they must become citizens not only formally but in substance.

Thus far, women in Germany are as ill-equipped for these tasks as for securing their rights. They still have a long way to go in order to become mentally and psychologically independent, and able to judge for themselves. Too many of them are still shaped in the traditional image of femininity. What is needed is to abandon the old model and to replace the former virtues of passivity, unconcerned subordination, and adaptation, with the virtues of reflection, critical thinking, and the courage to resist domination.

In Germany there are few historical models for such a change. For many generations the country has idealized the pious woman, subservient to husband, church, and throne. To this, the Nazis added a special note, degrading women to biological machines whose primary function was to give birth to as many children—future soldiers—as possible. Undoubtedly, there is today some awareness that these norms do not suffice, and certainly only a tiny lunatic fringe still pays homage to the Nazi idea. The lack of sensible historical models at least partly explains why the majority of women has no clear idea of what they should be. Nor has the public at large. Both male and female shuttle, so to speak, uneasily between present and past. This insecurity makes itself felt everywhere: in the ambivalent attitude towards working mothers; in taking for granted female labor while excluding women from the higher ranks; in granting them suffrage but discouraging them from political activity; in the overburdening of rural women and housewives; in granting personal freedom, while maintaining the traditional type of femininity as the ideal.

It will take a long time until the majority of German women arrive at a better understanding of their new position and of the new demands. Much depends on education, for which, however, the educators themselves still have to be educated. Some people have begun to formulate progressive programs. The goal is to make female students and teachers alike more intimately acquainted with the society they live in, and, above all, as has been pointed out by Marianne Grewe, to help them "get rid of their own prejudice as regards their inferiority . . . to give them better criteria for the evaluation of men, and for the social order in general."

Modern Families

FERDYNAND ZWEIG

Most evaluations of modern life require at least passing reference to the family, and the more critical ones usually dwell on the subject. The decline of the family has been a constant theme in European history since at least the early nineteenth century. Indeed, its collapse has been suggested so often that it is a wonder there is anything left still to decay. Clearly, many who have found modern life distasteful have exaggerated their laments about the breakup of the family. But this does not mean that they have not correctly identified trends, for no one denies that great changes have taken place in family structure.

There are several key problems in dealing with modern family history, aside from the difficulty of obtaining adequate information. To begin with, any valid judgment requires an evaluation of the quality of family life before the modern age. Most assessments of the modern family reflect, if only implicitly, deeply held beliefs about the premodern family. Those who find family life deteriorating and modern man bereft of the solidarity he needs, point to the strength and diverse functions of the premodern family. Yet we have seen that the premodern family may have had serious inadequacies, so that changes in family structure may conceivably have been good, not bad.

There are related disagreements about the facts of change. The modern family may be seen as a total contrast to its predecessors or as a modification only. Take, for example, the extended family. We have long imagined that premodern families united uncles, aunts, cousins, and grandparents with parents and children. This was a unit that could provide for itself and give guidance and support to all members. Recent work, however, suggests that the extended family was not united quite so literally as has been assumed. It did not, in western and central Europe, live under the same roof, and it regularly sent members to work for other families; yet there is little doubt that fairly close relationships existed. What happened, then, with modernization? A common assumption is that the extended family disappeared, and many observers believe this was a great loss. Yet studies of twentieth-century European workers reveal that their social life is centered almost entirely within the extended family circle. Great interest is taken in the doings of distant relatives. It is true that the extended family is sometimes (though not always) spread out geographically, but it has not literally disappeared. The question of the stability of marriage raises another set of factual problems. Without doubt, divorce has increased in Europe over the past hundred years. Yet family breakups may conceivably have declined, for we have no way of knowing the rate of desertions before legal divorce became widespread. Add to this the fact that before 1850 the early death of one marriage partner would frequently dissolve the marriage within a decade or so, and one may wonder how decisive the institution of divorce is in the history of the family. There is broad agreement on many trends in family history, but the facts are by no means entirely clear.

Family structure varies with social class and with region. Some historians write of the premodern family as though it were essentially the same everywhere. Other observers claim that family structure has become more homogeneous with modernization. The two views can be partially reconciled. It is possible that in the early stages of modernization families were differentiated by class. The middle class, for example, brought up its children distinctively; the working-class husband released the tensions and frustrations built up at his job by browbeating his wife. In the twentieth century, behavioral differences began to break down once again. Greater equality between marriage partners is now more common at all levels of society, as is reduction of family size, although the reduction has proceeded at different rates at different social levels. Yet important variations remain. The working class still marries younger than the middle class. It cares for its children differently—toilet training is begun earlier, for example, and physical discipline is stricter. These differences are not in all cases the same as those that could be found in the nineteenth century, but it does seem obvious that distinctive family patterns both reflect and cause key distinctions in social structure. This has to modify any overall generalizations about family evolution. Regional variations are important also. French parent–child relations are stricter than English, and far stricter than American. Divorce rates vary, from one country to the next, and only in part because of legal differences.

Finally, after one does the best possible job of getting the facts and making the necessary qualifications, there remains the question of interpretation. We can easily agree that, although its importance as a unit of consumption has increased, the family is no longer a key production unit. What does this mean for the family? For some observers it suggests decay, a loosening of ties, since many family members now work outside the home. For others it suggests a reduction of the tensions and bitterness that family economic relations once involved. No longer, for example, are twenty-five-year-olds normally under their father's economic control, unable to marry before he retires or dies. With this kind of family friction reduced, the family can become a closer emotional unit, with more affectionate ties between husband and wife and between parents and children.

Evaluations of the modern family are usually highly moralistic. They reflect what the analyst thinks a proper life should be—how much independence people should have, what the proper role of women is, what kind of care children deserve and need, and so on. In sum, the family remains at the center of a great deal of analysis of modern society and of the results of a modernization process, and the nature of the family engenders more debate than ever before. Today, many students of the family, heirs to a long line of pessimists (and some optimists) who have been proclaiming the decay of the family since the onset of industrialization, find it teetering on the brink of a new communal or individualized existence. Some simply believe that the conditions of modern society have proved progressively less compatible with family life: fathers drawn outside the home to work, children forced into schools, and people encouraged to replace familial with individualistic motivations. Others now see the first reactions to industrialization in the nineteenth century as immensely fruitful. They point particularly to the strength and intensity of the middle-class family, with the strong direction it provided for children. They find the twentieth century far different and far less appealing (thus implicitly rejecting modernization as a schema covering family history, with a distinction between industrial and postindustrial society).

Still others find the family alive and kicking, even healthier than it once was. Ferdynand Zweig, a sociologist, conducted an elaborate poll of English factory workers at the end of the 1950s and found that they had moved to a higher valuation of the family as a center for affection and recreation than ever before. Indeed, the family and its acquisitions and pastimes provide the basis for a new contentment, an adjustment to the pressures of industrial work. But not all is well. Zweig points to unresolved strains within the family that follow from new expectations and the lowering of the birthrate. One example of this is the new surge of married women into the labor force. He finds a certain blandness in the worker's family ties; the families are comfortable, not venturesome or intense. It would be possible to accept Zweig's judgments and paint a far harsher picture of the human values involved, as the second selection on the contemporary family suggests.

How does Zweig's picture fit any view of modernization? Clearly, this is not a traditional family pattern; it is leisure- rather than production-centered, possibly more influenced by women, and with more individually defined members, conscious of their freedom. But perhaps, within the structural constraints of modernization—notably the separation of production from the family and the need to seek employment outside the home—the contemporary working class is moving to restore something like a traditional family focus. Family history may not move with the tides of modernization, and the family may yet be the refuge for people who have been unable to adapt to a modern world.

Schopenhauer's simile likening human beings to hedgehogs, clustering together for warmth in winter, uncomfortable and pricking each other when

From Ferdynand Zweig, *The Worker in an Affluent Society* (New York: The Free Press, 1962). Reprinted by permission of Heinemann Educational Books Ltd.

too closely packed and miserable when kept apart, struck me during my enquiry as containing a sober truth about human behaviour. Schopenhauer interpreted this as human predicament, as a tragic dilemma. But there is no need to interpret this in a pessimistic way. As hedgehogs try to find the right distance so as not to prick each other and still keep warm, so also we are concerned to keep the right proportion of human warmth and freedom. There is no need to go to extremes to expose ourselves to constant pricking by packing ourselves too close, or to grow cold, deprived of the vivifying experience of human companionship. There is a large range of middle zones where the need for freedom of action and the need for human warmth are met with the intensity required, not being sacrificed to each other. Admittedly, it is not easy to reach this point and the point itself moves all the time, like a most sensitive magnetic needle. The right point depends not only on cultural patterns and social environment, but also on age, temperament, past experience, marital status and social status.

When I submitted for comment the statement: "We can say the least to those we love best," most agreed with me stating that they were afraid of upsetting their wives or being upset by them; obviously those whom we love have the greatest power to upset us. So all through the enquiry whenever the contacts with families of origin, neighbours or workmates were in question one could hear the same *leit-motiv*, "close but not too close," in various versions.

The other outstanding principle in personal contacts is the principle of substitution. When, for instance, contact with family of origin is largely lacking, other relationships such as closer contacts with neighbours develop. Where social clubs are very highly developed this may also affect other contacts. Apart from the need for human warmth, the time factor also plays its part, of course.

When a man is very happy at home, this often results in his complete isolation from other contacts; this was often expressed in the phrase "We keep ourselves to ourselves." I rarely heard the term "I keep myself to myself," it was mostly "we." A single man cannot keep himself to himself without the risk of becoming a recluse if not an outcast. In the places I visited between 15 and 20 per cent described themselves in these terms. The majority were older men but there were also young men among them, especially those who had just started their family life and were completely engrossed in it.

The question arises, what is general trend of behaviour in this respect: is the accent more on warmth or more on freedom? I would say that it is more on freedom, while the need for warmth is not so strongly felt as previously. Men suffering poverty and privation, men in a predicament, under strain and stress, need more sympathy and warmth, while men comfortably off, enjoying a good life, are more self-centred, desiring freedom more than anything else, freedom to enjoy life undisturbed. The warmth they need they can find in a small family circle, with their partners in the enjoyment of life. The wider circles of friends are to a large extent replaced by impersonal relationships, such as those developed around T.V. and other media of entertainment. A whole net of relationships which we may call "uncommitted" has grown between the viewer and the T.V. personalities. It is a diluted, mute, and single-track friendship, uncommitted and anonymous, which develops between the viewer and the personality, who is built up by the T.V. into something approaching an idol. A gracious gesture, a smile, open arms, a sweet word, are received by the viewer as addressed to him personally, filling his heart with warmth, without effort or struggle, without commitment and without fear of frustration or upset. It is a counterfeit of the real thing, but the counterfeit is cheap, giving the viewer in essence what he needs and leaving him free. The quest for freedom has assumed an unexpected aspect: the freedom to watch T.V. and the freedom to drive a car. . . .

Closely linked with these traits is his [the worker's] family-mindedness and home-centredness, as security, acquisitiveness and family-mindedness go well together. He seeks his pleasures and comforts at home more than ever. "I am a fairly domesticated animal," was a typical remark which I heard. Family life assumes a romanticized image of happiness and joy. Family life stands, in his mind, for happiness, enjoyment and relaxation. As he sits by his fireside and watches T.V. he feels free and happy. The wife doesn't snap at him as she used to; the children are no longer seen crawling and messing about on the floor, shouting and screaming. The foul air, the vermin, the outside, smelling lavatory, the broken chairs have been removed as if by magic. Instead there is a nicely furnished house of his own, or a council house which is a near equivalent to his own property. His main hobby is decorating his home and he is busy with his brush all the year round: "I never saw my father handling a brush, now it seems I have a use for my brush the whole year round." These contrasts may be slightly over-drawn in relation both to the present and the past, but I believe they have validity in relation to the general trend.

Part of a worker's home and family-centredness is his intense interest in his offspring. If he has no ambition for himself, he has plenty for his children. "In my days a man pushing a pram would have been a laughing-stock; now you see a great many men pushing their pram proudly," said an older man. He not only pushes the pram, he often washes the children and gives them baths, he reads them stories, follows their school records, calls at the school on parents' day, tries to fix them up with a good job or apprenticeship. "It is the finest thing there is to give the children every advantage," or "My boy has everything he wants," or "I scrubbed and scraped to give my children every chance," he may say.

This has an enormous effect on the father-image among the working classes. The bullying father or the father whose authority was used as a bogey has largely disappeared, and instead an older brother relation comes to the fore. The father is there to assist and help, to give guidance; but he is no more the master with a big stick. In my previous enquiries I often found the father-image distorted among the working classes and strongly imbued with the shadow of the Oedipus complex. The working-class child often had only the care and affection of the mother, while the father was an aloof figure. Now the powerful figure of the working-class "Mum" is receding, as in many workers' families the father steps into her place or occupies an equal place beside her, the more so as she often goes out to work. Anyway the balance of affection is nowadays more equitably distributed between the two parents. The changing father-image is an important factor in the changing ethos of the working classes. Whether a child suffers under arbitrary authority at home or enjoys a kindly and reasonable guidance has a great bearing on his character and outlook.

Somehow related to this is the process of softening in the worker, I would venture to call it his feminization. The workers' world was formerly known for its masculinity. The worker had little to do with children or womenfolk. He was a hard-working, hard-swearing and hard-playing man. His manners were often rugged and rough. His voice was often loud, his manner of speaking blunt and harsh. Now he has mellowed considerably. He smiles more frequently, his voice is softer, his manner of approach easier, freer, more obliging. The segregation of sexes, which used to be a marked feature in the worker's life, is on the decline. He marries earlier, he takes his wife or sweetheart out more frequently, he is more of a home-bird. The women around him imbue him with feminine values. He accepts his wife as his companion on more or less equal terms, especially when she goes out to work and earns her own living. The fear of being sponged on by women is not as prevalent as it used to be.

All this means that the worker is moving away from his mates. His home and family-centredness brings in its wake the tendency to keep aloof from his mates. Formerly he used to congregate with his mates, to "knock about" with them, to scheme with them, and there was a great deal of mutual aid. Now he sees his mates outside the works only occasionally, mostly on the sports ground or in a club, or at matches. No help, no scheming is required. There are no campaigns to wage, as little mutual help and assistance are needed. The Unions are taken for granted, and do their work without his help.

Social contacts with neighbours suffer the same fate. "Keeping oneself to oneself," either in the strictest sense or in a larger sense which includes seeing some friends occasionally, is on the ascendant. Is loneliness the outcome? No, the worker has no time for that. He is too busy decorating his house, "doing it himself," or watching T.V. "Nowadays there is no problem what to do with your spare time"—I heard.

In my enquiry I came across some Communist workers, not for the first time. What struck me about even the Communists was their lukewarm interest or lack of interest in the larger issues of the world or social problems at large; this showed a marked difference from the attitudes I had encountered previously. Their interest was primarily in their homes, their wives and children. They were also affected by the general mood and tendency towards domestication.

This moving away from his mates and strong home-centredness, with a romanticized idea of family life, fits well with another new characteristic, the "personalization" of the worker's mind. He is intensely interested in persons, in personal life, personal stories, personal troubles and successes. He is not interested in ideas or general problems or objective situations, but in personal relations. Social relations are soon transfigured and translated into personal terms. Not "what" but "who" is the main question. The press, radio and T.V. have contributed largely to this process. This personalization, as the term suggests, is nothing but a process of identification, a projection of his own personality.

Home-centredness and personalization, together with the decline in gregariousness, involves also the process of greater individualization. The term may be misleading. The colourful or eccentric personalities of a kind once common among the working classes are fewer in number. Workers are more of a pattern, cast in one mould. They are more conformist than ever, but still the tendency is to break away from the mass, to think of oneself not as one of the mass but as an individual, a person. The home-centredness has brought about greater self-centredness as the home is only an extension of the "I."

The worker wants little things instead of big things, he wants them for himself rather than for society at large, he wants better and wider opportunities for getting along. Old slogans, old loyalties tend to leave him cold. The class struggle interests him less and less. The idea of the working class as an oppressed or an exploited class or the romanticized idea of the working class as foremost in the struggle for progress and social justice, is fading from his mind and is more and more replaced by the idea of the working class as a class well established and well-to-do in its own right. "Working class but not poor" is his idea of himself. Class divisions are no longer marked out by hostility and segregation. They are still there, but class feelings are less active and less virulent. Also the ethos of class solidarity, of group movement, seems to be weakened, as a man thinks primarily of himself and his home. . . .

Is he happier than his father was? He is more contented, better pleased with himself, prouder of his achievements. Is he getting bored? Has he too much time on his hands? Has he already joined the leisured class? He is still very busy. The five-day week applies only in theory, as a great deal of overtime is worked at weekends. At home he is again kept very busy. The pressure on his leisure-time comes from many quarters. T.V.-watching for some programmes is almost obligatory. When he has a car or motor cycle, there are family outings to be undertaken. When he has a garden, as most working men have, he is kept busy gardening, whether he likes it or not. And when he has a house of his own or a council house, "Do-it-yourself" absorbs a great deal of his time. In spite of this, a considerable number of men take up constructive hobbies such as woodwork, model-making, making and repairing all sorts of things, arts and crafts, not to mention remunerative sidelines. They may not have "money to burn" but they often have enough to venture into new and exciting hobbies which were previously closed to them.

Have the worker's cultural horizons been enlarged, his cultural interests deepened? We can say that stomachs are being filled and bodily needs well taken care of in the affluent society, but whether minds and hearts are being filled is more doubtful. We saw, on the strength of the test paper for cultural horizons, that his cultural interests are still limited. The "two nations" may be a thing of the past in terms of economics but not in terms of education and culture.

The worker is now more prosperous than ever, and if prosperity is a prelude to art and learning we may hope that a rise in his cultural standards will come about in due course, but it is doubtful whether it would be an automatic process, taking place without a determined effort of social action. It is also doubtful whether it can be accomplished without breaking down the resistance of vested interests in mass entertainment. A good case could be made for a movement whose standard programme would be the establishment of common ownership of means of education and culture.

The Family Besieged

CHRISTOPHER LASCH

Writing specifically about American families, Christopher Lasch here sees a basic pattern to modern civilization that robs man of his worth in the outside world and returns him to the family for comfort, and then robs him of a solid family in turn. This picture of the family does not differ entirely from the more optimistic one offered by Ferdynand Zweig; Zweig, too, mentions the family as a source of superficial pleasure rather than emotional intensity. Lasch's view is also compatible in many respects with a pessimistic modernization theory, which would posit great change in the structure of society but immense deterioration in human content. In addition, his views should be juxtaposed to the patterns of women's modernization, for Lasch is particularly unhappy about the decline of male family values in the twentieth century.

Lasch clearly does not believe in a single modern personality type. For him, the twentieth century sees the elaboration of a shallow narcissistic personality, away from the achievement orientation of nineteenth-century individualism, which was in turn based on intense rather than friendly parent–child ties. Lasch posits then an ongoing structural process, that of industrialization, but two distinct stages in mentality. His judgment should be tested against other views of the contemporary family as well against the implied success of the nineteenth-century family. Were parents so successful in raising children in the past?

By implication, Lasch would reject also the idea that the contemporary family is returning to a pattern rather like that of preindustrial society, with greater husband–wife mutuality; or if it is returning, it is doing so amid such vast social changes, requiring strong individual personalities, that it fails to meet the challenges of contemporary life. Lasch is profoundly pessimistic. He sees no value in modern leisure patterns as a source of individual development or strong family training. If he is accurate in describing a contemporary morass, and the family's decay within it, what can the remedy possibly be?

The rise of bourgeois society enlarged the boundaries of freedom, but it also created new forms of enslavement. Capitalism created unprecedented

Excerpted from *Haven in a Heartless World: The Family Besieged*, by Christopher Lasch, pp. 167–74, 176–77, 183. © 1977 by Basic Books, Inc., Publishers, New York.

abundance but simultaneously widened the gap between rich and poor. The conquest of nature liberated mankind from superstition but deprived it of the consolation of religion. The spread of education, designed to make the masses more critical of established authority, encouraged a certain cynicism about official protestations but also made the masses avid consumers of advertising and propaganda, which kept them in a chronic state of uncertainty and unsatisfied desire. Private property and the nuclear family, which in the nineteenth century provided new supports for political freedom and personal autonomy, contained within themselves elements fatal to their own existence. When the democratic revolutions freed property from feudal restrictions, they also removed the obstacles to its accumulation and brought about a situation in which the most characteristic form of "private" property would be the multinational corporation. As for the family, its isolation from the marketplace, from the ravages of which it provided a refuge, was precarious from the beginning.

From the moment the conception of the family as a refuge made its historical appearance, the same forces that gave rise to the new privacy began to erode it. The nineteenth-century cult of the home, where the woman ministered to her exhausted husband, repaired the spiritual damage inflicted by the market, and sheltered her children from its corrupting influence, expressed the hope that private satisfactions could make up for the collapse of communal traditions and civic order. But the machinery of organized domination, which had impoverished work and reduced civic life to a competitive free-for-all, soon organized "leisure" itself as an industry. The so-called privatization of experience went hand in hand with an unprecedented assault on privacy. The tension between the family and the economic and political order, which in the early stages of bourgeois society protected the members of the family from the full impact of the market, gradually abated.

The withdrawal into the "emotional fortress" of the family took place not because family life became warmer and more attractive in the nineteenth century, as some historians have argued, but because the outside world came to be seen as more forbidding. Nor did the family's withdrawal take place without a struggle. Older patterns of male conviviality gradually gave way to a life centered on hearth and home, but in the first half of the nineteenth century, the new domesticity still met with resistance, which crystallized in protracted battles over temperance, the rights of women, and the attempt to suppress popular amusements and festivities that allegedly distracted the lower orders from familial duties.

Seasonal holidays and festivals, so important to the life of preindustrial societies, disappeared from Western Europe and the United States not because the working class suddenly discovered the delights of polymorphous sexuality but because the champions of temperance and sobriety—the prohibitionists, the feminists, the Society for the Prevention of Vice, the Society for the Prevention of Cruelty to Animals, the Animals' Friend Society—

stamped them out as occasions for drunkenness, blood sports, and general debauchery. Bourgeois domesticity did not simply evolve. It was imposed on society by the forces of organized virtue, led by feminists, temperance advocates, educational reformers, liberal ministers, penologists, doctors, and bureaucrats.

In their campaign to establish the family as the seat of civic virtue, the guardians of morality dwelled on the dangers lurking in the streets, the demoralizing effects of "civilization," the growth of crime and violence, and the cutthroat competition that prevailed in the marketplace. They urged right-thinking men and women to seek shelter in the sanctuary of the family. From the beginning, the glorification of domestic life simultaneously condemned the social order of which the family allegedly served as the foundation. In urging a retreat to private satisfactions, the custodians of domestic virtue implicitly acknowledged capitalism's devastation of all forms of collective life, while at the same time they discouraged attempts to repair the damage by depicting it as the price that had to be paid for material and moral improvement.

Nineteenth-century doctors, reformers, and public health officers, like missionaries, regarded themselves as agents of enlightenment, bearers of civilization to the heathen. Like their ecclesiastical counterparts, they believed it their mission to stamp out debauchery and superstition. Neither the disinterested benevolence with which they performed their duties, the dangers they suffered, nor the personal sacrifices they endured gave them an understanding of the customs they were attempting to eradicate. In rural France, doctors reported that peasant husbands unfeelingly exposed their wives to syphilis and that their wives ignored the health of their children. After the domestic revolution engineered by themselves, on the other hand, "unity reigned in the families," in the words of one practitioner, "and this true solicitousness, which means the sharing equally of trouble and joy, fidelity between the spouses, fatherly tenderness, filial respect and domestic intimacy," became the general rule.

The new religion of health, though based on modern science and technology, was no more tolerant of other religions than was Christianity itself. The medical mode of salvation, no less than its predecessors, asserted exclusive rights to virtue and truth. But whereas the missionaries, for all their ignorance of the peoples to whom they ministered, sometimes defended their elementary human rights against the state's attempt to enslave or otherwise exploit them for profit, the medical profession worked hand in hand with the state to modernize the backward sectors of European and American society. This partnership proved to be more effective than Christianity in improving not only the health of the poor but their "morals" as well.

The attack on disease was part of a general attack on preindustrial customs. It went hand in hand with the suppression of public executions, the movement to institutionalize the insane, and the campaign to replace public riot and licentiousness with domestic bliss. Doctors were among the earliest exponents of the new ideology of the family. They extolled domesticity on the grounds that it encouraged regular habits, temperance, and careful attention to the needs of the young. They saw the family as an asylum, analogous in its functions to the hospital, the insane asylum, and the prison. Just as doctors and penologists hoped to cure sickness, madness, and crime by segregating the patient in a professionally supervised environment devoted to his care, they hoped to mold the child's character in the home.

The therapeutic conception of insanity, disease, and crime repudiated theological assumptions of their inevitability and relieved the patient of responsibility for his actions, insisting that he was neither possessed nor willfully sinning, but sick. The new conception of the family as an asylum similarly repudiated fatalism and the assumption of original sin, insisting on the child's innocence and plasticity. The medical profession saw itself as the successor to the church, just as theorists of bourgeois domesticity for a long time upheld marriage as the successor to monasticism. Whereas the church, in attempting to stamp out sex, had merely made it an obsession, these theorists maintained, marriage put sex at the service of procreation and encouraged a healthy acceptance of the body. This affirmation of the physical side of life had demonstrably better effects on the health of the individual and the community, according to bourgeois moralists, than the church's denial of the body.

From the beginning, a medical view of reality thus underlay attempts to remodel private life. The struggle between the new remissions and the old proscriptions, between personal fulfillment and self-sacrifice, between the ideology of work and the ideology of creative leisure, began in the nineteenth century. Liberal clergymen themselves participated in the campaign to transform religion into moral and mental hygiene. They allied themselves with a nascent feminism and with the campaign to feminize society by extending the domesticating influence of women to institutions beyond the home. The religion of health had a special appeal to women because of its concern with personal relations, its attempt to substitute domestic enjoyments for the rough and brutal camaraderie of males, and its glorification of the child and of maternal influence on the child's development. The conflict between the work ethic and the therapeutic point of view, which became sharper as the century wore on, also presented itself as a conflict between masculine and feminine "spheres"—the split between business and "culture," the practical and the aesthetic, so characteristic of bourgeois society and of American society in particular. As late as the 1950s, John R. Seeley and his associates found the same division in the suburbs of Toronto, where women joined with mental health experts in combating the competitive, work-oriented values of their husbands. Middle-class Canadian men valued material objects and their production, while their wives concerned themselves with the management of personal relations. Men valued achievement; women, happiness and well-being.

In the United States, relations between the sexes had entered a new stage by this time. When social scientists replaced clergymen as the most prominent purveyors of the new ethic, male resistance, at least among the educated, gradually declined. The once-familiar alignment of domestic forces, in which the father tacitly sides with the children's war against maternally imposed refinement, now survived only in folklore. The ideology of mental health, having routed the residual opposition of American males, effectively ruled the family, thus bringing domestic life under the growing domination of outside experts. The remarkable popularity of Benjamin Spock's *Baby and Child Care*, which went through more than 200 printings between 1946 and the mid-seventies, provided merely the most obvious example of this parental dependence on outside help and advice.

Outside advice, however, weakens parents' already faltering confidence in their own judgment. Thus although Spock urges parents to trust both their own and the child's impulses, he undermines this trust by reminding them of the incalculable consequences of their actions. Words "uttered in a thoughtless or angry moment" can "destroy the child's confidence"; nagging can lead to troubles that "last for years"; and the failure to give the child love and security can cause "irreparable harm." "In the face of this forbidding awareness," Michael Zuckerman writes, "Spock's appeals for confidence fade. He may know that mothers and fathers cannot come to any assurance of their own adequacy if they have to rely on physicians and psychiatrists in every extremity, but he is nonetheless unwilling to leave parents to their own intuitions at such junctures." The proliferation of medical and psychiatric advice undermines parental confidence at the same time that it encourages a vastly inflated idea of the importance of child-rearing techniques and of the parent's responsibility for their failure. Meanwhile, the removal of education and medical care from the household deprives parents of practical experience, during their own childhood, in taking care of children, nursing the sick, and housekeeping. In their ignorance and uncertainty, parents redouble their dependence on experts, who confuse them with a superabundance of conflicting advice, itself subject to constant changes in psychiatric and medical fashion. Because the "immature, narcissistic" American mother "is so barren of spontaneous manifestations of maternal feelings," according to one observer, "she studies vigilantly all the new methods of upbringing and reads treatises about physical and mental hygiene." She acts not on her own feelings or judgment but on the "picture of what a good mother should be."

Thus the family struggles to conform to an ideal of the family imposed from without. The experts agree that parents should neither tyrannize over their children nor burden them with "oversolicitous" attentions. They agree, moreover, that every action is the product of a long causal chain and that moral judgments have no place in child rearing. This proposition, central to the mental health ethic, absolves the child from moral responsibility while leaving that of his parents undiminished. Under these conditions, it is not surprising that many parents seek to escape the exercise of this responsibility by avoiding confrontations with the child and by retreating from the work of discipline and character formation. Permissive ideologies rationalize this retreat. When parents cannot altogether avoid disciplinary decisions, they seek to delegate them to other authorities. The father cites the demands of his work as an excuse for assigning daily discipline to his wife. She in turn avoids the most painful encounters by invoking the ultimate authority of the father, threatening children with a fearful reckoning when he finally returns to the scene. Both parents shift much of the responsibility for the child's development to his peers—against whom, in the absence of firm standards of their own, they also measure the child's academic, athletic, and psychological progress. Seeley and his associates found that upper-middle-class parents in "Crestwood Heights" hesitated to impose their own tastes on the child and left the formation of taste to the child's peers. "Crestwood parents who would deem it morally wrong and psychologically destructive to regulate the expression of their children's tastes, after self-examination realized and stated that they were able to afford these views because . . . in these areas the peer group performed a satisfactory policing function for them." Permissiveness thus rests, in part, on peer-group control.

The peer group not only regulates taste, it puts forward its own version of ideal family life. It circulates information about parental regulations currently in force, about regulations that are violated with impunity, about what the world upholds as the norm of parenthood. The child's mastery of this information gives him an important tactical advantage in negotiations with his parents. If he can show that they have departed from established norms, he further weakens their self-confidence. Having made it clear that their own actions are to be submitted to the same standards of justice to which the child himself is expected to conform, parents find it difficult to specify those standards. In theory, justice derives from reason, but community practice turns out to be the only reliable guide. The child knows more about this ambiguous and constantly shifting practice than his parents do, and he skillfully exploits their uneasiness. Parental training has collapsed not because of the inevitable supersession of parents' technical knowledge but because organized interest groups, such as the health and welfare professions and the adolescent peer group, have a stake in promoting their own conceptions of the world, which compete with those of the family. Like the health industry, the peer group spreads information that parents cannot hope to master in its complexity but on which they nevertheless depend in their unsuccessful struggles to discipline their children and at the same time to retain their devotion.

Relations within the family have come to resemble relations in the rest of society. Parents refrain from arbitrarily imposing their wishes on the child, thereby making it clear that authority deserves to be regarded as valid only insofar as it conforms to reason. Yet in the family as elsewhere, "universalistic" standards prove on examination to be illusory. In American society, most rules exist only to be broken, in the words of a popular axiom. Custom has reestablished itself as in many ways the superior of reason. The administration of justice gives way, in a therapeutic society, to a complicated process of negotiation. Just as prices in the neocapitalist economy, allegedly determined by the impersonal laws of supply and demand, are really fixed by negotiations among corporations, unions, and government (with the corporations taking the leading role), so justice is fixed by means of similar bargains among interested parties. In learning to live by the law, therefore, the child actually learns how to get around the law, in the first place by getting around his parents. . . .

If parents attempt to intervene in their children's lives, family comedies depict them as objects of amusement or contempt. Thus Mother ineffectually attempts to uphold old-fashioned ideas of decorum and refinement, which Father collaborates with the younger generation in subverting. Father's well-meaning attempts to instruct, befriend, or discipline the young lead to situations that expose his incompetence. Having nothing of value to pass on to his sons, he reserves most of his affection, what there is of it, for his daughters. Yet he makes no attempt to keep his daughter to himself. He makes way for her suitors without complaint, even encouraging their courtship. According to Martha Wolfenstein and Nathan Leites, the ease with which fathers welcome sons-in-law as boon companions exposes another important theme in American popular culture: the sharing of a woman by two friends or "buddies." As sex becomes more casual, the jealousy of the male subsides. He not only tolerates promiscuity in his women but finds it titillating, largely because women know how to keep promiscuity within the bounds of what is called sexiness. . . .

The contemporary cult of sensuality implies a repudiation of sensuality in all but its most primitive forms. The fascination with personal relations, which becomes increasingly intense as the hope of political solutions recedes, conceals a thoroughgoing disenchantment with personal relations. Ideologies of impulse gratification and pleasure seeking gain the ascendancy at the very moment that pleasure loses its savor. A narcissistic withdrawal of interest from the external world underlies both the demand for immediate gratification—resoundingly endorsed by advertising, mass promotion, and the health industry—and the intolerable anxiety that continually frustrates this demand. The more the "liberated" man clamors for fulfillment, the more he succumbs to hypochondria, to melancholy, or to a suicidal self-hatred that alternates, not with occasional heights of rapture, but with a chronic mild depression, the dominant mood of the times.

Mirage of Health

RENÉ DUBOS

A continuing interest in health is an important feature of modern society. Indeed, a sense that health has improved and will improve further is basic to a view of social progress (and to the claims of that most successful of the modern professions, medicine). René Dubos, a doctor, raises a host of questions about our actual health in relation to the past, our assumptions about health, and the prospects for health in the future. He suggests that gains commonly associated with medicine actually have a broader base; is our faith in medicine thus too narrow to assure further gains in the future? He points also to the selective quality of the improvements we have achieved—the age groups affected—and to areas such as mental health in which we must ask how far we have slipped behind, rather than how much we have improved.

In terms of modernization, Dubos admits the importance of structural change—the massive alteration of technology—though he raises familiar questions about its impact on the environment and the quality of human life. The implications about a modernization of mentality are less clear. On the one hand, beliefs about health, and certainly about medicine, have altered; but Dubos also writes of human strivings and failings that he holds to be general features of a quest for health, not specifically Western or modern. Is he suggesting that the modern dilemma is that the structure of civilization has changed, but its values have not kept pace? We return here to questions that arose with the discussion of the first dents in traditional religions and superstitious belief. Have we simply switched our faith, holding that medicine is now the magic that will pull us through a still-uncontrolled environment (but now a technological more than natural environment)? Or do we believe that man—individual man and mankind in general—has acquired control, perhaps with the help of a pill or two? If we do believe in control, Dubos foresees a host of problems in putting this belief into practice as he challenges the idea that we have regulated our own health in the recent past as much as we might believe, and as he questions the importance claimed by the contemporary guardians of our health.

. . . While modern science can boast of so many startling achievements in the health fields, its role has not been so unique and its effectiveness not

From pp. 19-21, 44-46, 132-39, 223-25, and 226 in *Mirage of Health* by René Dubos, Volume Twenty-Two of the World Perspective Series, edited and planned by Ruth Nanda Anshen. Copyright © 1959 by René Dubos. Reprinted by permission of Harper & Row, Publishers, Inc.

so complete as is commonly claimed. In reality, as already stated, the monstrous specter of infection had become but an enfeebled shadow of its former self by the time serums, vaccines, and drugs became available to combat microbes. Indeed, many of the most terrifying microbial diseases—leprosy, plague, typhus, and the sweating sickness, for example—had all but disappeared from Europe long before the advent of the germ theory. Similarly, the general state of nutrition began to improve and the size of children in the labor classes to increase even before 1900 in most of Europe and North America. The change became noticeable long before calories, balanced diets, and vitamins had become the pride of nutrition experts, the obsession of mothers, and a source of large revenues to the manufacturers of colored packages for advertised food products.

Clearly, modern medical science has helped to clean up the mess created by urban and industrial civilization. However, by the time laboratory medicine came effectively into the picture the job had been carried far toward completion by the humanitarians and social reformers of the nineteenth century. Their romantic doctrine that nature is holy and healthful was scientifically naïve but proved highly effective in dealing with the most important health problems of their age. When the tide is receding from the beach it is easy to have the illusion that one can empty the ocean by removing water with a pail. The tide of infectious and nutritional diseases was rapidly receding when the laboratory scientist moved into action at the end of the past century.

The great increase in over-all expectancy of life during the past hundred years in the Western world is properly quoted as objective evidence of improvement in the general health condition. It is often overlooked, however, that this increase has been due not so much to better health in the adult years of life as to the spectacular decrease in infant mortality. The control of childhood diseases, in turn, resulted more from better nutrition and sanitary practices than from the introduction of new drugs. It is remarkable, in contrast, that little practical progress has been made toward controlling the diseases that were not dealt with by the nineteenth-century reformers. Whereas the Sanitary Revolution did much to eliminate the most common microbial diseases, it has had no counterpart in dealing with the ailments of the adult years of life and of old age.

The nineteenth-century sanitarians believed that health and happiness could be found only through a return to the ways of nature. Modern man, probably no wiser but certainly more conceited, now claims that the royal avenue to the control of disease is through scientific knowledge and medical technology. "Health is purchasable," proclaimed one of the leaders of American medicine. Yet, while the modern American boasts of the scientific management of his body and soul, his expectancy of life past the age of forty-five is hardly greater today than it was several decades ago and is shorter than that of many European people of the present generation. He claims the highest standard of living in the world, but ten per cent of his income must go for medical care and he cannot build hospitals fast enough to accommodate the sick. He is encouraged to believe that money can create drugs for the cure of heart disease, cancer, and mental disease, but he makes no worth-while effort to recognize, let alone correct, the mismanagements of his everyday life that contribute to the high incidence of these conditions. He laughs louder than any other people, and the ubiquitous national smile is advertised *ad nauseam* by every poster or magazine, artist or politician. But one out of every four citizens will have to spend at least some months or years in a mental asylum. One may wonder indeed whether the pretense of superior health is not itself rapidly becoming a mental aberration. Is it not a delusion to proclaim the present state of health as the best in the history of the world, at a time when increasing numbers of persons in our society depend on drugs and on doctors for meeting the ordinary problems of everyday life? . . .

Man, needless to say, is as susceptible as are animals or plants to sudden changes in his physical environment and to attack by new parasitic invaders. No technical knowledge can ever protect him completely from assaults and disturbances that he cannot possibly foresee. As many examples of unexpected external threats that changed the course of history will be presented in subsequent chapters, it does not seem necessary to labor the point further at this time. Instead, we shall consider now another type of disturbing influence which is apparently peculiar to mankind and has its origin in the fact that physiological requirements are no longer the mainsprings of human behavior. There is no doubt that man's own caprices and vagaries constitute the most insuperable obstacles to the achievement of the millennium and to the success of utopias.

It is a universal trait among men that as soon as their physiological needs are satisfied they develop new wishes and urges, which in turn are soon replaced by other desires. In man, at least, satisfaction is commonly followed by boredom. Food in abundance, supplying all the required nutritional elements, may solve the problem of eating for animals, but it does not do so for man. Even the most pampered cat or dog will happily eat day in and day out a standardized diet canned in Chicago with scientific but monotonous perfection. In contrast, the more man becomes civilized or at least urbanized, the more he is likely to lose the experience of honest physiological hunger and to replace it by nonphysiological needs born out of the pleasure of eating. This pleasure soon becomes an end in itself, replacing the physiological purpose from which it had originated. Cabbage and turnips would provide all the ascorbic acid required by the human body, yet millions of American mothers would believe their families on the brink of vitamin starvation unless fresh orange juice was on the breakfast table every morning. Two centuries ago tea and coffee were at best sophisticated luxuries for the favored few. The American citizen today believes that he cannot function effectively if deprived of caffeine stimulants. The taste and color of the dietary product, the package in which it is distributed, and the customs associated with its use are as essential factors in human nutrition as are the intrinsic values of the food or of the stimulant. And it is well known that fashions in tastes, colors, packages, and customs change fast in the modern world. The shelves of the supermarket constitute the colorful and rapidly moving record of the transformation into life necessities of tastes and habits newly acquired from social or advertising pressures.

In brief, it is certain that social criteria are far more influential in the selection of food than are preoccupations with optimal growth rates and with the adequate performance of biochemical processes. In order to be acceptable, diets must of course satisfy the needs of the body, but even more imperatively must they be compatible with the habits of the group as well as with the respect of its taboos—and this often imposes strange strictures upon the chemical concepts of nutrition. The changes in ideals of women's figures in the course of ages reflect well the capricious basis of dietary customs.

While scientists can cite the Venus of Milo and a few Greek-inspired goddesses as famous examples of feminine beauty compatible with scientific nutritional standards, it seems that this physical type is more popular as a museum piece than in the world of the living. In some parts of Latin America and of the Orient the plump, well-padded woman has far greater sex appeal; hence the sweet desserts which supplement her meals and occupy her idle hours. With us, in contrast, it is the tall, lanky girl who becomes the fashionable model or actress; hence her vitamin-rich but calorieless breakfast and the leaf of lettuce for lunch. The desire to look emaciated is not new in the history of fashion. In the sixteenth century Montaigne wrote of women swallowing sand to ruin their stomachs in order to acquire a pale complexion. During the nineteenth century the proper attitude at a romantic dinner was affected indifference to food, and it became fashionable among men to pretend a passion for languid, ethereal womanhood. As a response, young women were inspired to drink lemon juice and vinegar in order to kill their appetites and thus become more attractive. Repetitious indeed are the tricks used by the sexes to attract each other. . . .

It is generally assumed that the discoveries which led to the use of antibacterial drugs during the past two decades constitute scientific feats that transcend those of the past both in theoretical and in practical importance. In reality, as we have seen, these achievements do not mark the beginning of a new era, but are merely advances along a road that medicine has been traveling for countless centuries. For example, the introduction of the cinchona bark for the treatment of fever in the seventeenth century and the discovery during the nineteenth century that its effective constituent, quinine, has a suppressive effect on malaria parasites constitute achievements equal in scientific quality and in practical consequences to any of those made during the more recent era.

The provincial attitude of our time with regard to these discoveries comes in part from the unequal importance of various parasites in different parts of the world. Malaria, other protozoan infections, and worm infestations are the source of physiological and economic misery in most underprivileged areas. On the whole, however, the wealthy countries of the Western world suffer relatively little from these afflictions. Except in time of war or when his financial interests are involved, the white man is but mildly interested in diseases with which he has little personal contact. In contrast, his selfishness makes him endow with scientific glamour any discovery that bears on his own well-being. Millions upon millions of human beings in Asia, Africa, and Latin America suffer and die every year from hookworm disease, African sleeping sickness, or malaria. Yet discovery of a drug effective against these maladies has little chance of making headlines, whereas any fact having to do with diseases of importance to the Western world becomes a sensational event. The antibacterial drugs introduced since 1935 owe their unique importance to the fact that they are effective against some of the diseases which were most important for the white man in the Western world a few decades ago.

To be regarded as miracles, furthermore, events must either have occurred in the very remote past or have been published in yesterday's newspaper. Among antibacterial drugs only penicillin and the various mycins developed during or after World War II still rate as miracles, but the sulfonamides which date from 1935 are beginning to be regarded as antiquated drugstore articles. As to the therapeutic achievements of the pre-1930 era, they receive only the lip service paid to the irrelevant truths in some dusty old tome.

It is easy to see how the appearance of the new antibacterial drugs on the medical scene gave rise to the illusion that the age-old problem of infection had finally been solved. A few diseases almost universally fatal could now be cured—subacute endocarditis and certain forms of bacterial meningitis, for example. The course of other infectious processes could be interrupted with incredible rapidity—as in the case of acute streptococcal infections, pneumococcal pneumonia, bacillary dysentery, gonorrhea, syphilis, etc. Surgical sepsis became a rarity, thus widening the potentialities of the surgeon's skill. It is obvious that these triumphs of modern chemotherapy have transformed the practice of medicine and are changing the very pattern of disease in the Western world, but there is no reason to believe that they spell the conquest of microbial diseases. While it is true that the mortality of many of these afflictions is at an all-time low, the amount of disease that they cause remains very high. Drugs are far more effective in the dramatic acute conditions which are relatively rare than in the countless chronic ailments that account for so much misery in everyday life. Furthermore, as we have seen, the decrease in mortality caused by infection began almost a century ago and has continued ever since at a fairly constant rate irrespective of the use of any specific therapy. The effect of antibacterial drugs is but a ripple on the wave which has been wearing down the mortality caused by infection in our communities.

Most concepts concerning the nature, epidemiology, and control of microbial diseases were formulated during the nineteenth century. This was a time of widespread and killing epidemics, either introduced from the outside, as were cholera and yellow fever, or bred from misery and unsanitary living conditions. Very much the same state of affairs prevails in many parts of the world today, but, on the whole, the great plagues of the past have been brought under some form of control. However, it is only because scientists still think in nineteenth-century terms that these achievements are regarded as having brought about the final conquest of microbial diseases. The appalling number of deaths caused by these diseases was in everybody's mind during the period when the germ theory began to yield its fruits, and it was natural that the lowering of mortality should be the first goal of the medical and social campaigns organized against infection. Now that this goal has been reached, the time has come to realize that mortality rates do not constitute adequate yardsticks for measuring the importance of medical problems. If one were to use as criteria the amount of life spoiled by disease, instead of measuring only that destroyed by death; or the number of days lost from pleasure and work because of so-called minor ailments; or merely the sums paid for drugs, hospitals, and doctors' bills, the toll exacted by microbial pathogens would seem very large indeed. Microbial diseases have not been conquered. Rather, physicians and scientists have resigned themselves to the belief that a relative protection against them can be bought at the cost of a huge ransom.

One might assume that the persistence of microbial diseases is merely a temporary situation, a problem soon to be solved by the discovery of new and more powerful drugs. In reality, there are limitations inherent in drug therapy even under the most favorable conditions. Some of these limitations are technical and cannot be discussed here. Others are more fundamental in character, having their basis in the very philosophy of disease control.

As we have seen and shall again discuss in the following chapter, the characteristics of the total environment—physical and social—determine in a large measure the types of diseases most prevalent in any given community. The belief that disease can be conquered through the use of drugs fails to take into account the difficulties arising from the ecological complexity of human problems. It is an attitude comparable to the naïve cowboy philosophy that permeates the wild West thriller. In the crime-ridden frontier town the hero, singlehanded, blasts out the desperadoes who were running rampant through the settlement. The story ends on a happy note because it appears that peace has been restored. But in reality the death of the villains does not solve the fundamental problem, for the rotten social conditions which had opened the town to the desperadoes will soon allow others to come in, unless something is done to correct the primary source of trouble. The hero moves out of town without doing anything to solve this far more complex problem; in fact, he has no weapon to deal with it and is not even aware of its existence.

Similarly, the accounts of miraculous cures rarely make clear that arresting an acute episode does not solve the problem of disease in the social body— nor even in the individual concerned. Gonorrhea in human beings has been readily amenable to drug therapy ever since 1935; its microbial agent, the gonococcus, is so vulnerable to penicillin and other drugs that the overt form of the disease can now be arrested in a very short time, and at a very low cost. Yet gonorrhea has not been wiped out in any country or social group. The reason is that its control involves many factors, physiological and social, not amenable to drug treatment. These factors range all the way from the ill-defined conditions which allow the persistence of gonococci without manifestation of disease in the vagina of "successfully" treated women to the economic and psychological aspects of the social environment which favor loose sexual mores and juvenile delinquency.

Other limitations of drug therapy can be illustrated by the attempts to control bovine mastitis, a disease in which the udder of dairy animals can be infected with various types of bacteria. As streptococci used to be the microbes most commonly found in bovine mastitis, it was thought that control of the disease could be readily achieved by treatment with penicillin. It was soon recognized, however, that elimination of streptococci was often followed by appearance of other types of bacteria which took their place in the udder. Mastitis cannot be controlled merely by attacking the bacteria associated with a particular outbreak of the disease. Control can be achieved only by changing the practices of animal husbandry which permit the bacteria to become established and to multiply in the udder. Translated into terms applicable to human diseases, it signifies that drugs cannot be effective in the long run until steps have been taken to correct the physiological and social conditions originally responsible for the disease that is to be treated.

It is a remarkable fact that the greatest strides in health improvement have been achieved in the field of diseases that responded to social and economic reforms after industrialization. The nutritional deficiencies that were so frequent in the nineteenth century have all but disappeared in the Western world, not through the administration of pure vitamins but as a result of over-all better nutrition. The great microbial epidemics were brought under control not by treatment with drugs but largely by sanitation and by the general raising of living standards. In contrast, the cancers, the vascular disorders, the mental diseases, which were not affected by the sanitary movement, have remained great health problems and their solution is not yet in sight. It is legitimate to hope, of course, that vigorous research will yield drugs for the relief of patients suffering from these diseases, but it can be predicted that drug treatment will not provide the real solution to the problem.

The need is to discover and to reform those aspects of the physical and social environment which have brought about an increase in the prevalence of the diseases peculiar to our time. Atmospheric pollution, the exposure to certain chemical agents, the defects in nutritional regimens, the competitive way of life, etc., all have been implicated and probably play some part in disease causation. Many surprises certainly remain in store. The one characteristic of our civilization is the rapidity with which it changes all our ways of life, without too much, if any, concern for the long-term effects of the changes. Man can eventually become adapted to almost anything, but adaptation demands more time than is allowed by the increased tempo at which changes are presently taking place.

The relation of insulin to diabetes illustrates another type of difficulty in the control of disease by the use of drugs. Thanks to insulin, many millions of diabetic persons all over the world can now live long, happy, and useful years. Unfortunately, effective control of the symptoms of diabetes is not synonymous with cure of the diabetic patient, let alone with conquest of the disease. Even when adequately treated with insulin, the diabetic individual is at risk of developing vascular disorders during old age. Still more important from the social point of view is the fact that his children are likely to inherit a tendency to the disease. Thus, the very effectiveness of insulin therapy is bringing about an increase in the prevalence of diabetes in our communities, and a time may soon come when it will prove necessary to weigh the distant consequences of this biological situation. If the tendency to diabetes should become a frequent trait in human beings and if the need for insulin or for an adequate substitute should continue to increase, society may face medical, economic, and ethical problems for which it is not prepared at present. Fortunately there is evidence that treatment with insulin or with drugs having a similar action is not the only possible approach to the control of diabetes. It has been observed that the disease is on the whole less severe in situations where there is a shortage of food, for example, as normally occurs in Asiatic countries or as occurred during the war in the parts of Europe that were under German occupation. Clearly the problem is one that demands the most sophisticated medical statesmanship. Its solution transcends treatment of symptoms in the individual patient and might require social reforms reaching even into the field of ethics. . . .

Modern man believes that he has achieved almost complete mastery over the natural forces which molded his evolution in the past and that he can now control his own biological and cultural destiny. But this may be an illusion. Like all other living things, he is part of an immensely complex ecological system and is bound to all its components by innumerable links.

Moreover, as we have seen, human life is affected not only by the environmental forces presently at work in nature but even more perhaps by the past.

Any attempt to shape the world and modify human personality in order to create a self-chosen pattern of life involves many unknown consequences. Human destiny is bound to remain a gamble, because at some unpredictable time and in some unforeseeable manner nature will strike back. The multiplicity of determinants which affect biological systems limits the power of the experimental method to predict their trends and behavior. Experimentation necessarily involves a choice in the factors brought to bear on the phenomena under study. Ideally, the experimenter works in a closed system, affected only by the determinants that he has introduced, under the conditions that he has selected. Naturally, however, events never occur in a closed system. They are determined and modified by circumstances and forces that cannot be foreseen, let alone controlled. In part this is because natural situations are so complex that no experimental study can ever encompass and reproduce all the relevant factors of the environment. Furthermore, human behavior is governed not only by biological necessities but also by the desire for change. When surfeited with honey man begins to loathe the taste of sweetness, and this desire for change per se introduces an inescapable component of unpredictability in his life.

It is the awareness of these complexities which accounts for the clumsiness of the scientific language used in reporting biological events. The scientist emphasizes ad nauseam that what he states is valid only "under conditions of the experiment." As if apologetically, he is wont to qualify any assertion or general statement with the remark, "All other things being equal—which they never are . . ." Because things are never the same, almost everyone admits that prediction is always risky in political and social fields. But it is not so generally recognized that the same limitations apply to other areas usually regarded as falling within the realm of the so-called exact sciences, for instance, the epidemiology of disease.

Many examples have been quoted in earlier chapters to illustrate the unexpected and far-reaching effects that accidental circumstances have exerted in the past on the welfare of man. The introduction of inexpensive cotton undergarments easy to launder and of transparent glass that brought light into the most humble dwelling, contributed more to the control of infection than did all drugs and medical practices. On the other hand, a change in fur fashion brought about a few years later an outbreak of pneumonic plague in Manchuria; the use of soft coal in English grates caused chimney sweeps to develop cancer; Roentgen's discovery endangered the lives of scientists and physicians exposed to X rays in the course of their professional activities. Likewise oil and rubber may in the future come to be regarded as having been the indirect causes of disease and death. In addition to the human beings killed or maimed in automobile accidents, many are likely to suffer, directly or indirectly, from the air pollution brought about by the widespread use of oil and rubber. Furthermore, neuroses peculiar to our time may someday be traced to the speed and power that rubber and oil have made possible, as well as to the frustrations caused by crowded city streets and highways.

Human goals, which condition social changes, profoundly affect the physical and mental well-being of man. And, unfortunately, the most worth-while goals may have results as disastrous as those of the most despicable ambitions. Industrial imperialism was responsible for an enormous amount of misery among children during the early nineteenth century. But, as we have seen, the present philosophy to assure the survival of all children and to protect them from any traumatic experience also is likely to have unfortunate consequences by interfering with the normal play of adaptive processes. . . .

Technology is now displacing philosophical and religious values as the dominant force in shaping the world, and therefore in determining human fate. What man does today and will do tomorrow is determined to a large extent by the techniques that expert knowledge puts at his disposal, and his dreams for the future reflect the achievements and promises of the scientists. From them he has acquired the faith—or rather the illusion—that society can be planned in a manner that will assure plenty, health, and happiness for everyone and thus solve all the great problems of existence.

Part 5

THE NATURE OF

MODERN PEOPLE

Most historians are reluctant to define the central characteristics of the modern outlook, and perhaps the modern outlook is too complex and varied to be described clearly. Yet many social scientists believe the modernization process has had a certain direction, and it is important, after having considered some of the major features of the process, to talk about its possible end results or at least about the results to date.

The four selections that follow are written by social scientists (though one is more a humanist historian), and that is almost all they have in common. Different professional training and experience lead to different evaluations of the nature of modernization. Different approaches—the attempt to provide a general model, for example, as against a study of a particular class, region, or activity—lead to different evaluations of the extent of the process. Fortunately students of the modernization process in Europe are not forced simply to weigh one contemporary evaluation against another. They can apply their understanding of key stages in the history of society during recent centuries. They can compare current institutions and values to those that antedate modernization. Perhaps out of this mix will come some sense of what modern man is like, how new he is, and what his prospects are.

The selections do assume that modernization, or some key change at least, has occurred; we differ from our past. The differences center on the angle from which modernization is viewed (play versus work, for example) and above all on the evaluation of the quality of the result. And here, instead of pretending to resolve the dichotomy between optimism and pessimism, three final issues must be raised. The optimists, who hold that the modern mentality is becoming increasingly rational and effective, may wear blinders, deliberately shutting themselves off from the pain of modern life, staying close to surface beliefs in progress and science. Can they pretend to describe the modern world when most artistic movements of the twentieth century are busily portraying a deeper, and on the whole more frightening, reality beneath or apart from reason? As to the pessimists, the key question is the historical quality of their view. Are they blaming modern structures and ideas for sorrows that are inherent in the human condition (which the optimists admittedly ignore)?

How much have the incidence, nature, and importance of madness increased? How lacking is the modern family compared to its preindustrial progenitor?

And of course, for optimists and pessimists alike, the final issue involves the future. The more optimistic statements about modernization risk a closed quality: We are close to perfection and, at most, can hope for more of the same in the future, abetted perhaps by further gains in technology and knowledge. But, if this modern world exists, how long can it last, and how adaptable will modern people be to really fundamental change? On the other hand, if modernization represents humanity gone awry (not just tragic, but newly tragic), how can we escape? Can we really recapture the past, and do we understand our misfortune well enough to wish to do so?

BIBLIOGRAPHY

The twentieth-century French peasant has received considerable attention from scholars, who disagree about the extent of traditional behavior in rural society. See Gordon Wright, *Rural Revolution in France: The Peasantry in the Twentieth Century* (Stanford, 1968), and Robert T. and Barbara G. Anderson, *Bus Stop for Paris* (New York, 1966). Lawrence W. Wylie, ed., *Chanzeaux: A Village in Anjou* (Cambridge, Mass., 1966), studies a particularly conservative region; see also Wylie's *Village in the Vaucluse* (Cambridge, Mass., 1957). A fine study of leisure is Michael Smith, Stanley Parker, and Cyril Smith, eds., *Leisure and Society in Britain* (London, 1973).

The modernization model has often been applied to studies of non-Western societies; see Ronald P. Dore, ed., *Aspects of Social Change in Japan* (Princeton, 1967), and M. B. Jansen, *Changing Japanese Attitudes Toward Modernization* (Princeton, 1965). Cyril E. Black, *The Dynamics of Modernization: A Study in Comparative History* (New York, 1966), sketches a general history of the subject.

The modern mentality is discussed in Daniel Lerner, *The Passing of Traditional Society* (New York, 1964). For critiques, see Robert Nisbet, *Social Change and History: The Western Theory of Development* (New York, 1969); Dean C. Tipps, "Modernization and the Study of National Societies, A Critical Perspective," *Comparative Studies in Society and History* (1973), pp. 199–226; and Reinhard Bendix, "Tradition and Modernity Reconsidered," *Comparative Studies in Society and History* (1967), pp. 292–346.

Herbert Marcuse, *One Dimensional Man* (Boston, 1964), is a criticism of modernity somewhat related to Laing's. Fritz R. Stern, *The Politics of Cultural Despair: A Study in the Rise of the Germanic Ideology* (Berkeley, 1961), traces some earlier manifestations of intellectual hostility to modernity.

The Vanishing Peasant

HENRI MENDRAS

As the peasantry epitomized the character of traditional society, to the extent that generalizations about the one may too easily be used to describe the other, so modernization seems ultimately to destroy the peasant spirit. Some of the earliest modernizing societies lacked a peasantry in the ordinary sense; the earlier selection by Keith Thomas suggests that key aspects of the peasant mentality were being eroded in Britain as early as the seventeenth century. Elsewhere the peasant spirit was stronger, for example, as it confronted a modern educational system in France as late as the nineteenth century. But structural modernization, through expansion of the cities and industrial production, everywhere reduced the relative numbers and economic importance of the peasantry. Henri Mendras, a noted French sociologist, argues that in recent decades the final vestiges of the peasant mentality have been disappearing as well. Here indeed is one measure of how far modernization has gone and what it means in terms of traditional values: The farming population is converted to a market orientation and the behavior, including the family relationships, that goes with such orientation. It is important to recall that this process was not sudden, that an identifiable peasantry long held out against complete change. Indeed, against Mendras' argument, we may see remnants of the peasant outlook even in city dwellers who have preserved some of the habits of their ancestors—reactions to health problems, for example.

Mendras does more than note the disappearance of a basic way of life. He mourns it. The erosion of the peasantry is not an unalloyed triumph of progress over superstition. Mendras reminds us that the peasantry had virtues whose absence may endanger the civilization that uprooted them. Certain kinds of family ties, an attachment to the soil and a willingness to conserve resources to protect future generations, a sense of continuity—these qualities and more may now be irrevocably lost. How much will we suffer as a result? Can we strive to restore some of the solidarity that a peasantry traditionally offered? Should we in fact abandon the basic course of modernization in favor of a return to a more tested social structure, and can we do so even if we wish?

Most historians of agriculture in this country have admired the "French prudence" (*sagesse française*) that kept the nation from pushing the agricultural revolution of the eighteenth century to extreme social consequences and enabled us to conserve a large peasant class, while the British, yielding to the logic of the industrial economy, sacrificed their agriculture to the development of industry. In a way, France stopped in her tracks; she paused for a century and a half while her peasants, though slowly accepting technological innovations, remained peasants.

Today, the second agricultural revolution is upsetting every structure, and the dependable equilibrium has been disturbed. Agriculture, in its turn, is becoming "industrialized," and the French peasantry is being destroyed, one hundred fifty years later, by what we call industrial civilization. Suddenly we feel very close to the eighteenth century. We are rediscovering that nature can be subdued by technology, that agrarian history is marked by constant advances, innovations, and improvements, and that the farmers are living in turmoil.

We live essentially on ideas that were bequeathed us by the nineteenth century, and are today obviously anachronistic. It is important to revise these ideas and to look at the countryside with a new eye; otherwise we will remain blind to the great movement that is carrying the agrarian societies of the entire world toward a complete remodeling of their technology and their social equilibrium. The disappearance of the peasant in countries that have industrialized the most rapidly is due less to the force of economic circumstances than to the misapplication to agriculture of analytical methods, legislative measures, and administrative decisions that were not designed for it.

In countries such as England or the United States, where it was wholly subordinated to the logic of industrial society, agriculture remains an irreducible political and social problem, which seriously concerns leaders in Washington and London. . . .

Peasant society is subdivided into local communities that exist in relative demographic, economic, and cultural autarchy. According to Marx's famous image, the French peasantry of the last century resembled "potatoes in a sack," each community being a social entity, each being unique although all the communities were of the same kind.

Each community is a face-to-face group in which everybody knows everyone else in all his aspects. Its social relations are thus personal and not functional or segmentary. The community unites peasants (independent farmers, stockbreeders, landowners, cultivators, or salaried workers and their families, and nonpeasants (notables, artisans and merchants, and so on); but the

Reprinted from *The Vanishing Peasant* by Henri Mendras by permission of the M.I.T. Press, Cambridge, Massachusetts. Published in French by S.É.D.É.I.S., Paris, under the title *La Fin des Paysans, Innovation et Changement dans l'Agriculture Française.* English translation copyright © 1970 by The Massachusetts Institute of Technology.

dominant tone of the society is set by the peasants. Power belongs normally to the notables, who are in a marginal position between the local community and the broader society. The principal cleavages are often hierarchial in nature, according to a scale of socioeconomic prestige. If not, they can be of an ideological, ecological, or family nature in the larger sense: there is often no clear distinction between blood relatives and business connections. Finally, categories of age and sex are in general strongly individualized.

In communities as highly structured as this, everything contributes to the stability of the whole, and change can be introduced only by consensus, so slowly as to deny that it is change. These communities are not inflexible, but, except in a grave crisis, they evolve slowly to the rhythm of generations. Every innovation, whether it be technological, economic, or demographic, comes from the outside. In the words of Albert Dauzat, a man hardly to be suspected of prejudice on this subject, "The countryside has created nothing; everything comes to it from the city—dress, customs, songs. . . ." and one could add machines and technology.

In such a social system, the individual does not have to adapt himself to new decisions or make decisions himself; neither does he have to express or reveal himself to others, who know him from every point of view. Hence he has a tendency to remain true to himself and to the image others have of him. Showing or expressing sentiments and personal opinions is not encouraged by the code of values and norms. . . .

The agricultural revolution of the eighteenth century required more than a hundred years to carry its advances into the French countryside. It took place in the rhythm of a traditional society that industry had not yet modified. While it brought social change, supported and sometimes accelerated by political revolution, the essential character of village society remained unaltered. After a century of continual rural exodus, the present revolution in France is reducing the number of farmers at the bewildering rate of 160,000 per year, both through the death of farmers without successors and through the movement of young farmers into other professions. Those who remain become correspondingly richer and can meet the new exigencies of economy and technology, but not without completely upsetting village society. . . .

The ease with which peasants formed in the traditional world can move in a modern world is a source of constant surprise to the observer. Provided that they enter into a coherent and significant economic game, "economic motivations" come to young farmers with disconcerting rapidity. Moreover, when they travel from their farms, these untrained country bumpkins show an amazing aptitude for creating new institutions that are perfectly adapted to modern conditions, such as c.e.t.a. (Center for Technical Farm Studies). . . . Under their constant pressure, modern methods of farm accounting have been introduced in France, and it is in response to their demands that rural economics has come out of its age-old lethargy.

What truth is more self-evident, what fact better substantiated, than the peasant's individualism and love of his land? He gives his life's blood to enlarge his fields, and then fences himself in on his property with fierce independence, like a petty king in his kingdom. Nevertheless for half a century it is in the area of agriculture that cooperation has known its greatest success. Buying and marketing cooperatives, mutual insurance societies, farm credit associations . . . —no other sector of production can offer such a variety of cooperative organizations. Today some farmers are attempting the final step by joining their lands and grouping them into larger units where each product constitutes a workshop under the responsibility of one of the cooperating parties. Such experiments in "group farming" are not proceeding without difficulties, in the absence of legislation and established customs; for these pioneers must invent everything themselves until such time as economists, legislators, and public authorities have codified their experiments.

In devoting themselves enthusiastically to this total remodeling of their social and technical structures, the farmers have the feeling that they are making up for lost time and creating a place for themselves in the era of industrial civilization. Once the crisis of adjustment has passed, they hope in a confused way to rediscover the equilibrium their fathers knew. Having assimilated some new techniques and accepted some economic regulations, they expect to recreate a system of cultivation and independent farming as durable as the previous one. But modern technological civilization lives on continual change and dooms the quietude of immutable habits. Far from rediscovering traditional stability, the peasant will in his turn settle into the perpetual change of technological innovation and economic contingency. Furthermore, he is setting up, more or less consciously, the institutions that will help him to do this. Centers of management and rural economics study the evolution of markets and direct the management of farm workers accordingly. Services for agronomical research and agricultural extension complete the chain that progressively adapts the scientific discoveries of the laboratory so that they can be used by the farmer in his field.

Peasant values, so highly esteemed since the time of Xenophon and Virgil, and heretofore at the very heart of our Western civilization, will not be able to survive the shakeup of their ancient stability. The eternal "peasant soul" is dying before our eyes, just as is the patriarchal family domain founded on subsistence polycultivation. It is the final battle of industrial society against the last stronghold of traditional civilization. What we are undertaking here, then, is not simply a study of a new agricultural revolution but a study of the disappearance of traditional peasant civilization, which is a fundamental element of Western civilization and Christianity, and its replacement by the new modern technological civilization, which will often take on different forms in the country from those it presently assumes in the city. . . .

In most French regions the farmers are still . . . "real" peasants. The sentiments that tie them to their land have until now been the subject of only one pilot study of a limited region: the reader will find below its hypotheses and major conclusions. It is enough to point out here how impossible it is to isolate the land from its entire natural setting, human and social. For the farmer the word "land" evokes simultaneously the soil he works, the farm that has supported his family for generations, and the profession he follows, as well as the peasant condition and the whole body of the nation's farmers. During an interview he jumps from one meaning to another without seeming to realize that these meanings are separate and distinct; and at the same time he says repeatedly that the sentiments evoked by this word are ineffable, that they exist but cannot be expressed. To make them understood, he calls on the interviewer's experience: "If you're from the country, you know what I mean."

On the other hand, a big farmer from the Paris basin can refuse to purchase the fields he works because it is economically more advantageous for him to rent them and invest his capital in livestock and machinery. During an interview, his "economic rationality" is visibly in conflict with his "peasant sentiments," as when he seeks to justify his refusal to buy his land by showing his contempt for it: "It's a poor piece of land where a man wouldn't want to settle his family." Or again, by reducing it to nothing: "This piece of land is like any other . . . nowadays the land doesn't count any more. . . ." To reduce to naught or curse the land one refuses to own betrays sentiments similar to those the "peasant" feels but refuses to express. However, other farmers are able to analyze the origin of these sentiments, if not their content, in astonishingly lucid terms: "To know one's land, to improve it, takes a long time! And the more you know it, the more you become attached to it." Such statements, almost evangelical in tone, are an admission of the fact that sentiment and ownership go together: "What belongs, belongs . . . a peasant is a proprietor of the land. . . . When a man is a proprietor, he has a feeling and a concern for the land." As opposed to the big farmer, and contrary to all economic analysis, a small proprietor can state: "Rented land is expensive and amounts to nothing."

Thus the peasant has a deep conviction that his field is unique because he is the only one to know it, to love it and to own it: knowledge, love, and possession are inseparable. And even when the farmer behaves in a rational economic fashion with respect to land as capital, his feelings for the soil are no less diffuse or deep; he identifies it intimately with his family and his profession, thus with himself. It can be said that these feelings are largely the product of a historical situation that is on the way to extinction, and that they will outlive it by some years. Moreover, they are already disparaged by the ideology that the new generation is fashioning for itself. Young people think that the cultivators should be relieved of land ownership, and that the latter should be considered solely as a factor of production, by farmers as well as by public authorities and capitalists. . . .

As mechanization became general, the concept of technological and urban time invaded agricultural work and introduced into it the new unit of the hour. This concept came first with the threshing contractor, who asked to be paid by the hour; soon the farmer who came with his machine to plow his neighbor's field did the same; and today young farmers, mindful of how profitable their tractors or harvester-threshers can be, keep a notebook in which they carefully record their hours of work and the liters of fuel burned. For the first time abstract time, made up of equal units, has entered into agricultural work. It is tending gradually to modify the time scale of an ever-increasing number of tasks. Though the process of replacing one concept of time by another can be seen through many easily-measurable indices and hence can be observed by the sociologist with exceptional clarity, no study has yet been conducted on this subject.

Hourly time already existed in country life. Every farm kitchen displayed proudly a clock with a long pendulum, and most of the farmers had pocket watches. According to the French Institute of Public Opinion, 47 percent of farmers did not carry a watch on their persons in 1953 (compared with 34 percent of the population as a whole). In daily life these instruments served to indicate the progress of the day more than to fix the time exactly or indicate the beginning or end of some activity. Witness to an external civilization, they were employed to "tell time" only when in contact with this civilization, when one must be "on time": to send the children to school, to catch the train or bus, to attend a meeting. And in the latter case, if it was an appointment with neighbors or other country people, everyone knew it was not necessary to be punctual.

Today, on the contrary, as meetings become more frequent all the time, young people particularly want them to start punctually in order not to "lose time"; this is one of the indices which reveal the passage from the peasant to the modern concept of time. In the past, since the means of transportation were slow, people would go to town for the day or half a day if they had a meeting. The meeting began when everyone had arrived at the city hall, the cooperative, or the school. People took advantage of the trip to do other errands or to chat with each other. Now they take the car or the motorbike in order to arrive in time for the meeting and leave immediately afterward if work is pressing. This change in customs was surprising to the rural researcher who went from a French village to an American one in 1950; today it can be observed in every French village.

One must not, however, conclude from our analysis that this concept of "flowing, dreamy" time, vague and slow-moving, was of no value whatever. Just as the Mediterranean peoples, in particular the Greeks, like to "while away the time," so too Mexican peasants are always ready to put off till tomorrow what they can avoid doing today. Most French peasants, on the contrary, do not allow themselves to waste time. Time is so closely connected with the work experience that wasted time is wasted work; it is laziness to put off till tomorrow what one can do today. These two examples suffice to show how dangerous it would be to settle for a simplistic contrast between two extreme types. In each civilization the notion of time is closely linked to the system of values and the organization of daily life. In France we would have to undertake a study, region by region, to try to explain why some have rapidly accepted certain elements of modern time and others have proved more resistant. . . .

But, some will say, how are our traditionalist peasants going to shed the old self so abruptly and take on a new self? The peasant soul will survive the cataclysm that you forecast, if, indeed, it is to come. One has only to open a newspaper to dismiss this objection: there one sees article after article on progressive young farmers, on demonstrations, on conferences where the vocabulary of technical and economic efficiency has replaced the political and moral vocabulary that was in style only a few years ago.

On this point our studies are convincing: if economic structures are changed within a region, they will within a few years change the mentality of the inhabitants. It is striking to see the ease with which peasants formed in a traditional economic and social system can be moved to a modern system, given a few conditions—particularly that the coherence of the new system be rapidly established, visible, and comprehensible. It does not take the young farmers long to acquire "economic motivations," if only these have a meaning and are part of a coherent economic game that permits a glimpse of a successful future.

With astonishingly sure intuition they create entirely new institutions perfectly adapted to modern conditions. . . . But in reconstructing a new society on the dismantled structures of family, farm, and village, they sound the knell of the last vestiges of the peasantry in France, who will not survive their generation.

Thus, with them, the peasantry will itself be extinguished. And what will a world without peasants be like?

Modern Man at Play

JOHAN HUIZINGA

There is little doubt that the values of modern society remain confused in the area of play and leisure. In a period when more and more time is spent not working (due to shorter work days, longer vacations, and earlier retirement), we continue to define work as reality. Our schools, among other things, train students for the job with an often narrow passion. Yet there are observers who hold that leisure, defined as nonwork time in which an individual chooses his diversion, is a phenomenon of modernization.

In this selection, Johan Huizinga, a noted Dutch historian whose interests ranged from the Middle Ages to assessments (rather pessimistic ones) about modern life, judges that modernity has indeed brought a distinct trend in the area of play, and an unfortunate one. His views should be compared with the specific assessments of leisure and recreation in premodern societies and during industrialization. Insofar as he focuses on play, which is by nature particularly childlike, his opinions relate also to changes in the treatment and conception of childhood and youth. Quite possibly, in our desire to find purpose in activity (of which education and educational toys are one expression), we have indeed limited the play spirit.

But do we need play? What is it, in contrast to other uses of leisure? Huizinga ironically suggests that we are substituting play for seriousness in work. Yet one could argue that modern life is excitingly recasting the definitions of seriousness and nonseriousness. But, if this is the case, it is largely unwitting. The modern form of life is so new, such as the amounts of time available for nonwork, that we may be having difficulty in defining our own mentality, in adjusting our values to our behavior.

Huizinga certainly points to an area of great unclarity, far removed from most of the standard valuations of the gains and losses involved in modernization. His own judgment coincides with a pessimistic modernization thesis: We have lost a valued part of our own tradition. It coincides also with many of the criticisms of contemporary leisure that are made without definite historical criteria: Modern men do not know how to relax; we are dominated by remote commercial media rather than really choosing our own leisure; mass taste is degraded, regimented taste. Have we lost a vital capacity to enjoy, to indulge in purposeless expression, and with this a key source of mental balance? Or are we groping to use our undeniably increased material resources to make life itself a form of play?

The question to which we address ourselves is this: To what extent does the civilization we live in still develop in play-forms? How far does the play-spirit dominate the lives of those who share that civilization? The 19th century, we observed, had lost many of the play-elements so characteristic of former ages. Has this leeway been made up or has it increased?

It might seem at first sight that certain phenomena in modern social life have more than compensated for the loss of play-forms. Sport and athletics, as social functions, have steadily increased in scope and conquered ever fresh fields both nationally and internationally.

Contests in skill, strength and perseverance have, as we have shown, always occupied an important place in every culture either in connection with ritual or simply for fun and festivity. Feudal society was only really interested in the tournament; the rest was just popular recreation and nothing more. Now the tournament, with its highly dramatic staging and aristocratic embellishments, can hardly be called a sport. It fulfilled one of the functions of the theatre. Only a numerically small upper class took active part in it. This one-sidedness of mediaeval sporting life was due in large measure to the influence of the Church. The Christian ideal left but little room for the organized practice of sport and the cultivation of bodily exercise, except insofar as the latter contributed to gentle education. Similarly, the Renaissance affords fairly numerous examples of body-training cultivated for the sake of perfection, but only on the part of individuals, never groups or classes. If anything, the emphasis laid by the Humanists on learning and erudition tended to perpetuate the old under-estimation of the body, likewise the moral zeal and severe intellectuality of the Reformation and Counter-Reformation. The recognition of games and bodily exercises as important cultural values was withheld right up to the end of the 18th century.

The basic forms of sportive competition are, of course, constant through the ages. In some the trial of strength and speed is the whole essence of the contest, as in running and skating matches, chariot and horse races, weight-lifting, swimming, diving, marksmanship, etc. Though human beings have indulged in such activities since the dawn of time, these only take on the character of organized games to a very slight degree. Yet nobody, bearing in mind the agonistic principle which animates them, would hesitate to call them games in the sense of play—which, as we have seen, can be very serious indeed. There are, however, other forms of contest which develop of their own accord into "sports." These are the ball-games.

What we are concerned with here is the transition from occasional amusement to the system of organized clubs and matches. Dutch pictures of the 17th century show us burghers and peasants intent upon their game of *kolf*; but, so far as I know, nothing is heard of games being organized in clubs or played as matches. It is obvious that a fixed organization of this kind will most readily occur when two groups play against one another. The great ball-games in particular require the existence of permanent teams, and herein lies the starting-point of modern sport. The process arises quite spontaneously in the meeting of village against village, school against school, one part of a town against the rest, etc. That the process started in 19th-century England is understandable up to a point, though how far the specifically Anglo-Saxon bent of mind can be deemed an efficient cause is less certain. But it cannot be doubted that the structure of English social life had much to do with it. Local self-government encouraged the spirit of association and solidarity. The absence of obligatory military training favoured the occasion for, and the need of, physical exercise. The peculiar form of education tended to work in the same direction, and finally the geography of the country and the nature of the terrain, on the whole flat and, in the ubiquitous commons, offering the most perfect playing-fields that could be desired, were of the greatest importance. Thus England became the cradle and focus of modern sporting life.

Ever since the last quarter of the 19th century games, in the guise of sport, have been taken more and more seriously. The rules have become increasingly strict and elaborate. Records are established at a higher, or faster, or longer level than was ever conceivable before. Everybody knows the delightful prints from the first half of the 19th century, showing the cricketers in top-hats. This speaks for itself.

Now, with the increasing systematization and regimentation of sport, something of the pure play-quality is inevitably lost. We see this very clearly in the official distinction between amateurs and professionals (or "gentlemen and players" as used pointedly to be said). It means that the play-group marks out those for whom playing is no longer play, ranking them inferior to the true players in standing but superior in capacity. The spirit of the professional is no longer the true play-spirit; it is lacking in spontaneity and carelessness. This affects the amateur too, who begins to suffer from an inferiority complex. Between them they push sport further and further away from the play-sphere proper until it becomes a thing *sui generis*: neither play nor earnest. In modern social life sport occupies a place alongside and apart from the cultural process. The great competitions in archaic cultures had always formed part of the sacred festivals and were indispensable as health and happiness-bringing activities. This ritual tie has now been completely severed; sport has become profane, "unholy" in every way and has no organic connection whatever with the structure of society, least of all when prescribed by the government. The ability of modern social techniques to stage mass demonstrations with the maximum of outward show in the field of athletics does not alter the fact that neither the Olympiads nor the organized sports of American Universities nor the loudly trumpeted international contests have, in the smallest degree, raised sport to the level of a culture-creating activity. However important it may be for the players or spectators, it remains sterile. The old play-factor has undergone almost complete atrophy.

This view will probably run counter to the popular feeling of to-day, according to which sport is the apotheosis of the play-element in our civilization. Nevertheless popular feeling is wrong. By way of emphasizing the fatal shift towards over-seriousness we would point out that it has also infected the non-athletic games where calculation is everything, such as chess and some card-games.

A great many board-games have been known since the earliest times, some even in primitive society, which attached great importance to them largely on account of their chanceful character. Whether they are games of chance or skill they all contain an element of seriousness. The merry play-mood has little scope here, particularly where chance is at a minimum as in chess, draughts, backgammon, halma, etc. Even so all these games remain within the definition of play as given in our first chapter. Only recently has publicity seized on them and annexed them to athletics by means of public championships, world tournaments, registered records and press reportage in a literary style of its own, highly ridiculous to the innocent outsider.

Card-games differ from board-games in that they never succeed in eliminating chance completely. To the extent that chance predominates they fall into the category of gambling and, as such, are little suited to club life and public competition. The more intellectual card-games, on the other hand, leave plenty of room for associative tendencies. It is in this field that the shift towards seriousness and over-seriousness is so striking. From the days of *ombre* and *quadrille* to whist and bridge, card-games have undergone a process of increasing refinement, but only with bridge have the modern social techniques made themselves master of the game. The paraphernalia of hand-books and systems and professional training has made bridge a deadly earnest business. A recent newspaper article estimated that yearly winnings of the Culbertson couple at more than two hundred thousand dollars. An enormous amount of mental energy is expended in this universal craze for bridge with no more tangible result than the exchange of relatively unimportant sums of money. Society as a whole is neither benefited nor damaged by this futile activity. It seems difficult to speak of it as an elevating recreation in the sense of Aristotle's *diagoge*. Proficiency at bridge is a sterile excellence, sharpening the mental faculties very one-sidedly without enriching the soul in any way, fixing and consuming a quantity of intellectual energy that might have been better applied. The most we can say, I think, is that it might have been applied worse. The status of bridge in modern society would indicate, to all appearances, an immense increase in the play-element to-day. But appearances are deceptive. Really to play, a man must play like a child. Can we assert that this is so in the case of such an ingenious game as bridge? If not, the virtue has gone out of the game.

The attempt to assess the play-content in the confusion of modern life is bound to lead us to contradictory conclusions. In the case of sport we have an activity nominally known as play but raised to such a pitch of technical organization and scientific thoroughness that the real play-spirit is threatened with extinction. Over against this tendency to over-seriousness, however, there are other phenomena pointing in the opposite direction. Certain activities whose whole *raison d'être* lies in the field of material interest, and which had nothing of play about them in their initial stages, develop what we can only call play-forms as a secondary characteristic. Sport and athletics showed us play stiffening into seriousness but still being felt as play; now we come to serious business degenerating into play but still being called serious. The two phenomena are linked by the strong agonistic habit which still holds universal sway, though in other forms than before.

The impetus given to this agonistic principle which seems to be carrying the world back in the direction of play derives, in the main, from external factors independent of culture proper—in a word, communications, which have made intercourse of every sort so extraordinarily easy for mankind as a whole. Technology, publicity and propaganda everywhere promote the competitive spirit and afford means of satisfying it on an unprecedented scale. Commercial competition does not, of course, belong to the immemorial sacred play-forms. It only appears when trade begins to create fields of activity within which each must try to surpass and outwit his neighbour. Commercial rivalry soon makes limiting rules imperative, namely the trading customs. It remained primitive in essence until quite late, only becoming really intensive with the advent of modern communications, propaganda and statistics. Naturally a certain play-element had entered into business competition at an early stage. Statistics stimulated it with an idea that had originally arisen in sporting life, the idea, namely, of trading records. A record, as the word shows, was once simply a memorandum, a note which the innkeeper scrawled on the walls of his inn to say that such and such a rider or traveller had been the first to arrive after covering so and so many miles. The statistics of trade and production could not fail to introduce a sporting element into economic life. In consequence, there is now a sporting side to almost every triumph of commerce or technology: the highest turnover, the biggest tonnage, the fastest crossing, the greatest altitude, etc. Here a purely ludic element has, for once, got the better of utilitarian considerations, since the experts inform us that smaller units—less monstrous steamers and aircraft, etc.—are more efficient in the long run. Business becomes play. This process goes so far that some of the great business concerns deliberately instil the play-spirit into their workers so as to step up production. The trend is now reversed: play becomes business. A captain of industry, on whom the Rotterdam Academy of Commerce had conferred an honorary degree, spoke as follows:

> "Ever since I first entered the business it has been a race between the technicians and the sales department. One tried to produce so much that the sales department would never be able to sell it, while the other tried to sell so much that the technicians would never be able to keep pace. This race has always continued: sometimes one is ahead, sometimes the other. Neither my brother nor myself has regarded the business as a task, but always as a game, the spirit of which it has been our constant endeavour to implant into the younger staff."

These words must, of course, be taken with a grain of salt. Nevertheless there are numerous instances of big concerns forming their own Sports Societies and even engaging workers with a view not so much to their professional capacities as to their fitness for the football eleven. Once more the wheel turns.

Modern Man

ALEX INKELES

In the following description, modern man seems very new and quite a good fellow, well adjusted to a changing environment. Do these virtues—which sound remarkably like those urged by Enlightenment philosophers and middle-class optimists long ago—really describe the evolution toward a modern outlook? Are they consistent, for example, with changes in family relationships, where dignity and even democracy might be concretely expressed? Do they leave sufficient room for national or class differences in values?

Inkeles' approach makes one thing quite clear: For him, rural tradition must not be idealized; it is full of hardship and confusion. Hence movement to the city is actually an opportunity not only for higher earnings, but for a much more constructive human personality.

Inkeles discusses the variety of causes necessary to produce a modern outlook, most of them going back at least a century in European experience. He leaves room also for a gradual evolution toward modern values, and this is an important qualification to what might otherwise seem a simplistic approach. Urban man is not necessarily modern; pockets of tradition remain, and even when they begin to collapse there may be many stages before full modernization is attained.

This basic approach to defining modern values has been used by a number of social scientists studying the modernization process outside the Western world. Inkeles has applied his criteria of modernity to studies of Russia. Others have used similar characteristics in assessing the extent of modernization in Japan and elsewhere. They might disagree with Inkeles on some specific points (many definitions stress the secularism of the modern outlook, for example, whereas Inkeles tries to integrate religion), but they would agree that modernity is definable and good.

But what is the modern man, and what makes him what he is? The answer to this question is inevitably controversial, and almost no one enters on a discussion of it without arousing a good deal of emotion. The reasons

From Chapter 10, "The Modernization of Man," by Alex Inkeles in *Modernization: The Dynamics of Growth* edited by Myron Weiner. © 1966 by Basic Books, Inc., Publishers, New York.

are not hard to find. In the first place, the change from more traditional to more modern qualities in man often means someone must give up ways of thinking and feeling that go back decades, sometimes centuries; and to abandon these ways often seems to be abandoning principle itself. For another thing, the qualities that make a man modern often do not appear to be neutral characteristics that any man might have, but instead represent the distinctive traits of the European, the American, or the Westerner that he is bent on imposing on other people so as to make them over in his own image. In the third place, many of the characteristics that are described as modern, and therefore automatically desirable, in fact are not very useful or suitable to the life and conditions of those on whom they are urged or even imposed. These are most serious issues, and we shall return to them briefly after sketching some details of what we mean by modern man.

The characteristic mark of the modern man has two parts: one internal, the other external; one dealing with his environment, the other with his attitudes, values, and feelings.

The change in the external condition of modern man is well known and widely documented, and it need not detain us long. It may be summarized by reference to a series of key terms: urbanization, education, mass communication, industrialization, politicalization. These terms signify that in contrast to his forebears living in the traditional order of his society, the modern man is less likely to work the land as a farmer and is more likely to be employed in a large and complex productive enterprise based on the intensive use of power and advanced technologies. The various economies yielded by the concentration of industry in certain sites and the further demands of those industrial concentrations make it likely that the contemporary man will live in a city or some other form of urban conglomeration. Here, he will experience not only crowding but access to all manner of resource and stimulation characteristic of urban life. Inevitably, one of these stimuli will be the media of mass communication: newspapers, radio, movies, and perhaps even television. His experience of new places and ideas will be augmented by the impact of schooling, if not directly for him, then for his children, who may carry the influence of the school into the home. He is much more likely to have some connection with politics, especially on the national scale, as he is more exposed to mass communication, more mobilized in the surge of urban life, more courted by the competing political movements that seek his support as he may enlist their aid to replace that of the chief, the patron, or the family head whose assistance he would ordinarily have sought in his native village. Indeed, another mark of the contemporary man is that he will no longer live enmeshed in a network of primary kin ties, perhaps supplemented by ties to a small number of fellow villagers, but rather will be drawn into a much more impersonal and bureaucratic milieu in which he is dependent for services and aid in times of distress on persons and agencies with which he has a much more formal and perhaps tenuous relationship.

These are all attributes of his life space that may impinge on the modern man, but in themselves they do not constitute modernity. The densest urban centers may still shelter the most traditional network of human relations: the media of mass communication may mainly disseminate folk tales and traditional wisdom, factories may run on principles not far different from those of the estate or the hacienda, and politics may be conducted like an extension of the village council. Although his exposure to the modern setting may certainly contribute to the transformation of traditional man, and although that setting may in turn require new ways of him, it is only when man has undergone a change in spirit—has acquired certain new ways of thinking, feeling, and acting—that we come to consider him truly modern.

Although there is no single standard definition of the modern man that all accept and use, there is quite good agreement among students of the modernization process as to the characteristics that distinguish the more modern man from the more traditional. To convey my impression of his traits, I have chosen to describe him in terms of a series of attitudes and values that we are testing in a study of the modernization process among workers and peasants in six developing countries. This permits me not only to present the characteristic profile we define as modern but also to indicate some of the questions we are using to study its manifestation in concrete cases. The order in which these characteristics are presented here is not meant to suggest that this is the actual sequence in the process of individual modernization. So far, we are not aware that there is a clear-cut sequence, but rather have the impression that the process develops on a broad front with many changes occurring at once. Neither does the order in which the characteristics are given suggest the relative weight or importance of each characteristic in the total syndrome. Here, again, we have yet, through our scientific work, to assess the relative contribution of each characteristic to the larger complex of attitudes, values, and ways of acting that we consider modern. We do, however, assume that this complex of attitudes and values holds together: that in the statistical sense it constitutes a factor, and a relatively coherent factor. In time, our scientific evidence will show whether or not this is a reasonable assumption.

The first element in our definition of the modern man is his readiness for new experience and his openness to innovation and change. We consider the traditional man to be less disposed to accept new ideas, new ways of feeling and acting. We are speaking, therefore, of something that is itself a state of mind, a psychological disposition, an inner readiness, rather than of the specific techniques or skills a man or a group may possess because of the level of technology they have attained. Thus, in our sense, a man may be more modern in spirit, even though he works with a wooden plow, than someone in another part of the world who already drives a tractor. The readiness for new experience and ways of doing things, furthermore, may express itself in a variety of forms and contexts: in the willingness to adopt a new drug or sanitation method, to accept a new seed or try a different fertilizer, to ride on a new means of transportation or turn to a new source of news, to approve a new form of wedding or new type of schooling for young people. Individuals and groups may, of course, show more readiness for the new in one area of life than another, but we can also conceive of the readiness to accept innovation as a more pervasive, general characteristic that makes itself felt across a wide variety of human situations. And we consider those who have this readiness to be more modern.

The second in our complex of themes takes us into the realm of opinion. We define a man as more modern if he has a disposition to form or mold opinions over a large number of the problems and issues that arise not only in his immediate environment but also outside of it. Some pioneering work on this dimension has been done by Daniel Lerner, of the Massachusetts Institute of Technology, who found that the individuals within any country, and the populations of different countries, in the Middle East varied greatly in their ability or readiness to imagine themselves in the position of prime minister or comparable government leader and thus to offer advice as to what should be done to resolve the problems facing the country. The more educated the individual and the more advanced the country, the greater was the readiness to offer opinions in response to this challenge. The more traditional man, we believe, takes an interest in fewer things, mainly those that touch him immediately and intimately; and even when he holds opinions on more distant matters, he is more circumspect in expressing them.

We also consider a man to be more modern if his orientation to the opinion realm is more democratic. We mean by this that he shows more awareness of the diversity of attitude and opinion around him, rather than closing himself off in the belief that everyone thinks alike and, indeed, just like him. The modern man is able to acknowledge differences of opinion without needing rigidly to deny differences out of fear that these will upset his own view of the world. He is also less likely to approach opinion in a strictly autocratic or hierarchical way. He does not automatically accept the ideas of those above him in the power hierarchy and reject the opinions of those whose status is markedly lower than his. We test these values by asking people whether it is proper to think differently from the village headman or other traditional leader and, at the other end, by inquiring as to whether the opinions of a man's wife or young son merit serious consideration when important public issues are being discussed. These questions prove to be a sensitive indicator in helping us to distinguish one man from another and, we believe, will be an important element in the final syndrome of modernity we shall delineate.

A third theme we deal with at some length is that of time. We view a man as more modern if he is oriented to the present or the future, rather than to the past. We consider him as more modern if he accepts fixed hours, that is to say, schedules of time, as something sensible and appropriate, or possibly even desirable, as against the man who thinks these fixed rules are something either bad or perhaps a necessity, but unfortunately also a pity. We also define a man as more modern if he is punctual, regular, and orderly in organizing his affairs. These things can be very complicated, and this is a good opportunity to point out that it is a mistake to assume that our measures of modernity differentiate between traditional and nontraditional people as they would ordinarily be defined. For example, the Maya Indians had a better sense of time than their Spanish conquerors and they preserve it to this day. The qualities we define as modern can, in fact, be manifested in a people who seem to be relatively unmodern when you consider the level of technology or the amount of power they have. We are talking about properties of the person, which in turn may be a reflection of the properties of a culture that could emerge in any time or place. Indeed, when I described this list to a friend of mine who is doing an extensive study of Greece, he said, "My goodness, you are talking about the ancient Greeks!" He said there were only two respects in which the Greeks did not fit our model of the modern man. And, of course, the Elizabethan Englishman would also fit the model. So, this concept is not limited to our time. "Modern" does not mean merely contemporary in our approach.

A fourth theme that we include in the definition is planning. The more modern man is oriented toward and involved in planning and organizing and believes in it as a way of handling life.

A fifth, and important, theme we call efficacy. The modern man is the one who believes that man can learn, in substantial degree, to dominate his environment in order to advance his own purposes and goals, rather than being dominated entirely by that environment. For example, a man who believes in efficacy is more likely to respond positively to the question, "Do you believe that some day men may be able to develop ways of controlling floods or preventing destructive storms?" The more efficacious man, even though in fact he has never seen a dam, would say, "Yes, I think that some day man could do that."

Sixth, an element we consider part of the modern complex and include in our set of themes is calculability. By our definition, the modern man is one who has more confidence that his world is calculable, that other people and institutions around him can be relied on to fulfill or meet their obligations and responsibilities. He does not agree that everything is determined either by fate or by the whims of particular qualities and characters of men. In other words, he believes in a reasonably lawful world under human control.

The seventh theme that we stress is dignity. The more modern man, we feel, is one who has more awareness of the dignity of others and more disposition to show respect for them. We feel this comes through very clearly in attitudes toward women and children.

The modern man has more faith in science and technology, even if in a fairly primitive way. This provides our eighth theme.

Ninth, we hold that modern man is a great believer in what we call, for this purpose, distributive justice. That is to say, he believes that rewards should be according to contribution, and not according to either whim or special properties of the person not related to his contribution.

You could easily extend this list; you could also divide some of these items into still others; but I think this will serve to give an idea of the complex of attitudes and values that we consider important in defining the modern man. We have chosen to emphasize these themes because we see them as intimately related to the individual's successful adjustment as a citizen of a modern industrial nation. They are qualities that we feel will contribute to making a man a more productive worker in his factory, a more effective citizen in his community, a more satisfied and satisfying husband and father in his home.

We must of course, acknowledge that the nine themes just described are not the only way to approach the definition of modernity. Although we have stressed certain themes that cut across numerous concrete realms of behavior, some students of the problem prefer to emphasize attitudes and behavior relating mainly to certain important institutional realms, such as birth control or religion. . . . For each of these realms, one can define a position that can be considered more modern and an attitude one can define as more traditional, although at times the process of definition becomes very complex.

There is, for example, a very widespread notion that people lose their religion merely because they leave the countryside and go to the city. As a matter of fact, exactly the contrary is very often the case. There are two forces that bring this about. In the first place, really to practice your religion well, you must be a reasonably well-composed, well-contained individual. The person who is emotionally disturbed neglects his social obligations and involvements. Despite the idyllic image that many people have of the countryside, the great majority of the world's peasants are in a state of culture shock produced not by modernity but by the hard conditions of rural life. When a man goes to the city, and especially if he secures a job in industry, he comes to have much more respect and becomes much more self-controlled. This makes it more feasible for him to practice his religion. He turns to things that he previously neglected in his effort just to hold himself together. He reintegrates himself, if you like, with the formal things around him, one of which is his religion.

The second factor that may contribute to facilitate religious practice in the city is economic. To practice your religion generally costs something. For example, you may have to buy candles. If there is a religious ceremony, usually the religious specialist who performs the ceremony must be given some kind of payment. Something is required of you. If you are living a sufficiently marginal existence as a peasant, this may be one of the costs you forgo. When you get to the city and earn a more stable and steady income, you may be more willing to underwrite these costs. So, on this issue we are actually taking a rather unorthodox position and predicting that our city workers are going to be more rather than less religious, if not in spirit at least in terms of performing their formal religious obligations.

So much for our conception of the qualities that make a man modern. What can we say about the forces that produce such a man, that most rapidly and effectively inculcate in a population those attitudes, values, needs, and ways of acting that better fit him for life in a modern society? Just as modernity seems to be defined not by any one characteristic, but by a complex of traits, so we find that no one social force, but rather a whole complex of influences, contributes to the transformation from traditional to modern man.

Within this complex of forces, however, one certainly assumes pre-eminence: namely, education. Almost all serious scientific investigations of the question have shown the individual's degree of modernity to rise with increases in the amount of education he has received. Some reservations must be introduced, of course, to qualify this statement. In many countries, the weakness of the nation's resources permits schooling to be only of very poor quality, and the pressures on the poorer people force the children to be quite irregular in their attendance. In a number of countries, it has been observed that if children can obtain only two or three years of schooling, and especially if they do so under conditions where their environment does not particularly reinforce or support the school, there the effects of education on modernization will be very modest indeed. Similarly, the degree of traditionalism of the school itself plays some role. Little or no change toward modernity is evident in the more traditional schools that devote themselves mainly to passing on religious practices or inculcating and preserving traditional lore and skills. This is a characteristic of schools not only at the primary level; it may apply to those offering nominally advanced education. The "finishing" schools for young ladies from polite society in the United States may be taken as an example. Allowing for reservations of this sort, we may still say that education, especially in schools emphasizing the more modern type of curriculum, seems to be the most powerful factor in developing a population more modern in its attitudes and values. This effect depends in part on the direct instruction provided, but we assume as well that the school as a social organization serves as a model of rationality, of the importance of technical competence, of the rule of objective standards of performance, and of the principle of distributive justice reflected in the grading system. All these models can contribute to shaping young people in the image of the modern man as we have described him.

There is little agreement as to the rank order of influences other than education that we see affecting the degree of modernization of individuals. Many analysts of the problem propose the urban environment as the next most important input. The city is itself a powerful new experience. It encourages, and indeed to some degree obliges, the individual to adopt many new ways of life. By exposing men to a variety of ways of living, a wide range of opinions and ideas, increased mobility, more complex resources of all kinds, it accelerates the process of change. At the same time, in the city the prospect is greater that the individual will be relatively free from the obligations and constraints placed on him in the village by his extended kinship ties, the village elders, and the tight community of his neighbors. These structural differences free the individual to change; but, of course, they do not in themselves guarantee that he will change in ways that make him more modern. In many cities, there are powerful examples of rationality, of the use of technology to master the physical demands of life, of rewards adjusted to technical skill and competence, of the value of education, and of the guarantee of human dignity under law. But many great cities also provide powerful lessons that run counter to these modernizing influences on every score. If they breed a new type of man, they hardly make him in the image we have called modern. In addition, under conditions of very rapid growth, the city is often unable to absorb and integrate all the in-migrants, so that on the outer edges or in the older districts of the city, huge slum communities may develop in which people are in the city but not of it, cut off from many of its benefits and from the modernizing influence of urban life.

One source of modernization which generally accompanies urbanization but is also an independent influence is mass communication. Almost all studies of the growth of individual modernization show that those who are more exposed to the media of mass communication have more modern attitudes. Since such exposure, especially in the case of the newspaper, depends on literacy and education, it is important to stress that the modernization effects of the mass media can be shown to exert their influence within groups at almost any educational level. Of course, there remains the possibility that it is the man with modern attitudes who seeks out the mass media, rather than that the media make the man modern, but there seems little reason to doubt that influence is at least mutual. These media greatly enlarge the range of human experience with which the individual can have contact, even if only vicarious. They constantly present and illustrate new tools, items of consumption, means of transportation, and a myriad of new ways of doing things. They show examples of efficacious behavior of the most powerful kind in the building of dams, the taming of floods, the irrigation of deserts, and even the conquest of space. They also provide models of new values and standards of behavior, some of which are far beyond the reach of most men, but many of which can be copied and do influence behavior directly. As in the case of urban influences, we must acknowledge that the media of communication can and often do carry messages that mainly reaffirm traditional values, beliefs, and ways of acting or disseminate a concept of the new that is nevertheless not congruent with the model of the modern man here described.

Another source of modernizing influence is the development of the national state and its associated apparatus of government bureaucracy, political parties and campaigns, military and paramilitary units, and the like. The more mobilized the society, the more dedicated the government to economic development and spreading the ideology of progress, the more rapidly and widely may we expect the attitudes and values of modernity to expand. Some of the agencies of the state—in particular, the army—may play an especially important role in introducing men to the modern world, both in the direct instruction they offer and indirectly in the model of routine, scheduling, technical skill, and efficacy that inheres in many of their operations. Here again, however, we must acknowledge that the power of the state may also be used to reinforce more traditional values: politics may be conducted in a way that hardly sets an example of modern behavior, and armies may be run so as scarcely to induce a man to exert himself, to practice initiative, or to respect the dignity of others.

One last source of modernizing influence that we may cite . . . is the factory or other modern productive and administrative enterprise. Certain features of the modern factory are relatively invariant, and they communicate the same message, no matter what the cultural setting in which they may be installed. In them there is always an intense concentration of physical and mechanical power brought to bear on the transformation of raw materials; orderly and routine procedures to govern the flow of work are essential; time is a powerful influence in guiding the work process; power and authority generally rest on technical competence; and, as a rule, rewards are in rough proportion to performance. In addition, a factory guided by modern management and personnel policies will set its workers an example of rational behavior, emotional balance, open communication, and respect for the opinions, the feelings, and the dignity of the worker which can be a powerful example of the principles and practice of modern living.

In modern times we are experiencing a process of change affecting everything, yet controlled by no one. It is, in a sense, strictly spontaneous; yet it is in some ways the most strictly determined process history has yet known. Since no one can escape it, no one may be unconcerned with it. Man himself is being transformed. Many evils are being erased, but no end of new forms of corruption and wickedness may be loosed in the world. Some people in backward countries are ready to believe that any change is for the good. Others feel that much they now have is superior to what is being offered, and they are deeply convinced that many of the changes the contemporary world is introducing into their lives are no improvement, while others are positively disastrous. I have pointed to a set of qualities of mind that I call modern, which I believe have much to recommend them. They are not compatible in all respects with qualities that are widespread in traditional cultures, but I believe they are qualities men can adopt without coming into conflict, in most cases, with what is best in their cultural tradition and spiritual heritage. I believe they represent some of the best things in the modernization process. But whether we view them as positive or negative, we must recognize these qualities that are fostered by modern institutions, qualities that in many ways are required of the citizens of modern societies. We must, therefore, come to recognize them, to understand them, and to evaluate them as important issues in contemporary life.

The Horror of Modernization

R. D. LAING

Early in the modernization process, important intellectual criticism developed. Conservative intellectuals criticized excessive rationalism and individualism, which they believed endangered public order. By the later nineteenth century, attacks on modern values came even from intellectuals who were not politically conservative, but who thought that society was deteriorating as it moved away from traditional values. It was probably inevitable that many intellectuals would resent a society that placed so much emphasis on material achievement. The intellectuals' uncertainty about their own role in such a society encouraged their frequent hostility.

So intellectual attacks on modernity have a considerable history. They result in part from the impact of the modernization process on an articulate social group, which does not necessarily mean that they are biased or wrong.

R. D. Laing is a British psychoanalyst with a particular interest in schizophrenia. His training thus differs considerably from that of the sociologist Inkeles. Yet his list of the characteristics of modern man is by no means completely different. He argues that modern man is new, that modern man claims rationality, and so on. But Laing views these attributes from a completely different perspective. It is possible, of course, that he is talking only about *some* modern people, not *all*, or about people only at certain times or in certain moods. But Laing does not think this is so. Like Inkeles, he finds it possible to describe modern man, period.

Laing places the development of modern education and family structure, including childhood, in the forefront of his attack (and tangentially he also questions the scientific way of knowing). Above all, he contrasts modern values with those of the past, even though he does not describe the past in detail. Premodern man had faith and dreams. He could accept a creative madness. He was not alienated.

So in a sense we come full circle, to the question of insanity and the modern mind. Laing invites us to evaluate premodern as well as modern people. And if he is right that modern society has deteriorated, is this a cause for hope or despair? Are there values from the past that we should try to recover, and, given the enormous impact of modernization, do we have any hope of success if we do try? Can we, if we are complacently, scientifically modernized, even grasp the world that Laing experiences?

Few books today are forgivable. Black on the canvas, silence on the screen, an empty white sheet of paper, are perhaps feasible. There is little conjunction of truth and social "reality." Around us are pseudo-events, to which we adjust with a false consciousness adapted to see these events as true and real, and even as beautiful. In the society of men the truth resides now less in what things are than in what they are not. Our social realities are so ugly if seen in the light of exiled truth, and beauty is almost no longer possible if it is not a lie.

We live in a moment of history where change is so speeded up that we begin to see the present only when it is already disappearing.

It is difficult for modern man not to see the present in terms of the past. The white European and North American, in particular, commonly has a sense, not of renewal, but of being at an end: of being only half alive in the fibrillating heartland of a senescent civilization. Sometimes it seems that it is not possible to do more than reflect the decay around and within us, than sing sad and bitter songs of disillusion and defeat.

Yet that mood is already dated, at least insofar as it is not a perennial possibility of the human spirit. It entails a sense of time, which is already being dissolved in the instantaneous, stochastic, abrupt, discontinuous electronic cosmos, the dynamic mosaic of the electromagnetic field.

Nevertheless, the requirement of the present, the failure of the past, is the same: to provide a thoroughly self-conscious and self-critical human account of man.

No one can begin to think, feel or act now except from the starting point of his or her own alienation. We shall examine some of its forms in the following pages.

We are all murderers and prostitutes—no matter to what culture, society, class, nation, we belong, no matter how normal, moral, or mature we take ourselves to be.

Humanity is estranged from its authentic possibilities. This basic vision prevents us from taking any unequivocal view of the sanity of common sense, or of the madness of the so-called madman. However, what is required is more than a passionate outcry of outraged humanity.

Our alienation goes to the roots. The realization of this is the essential springboard for any serious reflection on any aspect of present interhuman life. Viewed from different perspectives, construed in different ways and expressed in different idioms, this realization unites men as diverse as Marx, Kierkegaard, Nietzsche, Freud, Heidegger, Tillich and Sartre.

More recent voices in the United States continue to document different facets of our fragmentation and alienation, whether it is the exposure of sham, the spatialization and quantification of experience or the massive economic irrationality of the whole system.

All such description is forced to describe what is, in the light of different modulations of what is not. What has been, what might have been, what should be or might be. Can we describe the present in terms of its becoming what it is not-yet—a term of Ernest Block's, so frightening, so ominous, so cataclysmic, that it is sometimes easier to see the present already darkened by the shadow of a thermonuclear apocalypse, than either to envisage further declensions from that from which our nostalgia absents us, or to see a redemptive dialectic immanent in the vortex of accelerating change.

At all events, we are bemused and crazed creatures, strangers to our true selves, to one another, and to the spiritual and material world—mad, even, from an ideal standpoint we can glimpse but not adopt.

We are born into a world where alienation awaits us. We are potentially men, but are in an alienated state, and this state is not simply a natural system. Alienation as our present destiny is achieved only by outrageous violence perpetrated by human beings on human beings. . . .

Even facts become fictions without adequate ways of seeing "the facts." We do not need theories so much as the experience that is the source of the theory. We are not satisfied with faith, in the sense of an implausible hypothesis irrationally held: we demand to experience the "evidence." . . .

Natural science is concerned only with the observer's experience of things. Never with the way things experience us. That is not to say that things do not react to us, and to each other.

Natural science knows nothing of the relation between behavior and experience. The nature of this relation is mysterious—in Marcel's sense. That is to say, it is not an objective problem. There is no traditional logic to express it. There is no developed method of understanding its nature. But this relation is the copula of our science—if science means a *form of knowledge adequate to its subject*. The relation between experience and behavior is the stone that the builders will reject at their peril. Without it the whole structure of our theory and practice must collapse.

Experience is invisible to the other. But experience is not "subjective" rather than "objective," not "inner" rather than "outer," not process rather than praxis, not input rather than output, not psychic rather than somatic, not some doubtful data dredged up from introspection rather than extrospection. Least of all is experience "intrapsychic process." Such transactions, object relations, interpersonal relations, transference, countertransference, as we suppose to go on between people are not the interplay merely of two objects in space, each equipped with ongoing intrapsychic processes.

This distinction between outer and inner usually refers to the distinction between behavior and experience; but sometimes it refers to some experiences that are supposed to be "inner" in contrast to others that are "outer." More accurately this is a distinction between different modalities of experience, namely, perception (as outer) in contrast to imagination, etc. (as inner). But perception, imagination, fantasy, reverie, dreams, memory, are simply different *modalities of experience*, none more "inner" or "outer" than any other.

Yet this way of talking does reflect a split in our experience. We seem to live in two worlds, and many people are aware only of the "outer" rump. As long as we remember that the "inner" world is not some space "inside" the body or the mind, this way of talking can serve our purpose. (It was good enough for William Blake.) The "inner," then, is our personal idiom of experiencing our bodies, other people, the animate and inanimate world: imagination, dreams, fantasy, and beyond that to ever further reaches of experience.

Bertrand Russell once remarked that the stars are in one's brain.

The stars as I perceive them are no more or less in my brain than the stars as I imagine them. I do not imagine them to be in my head, any more than I see them in my head.

The relation of experience to behavior is not that of inner to outer. My experience is not inside my head. My experience of this room is out there in the room.

To say that my experience is intrapsychic is to presuppose that there is a psyche that my experience is in. My psyche is my experience, my experience is my psyche.

Many people used to believe that angels moved the stars. It now appears that they do not. As a result of this and like revelations, many people do not now believe in angels.

Many people used to believe that the "seat" of the soul was somewhere in the brain. Since brains began to be opened up frequently, no one has seen "the soul." As a result of this and like revelations, many people do not now believe in the soul.

Who could suppose that angels move the stars, or be so superstitious as to suppose that because one cannot see one's soul at the end of a microscope it does not exist? . . .

Can human beings be persons today? Can a man be his actual self with another man or woman? Before we can ask such an optimistic question as, "What is a personal relationship?," we have to ask if a personal relationship is possible, or, *are persons possible* in our present situation? We are concerned with the possibility of man. This question can be asked only through its facets. Is love possible? Is freedom possible?

Whether or not all, or some, or no human beings are persons, I wish to define a person in a twofold way: in terms of experience, as a center of orientation of the objective universe; and in terms of behavior, as the origin of actions. Personal experience transforms a given field into a field of intention and action: only through action can our experience be transformed. It is tempting and facile to regard "persons" as only separate objects in space, who can be studied as any other natural objects can be studied. But just as Kierkegaard remarked that one will never find consciousness by looking down a microscope at brain cells or anything else, so one will never find persons by studying persons as though they were only objects. A person is the me or you, he or she, whereby an object is experienced. Are these centers of experience and origins of actions living in entirely unrelated worlds of their own composition? Everyone must refer here to their own experience. My own experience as a center of experience and origin of action tells me that this is not so. My experience and my action occur in a social field of reciprocal influence and interaction. I experience myself, identifiable as Ronald Laing by myself and others, as experienced by and acted upon by others, who refer to that person I call "me" as "you" or "him," or grouped together as "one of us" or "one of them" or "one of you."

This feature of personal relations does not arise in the correlation of the behavior of nonpersonal objects. Many social scientists deal with their embarrassment by denying its occasion. Nevertheless, the natural scientific world is complicated by the presence of certain identifiable entities, re-identifiable reliably over periods of years, whose behavior is either the manifestation or a concealment of a view of the world equivalent in ontological status to that of the scientist.

People may be observed to sleep, eat, walk, talk, etc. in relatively predictable ways. We must not be content with observation of this kind alone. Observation of behavior must be extended by inference to attributions about experience. Only when we can begin to do this can we really construct the experiential-behavior system that is the human species.

It is quite possible to study the visible, audible, smellable effulgences of human bodies, and much study of human behavior has been in those terms. One can lump together very large numbers of units of behavior and regard them as a statistical population, in no way different from the multiplicity constituting a system of nonhuman objects. But one will not be studying persons. In a science of persons, I shall state as axiomatic that: behavior is a function of experience; and both experience and behavior are always in relation to someone or something other than self.

When two (or more) persons are in relation, the behavior of each towards the other is mediated by the experience by each of the other, and the experience of each is mediated by the behavior of each. There is no contiguity between the behavior of one person and that of the other. Much human behavior can be seen as a unilateral or bilateral *attempt* to eliminate experience. A person may treat another *as though* he were not a person, and he may act himself *as though* he were not a person. There is no contiguity between one person's experience and another's. My experience of you is always mediated through your *behavior*. Behavior that is the direct consequence of impact, as of one billiard ball hitting another, or experience directly transmitted to experience, as in the possible cases of extrasensory perception, is not personal.

Normal Alienation from Experience

The relevance of Freud to our time is largely his insight and, to a very considerable extent, his *demonstration* that the *ordinary* person is a shriveled, desiccated fragment of what a person can be.

As adults, we have forgotten most of our childhood, not only its contents but its flavor; as men of the world, we hardly know of the existence of the inner world: we barely remember our dreams, and make little sense of them when we do; as for our bodies, we retain just sufficient proprioceptive sensations to coordinate our movements and to ensure the minimal requirements for biosocial survival—to register fatigue, signals for food, sex, defecation, sleep; beyond that, little or nothing. Our capacity to think, except in the service of what we are dangerously deluded in supposing is our self-interest and in conformity with common sense, is pitifully limited: our capacity even to see, hear, touch, taste and smell is so shrouded in veils of mystification that an intensive discipline of unlearning is necessary for *anyone* before one can begin to experience the world afresh, with innocence, truth and love.

And immediate experience of, in contrast to belief or faith in, a spiritual realm of demons, spirits, Powers, Dominions, Principalities, Seraphim and Cherubim, the Light, is even more remote. As domains of experience become more alien to us, we need greater and greater open-mindedness even to conceive of their existence.

Many of us do not know, or even believe, that every night we enter zones of reality in which we forget our waking life as regularly as we forget our dreams when we awake. Not all psychologists know of fantasy as a modality of experience, and the, as it were, contrapuntal interweaving of different experiential modes. Many who are aware of fantasy believe that fantasy is the farthest that experience goes under "normal" circumstances. Beyond that are simply "pathological" zones of hallucinations, phantasmagoric mirages, delusions.

This state of affairs represents an almost unbelievable devastation of our experience. Then there is empty chatter about maturity, love, joy, peace.

This is itself a consequence of and further occasion for the divorce of our experience, such as is left of it, from our behavior.

What we call "normal" is a product of repression, denial, splitting, projection, introjection and other forms of destructive action on experience (see below). It is radically estranged from the structure of being.

The more one sees this, the more senseless it is to continue with generalized descriptions of supposedly specifically schizoid, schizophrenic, hysterical "mechanisms."

There are forms of alienation that are relatively strange to statistically "normal" forms of alienation. The "normally" alienated person, by reason of the fact that he acts more or less like everyone else, is taken to be sane. Other forms of alienation that are out of step with the prevailing state of alienation are those that are labeled by the "normal" majority as bad or mad.

The condition of alienation, of being asleep, of being unconscious, of being out of one's mind, is the condition of the normal man.

Society highly values its normal man. It educates children to lose themselves and to become absurd, and thus to be normal.

Normal men have killed perhaps 100,000,000 of their fellow normal men in the last fifty years.

Our behavior is a function of our experience. We act according to the way we see things.

If our experience is destroyed, our behavior will be destructive.

If our experience is destroyed, we have lost our own selves.

How much human *behavior*, whether the interactions between persons themselves or between groups and groups, is intelligible in terms of human experience? Either our interhuman behavior is unintelligible, in that we are simply the passive vehicles of inhuman processes whose ends are as obscure as they are at present outside our control, or our own behavior towards each other is a function of our own experience and our own intentions, however alienated we are from them. In the latter case, we must take final responsibility for what we make of what we are made of.

We will find no intelligibility in behavior if we see it as an inessential phase in an essentially inhuman process. We have had accounts of men as animals, men as machines, men as biochemical complexes with certain ways of their own, but there remains the greatest difficulty in achieving a human understanding of man in human terms.

Men at all times have been subject, as they believed or experienced, to forces from the stars, from the gods, or to forces that now blow through society itself, appearing as the stars once did to determine human fate.

Men have, however, always been weighed down not only by their sense of subordination to fate and chance, to ordained external necessities or contingencies, but by a sense that their very own thoughts and feelings, in their most intimate interstices, are the outcome, the resultant, of processes which they undergo.

A man can estrange himself from himself by mystifying himself and others. He can also have what he does stolen from him by the agency of others.

If we are stripped of experience, we are stripped of our deeds; and if our deeds are, so to speak, taken out of our hands like toys from the hands of children, we are bereft of our humanity. We cannot be deceived. Men can and do destroy the humanity of other men, and the condition of this possibility is that we are interdependent. We are not self-contained monads producing no effects on each other except our reflections. We are both acted upon, changed for good or ill, by other men; and we are agents who act upon others to affect them in different ways. Each of us is the other to the others. Man is a patient-agent, agent-patient, interexperiencing and interacting with his fellows.

It is quite certain that unless we can regulate our behavior much more satisfactorily than at present, then we are going to exterminate ourselves. But as we experience the world, so we act, and this principle holds even when action conceals rather than discloses our experience.

We are not able even to *think* adequately about the behavior that is at the annihilating edge. But what we think is less than what we know; what we know is less than what we love; what we love is so much less than what there is. And to that precise extent we are so much less than what we are.

Yet if nothing else, each time a new baby is born there is a possibility of reprieve. Each child is a new being, a potential prophet, a new spiritual prince, a new spark of light precipitated into the outer darkness. Who are we to decide that it is hopeless? . . .

It is not enough to destroy one's own and other people's experience. One must overlay this devastation by a false consciousness inured, as Marcuse puts it, to its own falsity.

Exploitation must not be seen as such. It must be seen as benevolence. Persecution preferably should not need to be invalidated as the figment of a paranoid imagination; it should be experienced as kindness. Marx described mystification and showed its function in his day. Orwell's time is already with us. The colonists not only mystify the natives, in the ways that Fanon so clearly shows, they have to mystify themselves. We in Europe and North America are the colonists, and in order to sustain our amazing images of ourselves as God's gift to the vast majority of the starving human species, we have to interiorize our violence upon ourselves and our children and to employ the rhetoric of morality to describe this process.

In order to rationalize our industrial-military complex, we have to destroy our capacity to see clearly any more what is in front of, and to imagine what is beyond, our noses. Long before a thermonuclear war can come about, we have had to lay waste our own sanity. We begin with the children. It is imperative to catch them in time. Without the most thorough and rapid brainwashing their dirty minds would see through our dirty tricks. Children are not yet fools, but we shall turn them into imbeciles like ourselves, with high I.Q.s if possible.

From the moment of birth, when the Stone Age baby confronts the twentieth-century mother, the baby is subjected to these forces of violence, called love, as its mother and father, and their parents and their parents before them, have been. These forces are mainly concerned with destroying most of its potentialities, and on the whole this enterprise is successful. By the time the new human being is fifteen or so, we are left with a being like ourselves, a half-crazed creature more or less adjusted to a mad world. This is normality in our present age.

Love and violence, properly speaking, are polar opposites. Love lets the other be, but with affection and concern. Violence attempts to constrain the other's freedom, to force him to act in the way we desire, but with ultimate lack of concern, with indifference to the other's own existence or destiny.

We are effectively destroying ourselves by violence masquerading as love.

I am a specialist, God help me, in events in inner space and time, in experiences called thoughts, images, reveries, dreams, visions, hallucinations, dreams of memories, memories of dreams, memories of visions, dreams of hallucinations, refractions of refractions of refractions of that original Alpha and Omega of experience and reality, that Reality on whose repression, denial, splitting, projection, falsification, and general desecration and profanation our civilization as much as on anything is based.

We live equally out of our bodies and out of our minds.

Concerned as I am with this inner world, observing day in and day out its devastation, I ask why this has happened?

One component of an answer . . . is that we can *act* on our *experience* of ourselves, others and the world, as well as take action on the world through behavior itself. Specifically this devastation is largely the work of *violence* that has been perpetrated on each of us, and by each of us on ourselves. The usual name that much of this violence goes under is *love*.

We act on our experience at the behest of the others, just as we learn how to behave in compliance with them. We are taught what to experience and what not to experience, as we are taught what movements to make and what sounds to emit. A child of two is already a moral mover and moral talker and moral experiencer. He already moves the "right" way, makes the "right" noises, and knows what he should feel and what he should not feel. His movements have become stereometric types, enabling the specialist anthropologist to identify, through his rhythm and style, his national, even his regional, characteristics. As he is taught to move in specific ways out of the whole range of possible movements, so he is taught to experience out of the whole range of possible experience. . . .

If human beings are not studied as human beings, then this once more is violence and mystification.

In much contemporary writing on the individual and the family there is assumed some not-too-unhappy confluence, not to say pre-established harmony, between nature and nurture. Some adjustments may have to be made on both sides, but all things work together for good to those who want only security and identity.

Gone is any sense of possible tragedy, of passion. Gone is any language of joy, delight, passion, sex, violence. The language is that of a boardroom. No more primal scenes, but parental coalitions; no more repression of sexual ties to parents, but the child "rescinds" its Oedipal wishes. For instance:

> The mother can properly invest her energies in the care of the young child when economic support, status, and protection of the family are provided by the father. She can also better limit her cathexis of the child to maternal feelings when her wifely needs are satisfied by her husband.

Here is no nasty talk of sexual intercourse or even "primal scene." The economic metaphor is aptly employed. The mother "invests" in her child. What is most revealing is the husband's function. The provision of economic support, status and protection, in that order.

There is frequent reference to security, the esteem of others. What one is supposed to want, to live for, is "gaining pleasure from the esteem and affection of others." If not, one is a psychopath.

Such statements are in a sense true. They describe the frightened, cowed, abject creature that we are admonished to be, if we are to be normal— offering each other mutual protection from our own violence. The family as a "protection racket."

Behind this language lurks the terror that is behind all this mutual back-scratching, this esteem-, status-, support-, protection-, security-giving and getting. Through its bland urbanity the cracks still show.

In our world we are "victims burning at the stake, signaling through the flames," but for some, things go blandly on. "Contemporary life requires adaptability." We require also to "utilize intellect," and we require "an emotional equilibrium that permits a person to be malleable, to adjust himself to others without fear of loss of identity with change. It requires a basic trust in others, and a confidence in the integrity of the self."

Sometimes there is a glimpse of more honesty. For instance, when we "consider society rather than the individual, each society has a vital interest in the *indoctrination* of the infants who form its new *recruits*."

What these authors say may be written ironically, but there is no evidence that it is.

Adaptation to what? To society? To a world gone mad?

The family's function is to repress Eros; to induce a false consciousness of security; to deny death by avoiding life; to cut off transcendence; to believe in God, not to experience the Void; to create, in short, one-dimensional man; to promote respect, conformity, obedience; to con children out of play; to induce a fear of failure; to promote a respect for work; to promote a respect for "respectability."

A	8
B	9
C	0
D	1
E	2
F	3
G	4
H	5
I	6
J	7